The Emergence
of Thackeray's Serial Fiction

The Emergence of Thackeray's Serial Fiction

Edgar F. Harden

GEORGE PRIOR
PUBLISHERS

To the memory of
Clayton Edgar Harden
and
Elizabeth Schraer Harden

To speak of [Thackeray's *Cornhill Magazine*], in truth, . . . is to feel the advantage of being able to live back into the time of the more sovereign periodical appearances much of a compensation for any reduced prospect of living forward. For these appearances, these strong time-marks in such stretches of production as that of Dickens, that of Thackeray, that of George Eliot, had in the first place simply a genial weight and force, a direct importance, and in the second a command of the permeable air and the collective sensibility, with which nothing since has begun to deserve comparison. They were enrichments of life, they were *large* arrivals, these particular renewals of supply. . . . These various, let alone numerous, deeper-toned strokes of the great Victorian clock were so many steps in the march of our age, besides being so many notes, full and far-reverberating, of our having high company to keep—high, I mean, to cover all the ground, in the sense of the genial pitch of it. . . . I witnessed . . . , with all my senses, young as I was, the never-to-be-equalled degree of difference made, for what may really be called the world-consciousness happily exposed to it, by the prolonged "coming-out" of The Newcomes, yellow number by number, and could take the general civilised participation in the process for a sort of basking in the light of distinction. The process repeated itself for some years under other forms and stimuli, but the merciless change was to come—so that through whatever bristling mazes we may now pick our way it is not to find them open into any such vales of Arcady. My claim for our old privilege is that we did then, with our pace of dignity, proceed from vale to vale.

Henry James, Notes of a Son and Brother

Contents

Acknowledgments

For the basic support that has made research for this book possible, I am greatly indebted to the President's Research Grants Committee of Simon Fraser University and especially to the Canada Council.

I should like to acknowledge the helpful assistance of the following individuals and repositories of Thackeray material: Warner Barnes; Alan Bell; Herbert Cahoon; A. V. Caudery; Robert L. Colby; Clive E. Driver; the Fitzwilliam Museum; Karl C. Gay; Phyllis M. Giles; Theodore Grieder; Holly Hall; Christina M. Hanson; John Harvey; Ann Hyde; Carolyn E. Jakeman; Alan Jutzi; Keneth W. Kinnamon; Thomas V. Lange; Sally Leach; Brotherton Collection, University of Leeds; Loyola Marymount University, Los Angeles; Kenneth Spenser Research Library, University of Kansas; David I. Masson; John Murray, Ltd.; Virginia Murray; N. Frederick Nash; the Morris L. Parrish Collection, Princeton University Library; Nicholas Pickwoad; Joseph Rankin; Gordon N. Ray; Brian Rees; the Philip H. and A. S. W. Rosenbach Foundation; Evelyn W. Semler; Sarah S. Shaw; Hinda F. Sklar; Allen H. Stokes; John A. Sutherland; Lola L. Szladits; Oliver Van Oss; Robert L. Volz; Alexander D. Wainright; Washington University, Saint Louis.

For permission to quote from Thackeray manuscript material and for personal kindness, it is my pleasure to acknowledge the graciousness of Mrs. Edward Norman-Butler. For permission to consult and make published use of documents in their possession, I am grateful to the British Library; the Lockwood Memorial Library, State University of New York at Buffalo; Charterhouse School; Harvard University Library; Henry E. Huntington Library; University of Illinois Library at Urbana-Champaign; the Pierpont Morgan Library; Colonel G. A. Murray-Smith and the Trustees of the National Library of Scotland; the Henry W. and Albert A. Berg Collection and the Arents Collection, New York Public Library, Astor, Lenox and Tilden Foundations; the Fales Library, New York University; Punch Publications, Ltd.; the University of Rochester Library; the South Caroliniana Library, University of South Carolina; the Robert H. Taylor Collection, Princeton, New Jersey; the Humanities Research Center, University of Texas at Austin; and Yale University Library.

Various editors have kindly given permission for me to reprint material that originally appeared in their journals: brief portions of articles from *Papers on Language and Literature* and *PMLA*; half of an article from the *Journal of English and Germanic Philology*; and essentially entire articles from *Costerus*, *The Huntington Library Quarterly*, *Nineteenth-Century Fiction*, and *Studies in English Literature, 1500–1900*. I wish also to own a general debt to previous scholars, no matter what specific disagreements I may have with the work of some; it seems especially appropriate to acknowledge here the rich inheritance provided by the work of Gordon N. Ray, Kathleen Tillotson, and the late Geoffrey Tillotson.

In a work like this, which attempts to assimilate such a vast amount of detail, there will inevitably be errors. It will be no excuse to say that my efforts to be accurate have been exhausting, when they prove not to have been exhaustive as well. I can only apologize and hope for charitable understanding. For charity of a special kind that I have already received, I wish to thank the following people: Douglas Bush and Howard Mumford Jones, for being enduring examples; Andrew G. Hoover and Francis X. Roellinger, for long-sustained cheer and support; Stuart M. Sperry, for his continued wise and warm counsel; Peter L. Shillingsburg, who has read the manuscript with rigor and generosity, pointing out errors, challenging me in various ways to improve it, and offering the assistance that made such improvement easier to achieve; Robin Blaser and Robert H. Dunham, for their special, memorable care; and finally my wife and son, who endured.

E.F.H.

The Emergence
of Thackeray's Serial Fiction

1

Introduction

During the fifteen years since first I looked into the manuscript of *Vanity Fair* with a rather bewildered fascination, I have become increasingly aware that an adequate understanding of Thackeray's fiction would require, at the least, a mastery of the evidence provided by such documents. My own study of Thackeray's thematic concerns in his fiction and of the serial form of his novels has promoted a growing dissatisfaction with criticism that is not grounded in a thorough knowledge of his manuscripts and what they can teach us of the compositional processes that gave us these works. My two-fold sense that study of Thackeray in general, and my own work in particular, needed to be fundamentally informed by such an awareness—so far as we can gain it—has at length resulted in the completion of the present volume and leads me to contemplate a further work on the nonfictional prose.

Conventional opinion on this subject is succinctly expressed by the pronouncement that Thackeray "was a careless and hasty worker, submitting his manuscript to the printer at the last moment and evading the rigors of proof-reading."[1] When one of the most knowledgeable modern authorities on Victorian fiction, especially Thackeray's, can issue so uninformed yet *representative* a dictum, then an extensive study of the evidence—one that systematically presents and interprets the documents—is clearly needed. Such a broad assimilation of material and careful scrutiny of it will demonstrate that, contrary to general belief, the creative processes that produced Thackeray's serial fiction went on at great length, not in brief haste—through much rumination, not slap-dash scribbling—and through stages of growth that culminated in minute evolution during successive sets of proof.

I therefore have set out to show for the first time in adequate detail the surviving evidence of the compositional processes that resulted in the month-by-month appearance of his serial fiction from *Vanity Fair* through *Philip* (though with several exceptions, since the manuscripts of *Barry Lyndon* and, for the most part, *Pendennis* have apparently been lost, and that of the uncompleted *Denis Duval* has been exam-

ined at some length elsewhere).[2] In following the development of these
monthly installments, of course, one comes to trace the evolving over-
all forms of the novels themselves. The result is a history of movements governed by more or less strict requirements of time and space
but dramatically finding fulfillment as they grow into a discovery and
revelation of their integrity. A corresponding movement on our part
should profoundly revise our understanding of Thackeray the creator
by leading towards a new awareness of the dynamic relationship involving him, the special demands of the individual installment, and the
final total forms of the novels themselves. In no other way can we come
so close to the mysterious edge ultimately dividing us from the "other-
ness" that created these works.

The evidence cited here consists primarily of changes made by
Thackeray in the manuscripts and—from a comparison of the manuscripts with the first published texts—of the alterations introduced
by him during the often complex passage of his installments through
the press. The analysis is also supported, whenever possible, by evidence drawn from other materials, such as letters, diaries, outlines,
and proof sheets. For Thackeray, composition did not end until he
either had exhausted his repeated efforts to perfect the installment or
had been forced by the strokes of the clock to let it go out of his hands
for the last time. Since an understanding of this growth and these
evolving forms requires a corresponding attention to detail on our
part, the burdens placed upon us are considerable. Compensation may
perhaps be found in the possibility of gaining both a new awareness of
Thackeray's artistry (together with knowledge of Victorian serialization) and a reasonably comprehensive source for consultation that can
serve as a point of departure for future scholarly and critical endeavor.

The origins of the generally accepted view of Thackeray's compositional practices as a serial novelist extend back to Thackeray's lifetime
and involve issues such as the dignity of literature, the artist's attitude
towards his profession, his commitment to his work, the nature of his
chief artistic medium, and the circumstances of his personal life.
Therefore, in considering some of the major aspects of Thackeray's
compositional procedures, especially as a serial novelist, one might

appropriately begin by citing views of his contemporaries that relate to these issues and by providing at least a brief sketch of major developments leading to the present view. We may then discover a more adequate basis for understanding his compositional activity by re-examining some old assumptions, considering new evidence, following out some of its implications, and identifying directions in which it may lead us as scholars and critics.

The conception of Thackeray as a hasty and careless worker arose in part from his protracted disagreement with fellow writers—especially John Forster—over the dignity of literature.[3] In 1850, when remarks in *Pendennis* helped make the quarrel especially heated, Forster commented that Thackeray was disposed "to pay court to the non-literary class by disparaging his literary fellow-labourers." He suggested Thackeray was "conscious of the desire to be thought above his pursuits" (*The Examiner*, 19 January 1850, p. 35). Another critic wrote that "Mr. Thackeray does not appear to have any superabundant respect for authorcraft in itself." In addition, the same writer, who valued the dramatic form over all others, disparaged the artistic medium employed by Thackeray: "The serial tale . . . is probably the lowest artistic form yet invented; that, namely, which affords the greatest excuse for unlimited departures from dignity, propriety, consistency, completeness, and proportion" (*Prospective Review* 7 [1851]: 173, 158). Other critics of *Pendennis* had similar beliefs about qualities that they felt ought to characterize a novel but that they did not find in Thackeray's. One admitted that Thackeray's illness made a "claim upon indulgent criticism," but the critic nevertheless felt there was "in many small matters a want of fixed purpose," which he illustrated by listing over a dozen examples of minor inconsistency (*Fraser's Magazine* 43 [1851]: 85). Another asserted: "It is an established fact that Mr. Thackeray cannot or will not frame a coherent story, of which all the incidents flow naturally one from another, and are so necessarily connected with each other as to form a whole, whose completeness would be marred equally by taking away or by adding to it" (*The Spectator* 23 [1850]: 1213). Similar remarks continue to appear in subsequent Victorian criticism of Thackeray: he was aristocratically aloof from the profession of writing, including its necessary craftsmanship; he worked in an artistically inferior medium that invited carelessness; in writing he lacked the kind of sufficiently fixed purpose that both promotes consistency of detail and also successfully creates plot, not simply incident.[4]

Notably sympathetic commentary on Thackeray also contributed to this emerging picture. For example, "Theodore Taylor" (probably J. C. Hotten) stated that Thackeray was remarkable not only "for the clearness of his handwriting" but also "for the general neatness of his manuscripts. Page after page of that small round hand would be written by him absolutely—for he rarely altered his first draughts in any way—without interlineation, blot, or blemish of any kind."[5]

The chief contributor, however, was Anthony Trollope, a notoriously methodical writer, who firmly asserted of Thackeray: "It was his nature to be idle—to put off his work." For Trollope, a novelist was "to be placed in no lower level than that which he has attained by his highest sustained flight." Since he considered Thackeray's finest novel to be *Esmond*, Trollope emphasized its excellence, basically doing so at the expense of Thackeray's serial fiction, which he called a mode of writing "by no means very articulate, but easy of production and lucrative. But though easy it is seductive, and leads to idleness." Thus Trollope decided that *Esmond* was written with the necessary "elbow-grease": "a greater amount of forethought . . . than had been his wont." In *Esmond* Trollope saw a thoroughly planned "arrangement of . . . story." He argued that it was Thackeray's "only work . . . in which there is no touch of idleness"; it was "a whole," unlike the serial novels, in which there was "wandering"—"rather strings of incidents and memoirs of individuals, than a completed story." Constructing a chapter of his own book on the contrast between *Esmond* and *The Virginians*, the latter being taken as a particularly telling example of Thackeray's serial practice, Trollope rather obsessively repeated himself as he claimed the latter novel revealed "that propensity to wandering which came to Thackeray because of his idleness." Confidently depending upon his own impressionistic responses, and utterly failing to cite evidence—even of "wandering"—Trollope firmly maintained his viewpoint in spite of the evidence provided by the novels themselves and by Frederick Greenwood's 1864 *Cornhill* article concerning Thackeray's working papers for *Denis Duval*. Though Trollope recognized "how much collateral work [Thackeray] had given to the fabrication of [this] novel" and was ready to assume that "No doubt in preparing other tales . . ., a very large amount of such collateral labour was found necessary," he could see in this Thackerayan

forethought only a disturbing "irregularity." Thackeray, he continued
to insist, was not "a laborious man," because he could not (like Trollope) "bring himself to sit at his desk and do an allotted task day after
day."[6]

It is a notably stubborn, undiscerning argument, and its effects have
persisted into our own time, in spite of several objections, including
Herman Merivale's amusingly indignant reply: "According to him,
Thackeray wanted 'forethought,' which he calls the novelist's 'elbow-
grease.' Trollope wrote, regularly, so many words an hour, and therefore Thackeray should have done the same, and not so doing, wanted
forethought. Forethought indeed! Had not the man the eyes to see,
the heart to comprehend—that that very idleness—that very putting
off of the allotted hour of work—was Thackeray's forethought itself?
. . . There is more work, more thought, more truth, to spring out of
one morning lost in Thackeray's idleness, than in many gallons of
elbow-grease at so much industry per hour. . . . Idleness, with a
Thackeray, is simply 'getting ready.'"[7]

Trollope was willing to grant that no one to his knowledge had ever
accused Thackeray of "gross mistakes" (p. 56) in his writings, but
even George Saintsbury, one of Thackeray's warmest admirers, failed
to develop the possibilities of that statement. Instead, while discussing
the issue of artistic execution in *Pendennis*, Saintsbury made a significant concession before launching his defense: "Thackeray is often
accused—and it is not always easy to clear him from the charge—of
careless preparation of his books." He then went on, "but if he was a
careless 'putter forth,' he was often a very shrewd reviser, and most
certainly no indolent one."[8] Saintsbury's edition, moreover, furthered
this impression of carelessness, for it listed substantive variants from
Saintsbury's late-edition copy-texts, readings that generally were
omitted or modified in later editions—the implication being that
Thackeray corrected them after time for adequate reflection.

Although a number of modern studies, especially those concentrating upon structure and upon aspects of Thackerayan narrative, have
revealed elaborate patterns that clearly imply careful authorial forethought, the earlier arguments and assumptions have persisted—most
recently and strikingly in the work of John A. Sutherland, who while
inverting the chief Trollopian criticisms has still accepted their basic
premises, for he argues that Thackeray was a fundamentally lackadaisical writer, but that the novelist's works reveal the *virtues* of

Thackerayan carelessness. Sutherland goes beyond Trollope chiefly by claiming that *Esmond* was written in essentially the same manner as the serials, and by actually deriving his arguments from examined portions of manuscripts, though often doing so in a thoroughly impressionistic way.

Thackeray's own comments have also, of course, been drawn upon —though not thoughtfully enough—by critics, especially with the gradual publication of his letters and other documents, notably those contained in Gordon N. Ray's edition. Often Thackeray's remarks have been seized upon as confirming evidence of a fundamental carelessness—without appropriate attention to their context, tone, and implications. Like a number of other artists, he was not his own best critic: though constantly trying to excel, he had deep emotional needs that could never be satisfied by anything he did, except for brief moments. Thus on one occasion he told Jane Brookfield: "What a shame the Author dont write a complete good story. Will he die before doing so, or come back from America & do it?" (*Letters*, 2:685–86).

In making this remark he is responding in part to the installment he has just finished, number nineteen of *Pendennis*, where in beginning the final large movement of the novel he has had to loosen certain structural bonds in order to develop others and to begin a final tying together of the novel.[9] He looks forward to a work more tightly plotted and perhaps completed before publication—as *Esmond* turned out to be—but later he continues to speak of his novels, including *Esmond*, in the same way. A portion of *Pendennis* is "stupid . . . and yet how well written"; a part of *Esmond* "is clever but it is also stupid and no mistake"; *The Newcomes*, so far as it is written, is "not good. It's stupid"; *The Virginians*, as one can now easily predict, is "clever but stupid thats the fact," "most admirable" but also "devilish stupid" (*Letters*, 2:685; 3: 69, 299; 4: 80, 85n). In the works themselves, like the preface to *Pendennis*, Thackeray apologizes both for dullness and for artistic imperfections that he overtly associates in this instance with serial composition. The main point, however, is that Thackeray is not indifferent; he continues to be *bothered* by what are, after all, generally minor inconsistencies—which is not the usual response of a careless man. He insists, one should also notice, that serial writing has the compensating "advantage of a certain truth and honesty, which a work more elaborate might lose." But he is constantly, indeed compulsively, troubled by the minor imperfections that creep in—which even he is willing to admit are not major errors but "slip[s] of the pen and the printer."[10]

One might conclude that Thackeray is extremely concerned both with avoiding blunders and with achieving accuracy. His efforts to borrow unpublished papers, examine contemporary printed sources, secure early copies of forthcoming historical accounts or studies, and consult experts on points ranging from military history to matters of law are all documented by his correspondence, both published and unpublished. That kind of effort, sustained throughout his career, does not seem commensurate with the allegations of inadequate preparation.

Aside from the evidence of forethought and elaborate care provided by his correspondence and by the patterns that run through the published texts of Thackeray's serial novels, other pieces of documentation also survive. These include a fragmentary outline for a portion of *Vanity Fair's* ninth installment, historical notes for *Esmond* and *The Virginians*, a time scheme for certain events in *The Newcomes*, an outline for the major events in that novel's last nine installments, an outline for most of volume 1 of *The Virginians*, and a number of preliminary papers for *Denis Duval*. Our understanding of them is limited by the general absence of precise dates and of collateral notes, but we can probably assume that these documents, which range in their scope and serve a variety of functions, represent only a portion of the supplementary material used during the lengthy creation of these massive and intricate novels. At the very least, we would be well advised neither to assume that lack of fuller evidence means it never existed (three of these documents have been made public in the last five years), nor to base ambitious generalizations upon the papers that do survive, even were the space available here for examining them individually. It must suffice to say that Thackeray's historical research, the setting down of a time scheme, and the outlining of a sequence of developments are all not merely evidence of forethought and aids to memory, but are also modes of orientation and discovery. The growth of these discoveries, both up to and beyond their momentary fixing on individual surviving leaves of preliminary papers, we may never be able to trace in more than rough form, but the actual survival of these scattered leaves is enough to give us intimations of unsuspected complexity.

The further question of what *manuscript* antecedents might have

lain behind the version initially submitted to the printer each month
has never been pondered by previous criticism, nor has the use Thackeray made of secretaries been given sufficiently thoughtful attention
—so readily has it been assumed that there were no earlier manuscript
versions; hence, of course, secretaries could automatically be assumed
to be writing to dictation out of thin air, instead of copying—or, for
that matter, taking down oral revision—from a previously written
version. Close examination of the widely scattered Thackeray manuscripts, however, reveals not only passages in Thackeray's hand as
well as in those of secretaries that have the decided appearance of being copied, but also the occasional existence of discarded leaves in his
hand that were copied by an amanuensis or by himself for the version
submitted to the printer. Here too, then, is a major caution and a further suggestion of complex creation instead simply of the desperate
scribbling of a first and final draft.

The various time-factors also need to be considered. We know, for
example, that in the case of *Vanity Fair* Thackeray agreed to furnish
Bradbury and Evans with the text and illustrations for each installment by the fifteenth of each month (*Adversity*, p. 433), but that he
was still writing numbers five, seven, fifteen, and eighteen after that
date, and that he completed work on numbers nine, eleven, thirteen,
and fourteen, plus the final double installment close to publication date
(*Letters*, 2: 289, 305, 314n, 321, 327, 345–46, 352, 381, 392). Shortly
after finishing number fourteen, Thackeray himself commented: "At
the end of the month I always have a life-&-death struggle to get out
my number of Vanity Fair" (*Letters*, 2:346).

Here several issues arise. Since Thackeray was writing a variety of
pieces simultaneously with installments of *Vanity Fair*—notably for
Punch, which was also published by Bradbury and Evans—he had a
full month's activities, had carefully to juggle his tasks, and had the
printer's boy outside his door waiting for copy and corrected proof of
more than *Vanity Fair*. Such circumstances inevitably demanded
careful forethought and a judicious scheduling of his time. As he indicated to his mother on 16 March 1847, "It is work work, think think
all day. Men of my sort I suppose can do no otherwise—I am always
thinking of No IV or No V.&c—All things go very well in that respect"; and as he repeated some weeks later: "I am always thinking
about Vanity Fair" (*Letters*, 2: 286–87, 291). No wonder he was upset
when the unexpected intruded. Thus, amid difficulties concerning a

governess for his daughters, he informed his mother on 6 April 1847, "The Gloyne banishment has cost me a valuable day's work," and on 15 April he was agonizing over a further loss of time; in spite of the success of his earlier forethought, he announced himself "in a state of distraction with No V—I lost a whole week last week with our domestic perplexities . . . and must fly the house I see to get quiet." He broke off his letter: "I cant write—I'm thinking of V" (*Letters*, 2: 287, 289). What we see, then, is not idleness but a very energetic man deeply involved in his work, especially his novel.

One must also take a closer look at Thackeray's activity towards the end of the month during the appearance of a novel like *Vanity Fair*. Critics have generally assumed that Thackeray typically sent the anxious printer his manuscript for the complete installment on about the 28th or so of each month, together with his illustrations, and that he would then either cut a lengthy text or scribble out extra letterpress, or toss in extra illustrations, or do both in order to fill out his number. These assumptions need to be challenged, however, because evidence concerning both original and extra letterpress is generally lacking for this period of Thackeray's career, and because a text can be written and set up in type more quickly than a drawing can be made and executed in wood, which in turn can be done more rapidly than the drawing and etching of the full-page illustrations on metal plates—both kinds being required for each installment.[11]

It is more logical to suspect that *if* the manuscript were belated, it might have been sent to the printer in relays and portions of proof might have been corrected before the completion even of the basic manuscript (as distinguished from additional manuscript leaves composed after a text had already been set into type—written in order to fill out a short number, to make an artistically desired augmentation, or to do both together). Whether or not Thackeray sent the basic manuscript to the printer in relays during the composition of *Vanity Fair* and *Pendennis* we cannot say, though bits of evidence suggest he may have done so at times.[12] Stronger hints appear later, however; in the case of a novel like *Philip*, from Thackeray's numbering and from the independent, corroborative designations of the printer we can clearly see that *often* the procedure was to send the manuscript in relays and to return it in the same manner.

In addition to seeing the possibility of this procedure's use during creation of the earlier fiction, we can recognize that if the manuscript were quite belated, some drawings—especially those for the plates—would have to be sent in before the basic manuscript had been finished. Under such circumstances Thackeray would be illustrating a planned scene or providing an initial—often emblematic—for a chapter that had not yet been completed or perhaps even written. This too, of course, would require detailed forethought about the installment's structure and an awareness of its implications for the future. In short, the theory of belatedness, carried to an extreme, begins to work against itself.

But we need not assume that Thackeray's basic manuscript was still unfinished simply because he was working on the number at the end of the month. He may well have had to supply additional matter, to decide where it was to be inserted, and to determine what kind it was to be. Moreover, he had to read and correct proof, or to finish doing so—galley[13] and page proof, if there was time, otherwise only the latter, though not necessarily just one set, as we have seen. The printer, of course, also had proofreaders at work to detect compositorial errors and to raise queries for the author. How much time and care Thackeray gave to the different proofs of *Vanity Fair* is unclear, for not only is most of the manuscript missing, but so are the proofs, except for early fragments embedded in the present manuscript. The existence of errors in the printed text does not necessarily mean that the author failed to correct them in proof,[14] as has so easily and so often been assumed, or that they were even present in the revises. There are many imponderables, and we would be wise not to base generalizations about Thackeray's practices on the thin evidence concerning *Vanity Fair* and *Pendennis* or to assume that what seems to reveal aspects of his practices in composing and proofing these two novels, even if it could be shown to be true, necessarily reveals his later practices. The reverse is, of course, also true. Our need is to remain open and tentative, except where the evidence is firm.[15]

Where actual manuscripts and proof sheets exist, we can see that the only surviving portion of the *Vanity Fair* manuscript is itself largely a special instance of Thackeray's compositional procedures. Because it comes from his most famous novel and because it has been studied in some detail, critics are liable to think of it as a representative case. In fact, however, the circumstances surrounding it are unique, since almost a year elapsed between Thackeray's submission of an initial segment to Bradbury and Evans (after several rejections elsewhere) and the actual publication of the opening installment—an interval during which Thackeray made revisions that were extensive and significant, especially structurally. Even though we may never know what compositional activity lay behind the manuscript (especially its initial portion, which seems to have been at one point a relatively fair copy), we can still say that in no other novel can we identify changes of such magnitude during the course of writing.

Generalizations about the composition and proofing of his serial fiction must instead begin with the example of *The Newcomes*, but here too there are particular circumstances that must be recognized.[16] Although roughly half of the manuscript exists, there are no known proof sheets. With *The Newcomes* Thackeray was hardly ever belated in preparing the original manuscripts of his installments, being generally several months ahead of the publication dates, except towards the end. Since Richard Doyle, in spite of his dilatoriness, was retained as illustrator, Thackeray was free to travel abroad for months at a time. He was sent proofs while abroad, and after he returned them, a friend and fellow writer, Percival Leigh, read the revises. When Thackeray was in Italy, he expected proofs considerably in advance of publication, but even under these circumstances Bradbury and Evans did not furnish them—presumably because they wished to keep type standing for as short a time as possible. The only documented instance of their providing him in the same month with proof for several numbers concerns two installments of *The Newcomes*, numbers six and seven for March and April 1854, which they mailed to Italy on 11 February (*Letters*, 3:349)—the belatedness of his *publishers* almost costing him the opportunity for making changes in the March installment. Even though he had only hours at his disposal, Thackeray introduced a considerable number of refining changes into the proofs, extending from instances of a single word to one of almost a hundred. In short, his working over only a single set of proofs in this instance—which is one of the few of its kind we can document—reveals not carelessness but the reverse: both intensive and extensive labor.[17]

By the time he was completing *The Newcomes*, Thackeray's health had become severely and permanently damaged. Henceforth he was unable to stay significantly ahead of his deadlines, having instead to struggle with endlessly recurring attacks of illness. Though the pressures of time became more and more demanding, and though his anxieties increased, nevertheless his tenacious commitment to his art was unbroken. The manuscript of *The Virginians*, like all others, shows revisions made at different times before it was sent to the printer. Several installments provide brief evidence of several stages of proofing, but in the case of number eighteen for April 1859, proofs actually survive. They constitute the fullest documentation so far in Thackeray's career of an installment's passage through the press, for substantial portions from an earlier and a later set of page proof, together with the manuscript, exist in the Morgan Library. They show that in the earlier set of page proof Thackeray extended a passage of commentary at the end of the opening chapter so as to provide a further, more complex perspective. He also significantly augmented the ending of the next chapter by developing the dramatic implications of an already written portion of narrative, so as to create an ironic interplay with the augmented commentary of the previous chapter. When Thackeray received a subsequent set of page proof, he recognized that the installment now fitted satisfactorily into its allotted pages. If he were the careless, hasty, aloof workman he is assumed to be, that recognition would have been enough. Instead of being satisfied, however, he made further adjustments, including a dozen substantive changes.

The final stage of Thackeray's career, marked by his writing for the *Cornhill Magazine*, provides notably fuller documentation—especially concerning the actual proofing of installments. The initial number of *Lovel*, for example, passed through two stages of galleys—each of which reveals significant change and extensive care—before finally entering page proof, where further changes were made. Besides multiple levels of compositional activity apparent in the basic manuscript of this installment, therefore, we have clear evidence of three carefully proofed sequences marking the installment's passage through the press. Similar instances of careful correction and revision are documented throughout the rest of Thackeray's career—in the *Roundabout Papers*, for example, as well as in his fiction.

When we carefully move through the increasing evidence of Thackeray's compositional processes from *Vanity Fair* through *Denis Duval*, hints for a new view of Thackeray gradually emerge. Finally, we have the basis for saying that when manuscripts and proof sheets exist together they demonstrate conclusively that the author who set his hand to them was neither a careless nor a hasty worker, whether in composing the basic manuscript or in seeing an installment through the press, where he typically made revisions during a number of proof stages with an attention both minute and far-ranging.

In "De Finibus" for August 1862, he tells us that he cannot emulate Alexandre Dumas, for whom "the chapters, the characters, the incidents, the combinations were *all* arranged in the artist's brain ere he set a pen to paper" (emphasis mine). For all Thackeray's forethought, he had to work out various details of his conception during the processes of composition. So too, for all of Thackeray's careful writing, revising, and proofing, various details of his large-scale fiction escape perfect integration. In the same essay, when he acknowledges his shortcomings, blunders, and slips of memory, making reference to an error in volume 84 of the *Cornhill Magazine*, which would be published only in 1901, he is not merely saying that his errors will live after him, but is amusedly and resignedly acknowledging that the wish to eradicate error is inevitably defeated both by the temporal conditions of man's existence and by man's own hopelessly erring nature. We all, in different ways, stumble through life with at least one foot unaccountably wedged in a bucket. Part of our lack of graceful consistency no doubt comes also from our movement away from our own past, which is inevitably seen with a changed perspective—in Thackeray's case, typically a melancholy sense of unfulfillment. Looking back at the past represented by his own pages gives him "anything but elation of mind," he tells us in "De Finibus." "So you are gone, little printer's boy, with the last scratches and corrections on the proof, and a fine flourish by way of Finis at the story's end. The last corrections? I say those last corrections seem never to be finished" (*CM* 6 [1862]: 287–88). There is always further possibility as long as the process of our life continues, and especially as the impulse to write continues. Thackeray's concern with avoiding blunders and achieving accuracy, coherence, and fidelity of expression is an integral part of the larger process of searching, discovering, and unfolding that ultimately for him defines and justifies fiction: not the possession of truth, which is static and unreal, but the *striving* to find and "tell the truth. If there is not that, there is nothing" (*Pendennis*, 2:vi).

An awareness of these aspects of Thackeray's artistry should lead to the welcoming of a critical edition like *The Complete Works of William Makepeace Thackeray* that has been announced by J. Faust; it will include a text based upon the earliest surviving form, full illustrations, historical essays, textual essays, historical collation, and annotation. Perhaps we will now be able to see a Thackerayan novel more clearly than before as a series of overlays—each new installment, chapter, paragraph, and sentence being a possible overlay instead of merely a direct extension. Since Thackeray does not offer us a novel as a static construct, a seamless web, or a perfect organic whole, we would do well to move beyond our Neo-Aristotelian and New Critical vocabulary and expectations. We might then perceive that the "modes" of creation furnish an awareness for the reader to feel in his bones as he follows the so-called narrative, which is processive and various, not one thing.

Hence "overlay" is not quite the term, since it fails to express movement. We might think of the analogue of a Thackerayan narrative as an unhung variegated mobile, undulating and revolving as it proceeds, and which we perceive in moving to "follow" it. There is what we normally call order, which I have attempted to identify in earlier essays; but along with it is also "order" of a very different kind—"relation" is a better word—which it might be the task of future criticism to evoke. What we might seek is different from what we have seen, but we also have to look in a new way.

That, however, is only a possible shape of things to come. For the present, a firmer basis for our awareness must be established.

As the foregoing discussion suggests, and as the ensuing chapters will reveal, the significance of Thackeray's compositional activities lies especially in their particularity. Generalizations beyond those already made, however comfortable it might be to have them, are difficult to evolve precisely because of the highly idiosyncratic nature of each group of monthly efforts. This is as it should be, reality being concrete and particular, not abstract and general. A few additional introductory observations, however, can be made.

The demands of Thackeray's other creative interests, his active social life, and his steadily failing health, not only faced the novelist with difficult circumstances but also established constraints within which concentrated artistic efforts were encouraged. The very nature of serial creation and publication gave intermittent respite, but, even more, it freshly stimulated his abilities and called forth renewed commitment to his art, for he was not finished composing even when he had sent off the last relay of his monthly manuscript to the printer. The exigencies of producing a serial installment required repeated stages of creative activity in order to shorten a text by identifying weaker, expendable passages; to lengthen it by discovering further creative possibilities in material already set down; or to do both at once.

Again and again he came back to his manuscripts and then to his proofs—sometimes even before the basic manuscript was complete— making simple deletions, changes, and additions, but also reshaping, providing new interpretive contexts, refocussing perspectives, modulating tones, shifting emphases, anticipating future developments, and embodying new artistic discoveries. His modifying powers were so active that one suspects he used a secretary to take down and copy portions of his narratives partly in order to counteract his own irrepressible impulse to revise. Living constantly with these varied processes of creation as he formed his novels from month to month, accompanied by the ticking of the clock, Thackeray—amid all his distractions—was indeed possessed by a sacred rage that could not be extinguished except when he was overcome by waves of intense physical suffering. To study the composition of his major serial novels is, increasingly, to feel something of that anguish and to be deeply moved by the narrowing but invincible gaiety with which that central flame continued to burn.

2

Vanity Fair

Installments 1 and 2

Scholars have had difficulty deciding exactly when Thackeray began to
write the initial portion of *Vanity Fair*, for the evidence is sketchy.[1] A
number of other questions concerning this portion also remain unan-
swered and perhaps unanswerable. For example, to which publishers
was the manuscript submitted? During what period or periods was it
under consideration, and how long was the manuscript portion in each
instance? The scarcity of evidence should admonish us to assume as little as possible—not to believe, for instance, that the portion submitted
to a given publisher was thought of by Thackeray as a serial installment of thirty-two pages, for the nature of its publication could be
decided only after its acceptance, whether in the form of a three-vol-
ume novel, a serial appearing in a periodical (like *Barry Lyndon*, with
average installments of sixteen pages), a separate monthly serial (like
Martin Chuzzlewit, with installments of exactly thirty-two pages), or
some other form.

We know Thackeray told William Edmondstoune Aytoun that Henry Colburn refused the novel (*Letters*, 2:262), and we may suspect that
Thackeray's letter of 8 May 1845 to Colburn refers to *Vanity Fair*, assuming that the novelist requested its return because he interpreted
the publisher's delay as a tacit rejection. In this letter, however,
Thackeray calls the manuscript portion only "the commencement of a
novel" (*Letters*, 2:198n)—not its first installment. Henry Vizetelly,
whom Malcolm Elwin calls "one of the most reliable and entertaining
writers of Victorian literary memoirs,"[2] was apparently the only contemporary to publish statements drawing on personal experience
closely related to one of Thackeray's submissions. Writing forty-five
years after the event, Vizetelly evokes an afternoon in 1846 when
Thackeray arrived carrying "a small brown paper parcel," which he
then opened in order to show the engraver "two careful drawings."
Vizetelly (perhaps too confidently, considering the lapse of time) identifies them as "drawings for the page plates to the first number of

'Vanity Fair.'"[3] In fact, as we shall later see, one of them may have been *"Mr. Joseph in a state of excitement,"* for what came to be the second number. On the basis of no specified reason, Vizetelly feels "positive that . . . nothing beyond Number I. was written" (*Glances,* 1:285); his language, however, indicates that he is not repeating something Thackeray told him but is instead making an inference, perhaps from a memory of the parcel's approximate size together with a memory of there being two drawings, and is assuming that the parcel contained all of the extant manuscript. He writes that Thackeray said he was about to visit "Bradbury & Evans, and offer the work to them." Returning in "little more than half-an-hour Mr. Thackeray . . . gleefully informed me that he had settled the business." Vizetelly reports that the agreed-upon remuneration was "fifty guineas per part, including the two sheets of letterpress, a couple of etchings, and the initials at the commencement of the chapters" (*Glances,* 1:284). However, in a letter that seems to have been written in January 1846, soon after the event Vizetelly describes, Thackeray himself identified the sum as "60£ a number" (*Letters,* 2:225)—the same sum named in the later, formal agreement between author and publisher, which specifies "at least Two printed Sheets with two Etchings on Steel, and as many drawings on Wood as may be thought necessary" (*Adversity,* p. 433). Vizetelly also mistakenly feels "certain . . . that not so much as a hint about 'Vanity Fair' was conveyed to any other publisher" (*Glances,* 1:285) besides Bradbury and Evans except Chapman and Hall. An undated letter written by Thackeray during the *Cornhill* years, however, mentions his having "tried 3 or 4 publishers with Vanity Fair" (NLS; partly quoted in *Adversity,* p. 384), one of whom was presumably Colburn. Finally, Vizetelly claims that on the same day as the visit to Bouverie Street, which seems to have been early January 1846, Thackeray told him that *Vanity Fair* was to be the novel's title (*Glances,* 1:284); this too seems improbable.[4]

Turning from such uncertain testimony to the 113 manuscript leaves in the Morgan Library, one sees that a common numbering system unites fifty-four of the extant leaves (fols. 1–32, ⟨39⟩–⟨46⟩, and ⟨48⟩–⟨61⟩), which are numbered in pencil (except for fols. 1–11) and are written on whitish paper in Thackeray's slanted hand.[5] Brief changes in both slanted and upright script on some of these leaves apparently were made during a later stage of composition, as was the setting down of additional text (about which more will be said later) in the up-

right hand, for the most part on yellowish paper. Fols. 1–32, especially, which were sent to the Bradbury and Evans printing house in
1846, either in April (*Letters*, 2:233) or later that year, have the
appearance of fair copy. We shall probably never know the compositional activity that preceded this fifty-four-leaf portion of the
manuscript.[6]

If it is impossible to say how much of a sample Thackeray submitted
to the various publishers, including Bradbury and Evans, one can see
that the first thirty-two leaves mentioned above largely contain the
present text of chapters 1–4, together with an earlier version of chapter 6. All include brief alterations. Fol. 1 begins, "Chapr 1. Chiswick
Mall," but nowhere else in this initial section of the manuscript portion
did Thackeray set down a chapter division or chapter title. He clearly
thought of the first five leaves as a chapter, however, for fol. 6 begins:
"When Miss Sharp had performed the heroical act mentioned in the
last chapter, and had seen the Dixonary flying over the pavement of
the little garden . . . ." The text of the present chapter 3 begins with
the last line on fol. 12, but a portion of blank space at the bottom of fol.
25, prior to the text's continuing with the earlier version of chapter 6
on fol. 26, suggests that Thackeray may have intended a chapter break
at this point, even though he did not mark it. A blank space at the bottom of fol. 14 is more puzzling; it will be discussed below.

In setting down this neatly written text, Thackeray was apparently
copying an earlier version but also making revisions, several of which
may be cited as examples. He twice referred to a well-known novelistic
format (though it was not the one in which *Vanity Fair* was to appear),
for he indicated the probability that Jemima would never again be
mentioned in the novel, not "to the end of the third volume," and that
she would never again reenter "this world of history," above which he
added the words "three-volumed." Subsequently he deleted these references, replacing "third volume" with "time" (mistakenly retaining
"the") and substituting "little" for "three-volumed" (fol. 3). One cannot identify the manuscript as one of early 1845 on the basis of these
terms, however, for the date of the changes remains unknown. Although the terms are used generically, not literally, Thackeray apparently wanted in this passage to evoke a long stretch of time instead of
the confined space of a novel—even a lengthy one. He did not have the
same need in the final number, for there he did use the term, again in

its generic rather than literal sense: "Here it is—the summit, the end
—the last page of the third volume."[7]

Aside from making a number of careful adjustments to his narrative
by means of mostly very brief verbal changes, Thackeray also altered
in manuscript the names of several characters. He referred to Joseph
Sedley as Frank and Francis on fols. 11–13v, but began to set down
"Joseph" in uncorrected form on fol. 15, where an account of Jos's
Indian life began.[8] George Osborne was for a time given Mr. Sedley's
name of John (fol. 20), but whether it was simply a mistake or an early
means of showing a close relationship between George and his god-
father, the duplication did not occur thereafter. In one instance, not
only a name was changed but also the identity of a character to whom
an act was attributed. On fol. 1 Thackeray was in the process of showing how Miss Pinkerton herself was peering out of a window, pleased
by the appearance of Sedley's prosperous-looking coach at her gates
and apparently about to remark on it to her sister. The novelist decided, however, that the stern "roman nose of Miss Jemima Pinkerton
herself" would not be "somewhat flattened"; hence he cancelled the
last two words and continued: "rising over some geranium-pots in the
windows of that lady's own drawing room." He also recognized that
the dignified Miss Pinkerton would not be engaged in such publicly
visible peering and therefore he changed the nose to a "little red" one
and its owner to Miss Pinkerton's "good-natured" sister, now called
Jemima; but he forgot to cancel the word "herself," which he continued to use below in referring to "Miss Pinkerton herself, that majestic lady" (fol. 1), who was now to be named "Barbara" (fol. 2). A
number of such minor lapses always escaped Thackeray's attention, no
matter how often he went over his work seeking to improve it; they
seem the inevitable imperfections of this massive and intricate fiction.

Brief passages written on the versos of fols. 5, 13, and 20 also call
for attention. The first passage of the three seems to have been set
down on fol. 5v, not because it was an afterthought but because it was
to contain only a few lines and was to provide the initial chapter's ending: Becky's decisive rejection of the "Dixonary" (from "And the kind
creature" to "and so farewell to Chiswick Mall" [see p. 7]). This rejection, of course, is "the heroical act" to which Thackeray immediately
alludes in an uninserted passage at the top of fol. 6. The second passage also ends a scene and may likewise at the time have been intended

as a chapter ending. Extending from "On wh. of course" to "walked merrily off" (fol. 13*v*; see p. 17), it completes the scene in which Becky meets Jos Sedley, just before her first dinner in Russell Square. At this point, Thackeray may have begun to set down a retrospective narrative concerning Jos at the top of what is now fol. 15, where the first uncorrected use of his Christian name occurs: "Joseph Sedley was twelve years older than his sister Amelia." Blank space at the bottom of fol. 14 may therefore identify the twenty-five lines of that leaf—a narrative concerning Becky's Alnaschar visions (from "If Miss Rebecca Sharp" to "day-dreams ere now!" [pp. 17–18])—as a lengthy new ending for the proposed second chapter. If so, it would have been an ending that looks ahead to the failure of Becky's campaign against Jos that was to occur approximately two chapters later.

The third passage may represent either an interpolation or a chapter ending.[9] If it was the former, one must posit that the nighttime conversation between Mr. and Mrs. Sedley probably ended with the former's cry: "The girl's a white face at any rate" (fol. 20). The interpolation would then have begun with four words at the bottom of fol. 20 ("*I* don't care who") and continued, "marries him. Let Jos please himself," followed by a brief passage evoking the sounds and silence of night (fol. 20*v*; see p. 25). Alternatively, the four lines on the verso of fol. 20 may have represented the small surplus of the intended chapter conclusion—one that provided opposition to Becky's pursuit of Jos from Mrs. Sedley and acceptance from Jos's father.

After making a variety of changes, Thackeray sent his manuscript to the printer, though it is impossible to say whether in one unit or in relays (e.g., fols. 1–17, 18–25, and 26–32). We can see, however, that the shop foreman, generally following paragraph breaks, divided fols. 1–5, 5*v*, and the top five lines of fol. 6 among five compositors: an unknown man, Morgan, Smetham, Fitchett, and Combes. The group of Morgan, Fitchett, Meehan, Smetham, Combes, and Meehan again, set up the rest of fol. 6, plus fols. 7–17, the end of which coincides with the conclusion of the present chapter 3. The text of the present chapter 4 (fols. 18–25) was set up by Fitchett, Smetham, Morgan, and Combes, while the earlier version of chapter 6 (fols. 26–32)—then the final portion of the first installment—was set up, so far as one can see from the surviving manuscript, by the last three of these compositors, joined by Meehan, Sainte, and Austin, with Smetham and Sainte each doing two stints. Set into galley proof, this text extended over eleven "slips," nine of which were marked on the manuscript, presumably by a proof-reader.

These eleven "slips" either contained page divisions, including running heads and page numerals, or Thackeray in returning them to the printer asked for revised galley proof that was to contain such divisions. Only ten fragments of this initial or revised proof—or of both—survive; they are now part of the manuscript of the later version of chapter 6, having been pasted onto fols. 12–16 and 18–19 of the second installment. I shall designate these segments of proof frags. [A]–[J] in order to facilitate discussing them separately from the later manuscript leaves in which they are embedded. Collation of frags. [A], [D]–[F], [H], and [I] with the earlier manuscript version reveals no substantive variants beyond customary regularizing by the compositors: for example, "fought . . . with the coachman" (frag. [A]) for "fough . . . with coachman" (fol. 26). The same may be true of frag. [G], which reads "scuffling and running" for "scuffle and running" (fol. 31).

Frag. [C], however, reveals intervention of a kind that, while possibly compositorial, seems more probably to have been authorial: the creation of two new paragraph divisions. Fol. [B] seems to me to reveal prior authorial change in the deletion of two separate phrases, perhaps because of their mildly ribald and callous nature, that had appeared in the manuscript version of "THE NIGHT ATTACK." Thus, "A hackney coachman had been blown off his coach box in Southampton Row—a child of the Foundling hospital having occasion to leave his bed at night had been swept away—and whither? Ask the annals of Lamb's conduit—but the whirlwind tells no tidings" (fol. 26) became: "A hackney coachman had been blown off his coach-box, in Southampton Row—and whither? But the whirlwind tells no tidings" (frag. [B]).[10]

Frag. [J] is a portion of galley proof that contains a page division, for it starts with the last line of the previous page ("'He must propose to-morrow,' thought Rebecca. 'He called me'"), followed by the running head ("A NOVEL WITHOUT A HERO"), the recto page numeral ("35"), and the thirty-six lines of text that constituted the chapter's and first installment's intended conclusion. It begins with a passage set up from the surviving upper fragment of fol. 32 and includes in this portion of text one substantive variant; where fol. 32 reads, "asked him about his love—his love? Good Gad," the proof reads, "asked him about his love. Good Gad!"—an omission attributable either to the compositor or to Thackeray while correcting earlier proof.

Regardless how many sets of early proof there were, however, by the time Thackeray received the galley proof represented by frag. [J], he had a printed narrative centering on Becky's pursuit of Jos that extended over thirty-five proof pages and ended with disaster following the episode at Vauxhall. After depicting Miss Pinkerton's school and the departure of Becky and Amelia, Thackeray had shown something of Becky's bohemian past, her successful struggle with Miss Pinkerton, her arrival at Russell Square, and her determination to marry Jos. Subsequent to her first meeting and dinner with Jos, his tip-toeing departure, his return, and the plans for Vauxhall, the novelist had provided an account of an intimate evening at Russell Square that culminated in Becky's song, Jos's appreciative response, and his reappearance the next morning before luncheon to settle on a date for the party at Vauxhall: "The matter had not been fully arranged the night previous" (fol. 25).

Vauxhall then formed the substance of the installment's concluding portion of narrative. After an introduction that provided parodic samples of current novels (fol. 26; frag. [A]), especially of Newgate (fols. 26–27; frag. [B]) and supremely genteel fiction (fol. 27; frag. [C]), Thackeray turned to the occasion of the Vauxhall visit four or five days after the evening at Russell Square (fol. 28), Mr. Sedley's indifference to Jos's choice of a wife (fol. 28; frag. [D]), Mrs. Sedley's gradual acquiescence in Jos's choice of Becky (fol. 29; frag. [E]), preliminary events at the Royal Gardens (fol. 30; frags. [F] and [G]), and Jos's fatal ordering of the bowl of rack punch (fol. 31). One additional paragraph remains on the fragmentary fol. 31, recounting how Jos drank up all the rack punch and in his tipsy state attracted a considerable group of spectators, drawing from them "a great deal of applause." The same paragraph appears on frag. [H], and though the bottom half of fol. 31 is missing beginning at this point, frag. [H] supplies us with fifteen important additional lines of text. From them we learn that the boisterous comments directed at Jos by the onlookers "alarm" Amelia and Becky and produce "great anger" in George. When the imperturb-

ably affable Jos invites "all or any to come in and take a share of his
punch," George is "just on the point of knocking down a Hebrew gentleman from the Minories, who proposed to take advantage of this
invitation, who avoided that catastrophe by a timely retreat, when, by
great"; at this point, frag. [H] breaks off but not before revealing that
something happens to relieve the difficulties faced by George and the
ladies.

As the top of fol. 32 and as frag. [I] make clear, the event is the arrival of "Captain Tawney" to assist George and Jos, both of whom he
appears to know. Tawney's uniform seems to imply an intervention to
assist a known fellow-officer (George is in mufti, as we see in "*Mr.
Joseph in a state of excitement*"), while his name and yellow face indicate that he has served in a tropical climate, either the West Indies or
India[11]; his act of calling on Jos the next morning also suggests more
than one evening's acquaintance, as does the narrator's term, "his
friend Tawney" (fol. 32; see frag. [J]). In short, it appears that because
of Jos's helpless inebriation and George's need to protect Amelia and
Becky from the intrusive crowd and to be free to take the ladies home,
Thackeray required the presence of another male figure. His choice
was Captain Tawney. It may be that the creation of one of *Vanity
Fair*'s main characters—Dobbin—had its fortuitous beginning here
with the introduction of a mere supernumerary to keep the wheel of
the plot turning, but it is at least possible that Thackeray was both
serving a minor plot function and at the same time economically using
the occasion to introduce a figure whom he already intended as an important male character. One should notice also that acts of intervention crucially define Dobbin's role throughout the novel.[12]

It is certain, however, that the installment's emphasis on Becky's
pursuit of Jos left little room for further material: very little about
George and even less about a figure like Tawney, who was not a member of any romantic couple at the outset of the novel. Thackeray's main
preoccupation at this point was to bring his installment to a climax.
After having Captain Tawney shrewdly use Jos's mention of knocking
up the Archbishop of Canterbury as a pretext for conveying the fat
bacchanalian to his lodgings (fol. 32; frag. [I]), the novelist concluded
with a passage contained partly on the upper portion of fol. 32 and
partly on frag. [J]. Though Becky expects Jos to propose the next day,
the effects of rack punch keep him in agony and the reappearance of

Tawney causes him an excruciating embarrassment that leads to his
flight from London the next day. The final events, then, follow one another in a very rapid succession:

> His friend Tawney, came grinning with his lean yellow face, and asked
> him about his love. Good Gad! had he revealed it? All his modesty came
> rushing back upon him with redoubled force,—he felt awkward,
> wretched, humiliated beyond measure.
>
> The next day Amelia received a note from him, which the two girls
> opened trembling together, for they thought it contained the long-looked
> for declaration. But it contained only the following:—
>
> "DEAR AMELIA,—I leave town to-day for Cheltenham. Pray excuse me,
> if you can, to the amiable Miss Sharp for my conduct at Vauxhall, and
> entreat her to pardon and forget every word that I may have uttered
> when excited by that fatal supper. As soon as I have recovered, (for my
> health is very much shaken,) I shall go to Scotland for some months,
> and am
>
> > "Truly yours,
> > "JOSEPH SEDLEY."
>
> And so ended Miss Rebecca Sharp's first campaign in life. It was a de-
> feat; but it was honourable to the vanquished. She found that it was very
> necessary to keep her engagement with Sir Pitt Crawley, and so parted
> from her dear, dear, dear Amelia, whom she vowed she would love for
> ever, and ever, and ever. (frag. [J])

For whatever reason, publication was delayed until the end of December 1846, during which period, as is well known, Thackeray had
time to develop his conception of the novel. What we may suspect to
be an April type setting was apparently distributed and a new setting
composed in late November or in December.[13] Faced in late 1846,
then, with a text for the initial installment that was almost three pages
too long, but that had a rather hasty conclusion and that seems to have
had only limited space for illustrations—none evidently for the Vauxhall chapter—Thackeray had two rather unequal choices before him.
On the one hand he could have developed the concluding scene more
fully and thereby been forced to prune the earlier portions even further, reducing the whole text by four to five pages. On the other hand,
he could have removed the Vauxhall chapter, thereby leaving perhaps
four printed pages to be filled up with additional matter that would
have furnished a new serial ending. He chose the second alternative.
Especially in view of the artistic difficulty of deleting one-seventh of

his text, the latter choice was clearly the more plausible of the two. It meant altering the installment's structure, which coincided with Becky's "first campaign in life," but since the change only deferred a narrative climax, it was suited to the nature of a serial, which formalizes incompleteness. The choice had also the secondary advantage of conserving a portion of manuscript for inclusion in the second number.

In this last stage of adjusting his installment to the requirements of its serial appearance, Thackeray made no major changes to the texts of the first three chapters, though there were brief additions and deletions.[14] Though it is impossible to say at what point or points illustrations were inserted,[15] we can see that in the case of chapter 1 the text was augmented slightly by a chapter initial occupying the equivalent of seven lines and significantly by two internal wood-engravings taking up the space of twenty-eight and twenty-one lines respectively: the supercilious Miss Pinkerton writing her "billet" (p. 2) and the supercilious Jones reading the installment at his club (p. 5). The chapter's length was thereby increased from six pages to seven. Since only twenty lines of text now occurred on the last page, an endpiece was also added: showing the departing coach, it balanced the chapter initial's portrayal of the coach arriving.

Chapter 2 came to occupy eight pages instead of the seven represented by its letterpress, the difference being produced by a chapter initial of two lines (in effect) and an internal wood-engraving of thirty. Again Thackeray provided an endpiece as well—a rendering of Becky arm-in-arm with Amelia that illustrates the chapter's conclusion and in its surface appearance pointedly contrasts with the two previous illustrations, which provide it with an interpretive visual context: a demon, analogous to the figure evoked by Becky (p. 9), and Becky as puppeteer manipulating two female figures for an appreciative audience (p. 11). The third chapter was not notably extended by illustrations; it received only a brief initial and endpiece, showing Jos confronted and Jos fleeing. As a result of these additions, the first three chapters were now to occupy twenty-one pages; the remaining eleven were to be filled up by extending chapter 4 over two additional ones.

A chapter initial depicting Becky angling for a fat fish and an internal wood-engraving showing an audience of servants listening to the drawing room concert (p. 29) added the equivalent of thirty-four lines.[16] The two remaining additions were textual. Although, as I have said, it is not clear exactly when Thackeray inserted the first of these—a ten-

line paragraph that was added to the chapter's initial page—we can
see that it is thematically connected to the internal wood-engraving,
for it explains in detail that Becky not only established herself in the
favor of "the chiefs of the family," but also cultivated Mrs. Blenkinsop,
Sambo, and the lady's maid so successfully "that the Servants' Hall
was almost as charmed with her as the Drawing Room" (p. 22). Thackeray's major addition, however, was the passage of sixty-five lines
with which he gave the chapter and the installment a new ending.

His extant portion of narrative containing the immediate prelude to
the Vauxhall excursion ended, we remember, with the intimate evening at Russell Square, Jos's ensuing thought of possibly marrying
Becky, and his unprecedented reappearance prior to luncheon the next
day: "He had never been known to confer such an honor before on the
house in Russell Square. When was the party fixed for Vauxhall that
was the great question wh. brought him. The matter had not been fully
arranged the night previous" (fol. 25). Thackeray shortened the third
last sentence, deleted the last two, and then went on to develop his
concluding scene, which was to serve three objectives: further his plot,
lead to an aborted conclusion, and yet promise a decisive future development. In the deferred Vauxhall narrative, Thackeray had indicated
that during the interval of "four or five days" between the proposed
and the actual visit to the Gardens, Jos had visited Russell Square "almost every [day]" (fol. 28). Having shown only three occasions on
which Becky and Jos were together prior to the Vauxhall evening,
however, Thackeray now added a fourth dramatized meeting. His idea
for the scene's climax came from a phrase in the deferred narrative—
"He had been discovered holding her skein of silk" (fol. 28)—while the
novelist's immediate model for the scene was, of course, the intimate
evening of the day previous. As on that occasion, so here too George
Osborne is present for a while and then retires with Amelia, leaving
Becky alone with Jos. Before he goes, however, he adopts the bantering tone previously used by Mr. Sedley. The evening before, it was
Mr. Sedley who applauded Jos's solicitous offer of jelly to Becky and
his compliment with: "Bravo Jos!" (fol. 25; see p. 30); here, the same
bantering words are used by George to applaud Jos's solemn and clumsy presentation of flowers (p. 31). (Jos's accompanying gift of a pine-
apple recalls not only the jelly but more especially the chili of chapter
2, which Becky had also never tasted before.) This time Becky does not
sing; instead she resumes her work on the green silk purse and manip-

ulates Jos into the unforgettable position of giving her assistance: "'Will you help me, Mr. Sedley?' And before he had time to ask how, Mr. Joseph Sedley, of the East India Company's service, was actually seated *tête-à-tête* with a young lady, looking at her with a most killing expression; his arms stretched out before her in an imploring attitude, and his hands bound in a web of green silk, which she was unwinding" (p. 32). With the entrance of George and Amelia, Thackeray completed a striking tableau that he augmented with one of his most famous plates: "*Mr. Joseph entangled.*" Although we see that "Mr. Jos had never spoken," yet he does have the last, anticipatory word: "'Gad, I'll pop the question at Vauxhall" (p. 32). With a number of other modifications, all of a minor and very brief kind, Thackeray's composition of his initial serial number was now complete.[17]

The manuscript of number two opens with a chapter written entirely in Thackeray's upright hand on yellowish paper. A good deal has been made of the script by critics and such an emphasis is understandable, although it can be overdone. Gordon Ray, for example, believes that at the end of 1846 and the beginning of 1847 Thackeray "set about revising" what Ray takes to be "his 1845 chapters" in order "to make them convey his vision of well-to-do England as Vanity Fair." Ray also believes that the upright hand quickly reveals these changes: "The alterations which he made at this time (they are readily identifiable, being entered in his later, upright hand) may be studied in the fragmentary manuscript of *Vanity Fair* in the Pierpont Morgan Library" (*Adversity*, p. 386). Years later, however, Thackeray still refers to his slanted writing as his "own" hand, his "natural handwriting," not his "mean literary man's fist" (*Letters*, 2:808; 4: 420, 444) and mentions how at times he changes from one to the other because of his writing position, the particular pen he is using, the degree of haste he feels necessary, or simply because of the mood that happens to seize him (*Letters*, 3: 206, 329, 652; 4:234). Looking beyond circumstances or the motive of immediate personal convenience, however, one seems to see in his use of the upright script a motive more fundamentally related to the purpose of communication: the author's wish to ensure a more legible hand for his correspondents or his compositors. In writing his personal letters during 1847 he continued to use his slanted hand but here too came to employ his upright script more and more. This is one reason why Ray terms the upright Thackeray's "later" hand. But "later" than when? Until we can recover substantial manuscript portions of Thackeray's works before *Vanity Fair* it will be impossible to make a satisfactorily comprehensive statement on this subject.

Ray implies that Thackeray began to use an upright script in late 1846, thereby making possible a ready identification of late 1846 additions to the *Vanity Fair* manuscript; but one must point out in response that Thackeray used his upright hand long before that. In about 1835 he employed it in writing a number of explanatory phrases for a series of drawings known as "'The Count's' Adventures" (*Letters*, vol. 1, Appendix 5). The wish to provide a clear script also seems to have caused its appearance on the drawing for the frontispiece of *The Paris Sketch Book* of 1840.[18] By 1 June 1844 Thackeray had begun to set down correspondence in the upright hand, and during that year he often used it in parts of individual letters or throughout them; it frequently appears in his diary for that year as well (British Lib. Add MS 46899). During 1845 and 1846 he continued to use both scripts in his correspondence.[19] Furthermore, a specific example on fol. ⟨58⟩ indicates that a given alteration in the slanted hand may have accompanied composition or transcription in the upright hand and perhaps even followed some of that activity: on the latter leaf most of an insertion, located in the left margin, is in the upright script ("see them . . . they are!"), but its first two words, in the same dark ink, added near the right margin at the end of a slanted paragraph in lighter ink, were evidently influenced by the nature of the script into which he was making his addition, for these two words ("You should") are also in the slanted hand.

If we turn back to the manuscript of number one, we see that Thackeray also employs his upright hand several times in making pencilled alterations, but if we look at all instances of pencilled changes in the installment we notice that their occurrence forms no discernible pattern: *slanted*—"used to state subsequently" (fol. 8), "heard," "[Se]dley" (fol. 9), "Joseph" (fol. 11), "Joseph Sedley," "Joseph" (twice) (fol. 12); *upright*—"Joseph" (fol. 12); *slanted*—"Joseph," "rather loud," "Joseph" (four times), "Jos," "Joseph" (fol. 13); *upright*—"the period of wh. we write" (fol. 15); *slanted*—"he," "quite as finikin over their toilettes" (fol. 16), "as such perhaps some ladies of indisputable correctness & gentility will condemn the action as," "he," "his," "And this I set down as a positive truth" (fol. 19), "artful creature" (fol. 20); and then two notations in *upright* hand—"The wanderer" and "24 lines" (fol. 24). One concludes, therefore, that handwriting does not offer persuasive evidence for dating Thackeray's additions and corrections to the manuscripts of the first two installments; the question of their date remains open and perhaps unanswerable.

One must instead examine the nature of Thackeray's changes, beginning with the contents of chapter 5. Rather than beginning his new installment with the portion of narrative left over from the previous monthly number and then going on to follow Becky's experiences with the Crawleys, Thackeray precedes a rewritten version of the Vauxhall narrative with significant new exposition concerning the Captain and the Lieutenant, beginning with their acquaintance at school. Thackeray thereby commits himself not only to the character innovation and change of emphasis provided by the present chapter 5 but also, as we shall see, to a major compositional and structural principle that is to pervade the entire novel.

In chapter 5 the character of George is presented more fully and, in his appearance as a boy, at least, with a decisively altered emphasis, while that of the Captain receives its first clear definition. As one returns to the first installment and notes the delineation of George, one sees an uncomplicated figure who appears only in the final chapter and who is chiefly defined by good humor and by his attachment to Amelia. When the thunderstorm obliges the young people to remain at home together, "Mr. Osborne did not seem in the least disappointed" (fol. 21; see p. 26). George recalls how he was saved by Amelia from a beating when he cut the tassels off Jos's Hessian boots, and how he was tipped and awed by Jos, who no longer has that effect upon him. The hint of comfortable egoism in his character is strengthened when we see him good-naturedly propose that Becky use her talents as an artist to depict that earlier scene of the boots when his fate was the central issue.

After George and Jos have drunk "a fitting quantity of port-wine" (fol. 21; p. 26), George not only recalls these events but responds to Becky's histrionic flutter and especially to the sympathetic tears of Amelia "with a touched curiosity" and with a momentary surge of attraction towards the latter: "George . . . felt at that moment an extraordinary, almost irresistible, impulse to seize the above-mentioned young woman in his arms, and to kiss her in the face of the company" (fol. 22; see p. 27). It is an impulse of good-natured bibulous sympathy, of sexual attraction, and of publicly asserted possession all at once. Open in his acknowledgment that he does not understand Becky's French song, and playful in his partiality for the singing of Amelia and in his hint that he prefers to sit in the dark with his favorite (fol. 24; p. 29), he feels himself affronted only once: when, in the earlier version of the Vauxhall narrative, the crowd's satirical comments on Jos cause the ladies "inexpressible alarm" and provoke "great anger" (frag. [H]) on George's part—presumably both as the protector of the ladies and as the snobbish social superior of the crowd. Indeed, his outrage is about to be expressed violently, for he is "just on the point of knocking down a Hebrew gentleman from the Minories" (frag. [H]), when Captain Tawney makes his timely intervention.[20] Because Thackeray deferred this narrative and wrote his new conclusion to the first installment, however, up to this point in the novel readers see only a George who remains unruffled, exchanging a knowing glance and an arch smile with Amelia, bantering with Jos, and—like Amelia—leaving the room on a pretext so that Jos can enjoy in private the company of the girl he has come to see (p. 31). In the first number's final plate, *"Mr. Joseph entangled,"* which may well have replaced one already executed showing George about to knock down the Hebrew gentleman, George and Amelia again exchange knowing smiles and glances.

It would have been quite a shock for readers to discover—even across the interval of a month—that the good-natured George Osborne, who smilingly assisted Becky's and Amelia's plans for Jos, now, almost at the outset of the resumed narrative, was actively opposing the marriage; but that development did not occur for some time, both in the revised narrative and in the compositional sequence. Thackeray began instead with the schoolboy scene that grew out of his depiction of George in chapter 4 and out of his decision to introduce the contrasting figure of Dobbin. Here, as in chapter 4, we see George rescued from an angry bigger boy and here, as there, we see George's interest in telling others of a dispute in which he sees himself as the central figure. Instead of asking someone else to provide an artistic representation, however, here he himself delightedly furnishes the account, which is accompanied by various requests and by an expression of his love for Amelia. Yet, in the young George of chapter 5, readers could see not only traits with which they were familiar but also different ones—especially snobbishness, for the brief manifestation of that quality had appeared only in a portion of narrative that had already been written but not publĭshed. To one familiar with the manuscript of *Vanity Fair* and its composition, however, George's snobbishness is not new but newly weighted. Now Thackeray places emphasis upon that quality, for the novelist is presenting George not in terms of a partial contrast with Jos, as in number one, but in partial contrast with Dobbin. We are made to see in George precisely those qualities of Jos that Dobbin—though large, awkward, and shy, like Jos—generally lacks: pompousness and vanity. Unlike Dobbin, who from the start is nervous at asserting himself, the youthful George is scornful and pretentious, though these qualities are not immediately carried over into the older George Osborne. Even though young George is outmatched by Cuff, we see that he obviously models himself on that dandy—for example, in his wish to have a pony like Cuff—and we are thereby better prepared for George's later emergence as the affronted figure in the Vauxhall box.

It was in the manuscript of the schoolboy narrative (fols. 1–8 and the top of 9), then, that Thackeray offered a significantly altered portrayal of George's character, one that does not merely give a passing glimpse of his egoism but shows it in extended childlike openness. When the novelist came to write a bridge passage (fols. 9–11) between this narrative and the account of Vauxhall, he added further touches of development and preparation, like the older George's naïvely admiring glance at himself in the mirror. In this passage Thackeray termed George "Lieutenant Osborne" (fol. 9; p. 39) and stressed his identity as a military officer. As in chapter 4, George shows a good-humored freedom and playfulness, but his comments have a more perceptible, though still not blatant, tone of haughty smugness than did his earlier ironic praise of Jos's clumsiness: "Bravo, Jos!" (p. 31). The rest of Thackeray's attention near the end of chapter 5, however, as at its beginning, centers on Dobbin.

With "DOBBIN OF OURS" (p. 33) has come both the inflated "hero" and the deflation of the mock-heroic mode, as we immediately saw in the narrative of Cuff's fight with Dobbin. Now, towards the end of chapter 5, Amelia's perspective towards George is changed to harmonize with this thematic antithesis. She no longer sees George simply as a sweetheart and future husband, but as a "hero": looking at George just as he is about to admire himself in the mirror—when Becky sees through him—Amelia "thought in her little heart that in his Majesty's

army or in the wide world there never was such a face or such a hero"
(fols. 9–10; see p. 40). Dobbin, of course, continues to be George's ob-
verse. Jos had been quite ungainly, but Dobbin is superlatively, epical-
ly so: "His blushes, his stumbles, his awkwardness, and the number of
feet wh. he crushed as he went back to his place who shall describe or
calculate?" (fol. 8; see p. 39). In the first installment, Jos made "an exceedingly solemn and clumsy bow" (p. 31), but Dobbin now makes
"one of the clumsiest bows that was ever performed by a mortal" (fol.
10; p. 40). In George's words, "he is not an Adonis certainly." (In this
allusion one notices, parenthetically, an ironic hint of the coming death
of George, who sees himself as an Adonis in appearance at least.)

Dobbin has "just returned from yellow fever in the West Indies"
(fol. 10; see p. 40), perhaps like Captain Tawney, but two matters distinguish him from Tawney: his personal response to Amelia and the
mock-heroic perspective in which the narrator causes us to see him. As
he hears her come singing into the room, "the sweet fresh little voice
went right into the Captains heart and nestled there. . . . What a
blooming young creature you seem, and what a prize the rogue has
got! . . . he thought, before he took Amelias hand into his own, and as
he let his cocked hat fall" (fol. 10; see pp. 40–41).[21] With the introduction of this narrative mode in number two, Thackeray also enlarges
the novel's field of concern. Whereas in the first number, for example,
conversation among George, Jos, Amelia, and Becky was specified
only as "not especially witty or eloquent" (p. 27) and as "sentimental"
(p. 29), now the subject is loftier and the scope wider: "They talked
about war and glory and Boney and Lord Wellington and the last Gazette" (fol. 11; see p. 41). In the earlier serial part, Becky had evoked
the Emperor only in her exuberant tribute to the usefulness of the
French language for putting down Miss Pinkerton; here, in the second
part, Napoleonic warfare is introduced both as literal event and as a
metaphor that is to furnish the novel with a major thematic and structural principle.[22] Considering this evidence not only of continuity between chapter 5 and the manuscript of the first installment but also of
significant changes and differences, one suspects that chapter 5 was
composed in large part after the appearance of number one, which had
an announced publication date of 1 January 1847.[23] Further support-
ing evidence appears in the manuscript of the present chapter 6.

After composing chapter 5, Thackeray set down, also in upright
hand on yellowish paper, a revised version of the earlier Vauxhall nar-

rative, though only a few of the extensive alterations can be mentioned here. First, his opening sentence required change. Instead of satirizing the reader for "growing very weary of these little mean unromantic details about a vulgar stockbroker's family in Russell Square" (fol. 26), Thackeray stated his awareness "that the tune wh. I am piping is a very mild one" and begged "the good-natured reader" to keep in mind that his characters were behaving just as people do in common, everyday life. The details were not unromantic, because in fact his chief subject was love, as he now overtly announced in summarizing the progress of the second installment: "The argument stands thus— Osborne in love with Amelia has asked an old friend to dinner & to Vauxhall—Jos Sedley is in love with Rebecca. Will he marry her? That is the great subject now in hand" (fol. 12). Beginning with the present second paragraph, Thackeray then undertook to revise his parodies of contemporary fiction on fols. 12 and 13, economically pasting in three trimmed portions of proof from the earlier version's partial passage through the press and making brief, minor alterations in each of them. A final modified paragraph at the top of fol. 14 mockingly apologized for this illustrative treatise on fiction and its public, the "little disquisition" allegedly being required to fill out the chapter. At this point he passed over a brief discussion of rack punch in the original version (fol. 28), apparently deciding to incorporate a revision of this passage later in his present narrative. He also omitted mention of any interval between the proposed and actual visit to the Gardens, having now dramatized in chapter 4 an additional meeting between Becky and Jos and shown us one of Jos's actions during the interval that had been reported only briefly in the original version: "He had been discovered holding her skein of silk" (fol. 28).

Thackeray subsequently began his revised account of the Vauxhall journey: "Let us then step into the coach with the Russell Square party. . . . Every soul in the coach had agreed that on that night Jos would propose to make Rebecca Sharp Mrs. Sedley" (fol. 14). After reworking a subsequent portion of narrative and pasting in two more sections of proof, he continued: "Such was the state of affairs as the carriage crossed Westminster bridge. 'Keep clear of Jos & Amelia's little friend' Osborne whispered to Captain Dobbin" (fol. [15]). In short, Thackeray at this point added new material that continued to present George as a co-conspirator of Amelia's in promoting the marriage of Becky and Jos. As George's language suggests, his motive is love of Amelia, which causes him to identify closely with her feelings and wishes.

Though the novelist extended this characterization of George, his main attention shifted to Dobbin, whose inner response to George's injunction we now see: "Yes & of George & Amelia I suppose thought poor Dobbin to himself—and as he saw her take." But Thackeray cancelled the last five words and then went on: "so he contented himself by paying at the door for the whole party while Jos squeezed through the gate." The novelist then apparently returned to George's whispered comment and added the more audible and demeaning words: "and I say Dobbin just look to the shawls & things theres a good fellow." Thackeray apparently realized, however, that to hint at George's wish for Dobbin's absence emphasized the implausibility of George's having invited him in the first place and openly revealed the awkwardness of Thackeray's device for getting Dobbin on stage prior to the scene's climax. When Dobbin does feel "de trop" (fol. 17), time has passed and all members of the party have forgotten him. Meanwhile, Thackeray cancelled the sentence he had written about Dobbin's awareness and set down another version of it: "So while George paired off quite happily with Miss Sedley: and Jos squeezed through the gate into the Gardens with Rebecca at his side; honest Dobbin contented himself by giving an arm to the shawls & by paying at the door for the whole party" (fol. [15]).

Having gotten "the gawky young officer" into the novel and into distant attendance upon Amelia at Vauxhall, Thackeray emphasized how Dobbin has been touched by her. He thinks Amelia "worthy even of the brilliant George Osborne" and he watches "her artless happiness with a sort of fatherly pleasure" (fol. [15]) even as he feels the loneliness of his unpaired state. The delights of Vauxhall, which Thackeray had enumerated in the earlier version, a proof segment of which he here inserted, now became delights of which "Captain William Dobbin did not take the slightest notice" (fol. 16), even though Thackeray thereby had to sacrifice a visionary passage from the earlier version that was appropriate to the narrator but not to the unperceiving Dobbin: "[Simpson's] ghost may wander about now in the ghost of a royal property where the spirit of Madame Sacqui is still dancing on the apparition of a tight rope, and the old departed ham-cutters are carving slices scarcely more visionary than those wh. in life they supplied" (fol. 30).

Another reminder of the Napoleonic context, more mock-heroic in tone than the previous mention, follows as Dobbin, "having ⟨heard⟩ †attended under the gilt cockle-shell while† Mrs. Salmon performed the Battle of Borodino (a savage Cantata against the Corsican Upstart, who had lately met with his Russian reverses)," walks away trying to hum to himself this fierce music only to find that the melody in his heart is domestic: "the tune wh. Amelia Sedley sang on the stairs as she came down to dinner" (fol. 16). So too, though Dobbin has been asked to "look to the shawls & things" (fol. [15]), here it is his carrying of "Amelias white cashmere shawl" (fol. 16) that the narrator identifies for us. Following the insertion of a proof fragment of twenty-nine lines concerning Becky and Jos (fol. 16), the narrator's attention turns back to Dobbin, who finds himself totally forgotten as "the now united couples," the "mated pairs" (fol. 17), prattle away quite happily at supper without him.

Narrative focus then shifts to the climactic bowl of rack punch, the opening account of which is based upon the passage in the earlier version that Thackeray had deferred reworking until now. Another portion of proof carried the narrative to the point of intervention. As Thackeray had Dobbin "shouldering off a great number of the crowd" and ordering them all away, he originally wrote "roared," a word that may have been appropriate to Captain Tawney but not to this man, who had in fact just lisped out his command: "Be off you foolth!" Thackeray therefore substituted the word, "said," and showed us a man who, like his schoolboy self, is "most agitated" (fol. 18) when he asserts himself (though in later book form printings, unlike the manuscript and the parts issue, he no longer lisps the word, "fools"). George, on the other hand, who has just been about to knock down a prominent member of the crowd (though partly restrained by Amelia, the plate reveals), asserts himself with a callous egoism that blames his rescuer. He cries out, "Good Heavens Dobbin where *have* you been?" and then not only: "Take charge of Jos here whilst I take the ladies to the carriage," but, with an additional show of arrogance inserted by Thackeray: "Make yourself useful, & ⟨T⟩ take . . ." (fol. 18). After a single push from Osborne's finger has sent Jos back into his seat, where he remains as George escorts the ladies to the carriage, Jos confides to Dobbin "the secret of his loves."

Thackeray then took a final portion of proof and separated it into segments of eight and thirty-seven lines each. Between them, just after the end of the paragraph explaining how Dobbin got Jos safely home (fol. 18), the novelist set down three lines not present in the early version that show George's amused response to the incident and Amelia's pity for Becky: "George Osborne ⟨burst⟩ conducted the girls home in safety: and when the door was closed upon them and as he walked ⟨home⟩ across Russell Square laughed so as to astonish the watchman. Amelia looked very ruefully at her friend as they went up stairs, and kissed her, and went to bed without any more talking" (fol. 19). George's reaction, one should note, is that of a spectator with a developed sense of the ridiculous. It reveals no malice, being entirely consistent with his earlier amused responses to Jos: "Bravo, Jos!" (p. 31) and "[Dobbin] is [modest, like you]—but you are incomparably more graceful Sedley, Osborne added laughing" (fol. 9; see p. 39).

This amusement, moreover, found one additional expression. On the two segments of the final divided portion of proof, Thackeray changed the printed name, "Tawney," to "Dobbin"—where the Captain shrewdly induced Jos on a pretext to leave Vauxhall (fol. 18) and where the next morning Jos's "friend Tawney, came grinning with his lean yellow face, and asked him about his love. Good Gad! had he revealed it? All his modesty came rushing back . . ." (fol. 19). Finally, however, Thackeray made one more change, for he crossed out the second correction, "Dobbin," and gave the grinning question to "George Osborne." Dobbin, as we have just seen when he finds himself humming Amelia's song, laughs at his own awkward performance (fol. 16; p. 48). It is George who has thrice before laughed at Jos; here it is he who now asks the grinning question. All the same, however, we see absolutely no sign of his wishing to break up the courtship. Jos's "modesty," the very quality by which George has earlier been amused, here asserts itself in direly timorous form. The narrative then ends, as it had in the earlier version, with Jos's letter, the end of Becky's first campaign in life, and her departure for Sir Pitt Crawley's together with her vow to love Amelia "for ever, and ever, and ever" (fol. 19).

Thackeray, then, was presumably still satisfied with his earlier ending of the Vauxhall narrative and after marking places for insertion of woodblocks, including an apparent endpiece, evidently sent this portion of manuscript to the printer's, either together with that of chapter 5 or separately. The manuscript of each chapter has the names of two compositors on it; the opening stints are again unidentified.[24] However, even if appropriate space had been left for the indicated woodblocks (fols. 1, 4, 10, 12, 13, 16, and 19; see pp. 33, 35, 41, 43–45, 48, 51, and perhaps p. 54, whose illustration may have been intended as an endpiece), the narrative would have extended over only about nineteen pages (pp. [33]–51), leaving thirteen still to be filled. The question therefore becomes: how much space was taken up by chapter 7?

The manuscript of the latter is missing, yet one can offer a plausible guess at its length. One can see that the present chapter 8 originally existed on leaves written in the slanted hand that were numbered ⟨39⟩–⟨45⟩, preceded by an apparent fragment of fol. [38]; hence one assumes that the present chapter 7, though not originally separate from 8, came to occupy the interval: fols. [33] through the upper portion of fol. [38]. If they were written in the slanted hand, which seems likely, they would have carried the installment approximately to its twenty-fourth page, perhaps to the point in the present chapter where Becky sets out for Queen's Crawley in the carriage that is identified as carrying her into the wide world. The text found on the apparent bottom of fol. [38] and on ⟨39⟩–⟨45⟩, from the present chapter 8, would have extended the serial number to its thirty-first page, ending with the conclusion of Becky's letter to Amelia; as in the case of the preceding chapter, inclusion of the relevant wood-engraving or space for it would not have changed the page count, assuming appropriate calculations had been made for chapter headings and initials. It appears, then, that the novelist theoretically might have completed his second installment by incorporating the texts of the present chapters 7 and 8 as they then probably existed on fols. [33]–⟨45⟩; at most he would have needed an additional page, to be made up either of wood-engravings or letterpress. Following the disaster at Vauxhall, Becky would have met Sir Pitt, set out into the world for Queen's Crawley, and settled into life there, reporting her experiences in a long letter with protestations of eternal devotion to the Amelia whom she had promised to love forever at the end of her failed campaign against Jos in chapter 6. The serial number would have had a quite satisfactory neatness about it.

Thackeray, however, did not include Becky's letter. Instead, on leaves that are now missing, he revised what had been the ending of chapter 6 and extended the chapter's length by just over four pages— evidently after it was already in press. The narrative of the Vauxhall catastrophe and Jos's immediately ensuing letter had always been extremely rapid in pace, especially at its conclusion. It thereby had considerable dramatic effectiveness, especially as the end of a number but also, though to a lesser extent, merely as the end of a chapter. Thackeray came to sacrifice the sudden, powerful force of this ending, however, for he now had a new creative purpose regarding George Osborne: to establish clearer links between the schoolboy of chapter 5 and the young man of chapter 6 by showing how the former's snobbishness later expressed itself not merely in scattered hints but in full blatancy. Since the novelist had already made George Osborne the agent of Jos's emotional hangover and had shown Osborne's callousness the evening before as well, Thackeray had before him the ready possibility of a comic scene in which George laughingly dramatized for the physically suffering Jos his intoxicated foolishness of the previous evening and thereby extensively promoted Jos's emotional anguish.

Following brief mention of how Amelia looked forward not only to Becky's wedding but to her own (pp. 50–51), Thackeray continued in a thoroughly comic vein. After his previously conceived and probably executed wood-engraving showing a suffering but standing Jos, and after a previously written sentence about small beer, Thackeray now continued: "With this mild beverage before him, George Osborne found the ex-collector of Boggleywollah groaning on the sofa at his lodgings." Since George is not to be Jos's "friend," that term was omitted. Dobbin, now, is also present, "good-naturedly tending his patient of the night before," and exchanging with George "the most frightful sympathetic grins" (p. 51). As George had done when a boy (p. 37), now he also acts as a pugilistic connoisseur in alleging Jos's prowess as a fighter. Drawing on amusing details supplied by Jos's valet, George invents a story of a battered hackney coachman threatening Jos with legal measures and, with Dobbin's assistance, he carries the joke farther until a reply by Jos that combines braggadocio with an extremely "dreary and ludicrous" grimace overcomes Dobbin as well as George, so that both visitors "fired off a ringing volley of laughter." So far, the tone of the bantering is good-natured, as Dobbin's response testifies. At this point, however, comes the major revelation, for we now learn of George's snobbish opposition to the marriage of Becky and Jos:

> Osborne pursued his advantage pitilessly. He thought Jos a milksop. He had been revolving in his mind the marriage-question pending between Jos and Rebecca, and was not over-well pleased that a member of a family into which he, George Osborne, of the —th, was going to marry, should make a *mésalliance* with a little nobody—a little upstart govern-

ess. "You hit, you poor old fellow?" said Osborne. "You terrible? Why, man, you couldn't stand—you made everybody laugh in the Gardens, though you were crying yourself. You were maudlin, Jos. Don't you remember singing a song?"

"A what?" Jos asked.

"A sentimental song, and calling Rosa, Rebecca, what's her name, Amelia's little friend—your dearest diddle, diddle, darling?" And this ruthless young fellow, seizing hold of Dobbin's hand, acted over the scene, to the horror of the original performer, and in spite of Dobbin's good-natured entreaties to him to have mercy.

The scene is very brief but effective, both in establishing more convincing grounds for Jos's subsequent flight and in dramatizing the decisive reappearance of young George in the grown Osborne. Thackeray then goes on to offer us an aesthetically desirable further expression of George's attitude towards the proposed marriage, his acknowledgment of having been affronted the night before, and his sense of being personally insulted by Jos's pompous manner. The novelist also provides yet further grounds for Jos's panicky departure:

> "Why should I spare him?" Osborne said to his friend's remonstrances, when they quitted the invalid, leaving him under the hands of Doctor Glauber [later book form printings read "Gollop"]. "What the deuce right has he to give himself his patronizing airs, and make fools of us at Vauxhall? Who's this little school-girl that is ogling and making love to him? Hang it, the family's low enough already, without *her*. A governess is all very well, but I'd rather have a lady for my sister-in-law. I'm a liberal man; but I've proper pride, and know my own station: let her know hers. And I'll take down that great hectoring Nabob, and prevent him from being made a greater fool than he is. That's why I told him to look out, lest she brought an action against him." (p. 52)

By this time, of course, Dobbin is troubled, but the damage has been done.

Thackeray went on to present a scene showing George with Becky and Amelia, with both of whom his relations were now going to be different, owing to the new prominence of callousness and snobbery in his character. First, he enjoys Becky's fruitless anticipation of Jos's arrival ("Sister Anne is on the watch-tower . . . but there's nobody coming" [p. 53]), and then he gives Amelia pain for the first time in the novel by describing to her "the dismal condition of her brother." Already "enjoying the joke hugely," he now delights in it even more when he sees Amelia's "piteous and discomfited mien." In bantering Rebecca "upon the effect of her charms on the fat civilian," George's

malice remains hidden from her, but in his joking promise to tell Dobbin of her indifference to him the hostility becomes sufficiently overt
for Becky to suspect its implications and to feel the danger most keenly: "'Has he been laughing about me to Joseph? Has he frightened him?
Perhaps he won't come.'—A film passed over her eyes, and her heart
beat quite thick." Along with his lack of fellow-feeling goes a lack of
perception, of course, so that he remains quite unconscious of having inspired distrust and hatred in Becky, but he cannot fail to see the
reproving look that Amelia now, also for the first time, gives him following Becky's quick ability to dramatize her own vulnerability to
George's unkindness. Even so, he feels only "some little manly com-
punction" and merely at having inflicted "unnecessary unkindness."
In implicitly accepting the necessary unkindness of disrupting the
anticipated marriage, he adopts for the first time a patronizing tone
towards Amelia: "My dearest Amelia, . . . you are too good—too
kind. You don't know the world. I do. And your little friend Miss
Sharp must learn her station." Finally, he tries to turn the conversation by saying: "'I only know [Jos] is a very foolish vain fellow, and
put my dear little girl into a very painful and awkward position last
night. My dearest diddle—diddle—darling!' He was off laughing
again; and he did it so drolly that Emmy laughed too" (p. 53). The pain
and discomfort, of course, was chiefly his snobbish sense of being himself affronted by banter directed at Jos, but, as Amelia's amusement
reminds us, the appropriate response to comic behavior is laughter.

A brief narrative concerning Amelia's attempt to prompt a visit
from Jos, a wood-engraving of Sambo presenting the fatal letter, and a
slightly expanded version of the letter carried the chapter to the bottom of its twelfth page. Slightly more than one full page was additionally supplied by an account of the preparations for Becky's departure
from Russell Square; into it Thackeray inserted several details that
reappeared in later chapters: the servants' jealousy and dislike of
Becky, which helped prepare for the rudeness of the groom in the
presumably already written chapter 7, and George's free-handedness,
which was to be an important element of the plot some numbers in the
future. The novelist also introduced a footnote with an illustration concerning the costumes of his characters and ended on the fourteenth
page with a modified version of his previous conclusion, as "Rebecca
and Amelia parted, the former vowing to love her friend for ever and
ever and ever" (p. 56).

These changes necessitated further alterations—likewise, presumably, in press. Thus after crossing Westminster Bridge, George no longer whispers to Dobbin that he should keep clear of Jos and Becky. Instead Thackeray inserted a sentence taking the party from the Bridge to the Gardens and continued with preparation for Jos's later attraction of the crowd's bantering attention: "As the majestic Jos stepped out of the creaking vehicle the crowd gave a cheer for the fat gentleman, who blushed and looked very big and mighty, as he walked away with Rebecca under his arm. George, of course, took charge of Amelia." Thackeray also added emphasis to Amelia's happiness— "She looked as happy as a rose-tree in sunshine"—and, significantly, withdrew it from George's. In the earlier manuscript, George had "paired off quite happily with Miss Sedley" (fol. [15]); now he just "paired off with" her (p. 47). Other, much more minor, changes also were made, but the reference to the chapter's brevity remained, either because Thackeray forgot about it or because he needed the letterpress and decided the five additional printed pages would merely extend the joke of his mock apology: "this chapter about Vauxhall would have been so exceeding short but for the above little disquisition [on fiction], that it scarcely would have deserved to be called a chapter at all" (p. 46).

Because the manuscript of chapter 7 is missing, one cannot be sure that its presumed five and one-half leaves carried it only to the point where Becky chooses to dream about Rawdon or where she sets off for Queen's Crawley inside the coach that "may be said to be carrying her into the wide world" (p. 62); the possibility exists that Thackeray may have had to add the last thirty-five to sixty-two lines of text and the wood-engraving occupying twenty-nine lines that together extended the installment's length by two additional pages. If so, we can welcome the wood-engraved portrayal of Becky in her true element, a world of men (p. 63), and we can be especially grateful for the encomium to stage coaching that ends the serial number with one of Thackeray's most distinctive retrospections, one that is splendid in its own right and also most effective in casting its shadow over the wood-engraved endpiece so as to help prefigure the tumbling of Becky's next house of cards (p. 64).[25]

The structural significance of Thackeray's inserting chapter 5, revising chapter 6, and then extending it, and concluding the installment with the present chapter 7 remains to be considered, especially because in making these changes Thackeray initiated the structural pattern that was to persist throughout the novel. Details from the preceding discussion will inevitably recur, but in the context of a new perspective that, one hopes, will justify the repetition. By intimately connecting chapter 5 with the opening chapter of the first installment, Thackeray began the symmetrical arrangement of monthly parts that represents his most interesting contribution to the form of the serial novel.[26] Geoffrey and Kathleen Tillotson offer thematic justification for chapter 5 and briefly explain how the structure of the new number recalls that of its predecessor by balancing Swishtail's against Miss Pinkerton's and showing how the schoolboy relations and snobberies extend into the adult world (Tillotson edition, p. xix). One might add that the prominent mock-heroic tone also enforces the parallelism. Yet there are also a number of specific events occurring in parallel sequence that provoke comparison and contrast. In chapter 1, Amelia's character and popularity contrast with Becky's character and unpopularity; the same antithesis exists in chapter 5 between Cuff and Dobbin. Therefore, in comparing the two underdogs, we see the pointed contrast between Becky and Dobbin, which is further developed in these two chapters and later. In chapter 1, when Miss Pinkerton is bidding farewell to Amelia, Becky enters and disrupts the parting; in chapter 5, when Cuff is beating George, Dobbin intervenes to defend the victim.

The first climax in chapter 1 consists of a battle between Becky and her mock-heroic opponent, Miss Pinkerton; the Dobbin-Cuff engagement obviously recalls that incident, not only because it is another battle but because both Becky and Dobbin are struggling against domineering bullies after having had an indecisive encounter with their rivals. Becky's "little battle" (p. 6) with Miss Pinkerton is fought for baser motives, of course, and with crueller weapons. She gains her objective—freedom—and then insults Miss Pinkerton amusingly but also gratuitously, snobbishly, and with malice. The second climax of chapter 1 comes as Becky sweepingly rejects Miss Jemima's generous if simple-minded present of the "Dixonary"; events in chapter 5 twice serve to contrast with her gesture. Cuff magnanimously offers assistance to Dobbin, who blushingly accepts it; as an indirect result, Dobbin receives a prize-book in Becky's "mother-tongue" (p. 9) and generously responds to that and to his ensuing monetary reward by giving "a general tuck-out for the school" (p. 39). The only section[27] of either chapter that does not fit into a joint pattern is the ending of chapter 5 (pp. 39–42); carrying forward the movement towards Vauxhall from the conclusion of the first number, it is intended, as I have indicated, to introduce Dobbin into the Vauxhall party and to dramatize Jos's increasing entanglement. By suspending the chronological development of the narrative, as he does for most of chapter 5, Thackeray is not only offering supplementary or entirely new perspectives on what he has already written but also presenting material in a sequence parallel to that of an earlier installment.

The middle of the first number, chapters 2 and 3, might be entitled "The Opening of the Campaign Against Joseph Sedley"; its structural counterpart, chapter 6, relates the close of that campaign. We begin with two coach rides, one to Russell Square and one to Vauxhall, and then enter two retrospective accounts: the narrator's unfavorable summary of Becky's past (pp. 9–13), including her attempts on the Reverend Mr. Crisp, and, in chapter 6, a survey of foolishly acquiescent attitudes towards a match between Becky and Jos (p. 46). After arriving in Russell Square and touring the Sedley home with Becky, Amelia gives her guest presents and important information about Jos's financial and bachelor status; the section ends as Becky silently vows to catch Jos (p. 15). After the arrival at Vauxhall in chapter 6, Becky also goes on a tour, this time with Amelia's brother through the Gardens; although Becky encourages Jos all she can, here it is his intention that remains unspoken (p. 50), and so her vow of chapter 2 remains unfulfilled. The ironic point of this comic pairing seems to be that his bumbling proves to be a match for her cunning.

In chapter 3 Mr. Sedley's mocking of Jos's appearance seriously alarms the timid dandy (p. 17), but when in chapter 6 George more selfishly and elaborately ridicules Jos's inebriated behavior (pp. 51–52), the effect is considerably more upsetting. Mr. Sedley's action, though coarse, contrasts favorably with George's conduct, for the young man's motives are as snobbish and pompous as anything in the behavior of his victim. George's mimicry, of course, rasps on the tender nerves of the suffering bacchanalian, who is not mollified as in chapter 3, but left alone to quiver at his exposed ludicrousness. Conse-

quently, while Becky could quickly recover from the embarrassments
of curry and chili (p. 20), Jos finds the aftereffects of rack punch and
mockery more agonizing and more enduring: he stays in bed all day
and dares not return to Russell Square (p. 54). Therefore, while chapter 3 ends with only a temporary setback for Becky, who fruitlessly
awaits a hesitant Jos in the drawing room, chapter 6 moves towards a
climax as Amelia watches George approach her father's house while
Becky looks out for a Jos who definitely will not come. In place of tip-
toeing Jos departing from Russell Square in chapter 3, we have the
note announcing his departure from London without calling again; it is
then Becky who must leave Russell Square permanently.

The concluding chapter of number two ironically establishes Sir Pitt
Crawley and, to a lesser degree, his younger son as counterparts to
Mr. Sedley and Jos. In chapter 4, Jos had arrived at Russell Square to
begin a new, if limited, series of adventures with Becky; chapter 7 begins as Becky arrives in Great Gaunt Street for an introduction to a
new and considerable series of experiences. The analogies are all comically inverted: here the place at a prosperous table of the coarsely jesting Mr. Sedley, whose notion of placating his victim consists of offering
him excellent champagne (p. 24), is taken by the coarsely jesting Sir
Pitt, offering Becky a drop of beer, demanding his pint for carrying her
baggage, and finally apportioning out the penurious fare of tripe and
onion (pp. 59–61).

The thunderstorm that keeps the young people indoors in chapter 4
leads to a cheerful evening at Russell Square, as Jos entertains Becky
with long stories about India (pp. 27–28) amid the festive accompani-
ments of music and refreshments, while in chapter 7 Becky spends a
much more quiet evening in the dark house on Great Gaunt Street,
though she finds entertainment in listening to Sir Pitt's extended confidences (p. 61). The first number ends as Jos fails to propose while
bound in Becky's green silk skein but prepares himself for Vauxhall
by vowing to "pop the question" there (p. 32); the second number ends
as Becky, after failing in her campaign against Jos, looks toward a new
quarry and prepares for Queen's Crawley by choosing to dream of
Rawdon (p. 62).

Since the concluding lament for things past has no structural counterpart in the first installment, one has further grounds for suspecting
that the passage was needed to fill out the number. Thackeray makes
his addition relevant, however, by its melancholy retrospectiveness.

Just as the Gardens in which Jos prepared for an imaginary future with Becky have now passed away, so too the evanescence of Becky's conveyance, as she moves towards her insubstantial future, has been revealed by time. The ultimate contribution of number one, then, was to provide a structural pattern for the creation of the second installment.

3
Vanity Fair
Installments 3 and 4

The nucleus of number three for March 1847 consisted of the remainder of the manuscript portion united by a common pencilled numbering system and by the use of the slanted hand on whitish paper: fols. ⟨39⟩–⟨46⟩ and ⟨48⟩–⟨61⟩, together with two fragments that begin and end Becky's initial letter to Amelia. The first fragment contains no pencilled number, for presumably it is the detached lower portion of fol. [38]; the second fragment is the upper half of fol. ⟨45⟩. Neither contains much revision, but such is not the case for the intervening leaves.

The major part of the letter was at one time written on five unnumbered leaves that were later identified as fols. ⟨39⟩–⟨44⟩.[1] Beginning with a narrative of her journey to Queen's Crawley, Becky intersperses a number of annoyed comments about Sir Pitt's stinginess. On one occasion, however, Thackeray at first went awry: in having Becky explain how the young gentleman from Cambridge intended to gain comical revenge on Sir Pitt by lashing the horses that Sir Pitt, as their proprietor, has penuriously kept at a slow pace, Thackeray made her write—presumably as a hypocritical appeal to Amelia's sensibilities—"of course I interceded for the poor animals" (fol. ⟨39⟩). Naturally, Becky would do no such thing, but would flash out with glee, which would be consistent with her previous irritation at Sir Pitt and would find expression in the letter, unrestrained by any implausible need for hypocrisy. Because of Sir Pitt's eagerness to take another paying passenger into the coach, Becky has been forced to make the journey *"outside for the greater part of the way"* (as she emphasizes) and in heavy rain as well, from which she has been protected only by the greatcoat kindly offered by the young gentleman. The guard and the Cambridge gentleman have already laughed at Sir Pitt's miserliness, and Becky has firmly said, "this meanness I hate." Hence, one suspects, Thackeray deleted the eight words about intercession that, even as hypocrisy, are so out of character for Becky and substituted instead the statement that when she understood the young gentleman meant to drive the rest of the way "and revenge himself on Sir Pitt's horses, of course I laughed too" (fol. ⟨39⟩). This is the same Becky who has said to Amelia in the second chapter: "Revenge may be wicked, but it's natural. . . . I'm no angel" (p. 9).

At the very bottom of fol. ⟨40⟩, Thackeray indicated Becky's intention to resume the history of the family with an account of Lady Crawley, but if he ever began to carry out this intention, the evidence has disappeared, for the top of the next leaf, after a cancelled phrase about the inside of the house, begins with a description of the Crawley coat of arms on its outside. Towards the bottom of fol. ⟨41⟩ Thackeray finally came to Lady Crawley and Pitt, whom he here presented as her son:

> Well, the great dinner bell rung—and we all assembled in the little green room where Lady Crawley always sits. She is a tall snuffy pompous old lady in grey silk—just like a schoolmistress in a word. With her was her son Mr. Crawley in full dress though his clothes look very old—He is a pale thin ugly silent young man with hay-coloured whiskers, and pink eyes and straw-coloured hair. Mr. Crawley said his mamma of whom he is the very picture—this is the governess of your sisters Miss Sharp.
> O said Mr. Crawley: and pushed out his head a little way by way of bowing. Miss Sharp continued my lady, you will be treated as one of the family of Queen's Crawley, and I hope that you will find everything conducive to your comfort and that we shall have every cause for mutual satisfaction.'—My lady is a speech-maker like horrid old Miss Pinkerton. I hate speech makers but of course I made a pretty speech in reply.

The narrative continued on fol. ⟨43⟩ as the butler entered to announce: "My lady is served." In answer to Sir Pitt's question about the nature of the dinner, Lady Crawley identified it as his favorite—portions of a black Hampshire pig, which the butler-butcher familiarly told Sir Pitt was "as fine a beast as ever I stuck a knife into," and which yielded for the dinner a leg of pork, black puddings, and pig's fry, in addition to some pig's head broth offered by Pitt to "Miss Ah— Miss Blunt." Thackeray immediately cancelled this passage, however, changed the nature of the animal, and continued along the line of "My lady is served" by having the butler identify the lamb and other constituents of the meal with their French names, against which Thackeray played the simple tune of Sir Pitt's blunt speech. It is the baronet's questions that now elicit the butler's remarks, while Pitt's offer of "potage" to "Miss Ah—Miss Blunt" prompts an exchange between his father and himself on the subject of French terms. Already at this stage Thackeray mentioned Lady Crawley's poor health, for he wrote that "as a great invalid" she "had a little private silver dish containing 3 mutton cutlets," while the "rest of the family dined upon the mouton aux navets." Perhaps because this statement was rather awkwardly placed, Thackeray deleted it, but he soon reintroduced the idea.

On fol. ⟨44⟩, in reply to a question of Sir Pitt's about the fate of the mutton shoulders, Lady Crawley says "loftily": "I presume they were eaten in the servants' Hall." Her comment only provokes the permitted license of Horrocks, however: "They was my lady . . . , and precious little else we get there neither"—at which Sir Pitt roars with laughter and continues his conversation with Horrocks by bringing up a modified version of the subject found in the preceding cancelled passage: the butchering of a pig. By this time, Thackeray had either remembered that in an earlier portion of manuscript narrative—the present chapter 7, now missing—he had already indicated that Lady Crawley was not Pitt's aristocratic mother but his plebeian stepmother, or else the novelist now decided to alter the identity of Lady Crawley and later went back to modify details in the previous chapter. Accordingly, it is ultimately Pitt, not she, who censures the children's laughter at the language of Horrocks, and when next we see Lady Crawley she is not haughty but terrified: "Put away the cards girls cried My lady in a great tremor—put down Mr. Crawley's books Miss Sharp."

In keeping with this altered or remembered identity, Thackeray revised his characterization of Lady Crawley on the previous three leaves. At the bottom of the first of these, fol. ⟨41⟩, he replaced "tall snuffy pompous old lady in grey silk" with "poor pale sickly looking body—gentle and with weak eyes," and "son" with "step son"; but then he deleted the whole passage ("Well . . . speech in reply") and set down a revised version on a fresh leaf that was inserted into the manuscript. With the ringing of the dinner bell, everyone assembles in the drawing room of the person who is now identified as "the second Lady Crawley and mother of the young ladies. She was a gardener's daughter and her marriage was thought a great match." Here we have a creation identical to the one found in the printed text of chapter 7, who is completely horticultural: "Rosa, daughter of Mr. G. Grafton of Mudbury" (p. 58). Now Becky's wit plays over Rosa Grafton Crawley as well as over Pitt, who is seen slightly more satirically than before:

"She looks as if she had been handsome once, and her eyes are always weeping for the loss of her beauty. She is pale and meagre and high-shouldered: and has not a word to say for herself evidently. Her step son Mr. Crawley was likewise in the room. He was in full dress as pompous as an undertaker. He is pale thin ugly silent he has thin legs, no chest, hay coloured whiskers and straw-coloured hair. He is the very picture of his sainted mother over the mantel-piece—Jemima of the noble house of Binkie." Later Thackeray penned in "Griselda" for the latter's name (it is "Grizzel" in chapter 7 [p. 58]). Other details remained much the same, except that now Lady Crawley no longer makes a pompous speech: "I hope you will be kind to my girls, said Lady Crawley—with her pink eyes always full of tears. Law Ma of course she will said the eldest: and I saw at a glance that I need not be afraid of *that* woman." Following this sentence, Thackeray drew a vertical line down through the remaining blank space on the leaf. Later he numbered all of them, the inserted leaf receiving the designation of fol. ⟨42⟩. On the next two leaves Thackeray completed his manuscript revisions concerning Lady Crawley. Sir Pitt now addresses her as "Betsy" instead of "my lady" and she calls him "Sir Pitt" (fol. ⟨43⟩). So too, in speaking of the shoulders of mutton, she now believes instead of presumes and speaks "humbly" instead of "loftily" (fol. ⟨44⟩).

After the approach of Pitt has caused the terrified Lady Crawley to order the girls to put away their cards and Becky to put down his books, Thackeray provided a contrasting dramatic event—Sir Pitt's tipsy reaching out for Becky at prayer time, apparently as the family is on its knees waiting for late arrivals: "and do you know the horrid man pinched me once or twice in the side at wh. the girls began to giggle Papas pinching Miss Sharp! roared out Miss Rosa at wh. I blushed, & Mr. Crawley looked as black as thunder, and Lady Crawley blushed too as well as her tallowy face would let her. Sir Pitt was evidently tipsy, and was beginning to break out in some frightful oaths when the door opened and the servants came in" (fol. ⟨44⟩). The scene ends in a discordant duet as Pitt reasserts his presence by expounding a chapter of Habakkuk, his father all the while hiccupping "in the drollest way" (fol. ⟨45⟩).

Thackeray may well have begun a passage of narrative commentary on the now missing bottom of fol. ⟨45⟩, following the end of Becky's first letter, and continued at the top of fol. ⟨46⟩ with a now-cancelled passage that focuses on Becky's pupils and comments on her having

referred to them as "insignificant little chits" (fol. ⟨41⟩): "Miss Sharp's
opinion with regard to the two young ladies whom she was to instruct
was made with her usual intelligence and fine feeling. They had been
educated by servants hitherto, the coachman imparted them instructions in the stable, the cook giving lectures ex cathedrâ in the kitchen,
the housemaids and gardeners completing the rest of their education"
(fol. ⟨46⟩). Taking up other members of the family in turn, Thackeray
then shifted his attention to the girls' mother—the subject he had just
clarified in the preceding leaves. Because Sir Pitt had found his first
wife, "the daughter of the noble Binkie . . . a confounded quarrelsome
high-bred jade," he took a complaisant, low-bred flower for his second
wife, whom Thackeray now identified as "Rose Dawson, daughter of
Mr. John Thomas Dawson gardener." Thackeray came to emend not
only the name of her father, however, but also his profession, deciding
that Sir Pitt would marry for money as well as for beauty and com-
plaisance; hence the novelist cancelled "gardener," wrote above it
"ironmonger of Mudbury," and soon referred to Rose, without correction, as "a tradesman's daughter" (fol. ⟨46⟩). Presumably later, in
preparing the second installment for the press, he forgot he had made
these changes. On a fol. [47], which apparently was later replaced,
Thackeray concluded his narrative of Rose Dawson Crawley, continuing in mid-sentence from the bottom of fol. ⟨46⟩, and took up Pitt
Crawley, going on at the top of fol. ⟨48⟩ with a now cancelled passage:
"a stingy fellow who never could be got to owe [more] than a halfpenny. Pitty [the character soon to be called Rawdon] Crawley's disposition was very different as we shall hear when we come to discuss
that gentleman's character. [New paragraph:] The tipsy old boor of a
baronet had a great respect for his eldest son, who by his constantly
frigid and haughty demeanour obtained great influence over him."
Gradually the novelist returned to Sir Pitt (fols. ⟨49⟩–⟨50⟩) and then
concluded this portion of narrative by mentioning Miss Crawley, Sir
Pitt's half-sister, and ironically commenting on the dignity that wealth
gives to an old lady (fols. ⟨50⟩–⟨51⟩).

After setting down the last six lines of his commentary at the top of
fol. ⟨51⟩, ending "foolish foolish dream," the novelist began for a moment an account of Miss Crawley's visit: "Twice a year a big carriage
drawn by fat horses driven by a fat coachman (the establishment of
maiden-ladies is always fat) used to drive up the avenue to Queen's
Crawley House or to the abode of the worthy rector of that parish"

(fol. ⟨51⟩). He cancelled these lines, however, and left the rest of the leaf blank. On a fresh leaf, perhaps intending the possible beginning of a new chapter, he went on instead with the subject that, just previous to his mention of Miss Crawley, he had promised to take up: "Miss Sharp . . . became as we shall hear speedily inducted into most of the secrets of the family" (fols. ⟨49⟩–⟨50⟩). This served as the theme of the next four leaves (fols. ⟨52⟩–⟨55⟩), where we see Becky ingratiating herself with her pupils, Miss Horrocks, Pitt, and especially the baronet. Finally, Thackeray mentioned the conflict between the two brothers of the family, Pitt and Pitty, and he emphasized Miss Crawley's partiality for the younger, concluding with eight lines at the top of fol. ⟨57⟩.

The novelist then took up the postponed subject of Miss Crawley's visit, the narration of which he turned over to Becky, whose second letter to Amelia begins at the top of a new leaf, fol. ⟨58⟩. In addition to parenthetical remarks that she has become Sir Pitt's secretary and that Lady Crawley is ill, Becky explains at length the effects of Miss Crawley's arrival upon the resident family members and also gives significant attention to a second visitor, "the young dandy & 'blood'" (fol. ⟨59⟩), Captain Crawley, and to the maneuvering of Mrs. Bute Crawley. Then taking over the narration from Becky, Thackeray once again began in an ironic tone of voice directed against the knowing Becky, who has failed to understand Mrs. Bute's purpose. He went on to show us in a private scene the further scheming of Mrs. Bute, concluding on fol. ⟨61⟩, the last surviving leaf in the manuscript written in the slanted hand.

Having completed this portion of narrative, Thackeray apparently looked over it and made a number of revisions in the same hand. For one thing, the awkwardness of two sons named Pitt and Pitty was removed, for the latter became "Rawdon" (fols. ⟨41⟩, ⟨55⟩, ⟨56⟩, and ⟨61⟩). Perhaps because he had just given Mrs. Bute Crawley the name of "Martha" (fol. ⟨61⟩), he now went back to fol. ⟨53⟩ and changed the Christian name of Miss Horrocks from "Martha" to "Sarah" on the four occasions when it occurred there. He omitted, however, to make the two necessary changes in the remainder of that long paragraph at the top of fol. ⟨54⟩, either because he overlooked the necessity or because he now decided to cancel the whole paragraph. For a reason that we shall see shortly, he realized that he did not need his lengthy explanation of how Becky flattered Miss Horrocks and finally gained

ascendancy over her by discovering the girl "engaged in earnest conversation with Mr Stock the second keeper" (fol. ⟨54⟩). It is difficult to
be sure that in cancelling this passage Thackeray decided to defer
making Miss Horrocks the mistress of Sir Pitt until the relationship
could be used to show his moral deterioration after Becky's departure,[2] for if he now did make such a decision, he imperfectly carried it
out by retaining another passage that very strongly hints at the existence of that relationship: "That odious pert ogling creature with the
red cheeks and the flaunting ribbons in her cap is Horrocks's daughter
and I *very much fear* Sir Pitt is,—but hush! What would Miss Pinkerton say at such stories? My dear I will tell them to Mrs. George
Osborne" (fol. ⟨45⟩).

Thackeray also turned his attention to a passage about Pitt, following shortly after the baronet's insistence that Pitt "Shut up [his] sar-
mons" during Miss Crawley's visit (fol. ⟨56⟩) so as not to antagonize
their wealthy, worldly relative. In response to Pitt's reply, "What is
money compared to our soul's ⟨salvation⟩ Sir?," the baronet taunt-
ingly interpreted the question to "mean that the old lady ⟨dont⟩
†won't† leave the money to you." Thackeray had continued: "this was
in fact the meaning of Mr. Crawley. No man for his own interest could
accommodate himself to circumstances more. In London he would let
a great man talk and laugh and be as wicked as he liked. but as he could
get no good from Miss Crawley's money why compromise his conscience? This was another reason why he should hate ⟨Pitty⟩ †Raw-
don† Crawley. He thought his brother robbed him. Elder brothers
often do think so; and curse the conspiracy of the younger ⟨sons⟩ †chil-
dren† wh. temporally deprives them of their fortunes" (fol. ⟨56⟩). This
passage, however, distracts attention from the major subject, Miss
Crawley, whom Thackeray immediately had gone on to discuss in further detail; more important, it is also significantly harsher than any
earlier portion of narrative concerning Pitt and baldly insists upon his
hypocrisy. In cancelling it, therefore, Thackeray not only removed a
distraction but also helped to make his narrative more subtle by placing the reader in what came more and more to be a distinctively Thackerayan position: where one cannot positively know truth but can only
infer it. Hence the novelist deleted the passage and replaced it in the
slanted hand with a question that extended Sir Pitt's taunt: "—and
who knows but it was Mr. Crawleys meaning?"

We now come to changes linked to writing in the upright hand, the first being Thackeray's removal of the passage where Sir Pitt tipsily gropes for Becky at prayer time and swears at being publicly detected. The novelist may have felt that depicting the blasphemous conduct of Sir Pitt would shock his audience's religious scruples and that showing even a limited awareness by Sir Pitt's young daughters of his sexual by-play with Becky would offend against other standards; a revision in the slanted hand had apparently already replaced their childish lisps with more mature pronunciation. One may also feel that Thackeray decided the tensions so suddenly and briefly introduced here were artistically inappropriate. It was undesirable on the very evening of Becky's arrival to expose her publicly to Sir Pitt's sexual advances, for that would logically have undermined her position in the family and created firm opposition to her—notably in Pitt, for example, who was about to be the object of Becky's successfully flattering attention. Thackeray had already satisfactorily revealed Sir Pitt's private interest when the baronet visited her room with only Horrocks for a witness (fol. ⟨40⟩). The deletion required that a syntactical bridge passage be inserted—"& after him"—between "Sir Pitt came in . . . unsteady in his gait" and "the butler" (fol. ⟨44⟩; from the handwriting alone one cannot be sure whether or not the deletion was made some time after the rest of this portion of the Queen's Crawley narrative existed in an early form (fols. ⟨45⟩–⟨61⟩). If it was, then Thackeray may also have been influenced by a clearer and more complex sense of the gradualness with which Sir Pitt discovers his need of Becky (fols. ⟨52⟩–⟨55⟩). The novelist may also have felt he was unduly complicating the scene with the variety of Sir Pitt's sexual interests, for immediately afterwards the overdressed Miss Horrocks comes in, jealous of Becky merely for her presence in the household. In this latter detail we may perhaps see the immediate reason behind Thackeray's deletion of the subsequent passage about Becky and Miss Horrocks, for, as is implicit here, Becky will neutralize the influence of Miss Horrocks not by learning of an involvement with the second keeper but simply by her own clever presence, which will impede the development of Miss Horrocks's relationship with Sir Pitt.

Thackeray's remaining significant changes seem to have been accompanied and prompted by four major insertions totalling nineteen leaves in his upright script and by a number of briefer additions in the same hand—some or all of them possibly after the appearance of number two for February. In terms of narrative sequence the first of these came on the fragment containing the beginning of Becky's first letter to Amelia, which seems to have been the lower portion of fol. [38]. Thackeray pasted it in the middle of a full-sized yellowish leaf and inscribed above it: "Chap," "PRIVATE & CONFIDENTIAL," and "The girl on the chair," plus a square to indicate the woodblock's position, and the numeral "1" for the leaf itself. Subsequently, fols. ⟨39⟩–⟨44⟩ were redesignated fols. 2–7. The end of Becky's letter was now also a fragment, for Thackeray separated the top half of fol. ⟨45⟩, on which it was written, from the lower half. After this came his first major insertion in the upright hand: three yellowish leaves first numbered fols. 8–10 but then redesignated fols. 9–11—either because Thackeray had misnumbered them or because he wrote the last two first, beginning "I have heard a brother of the story-telling trade at Naples" (fol. ⟨9⟩ 10; see p. 72), and then decided he needed a transition between Becky's letter and his commentary.

He took his cue for beginning fol. ⟨8⟩ 9 from a short passage at the top of fol. ⟨46⟩ 12 that was now to be cancelled, in which he ironically distanced himself as narrator from Becky, whose initial account of the family at Queen's Crawley had just ended: "Miss Sharp's opinion with regard to the two young ladies whom she was to instruct was made with her usual intelligence and fine feeling. . . ." Possibly he also set down a modified version of writing that may have been on the lower half of fol. ⟨45⟩. In any event, on fol. ⟨8⟩ 9 he now pointed out the baleful potential for Amelia of her relationship with Becky—an important future element of the plot—and, with the awareness of Becky's later self-congratulation at having allegedly been able to see through Mrs. Bute's artifices, Thackeray's irony now played not over Becky's indifference to her pupils but over the limited perceptiveness of her wit: "Everything considered, I think it is quite as well for our dear Amelia Sedley in Russell Square, that Miss Sharp and she are parted—Rebecca is a droll funny creature to be sure: and those descriptions of the poor lady weeping for the loss of her beauty, and the gentleman 'with hay-coloured whiskers & straw-coloured hair' are very smart doubtless and show a great deal of knowledge of the world." Presumably in conjunction with the writing of this passage Thackeray also deleted mention of Sir Pitt's pinching and swearing at prayer time. Becky is now distracted, as a newly added comment points out, by her own pro-clivities: "That she might when on her knees have been thinking of something better than Miss Horrocks's ribbons has possibly struck both of us" (fol. ⟨8⟩ 9; see p. 71).

As the last three words indicate, in this passage Thackeray has be-gun to move in terms of emotional distance not only away from Becky but close to the reader, whom he now addresses overtly as he alludes to the novel's title for the first time and as he evokes the narrator-audience relationship depicted on the wrapper of the monthly num-bers: "But my kind reader will please to remember that these histories in their gaudy yellow Covers, have 'Vanity Fair' for a title and that Vanity Fair is a very vain wicked foolish place, full of all sorts of hum-bugs and falsenesses and pretentions, and while the moralist who is holding forth on the cover, (an accurate portrait of your humble ser-vant) proposes to wear neither gown nor bands, but only the very same long-eared livery, in wh. his congregation is arrayed: yet, look you, one is bound to speak the truth as far as one knows it, whether one mounts a cap & bells or a shovel-hat, and a great deal of disagree-able matter must come out in the course of such an undertaking" (fol. ⟨8⟩ 9; see pp. 71–72).

He went on with a passage implicitly likening himself to cartogra-phers at the Admiralty whose charts include not only areas for naviga-tion but also dangerous impediments which the mariner-reader must know about in order to avoid. Thackeray cancelled this passage, how-ever—possibly because its claims for the novelist were too grandiose and one-sided. After a blank space at the bottom of fol. ⟨8⟩ 9, the text continued at the top of the next leaf with a passage that evoked instead a two-sided and more ambiguous relationship between narrator and audience. The narrator is not a highly knowledgeable specialist chart-ing waters and dangers for others but a man like the members of his audience. On the one hand, like his brother of the trade at Naples, he evokes their passionate, though naïve, indignation at villainy partly because he shares their moral involvement and partly because he is sufficiently detached that he can seek money from them at the same time. On the other hand, like the actors at Paris, he has an honest, naïve reluctance to dramatize evil—precisely because he shares his audience's propensity to denounce it. Hence, he tells us, "you may see that it is not from mere mercenary motives, that the present performer is desirous to show up & trounce his villains,—but because he has a sincere hatred of them wh. he cannot keep down, and wh. must find a vent in suitable abuse & bad language."

As the narrator himself realizes, however, such abuse will not be a part of the "present number," which "will be very mild" (fol. ⟨9⟩ 10; see p. 72). What he is revealing to us instead is not only his discomfort at being effaced behind a "heartless" mask with which his audience might identify him (fol. ⟨10⟩ 11; p. 72), but also his wish to remind us that we are reading a comedy, the pleasures of which, he tells us, lie in loving goodness, laughing at silliness, and repudiating villainy. Furthermore, he wishes to offer us a summary statement of what he takes to be the purpose of comedy. For these reasons he announces that he will not remain effaced but will on occasion detach himself from his characters and comment on them. Men in their generations are indeed like the leaves of the trees, as he had written (quoting Homer's Greek) and then deleted on fol. ⟨8⟩ 9; but that tragic awareness, which is one of the bases of heroic aspiration, is inappropriate here, for Thackeray's focus falls not on life's brevity but on the hardihood of the ungodly: "Such people there are living & flourishing in the world—Faithless Hopeless Charityless—let us have at them dear friends with might & main. Some there are, & very successful too, mere quacks & fools— it was to combat & expose such as those no doubt, that Laughter was made" (fol. ⟨10⟩ 11; see p. 72).

In addition to such reasons for writing this long insertion, one can see, with Gordon Ray, Thackeray's wish to make a public statement of his sense of professional responsibility. He had recently done so in the conclusion of *The Book of Snobs*, and on 24 February 1847, in a private letter to the editor of *Punch*—written apparently while Thackeray was still working on this installment of his novel, to which he alludes— he did so again, referring to himself as one of those "who set up as Satirical-Moralists" and who have "such a vast multitude of readers whom we not only amuse but teach. And indeed, a solemn prayer to God Almighty was in my thoughts that we may never forget truth & Justice and kindness as the great ends of our profession. There's something of the same strain in Vanity Fair" (*Letters*, 2:282; quoted *Adversity*, p. 385). One may also agree with John Sutherland in suspecting that this passage of commentary, which came to occupy fifty-nine lines of type, may also have been consciously intended to extend the chapter by a page.[3]

In his upright script Thackeray marked the beginning of another chapter at the top of fol. ⟨46⟩, which he renumbered 12. The major change here, the second in the installment, came on three yellowish leaves in the upright hand; these were numbered fols. 13–15 but drew in part on a replaced fol. [47], for the text on the new leaves begins and ends in mid-sentence. Altogether the three leaves contain slightly more than would normally be found on a full leaf in the slanted script. If one follows the hint provided by the passage of commentary added at the end of the previous chapter, he will single out at least one passage as a probable addition to the text of fol. [47]; coming after the narrative, beginning on fol. ⟨46⟩ 12, of the second Lady Crawley's demoralization following her marriage to Sir Pitt, it too evokes the novel's generalizing title: "O Vanity Fair, Vanity Fair!—this might have been but for you a cheery lass:—Peter Butt & Rose a happy man & wife, in a snug farm with a hearty family, and an honest portion of pleasures cares hopes & struggles. But a title and a coach & four are toys more precious than happiness in Vanity Fair: and if Harry the Eighth or Bluebeard were alive now, and wanted a tenth wife, do you suppose he could not get the prettiest girl that shall be presented this Season?" (fol. 13; see p. 74).

Having cancelled the earlier passage mentioning the daughters' lack of education (fol. ⟨46⟩ 12), Thackeray now composed another, partly modified, version of their education: "they were very happy in the servants hall: and in the stables; and the Scotch gardner having luckily a good wife and some good children they got a little wholesome society and instruction in his lodge, wh. was the only education bestowed upon them until Miss Sharp came" (fol. 13). This discussion led to the identification of Pitt as the person whose influence brought about the employment of a governess. Pitt now became the narrative subject, in preparation for a link with fol. ⟨48⟩, which began with the following passage, part of which I have quoted before and all but the last sentence of which is now cancelled: "a stingy fellow who never could be got to owe [more] than a halfpenny. . . . The tipsy old boor of a baronet had a great respect for his eldest son, who by his constantly frigid and haughty demeanour obtained great influence over him. After leaving college he became private Secretary to Lord Binkie, and was then appointed attaché to the Legation at Pumpernickel wh. post he filled with perfect honor, and brought home dispatches consisting of Strasburg-pie to the foreign minister of the day."

Thackeray may have intended to tear off the bottom of fol. [47] and retain that fragment, for the second inserted leaf ends in the middle of a sentence, followed by a vertical line drawn through a portion of blank space after the words, "At Eton he was called Miss Crawley; and there I am sorry to say his younger brother Rawdon [here set down for the first time in uncorrected form] used to lick him violently. But though his parts were not brilliant he made up for his" (fol. 14; see p. 74). If such was the case, however, Thackeray changed his mind, for he went on to write a third leaf and perhaps at this stage to cancel the passage at the top of fol. ⟨48⟩. There was no need to retain its mention of Sir Pitt's respect for his elder son, for fols. 13 and 14 indicated how the father was awed by Pitt. Similarly, Thackeray did not need to mention the difference between Pitt and Rawdon, for fol. 14 showed us Pitt's frigid, haughty demeanor and the contrasting proclivities of his younger brother. Thackeray had some difficulty, however, in making a transition to fol. ⟨48⟩. After completing the sentence on the bottom of fol. 14, he began: "After leaving college," but altered it to "At college," having decided to devote a paragraph to Pitt's university career, especially his preparation for following public life under the patronage of Lord Binkie. The novelist then wrote his bridge passage, which contained a brief hint of the stinginess mentioned in the cancelled lines on fol. ⟨48⟩: "On quitting Christchurch—without a debt and with the sincere regards of the Dean—he became" (fol. 15). After drawing a vertical line through the remaining blank space the novelist decided to delete his final words, however, and to accept his earlier language on the following leaf: "After leaving college he became private Secretary to Lord Binkie" (fol. ⟨48⟩; see p. 75). An additional insertion concerning Pitt involved cancellation of a harsh remark about Pitt's mental ability and of a cynical, awkward, partly redundant comment about the failure of his diplomatic career: "And here again it may be said that his misfortunate star pursued him, for he was such a fool and so solemn that it is a wonder Government did not see his merit and look to his rapid advancement." In place of this sentence, Thackeray added a brief phrase in his upright hand that identified Pitt's new vocation: he gave up his diplomatic career "and began to turn Country gentleman" (fol. ⟨48⟩).

After inserting fols. 13–15, Thackeray changed the designations of the chapter's remaining leaves from fols. ⟨48⟩–⟨51⟩ to 16–19 and he added a short passage in the upright hand to each of the first three. On fol. ⟨48⟩ 16, he took up a cue provided by a phrase about how Pitt dominated the house with his spiritual exercises, "in wh. and after some time he brought his father to join." Now we learn that Pitt also engaged in spiritual warfare with his uncle, thereby providing further cause for dispute between Sir Pitt and Bute: "He patronized an independent meeting house in Crawley parish, much to the indignation of his uncle the Rector and to the consequent delight of Sir Pitt, who was induced to go himself once or twice, wh. occasioned some violent sermons at Crawley Parish Church directed point-blank against the Baronets old Gothic pew there. Honest Sir Pitt did not however feel the force of these discourses, as he always took his nap during sermon-time" (see p. 75). On fol. ⟨49⟩ 17, Thackeray added a sentence that overtly explained what might have been hastily interpreted by readers as a contradiction in the baronet's character: "for boor as he was Sir Pitt was a stickler for his dignity while at home, & seldom drove out but with 4 horses, and though he dined off boiled mutton had always 3 footmen to serve it" (see p. 76). Finally, just before the place where the narrative shifted from Sir Pitt to Miss Crawley, Thackeray cut a strip out of the middle of ⟨50⟩ 18 and joined the remaining top and bottom pieces with a strip of yellowish paper on which was written a passage of generalizing commentary that again evoked the novel's title: "O Vanity Fair Vanity Fair! Here was a man, who could not spell, and did not care to read—who had the habits & the cunning of a boor: whose aim in life was pettifogging: who never had a taste or emotion or enjoyment but what was sordid & foul: and yet he had rank & honors & power somehow & was a dignitary of the land & a pillar of the state. He was high Sheriff and rode in a golden coach, great ministers & statesmen courted him: and in Vanity Fair he had a higher place than the most brilliant genius or spotless virtue" (fol. ⟨50⟩ 18).

Thackeray apparently sent these nineteen leaves off to the printer and then took up the manuscript of what was to become chapter 10: fols. ⟨52⟩–⟨57⟩, on which he began a new numbering system, fols. 1–6. Here too there were several noteworthy additions. In showing Miss Crawley's partiality for Rawdon, Thackeray had originally indicated that "she purchased his commission for him, and though it was war time had interest enough to keep him at home" (fol. ⟨56⟩ 5). The implication of Rawdon's cowardly acquiescence was not wanted, however, so Thackeray had already cancelled most of this language and in slanted hand had modified it to read: "she bought him his commission

as Cornet & Lieutenant Crawley." The beginning of the next sentence
still created a problem, however, by alluding to what had been deleted:
"His reputation for courage did not suffer for to do him justice he was
as brave as a Lion, and had already, apropos of play of wh. he was
immoderately fond, fought three bloody duels in wh. he gave ample
proofs of his contempt for death" (fols. ⟨56⟩ 5–⟨57⟩ 6). Thackeray responded by deleting all but the last five words, which ended the sentence at the top of fol. ⟨57⟩ 6, and at the bottom of the latter leaf
penned a substitution in his upright script. Taking up Becky's description of Rawdon as a "young dandy & *'blood'*" (fol. ⟨59⟩ 14), Thackeray
now wrote a more extended explanation: "A perfect and celebrated
'blood' or dandy about town was this young officer—Boxing, rat-hunt-
ing, the fives' court and four-in-hand driving were then the fashion of
our British aristocracy: and he was an Adept in all these noble scien-
ces. And though he belonged to the household troops, who as it was
their duty to rally round the Prince Regent had not shown their valour
in foreign service yet, Rawdon Crawley had already (apropos of play
of wh. he was immoderately fond) fought three bloody duels in wh. he
gave ample proofs" (fol. ⟨57⟩ 6).

In the earlier manuscript, after these six leaves Thackeray had
Becky write a second letter to Amelia (fols. ⟨58⟩–⟨60⟩) in which she
introduced not only Rawdon but also another new character, whose
first act was to encourage Rawdon's wish to dance with Becky: "I'll go
and play a country-dance said Mrs. Bute Crawley very readily (she is
a little black-faced old woman in a turban rather crooked and with very
twinkling eyes)" (fol. ⟨59⟩). Even though Becky knows this woman is
"the proud Mrs. Bute Crawley, first cousin to the Earl of Tiptoff, who
won't condescend to visit Lady Crawley" except during visits by Miss
Crawley, Becky knowingly claims to understand that Mrs. Bute's
friendliness and invitations to Becky are motivated by the wish to
secure free instruction for her daughters. Thackeray followed this
letter with a private conversation between the rector and his wife revealing that Becky was being used as a pawn in Mrs. Bute's strategy
against Rawdon, the subtlety of which escapes both Becky and also
Mrs. Bute's avaricious but stupid and boozy husband. The narrator
concluded this revealing domestic scene with a statement ironically
summarizing the relationship of the parish inhabitants to the Crawley
brothers: "Thus it will be seen that the parishioners of Crawley were
equally happy in their Squire, and in their rector" (fol. ⟨61⟩).

Thackeray apparently came to see, however, that he was proceeding too quickly. Earlier, in a passage written in the slanted hand—perhaps on the bottom of fol. ⟨45⟩, which immediately preceded the leaves that now make up chapter 9, "FAMILY PORTRAITS"—he had briefly sketched Bute Crawley:

> In life he was a tall stately jolly shovel-hatted man far more popular in his county than the Baronet his brother. At college he pulled stroke oar in the Christ-Church boat, and had thrashed all the best bruisers of the 'town'. He carried his taste for boxing and athletic exercises into private life: there was not a fight within twenty miles at wh. he was not present nor a race: nor a coursing match nor a regatta nor a ball nor an election nor a visitation-dinner nor indeed a good dinner in the whole county but he found means to attend it. You might see his bay-mare and gig-lamps a score of miles away from his Rectory House whenever there was any dinner-party at Fuddleston or at Roxby or at Wapshot Hall, or at the great lords of the county, with all of whom he was intimate. He had a fine voice, sung 'A southerly wind and a cloudy sky' and gave the 'whoop' in chorus with general applause.

Thackeray, however, had not explained Bute's financial condition and the related hostility between the brothers concerning Miss Crawley's disposition of her wealth; he had only hinted at these matters when he made Sir Pitt curse Bute's interest in tithes, curse his brother's longevity, and mock the man and his evidently formidable wife with the phrase "Buty & the Beast" (fol. ⟨40⟩ 3). Nor had Thackeray shown Mrs. Bute's responses to Becky's arrival and successful ingratiation of herself into the rival brother's house. These matters came to appear, however, in the installment's third major insertion; written in the upright hand on yellowish leaves, it deals with the family at the rectory and with the background of Mrs. Bute's maneuvering (fols. 7, 8, 9a, and 9–12).

The first of these in the present narrative sequence begins with a brief transition from "these honest folks at the Hall" to "their relatives and neighbours at the Rectory" and with the ironic revelation that Bute's wife "had no little influence in the end on Miss Rebecca Sharp's history" (fol. 7). Then turning to Bute, Thackeray wrote an introductory sentence and pasted in his earlier paragraph set down in the slanted hand. After a concluding sentence about Bute ("He rode . . . the county") written in the slanted hand partly on the old fragment and partly on the new, Thackeray went on in his upright script with exposition concerning Mrs. Bute's marriage, her husband's ruinously inept bet on the Derby, and his monetary struggles with his brother, concluding with the ironic, generalizing comment: "These money transactions, these speculations on life and death—these silent battles for reversionary spoil make brothers very loving towards each other in Vanity Fair. I, for my part, have known a five-pound note to Interpose and knock up a half century's attachment between two brethren: and can't but admire as I think what a fine and durable thing Love is among worldly people" (fol. 8). He then wrote "break a line" and drew a vertical line down through the bottom portion of the leaf. Fol. 8 and the new segments of 7, therefore, may have been written after fol. 9a or 9; alternatively, except for the paragraph in slanted script, fols. 7 and 8 may contain a revised version of an earlier leaf or leaves in the upright hand.

Fols. 9a and 9 also constitute a minor puzzle, mainly because of the anomalous numbering. Fol. 9a, which inexplicably contains the cancelled designation "24," was probably written first. Beginning, "It cannot be supposed that the arrival of such a personage as Rebecca at Queens Crawley and her gradual establishment in the good graces of all people there could be unremarked by Mrs. Bute Crawley," the novelist went on to explain how keenly calculating an eye the rector's wife kept on her brother-in-law's establishment in her role as "spy." Following the latter word, Thackeray began a new paragraph that explained how Mrs. Bute wrote to Miss Pinkerton for information concerning Becky: "Mrs. Bute Crawley very soon found that the new governess had been educated at Miss Pinkerton's Academy Chiswick Mall, where she herself had received her accomplishments: and of course she soon had a pretext for writing to her old Instructress (Sir Huddleston Fuddleston had 2." At this point, at the bottom of fol. 9a, Thackeray either continued on a new leaf that he later cancelled together with the beginning of this paragraph, or he broke off, deleted these few lines, and possibly went on directly to the letter itself on fol. 10. In either case, he evidently chose to omit the introductory material because by quoting the letter itself he would make the passage redundant. Later he apparently went back and wrote three-quarters of a new leaf which he misnumbered "24" and then "9." The new leaf supplied what fol. 9a had promised but not provided: specific news that Mrs. Bute received concerning Becky, and her initial response to that news. Hence Thackeray, drawing in part upon Becky's description of the rector's lady on

fols. ⟨59⟩–⟨60⟩, provided three short paragraphs that now immediately precede the letter to Miss Pinkerton and neatly characterize Mrs.
Bute, especially with the brilliantly incisive passage: "Then the report
would come—The new governess be a rare manager—Sir Pitt be very
sweet on her—Mr. Crawley too. He be reading tracts to her—What
an abandoned wretch! said little eager active black-faced Mrs. Bute
Crawley" (fol. 9).

The letters exchanged between Mrs. Bute and Miss Pinkerton, with
perfectly matched postscripts, are found on fols. 10–12, which complete the upright insertion. As a result of this new material, we now
approach Becky's letter to Amelia (fols. ⟨58⟩–⟨60⟩, presently renumbered 13–15) from an ironic perspective, since we are newly aware of
the damaging information Mrs. Bute has been given by Miss Pinkerton
(fols. 11–12). To strengthen our awareness of Mrs. Bute's strategy,
Thackeray also made a brief insertion into Becky's letter, explaining
in upright script that Mrs. Bute complimented Becky upon her steps
"after the Captain & your poor little Rebecca had performed a dance
together," and marking the spot as the place for a wood-engraved
illustration of the dance. The word "poor" is of course marvellously
epitomizing, for while Becky believes that though she is financially and
socially disadvantaged her abilities will overcome these handicaps, as
they are now to some extent doing in the dance, we on the contrary
have a more deeply ironic understanding: the issue is indeed poverty,
which will apparently continue to remain her portion precisely because
the dance is being performed to the music of a hostile and knowledgeable antagonist. In the finished wood-engraving itself (p. 90), which
Thackeray already outlines here with a few quick strokes inside his
customarily blank square, we observe not only the foreground dancers
performing to the background figure's tune but perceive an unmistakable smirk on the latter's face. Like the implications of the prose itself,
only we, not Becky, are privileged to see it.

In addition to renumbering fols. ⟨58⟩–⟨61⟩ as 13–16 and identifying
in a headline the writer and recipient of Becky's letter, Thackeray also
added a brief description of Sir Pitt's and Bute's obsequious behavior
towards Miss Crawley: "You should see them struggling to Settle her
cushions or to hand her coffee!—'When I come into the country she
says (for she has a great deal of humour) I leave my toady Miss Briggs
at home—my brothers are my toadies here my dear'—and a pretty

pair they are!" (fol. ⟨58⟩ 13).[4] This passage was the basis for a full-page illustration, *"Miss Crawley's affectionate relatives"* (opposite p. 89).

Thackeray's fourth major addition to the installment in the upright script follows soon after, on fols. 17–20, 22, and 21—the last two leaves being misnumbered, like fols. 9a and 9.[5] The last three leaves contain a good number of revisions, unlike the first three, which are much smaller in size and may represent a reworked and augmented version of a replaced leaf of the same dimensions as fols. 20, 22, and 21. Beginning with a cancelled reference to apparently continuing "festivities," fols. 17–19 explain how Becky "won the heart" of Miss Crawley, as she had "of the country innocents whom we have been describing" (fol. 17). As a result, Becky attends Sir Pitt's ceremonious dinner at the side of Miss Crawley, and abuses the guests to the old lady after the festivity, "to the infinite amusement of her audience" (fol. 18). Afterwards she continues to join Rawdon at Miss Crawley's side (fol. 19).

Becky ministers to Miss Crawley's city-bred snobbery, but she misinterprets the old spinster's liberalism, as fol. 20 and the top of the following leaf reveal—even when the latter tells her she is foolish to ask whether it would be appropriate for Rawdon to elope with a poor girl: "Why you goose, Rawdon has not a shilling but what I give him. He . . . must repair his fortunes and succeed in the world" (fol. 22). The subject of Becky and Rawdon then concludes the chapter as Thackeray supplements Becky's letter to Amelia with information about Rawdon's increasing attention to Becky—a relationship aptly characterized by the metaphor of warfare as Becky rejects the dragoon's blundering note to her. With a reference to Lady Crawley's illness and isolation (fol. 22),[6] the novelist furthered the line of plot that will culminate in Sir Pitt's freedom to marry Becky. Thackeray also developed our awareness of Mrs. Bute's motives with the ironic observation: "how good it was of Mrs. Bute Crawley not to be jealous; and to welcome the young lady to the Rectory—and not only her but Rawdon Crawley her husbands rival in the old maids five per Cents!" (fol. 21).

Having indicated that Mrs. Bute frequently invited Miss Crawley, Rawdon, Becky, and Sir Pitt's two daughters, Thackeray rapidly went on:

and of an evening they would walk back together—
    Take care of that scoundrel my son—whispered Sir Pitt, in his elegant way. to his governess—Take care on um—you little zilly thing.

I can defend myself against the son & the father Sir, said she with a toss of her head. And so she could, that's the truth. (fol. 21)

Determining to evoke those crucial evening walks, however, he reworked this material in more extended form, beginning: "some of the party would walk back together—not Miss Crawley she preferred her carriage but the walk over the Rectory fields, and in at the little park wicket, & through the dark plantations, and up the checkered avenue to Queens Crawley was charming in the moonlight to two such lovers of the picturesque as Miss Rebecca & the Captain." Thackeray then evidently decided to epitomize this development by dramatizing a brief nocturnal scene between Rawdon and his captivator. Cancelling the last thirteen words, which were squeezed vertically along the side of the leaf, and recopying them in modified form below the now-deleted interchange between Becky and Sir Pitt, Thackeray showed her twinkling glances upward into a higher sphere and her coy puffing of Rawdon's cigar, to the responsive but largely inarticulate delight of the "heavy young dragoon." A final brief portion of text providing a revised and now choric version of the cancelled interchange with Rawdon's father then followed, concluding the chapter and number with a splendid summary and portent:

Old Sir Pitt, who was taking his pipe and beer, and talking to John Horrocks about a 'ship' that was to be killed, espied the pair so occupied from his study-window, and with dreadful oaths swore that if it wasn't for Miss Crawley, he'd take Rawdon and bundle un out of doors, like a rogue as he was.

"He *be* a bad 'n, sure enough," Mr. Horrocks remarked; "and his man Flethers is wuss, and have made such a row in the housekeeper's room about the dinners and hale, as no lord would make—but I think Miss Sharp's a match for 'n, Sir Pitt," he added, after a pause.

And so, in truth, she was—for father and son too. (p. 96)

In press Thackeray made a variety of alterations. In accordance with Rose Dawson's new background, a remaining allusion to her as "a gardener's daughter" on fol. ⟨42⟩ 5 was now detected and changed to "an ironmonger's daughter" (p. 68). Another reading, also earlier in the slanted hand, was largely replaced. Originally, on Becky's first evening in the country, "Mr. Crawley delivered an extempore prayer wh. lasted twenty minutes and then expounded a a chapter of Habakkuk. Sir Pitt hiccupped all the time in the drollest way" (fols. ⟨44⟩7– ⟨45⟩8), after which everyone received his candle and went to bed.

Thackeray apparently intended a deletion in this passage, for he drew a cancelling vertical slash through the middle of the bottom line of fol. ⟨44⟩ 7 ("Mr. . . . expounded a"), passing through the word "prayer," but this provided a syntactically imperfect cancellation. The ultimate result was Thackeray's softening at the proof stage of the prayer-time behavior of both men: "After Mr. Crawley had done haranguing and expounding, we received our candles, and then we went to bed" (p. 71). The deletion of Sir Pitt's hiccupping thus seems an extension of the earlier removal in manuscript of his tipsy pinching of Becky and the public exposure of that act. Clearly in keeping with a manuscript cancellation, Becky's strong suspicion that Miss Horrocks is Sir Pitt's mistress (fol. ⟨45⟩ 8) was now removed in press. Sir Pitt's swearing was also softened, as "d—" (fol. 12) became "hanged" (p. 73) and "be —" (fol. ⟨56⟩ 5) evolved into "be hanged" (p. 82).

Two other deletions, both in chapter 11, also deserve mention. The first removed the premonitory phrase, originally added in the upright script, concerning the ultimate effect upon Becky's life of Mrs. Bute's maneuvering—an addition that had ironically qualified the whole succeeding narrative of Becky's efforts to captivate the men at Queen's Crawley: "we must introduce the reader to . . . Bute Crawley & his wife, who had no little influence in the end on Miss Rebecca Sharp's history" (fol. 7; see p. 84). This deletion ("who . . . history") may at first seem puzzling, for although the "who" is syntactically ambiguous, further revision could have identified Mrs. Bute Crawley as the sole antecedent. The cause of the deletion therefore must be discovered elsewhere, in terms of broader artistic significance. On the one hand, Thackeray may have thought his phrase indicated the failure of Becky's efforts too clearly in advance for the maintenance of sufficient suspense. On the other, he could readily see that its removal would not destroy the ironic qualification but only narrow it, since we immediately thereafter learn—from a passage inserted into the manuscript—of the letter from Miss Pinkerton that provides Mrs. Bute with damaging information to use at an appropriate time against Becky, who is utterly unconscious of her potential victimization. By ending the sentence after "Bute Crawley and his wife" (p. 84), Thackeray shifted our attention from the outcome of Mrs. Bute's malice, which eventually had a whole series of reverberations, to her active potential for malice; at the same time he removed a suggestion that Becky was more a victim than an architect of her own failure. The second deletion that ought to be mentioned is less significant, but it does seem to show sensitivity—whether the publisher's or, more probably, Thackeray's—about possible contemporary response to his characterization of the rector, for on the same page a verbal portrait of Bute Crawley now appears without mention of him as one "of a sort of ecclesiastics who are becoming daily more rare in the country, but of whom most country districts contain a few specimens still" (fol. 7). Such an overt criticism might have been inflammatory to some readers and was tactfully cancelled.

A few additions were also made. The antagonism of siblings, earlier seen in the mutual hostility of Sir Pitt and Bute, and Pitt and Rawdon, was now reflected as well in the relationship of Sir Pitt's daughters, as Thackeray added the phrase, "She and her sister were engaged in constant battles" (p. 80), thereby also indicating Becky's neglect of them —an emphasis strengthened by a full-page illustration, "*Miss Sharp in her School-room.*" The most quantitatively significant addition, however, was the postscript to Becky's second letter (p. 91), which provided only four lines of letterpress but which established the basis for an illustration of the Miss Blackbrooks that Thackeray evidently needed to extend the text by one page, for the postscript and wood-engraving total thirty-four lines (including one blank), while the chapter's final page contains only thirty-one.

Only the first two chapters of number four for April 1847 survive in the Morgan manuscript (fols. 1–19), but they provide occasion for a number of observations. On 16 March Thackeray mentioned, "I am always thinking of No IV or No V. &c," and commented further, "All things go very well in that respect" (*Letters*, 2:286–87); only the following month did he begin to talk of impediments to composition. Thackeray may have begun the number with entirely fresh material, for the slanted script no longer appears, but it is possible that a number of the present leaves were recopied from texts originally set down in the slanted hand. One should also note that the wood-engraving of the two Miss Blackbrooks, which was used near the end of the third installment (p. 91), may have been intended for the space marked off in the middle of text on fol. 2 in illustration of the Osborne girls, just above the words "—a pair of fine black browed young ladies" (fol. 2; see p. 98). The present illustration of the latter together with Miss Wirt would have been inappropriate for that spot, having been prepared for only after an insertion into the manuscript: "the Miss Osbornes ⟨wondered more⟩ †and their governess, who stared after her as she went sadly away □ ⟨block of 3 figures⟩ wondered more† than ever what George could see in poor little Amelia" (fol. 5; see p. 100).

Thackeray may, in fact, have started this portion of narrative on what is now fol. 7: "We have talked of Shift self & poverty, as those dismal instructors under whom poor Miss Becky Sharp got her education—now Love was Miss Amelia Sedley's last tutoress, and it was amazing what a progress our young lady made under that popular teacher." If he did begin at this point and continued, say, to the bottom of fol. 8 ("too tired to write long letters"), however, he eventually decided to place ahead of it the material that now appears on fols. 1–5 and the upper third of fol. 6, ending "in honor of George Osborne" (see p. 102) and beginning with a sentence that alludes to the previous installment: "And now, while these things are befalling in the country, we must travel back to London by Sir Pitts coach, or that still more rapid conveyance the fancy, and have a little chapter about Miss Amelia." Later, in readying this chapter for the printer, Thackeray marked off space for a wood-engraved chapter initial, provided a title ("Chap XII, Quite a Sentimental Chapter"), and modified an already revised version of the opening sentence so as to produce the present reading: "We must now take leave of Arcadia, and those amiable people practising the rural virtues there, and travel back to London to enquire what has become of Miss Amelia" (fol. 1; see p. 97).

The Amelia we now find in fols. 1–6, moreover, turns out to be less spritely than we have seen her, less loved by George (in accordance with changes in earlier installments), and less popular with those of her own sex. Indeed, the Miss Osbornes and Miss Dobbins agree "in their estimate of her very trifling merits" (fol. 2). Thackeray presumably continued this account on two unnumbered and replaced leaves, one of which survives in the Morgan manuscript with the following cancelled writing: "Poor little tender heart! and so it goes on hoping & throbbing and longing and trusting. You see—it's not much of a life to describe—There's not much of what you call incident in it—Only one feeling for all the day; and one thought to sleep and wake upon. When will he come? Why didn't he come? he promised" (Album fol. 112).

These unnumbered leaves were then apparently replaced by two smaller ones on which Thackeray set down a narrative of George's neglect, incorporating into it a revised version of the above passage that may be taken as representative of Thackeray's admirable inability merely to transcribe a passage without attempting to improve it: "Poor little tender heart! and so it goes on hoping & beating and longing and trusting. You see it's not much of a life to describe. There's not much of what you call incident in it. Only one feeling ⟨from morning till night⟩ †all day†, when will he come? only one thought to sleep and wake upon—I believe George was playing billiards with Captain Cannon in Swallow Street, ⟨or trying his new horse⟩ †at the time when Amelia was asking Captain Dobbin about him:—† for he was a jolly sociable fellow and excelled in all games of skill" (fol. [4]). Thackeray continued on fol. 5 and the top of fol. 6 with a narrative that once more opened wider perspectives by placing in an ominous Napoleonic context the account of Amelia's snug, sheltered life in Russell Square. After completing what I take to be this possible interpolation (fols. 1–6) with Amelia's illusive belief that war was over and the celebration of peace was all in honor of George Osborne (p. 102), Thackeray indicated the break of a line and drew a vertical stroke through the blank space at the bottom of fol. 6.

He also wrote an addition to fol. 8, a leaf that originally may have ended with Amelia's belief that George, being busy with his regiment, was too tired to write long letters. If so, Thackeray added one more sentence—"I know where she kept that packet she had—and can steal in and out of her chamber like Iachimo"—before setting down the chapter's final portion on the verso of fol. 8 by rejecting the role of Iachimo for that of Moonshine, insisting that Amelia lacked the perfection of a heroine, and arguing the superiority of her warmheartedness. A marking for a terminal woodblock concluded the augmentation (fol. 8v). Like the putative insertion at the beginning of the chapter, this had structural significance, as we shall see.

After this sentimental chapter devoted to Amelia, Thackeray turned to a contrasting figure in a narrative unit eventually entitled "Sentimental & otherwise" (fol. 9). The chapter seems to fall into four manuscript units: fols. 9–12, written with a somewhat thin pen on grayish paper; fol. 13, containing only a few lines, which are written with the same pen but on longer and narrower buff paper (watermarked 1846)[7]; fols. ⟨13⟩ 14–16, written with a broader pen on buff paper that is longer still and also wider; and fols. 17–19, written on the same paper as the three preceding leaves but beginning with a somewhat thin pen and soon becoming broader. This evidence suggests that Thackeray may have written fols. 9–12 and several additional leaves before inserting fol. 13, going on with fols. 17–19 (still unnumbered, perhaps), and then replacing intervening leaves with the present fols. 14–16. In the text of fols. 9–12 we see George cultivating his reputation as an unattached bachelor among admiring regimental naifs like Stubble and Spoony, who think "that to be 'a regular Don Giovanni by Jove' was one of the finest qualities a man could possess" (fol. 9). Contrastingly, we observe Dobbin, who though loyal to George repudiates those values, publicly reveals George's engagement, and encourages him to visit Amelia (fols. 10–12). Apparently after beginning on a now replaced leaf an account of that visit, Thackeray decided to insert another contrast. On the bottom of fol. 12 he had revealed Amelia's romantic and sentimental fantasies about George: "perhaps he is bivouacking: perhaps he is attending the couch of a wounded comrade; or studying the art of war up in his own desolate chamber" (fol. 12); now, at the bottom of fol. 12 and at the top of fol. 13, he added the words: "And her kind thoughts sped away, as if they were angels and had wings, and flying down the river to Chatham & Rochester strove to peep into the barracks where George was.—It was as well the gates were shut and the sentry allowed no one to pass—so that the poor little white-robed angel could not hear the songs those young fellows were roaring over the whiskey-punch." Thackeray then set down a square to mark the place for a wood-engraving, together with a brief sketch of it, and drew a vertical line down through the rest of the leaf.

The next portion of the chapter seems to be a revised and recopied narrative of George's decision to make the visit, his using Dobbin's money to buy not a gift for Amelia but a pin for himself, his conversation with Amelia, his departure on "business," and the ominous scene at the Osborne home until George's reappearance during dinner (fols. ⟨13⟩ 14–16). In typical fashion Thackeray reworked what he set down on these leaves, most notably on fol. 16, where the emblematic figures in "the cheerful brass groupe" on the French clock eventually became not the unwilling "Jepththah sacrificing his daughter," but those of the more grimly purposeful "sacrifice of Iphigenia," and where several other changes added to the tone of dark comedy. Thus "down stairs" became "in the lower regions," the initial silence at dinner was broken as "[Osborne] growled out a blessing wh. sounded as gruffly as a curse," and the period immediately preceding George's arrival was slightly extended by the following sentence and a half: "Having concluded his ⟨remarks⟩ †observations† upon the soup, Mr. Osborne ⟨commenced a series of observations regarding the fish⟩ †made a few curt remarks respecting the fish† —also of a savage and satirical tendency, and cursed Billingsgate with an emphasis quite worthy of the place. Then he lapsed into silence and swallowed ⟨many⟩ †sundry† glasses of wine, looking more and more terrible" (fol. 16).

After indicating George's arrival and his good-humored remarks that contrasted with old Osborne's severity, to the especial delight of one "who need not be mentioned," Thackeray drew a vertical line through the remaining blank space, thereby completing this apparently reworked portion of the chapter. Except possibly for a few brief modifications, he evidently allowed the last three leaves to stand (fols. 17–19); containing the monetary discussion between George and his father and the ensuing scene where George refills his purse while old Sedley fails to do so, they present another contrast that effectively concludes the chapter.

Although the Morgan manuscript ends at this point, the structural implications of these nineteen leaves remain to be discussed. The pattern for number four, and indeed number five, was established by number three, the presence of which strengthens the theory that fols. 1–6 of the following installment were added ahead of fol. 7—in order to follow the pattern. The narrative in number three details Becky's progress at Queen's Crawley and ends by affirming her ability to be a match for Sir Pitt and his son. Contrastingly, number four develops Amelia's difficulties with George and concludes with Becky's success in finding a husband. Number five then shows us the waning of Becky's fortunes and concludes with Amelia's response to George's proposal of marriage.

The first chapters of each number begin by contrasting Amelia's fortunes with a change in Becky's. In chapter 8 Becky enters Queen's Crawley and begins to establish her position there (pp. 65–68); in 12 Amelia is rejected by the pompous, fashionable young ladies with whom she has to associate (pp. 99–101); and in 15 Becky is leeringly offered protection at Queen's Crawley by Sir Pitt, who believes her husband has abandoned her but is himself willing to make "a hideous attempt at consolation" (p. 129). Becky's covert amusement at the Crawleys in chapter 8 and her satire of them (pp. 68–71) finds its contrast in Amelia's timidity and her hero-worship of George (pp. 101–2), while the ironic structural counterpart in chapter 15 consists of Becky's feigned modesty and devotion to the Crawleys (pp. 129–31), which she affects in order to placate Sir Pitt and conceal for a time from Miss Crawley the news of her marriage. As the chapters end, three additional connections are made, this time by the narrator's comments about his own role. In number three the narrator asks us to recognize the difference between him and his characters so that we may be fully aware of his moral purpose: "to combat and expose" (p. 72) folly and evil while approving goodness. In number four we are requested to observe the distinction between selfishness and idolatry. While "shift, self, and poverty" (p. 102) instruct Becky and find their emblem in the orange blossoms of mercenary attachments, and while Amelia is guilty of an extravagant hero-worship, yet if we understand the superiority of the warm-hearted excess over the coldly calculating one, we can adequately sympathize with Amelia's love for George and value "this blind devotion" (p. 103), for it is directed towards another human being instead of solely towards one's self. The narrator reminds us at this point of his omniscience and his ability to play a dual part, but he renounces the betraying role of Iachimo for the approving role of Moonshine, since Amelia's love reflects faith, beauty, and innocence (p. 103), in contrast to the "Faithless, Hopeless, Charityless" (p. 72) rogues of chapters 8, 12, and—as we are about to see—15.

In the corresponding portion of number five the narrator explicitly recalls this passage while talking about Becky: "If, a few pages back, the present writer claimed the privilege of peeping into Miss Amelia Sedley's bed-room, and understanding with the omniscience of the novelist all the gentle pains and passions which were tossing upon that innocent pillow, why should he not declare himself to be Rebecca's confidante too, master of her secrets, and seal-keeper of that young woman's conscience?" (p. 134). Now, however, he goes on to expose rather than sympathize and approve. Moreover, by recalling the earlier passage, itself connected to the one at the end of chapter 8, in effect he asks us to compare the three of them and to notice how he applies the original purpose (8) to approve behavior in 12 and to undermine it in 15. Amelia, we are told in chapter 12, has "not a well-regulated mind"

(p. 103); instead of acting in a well-regulated and, by implication, selfish way, she manifests the genuine feeling that makes selfish, patterned behavior seem empty. As a result of this tripartite structure, we can in chapter 15 understand the earlier passages fully, for we again see the desire to serve one's self by worldly attachment; this time Becky manifests it and the ironic narrator calls such a desire the wish of a "properly regulated mind" (p. 134). This time, however, instead of sympathizing with its opposite, the narrator emphasizes the shortcomings of selfishness. Becky's hasty choice of the impecunious son when she might later have had the baronet clearly reveals how the calculations of human beings are inevitably limited by the incalculable. Therefore, we are placed in a position to evaluate, as Becky cannot in her eager greed, the improbability of her hope for Rawdon's future and Miss Crawley's money (pp. 135–36).

The middle portions of numbers three, four, and five begin with several examples of unequal human relationships: Sir Pitt rules the downtrodden Lady Crawley (pp. 73–74); George holds sway over his hero-worshippers, Amelia and the young men of the regiment (pp. 104–5); and Becky controls her love-conquered dragoon (pp. 137–38). After a series of protective gestures, Pitt's ambition (chapter 9) establishes a value with which we contrast Amelia's love (13) and compare the selfish ambitions of Becky and Mrs. Bute (16). On the other hand, Sir Pitt's prosperity (pp. 76–77) finds lateral counterparts in old Osborne's dominance (pp. 109–10) and then, ironically, in Miss Crawley's hysteria and Sir Pitt's impotent rage when they discover the identity of Becky's husband (pp. 142–43). The monetary security and hence dignity of Miss Crawley among her toadying relatives (pp. 77–78) sharply contrasts in number four with Amelia's doubts, which old Osborne's hostile behavior produces, about the future of her relationship with George (p. 110); both seem partly reflected in number five, where Rawdon's monetary anxiety is overcome by Becky's confidence about their financial future with his wealthy aunt (p. 143). Chapters 10, 13, and 17 then contrast the success of Becky, who neglects her pupils but in other ways makes secure her position at Queen's Crawley (pp. 79–82), and the success of George, who flatteringly gets money from his father (pp. 111–12), with the failure of old Sedley (p. 113), whose possessions are dispersed amid the disorder of a public auction (pp. 144–46).

Various threats and disasters begin the final portions of these three numbers. Mrs. Bute sees a threat in Becky's arrival at Queen's Crawley (pp. 85–86), while Briggs finds herself actually displaced by Becky's arrival in Park Lane (pp. 114–17). Napoleon furnishes the mock-heroic analogy to Becky in number five, as his arrival at Cannes threatens all Europe and causes John Sedley's ruin (pp. 151–53). The effects quickly follow in all three numbers: Mrs. Bute promotes Rawdon's interest in Becky and, in order to allow the young people intimacies such as evening walks home together, she even invites Rawdon to dinner (pp. 89–93). Number four refers to these efforts very clearly as a retrospective passage recalls how "Rawdon saw there was a manifest intention on Mrs. Bute's part to captivate him with Rebecca" (p. 119). After a shift of scene back to Park Lane, the parallel follows: the motives of personal gain that permeate Mrs. Bute's hospitality find echo in her nephew's wish that Miss Crawley invite George to dinner so that Rawdon may prepare the wealthy young man for plucking (p. 122). Number five then partly reverses this pattern as Osborne brutally rejects Amelia and as Sedley orders her to return George's gifts and letters (pp. 154–55); yet both men act from purely selfish motives, as do Mrs. Bute and Rawdon in their feigned generosity. Amelia, however, sadly returns the trinkets, although she keeps the letters and retains her love (p. 158). Number three ends as Becky is promised as a match for father and son (p. 96). The prophecy is fulfilled at the end of number four, when Sir Pitt proposes but is refused because she is married to the son (pp. 127–28); its contrast occurs at the end of number five (p. 160), when George proposes to Amelia, who of course joyously accepts him.

After using the same structural principle throughout *Vanity Fair*, Thackeray again employed it at the beginning of *Pendennis*. Gradually finding the nature of his material less and less amenable to the intricacies of such a highly articulated design, however, he came to relax this highly regular pattern of organization.[8] In the case of *The Newcomes* and later novels, for the most part he abandoned it.

4

The Newcomes

Installments 4, 5, 6, and 10

Since so little of the *Pendennis* manuscript seems to have survived [1]—
not even a single complete installment—one must turn instead to
Thackeray's ensuing serial novel. As his diary tells us, he began *The
Newcomes* on 9 July 1853 in Baden during a continental trip with his
two daughters (*Letters*, 3:668). He wrote numbers one and two during
the rest of July and finished number three on 15 August while visiting
Thun (*Letters*, 3:668–69). Despite illness, he had completed number
four by 31 August, when he arrived in London to conclude arrangements for illustrating the novel and to start it through the press (*Letters*, 3:300, 670). [2] Since he proposed spending several months during
the autumn in Paris and then wintering in Rome, he arranged on 1
September for Richard Doyle to do the illustrations; as Thackeray
wrote to his mother, "[I] feel almost sorry I am not to do them myself:
but it will be a great weight off my mind and I can now move about
Whithersumever I will" (*Letters*, 3:302). (This freedom of movement,
however, was to cost an unforeseen price.) Three weeks later he received the last proof sheets of number one for October, and soon after
its appearance he returned to the continent. In Paris during October
he apparently received and corrected the proof sheets of number two
and worked on number five, with Anne Thackeray as his amanuensis
(*Letters*, 3:313), completing it at the end of the month (*Letters*, 3:670).

Facts concerning the composition of number six are less clear, but it
appears from the manuscript that Thackeray brought with him a few
dictated or copied leaves of its opening chapter (17) when he came to
London on 11 November. He evidently wrote more leaves in London,
for several bear the mark of a favorite haunt—the Bedford Hotel,
Covent Garden. After a week's visit he planned a quick return to Paris
(*Letters*, 3:319) but was detained by influenza, a newspaper controversy over a sentence that had appeared in number one, and "by my
proofs" (*Letters*, 3:322)—presumably those of number three for December. He left London on 24 November and three days later set out

from Paris with his daughters for Rome, occasionally dictating to Anne along the way (*Letters*, 3:323). They arrived on 3 December, but after two weeks Thackeray had still not done "one word of writing" in Rome (*Letters*, 3:328). By the end of the month he apparently had sent the manuscript of number six to England, even though it was well short of what would be needed to fill the thirty-two-page installment. One can only conjecture the reason for sending an incomplete manuscript; perhaps he hoped to safeguard its arrival by entrusting it to someone who was then leaving for London, as was later the case with number eight (*Letters*, 3:351).[3]

Whatever the reason, it was here that Thackeray's difficulties with number six for March began. During the first part of January 1854 he wrote three more leaves to fill the necessary space in number six (*Letters*, 3: 350, 355), but the proofs of numbers six and seven were not sent to him in Rome by Bradbury and Evans until 11 February; by this time Thackeray was in Naples and did not receive them until ten days later—when it was almost impossible to correct and return them before the scheduled appearance of number six at the end of the month. Even more upsetting was his discovery that the proofs of number six contained "only 25 pages and a bit" (*Letters*, 3:350). He soon wrote to Percival Leigh,[4] the friend in London whom he had chosen to see *The Newcomes* through the press during his own absence. Apparently it had been agreed that the proofs were to be sent to Thackeray, who would correct and return them to London, where Leigh would check the revises[5]; if any extra letterpress remained, Leigh would have the authority to make deletions.[6] But for all Leigh's help, it was at once apparent that he had not inserted the three leaves written in January to fill up the number. Therefore, on 25 February 1854, Thackeray wrote Leigh from Naples, expressing thanks "for your letters & the pains you have taken with my numbers" but also pointing out: "It was for VI I sent the additions 2 months ago from Rome. There's no time to communicate now about it: and the mischief whatever it is is done. I might have had the proofs months ago. But what's the use of talking now? I hope you have eked out the number somehow: and trust in the Lord" (*Letters*, 3:349–50). Telling Leigh that he and his daughters were going to Florence, he asked: "Please write me Poste Restante there the fate of No VI" (*Letters*, 3:351).

But the fate of number five for February was now also in question—

for Leigh had assumed that the three leaves were for that installment
rather than for number six—as was the fate of numbers seven and
eight, for with the February installment now in print and the March
number short, Leigh might have to transfer a portion from number
seven, for April, and that would require a further transfer from number eight, which could not be tampered with because of its unity and
its special place in the novel's design (*Letters*, 3:355). Furthermore,
the time was too short and the distance too long to permit Thackeray
to produce more copy for needs that were still unclear to him and that
therefore required correspondence. Not surprisingly, Thackeray sent
an anxious letter to Leigh in early March inquiring about "the public
and No VI? You see now I cant tell what has happened to VI how the
Lacune has been filled up whether out of VII or from the overplus of
V and the copy wh. I sent for VI—nor will there be time for me this
month to get your reply, and send back copy if need be" (*Letters*,
3:354). He therefore desperately suggested that Leigh might "fill up
3 pages of your own noble invention—just going goose-step as it were
and making the story pretend to march" (*Letters*, 3:354–55); but then
he proposed that a notice "be affixed to No VII. to say that a portion
of the Authors MS. wh. was sent from abroad, has—in fine the scrape
must be met somehow." Exasperation at last burst out: "Confound
those 3 pages! wh. I got up trembling in a fever to supply in January!
and that my carelessness should have led you to suppose it was not for
No VI but Number V they were intended" (*Letters*, 3:355). The letter
ended more calmly, with a request that Leigh make two specific
changes in number seven.

In a footnote to the first letter, Gordon Ray writes: "This confusion
was apparently remedied. Parts V, VI, and VII of *The Newcomes*
have thirty-two pages each" (*Letters*, 3:350n). The major questions
remain, however: how was it all done? to what degree did Thackeray
accept the remedy? what implications does it have for students of this
novel and of Thackeray's art?

In order to answer such questions, one must first examine more closely
some of the limits, flexible though they were, within which the serial
novelist worked. Then, by following the growth of numbers four, five,

and six of *The Newcomes* from manuscript to their appearance in corrected state in the first book issue, one can determine how this portion
of the novel was shaped. A normal page of the published novel consisted of forty-seven lines of printed text; however, it is apparent that
a thirty-two-page number could not contain thirty-two such pages
(1504 lines), since separate pagination for the chapters and allotments
for the chapter headings, chapter initials, and internal wood-engravings all reduced the amount of space available for the text. As Thackeray's letter of 25 February 1854 makes clear, he felt that by adding
the text of three manuscript leaves to the "25 pages and a bit" in proof,
he would have sufficient letterpress: approximately twenty-eight full
pages, or 1316 lines. An estimate of the final text length had to be
made first at the manuscript stage, and since Thackeray could see that
one of his own manuscript leaves—whether in upright or slanted hand
—tended to yield somewhat more than one page of printed text of
The Newcomes and that three of Anne's tended to yield approximately
the same, he could make rough calculations. Actual measurement was
then made in the proof stages.[7] Thackeray indicated to his illustrator,
Doyle, in a letter of 5 June 1854, that a slip of galley proof for the July
installment typically contained the equivalent of two and one-half
pages of printed text. "Allow 12 lines for the chapters and letter
pieces, and with a string you can easily make your calculation" (*Letters*, 3:372). Doyle thereby had the basis for measuring the space
available for wood-engravings. If copy was scarce, Doyle could increase the size of the chapter initials ("letter pieces") and the size and
frequency of the wood-engravings placed within the text.[8] In the absence of Thackeray, final supervision was the responsibility of Leigh,
who had to decide what was to be done if the corrected, paginated, and
illustrated text was still too long or too short.

Number four, the initial portion of the Charterhouse manuscript,
provides a good example of the flexibility required of the novelist. The
manuscript indicates that number four was intended to consist of three
chapters, dealing with Ethel and her relations, Ridley's house and its
inhabitants, and the Colonel's and Binnie's dinner, ending with the
Colonel's interrupted last song. This conclusion would therefore have
balanced that of the novel's first chapter, where the Colonel sang his
song and then interrupted Costigan's performance in the Cave of Harmony. There proved to be too much copy, however, and the result was
an adjustment to meet the constraints of the serial format. The open-

ing chapter, "Ethel and her relations" (fol. 1), consists in manuscript of approximately six and one-third leaves in Thackeray's hand (fols. 1–3, 3v, 14–17) and slightly more than nine in Anne's (fols. 4–13), for a total of about nine and one-half pages of printed text. Chapter 11, originally entitled "RIDLEY'S" (fol. 18), consisted of eight full leaves in Thackeray's hand (fols. 18–25), representing eight and one-half pages of printed text and bringing the total to about eighteen. Chapter 12 was not marked as a chapter, though presumably it was intended as such, for it begins with a new portion of the narrative; no installment in the novel, moreover, contains less than three chapters. What is more notable about this portion of the manuscript, however, is the fact that it does not stop at what is now the end of chapter 12 but continues straight through to the end of what is now chapter 13: the statement that the novel will record no more of Thomas Newcome's musical performances. This part of the manuscript (fols. 26–36) also is entirely in Thackeray's hand: almost eleven leaves, which would have required eleven and three-quarters pages to print their text. In summary, then, Thackeray had a manuscript for number four that required twenty-nine and three-quarters pages (nine and one-half, eight and one-half, and eleven and three-quarters) if it was to be fully printed—almost two pages too many.

Realizing his predicament, Thackeray decided to take out the entire dinner scene (fols. 31–36), transferring it to the beginning of number five. In order to make up the deficit, Thackeray composed four additional leaves for insertion at the end of chapter 11, apparently beginning his augmentation at the bottom of fol. 25 with the words "At this time Mr. Honeyman comes" (see 1:117). He numbered these fols. 25a–25d, using them to offer a fuller exposition of J. J. Ridley's early life and to give us a lively further insight into Charles Honeyman by showing him in a private scene with Fred Bayham, who is now introduced here rather than in chapter 12.[9] Previously we had learned how J.J.'s parents thought him half-witted until "little Miss Cann took him in hand, when at length there was some hope of him" (fol. 22; 1:116), and how J.J. had been inspired by Miss Cann's music and Miss Flinders's books. Now, in the additional passage, Thackeray dramatized the conflict between J.J.'s dreams and the unwittingly cruel expectations of his parents by having them propose for him an apprenticeship to a tailor, by mentioning J.J.'s "frantic desperation," and by stressing that Miss Cann—with the assistance of Honeyman and Bagshot—actually "rescued him from that awful board" (fol. 25a; 1:118). Thackeray indicated as well that Miss Cann teaches J.J. the rudiments of drawing and mixing watercolors and that although he does not go through her course as brilliantly as she has expected, nevertheless he has the rare gift not only of imagining scenes from operas and books but of seeing the "beauties manifest in forms, colours, shadows of common objects" (fol. 25b; 1:118). In short, Miss Cann's role is more fully established and J.J.'s abilities and development more clearly articulated. The novelist now gave additional attention to the setting of Ridley's house in Walpole Street, but his chief remaining concern was introducing Fred Bayham and using him to characterize Honeyman's moral shortcomings, thereby revealing more clearly the nature of the skeleton in Honeyman's closet. Bayham, whose wonderfully evoked language and personality suddenly light up this portion of the novel, adds vibrancy to this chapter as well as to chapter 12 and therefore helps create greater expectancy for the dinner, at which he will be present, that has had to be deferred until the subsequent installment. Additionally, a knock at the door is now specified (fol. 25d; 1:121) to provide J.J. with an occasion for answering it.

During the proof stage or stages, Thackeray ended his final chapter after a small portion of the text furnished by fol. 31 had been used. Only a slight change was required: the manuscript reading, "One by one the guests now began to arrive," was altered in proof to become, "And now the carriages began to drive up, and the guests of Colonel Newcome to arrive" (1:128). Thackeray also inserted a passage of twenty-eight printed lines that not only helped to fill out the chapter but also raised an important issue that was later to recur—the question of whether it is appropriate for a gentleman to follow the career of an artist—and the novelist added two plot developments. Beginning, "I've settled it up-stairs with J.J.," and ending, "I shouldn't object," this passage provides Clive with an occasion to enunciate his decision to take a studio with J.J., possibly even to travel abroad with him, and it gives Colonel Newcome the opportunity to give his consent. Although the worldly Charles Honeyman demurs, Clive's enthusiastic celebration of painters is followed by his father's firm acquiescence: "'He shall follow his own bent,' said the Colonel; 'as long as his calling is honest it becomes a gentleman'" (1:124).

Number five now begins with the dinner, which takes up the whole of chapter 13, a change not reflected in the manuscript. Chapter 14, marked off in the manuscript as a separate narrative unit, starts again with the numeral 1, as we might expect of a chapter that was originally intended to inaugurate a new monthly part. The composition of the chapter seems to have begun with a dictation of three leaves to Eyre Crowe, Thackeray's amanuensis for much of *Henry Esmond*, who visited Thackeray in Paris in October 1853 (*Letters*, 3:310). Later Thackeray apparently inserted a bit more than a leaf to open the chapter as we now know it, up to the words, "with tears in his eyes" (1:137). The rest of the chapter is in Anne's hand (fols. 5–18), except for a few lines immediately preceding this portion and about twenty lines that close the chapter (fols. 17–18). Of the seventeen and one-quarter leaves of manuscript for chapter 14, then, Thackeray set down about two, for an estimated two printed pages; Crowe three, for an estimated two and one-quarter; and Anne twelve and one-quarter, for an estimated four; together they represented approximately eight and one-quarter printed pages. Chapter 15, entitled "THE OLD LADIES" in the manuscript, begins on the final leaf of the previous chapter (fol. 18). After a few lines written by Thackeray, the rest of the chapter was set down by Anne, except for the final two and one-half leaves (fols. 31–33), which are again in Thackeray's hand. The two and one-half leaves by him and the twelve and one-half by her could be expected to yield six and one-half pages of printed text. A final portion of the narrative, unmarked in the manuscript but presumably intended as a separate chapter (16), begins with a few words written down by Thackeray, the rest by Anne: twenty-five leaves (fols. 34–58), for an estimated eight and one-third printed pages. In summary, the manuscript leaves for the transferred opening chapter plus those for chapters 14–16 would seem to have required over twenty-nine pages to be fully printed (six, eight and one-quarter, six and one-half, and eight and one-third). Cuts therefore had to be made, and once more the changes were made in proof.

What is especially interesting, however, is the fact that in the proofs Thackeray also made several long additions, therefore requiring even more substantial deletions. Aside from various slight alterations throughout the installment, a number of minor cuts were made at the beginning of chapter 13 in the description of the Colonel's guests, chiefly in the case of Bayham, whose appearance and behavior were made less disreputable. More lengthy cuts were made in chapter 14, especially in five instances. The first of these is the most significant, for after Barnes's final turning aside of Clive's apology, the following words are removed: "& here Barnes could not help giving a little look at his cousin, wh. caused the latter young gentleman to feel sure that Barnes was perfectly aware of the previous night's transactions in spite of all his assertions to the contrary" (fol. 4). By omitting this passage, Thackeray did three things: he removed an uncharacteristic slip in Barnes's role; he took away from Clive an insight that makes him more perceptive than his father; and he moved the reader further into a position of being required to infer truth—a condition more in keeping with the perspective that usually governs a Thackerayan narrative. He also deleted a phrase characterizing the Colonel in this scene as a "prudent negociator of peace" (fol. 4), for diplomacy implies considerable hypocrisy in Thackeray's novels; thus Colonel Newcome is not a cagey maneuverer but a simple, moral man who asks his son to apologize because Clive's behavior was wrong and who leaves with his son when the youth's questions threaten to lead to further embarrassment. Thackeray also removed from the narrative immediately following this scene a long passage that inappropriately contrasted the childlike qualities of Clive's father with the young man's "shrewdness & experience" (fol. 5), his greater clarity of observation, and his newly formed tendency "to keep his own opinion & to question the experience of wh. his artless sire never doubted the value" (fols. 5–6). Such an antithesis is inappropriate at this early stage of the narrative, and especially after a scene in which only the Colonel has the maturity to seek apology and forgiveness—an apology that fails because of a crass egotism on Barnes's part that is not without a naïvety of its own. What remains in the printed narrative is not the young Clive's superiority of wisdom but of wit, together with his "tender admiration for his father's goodness" (1:139). The last two of these five deletions, made in what is now the text on page 140 of volume 1, remove minor information about Sir Brian's household in Park Lane.

All these cuts, however, are quantitatively outweighed by the addition in proof of the long passage that now closes the chapter following Peeping Tom's letter, which ended the manuscript chapter but which obviously called for a response. In the added scene that now follows we observe behavior that, though largely comic, also has somewhat sinister overtones, for Sir Brian, "the elder persecutor of the press," is joined by his son Barnes in what the narrator calls a "conspiracy for bribing or crushing the independence of a great organ of British opinion" (1:145). Although the *Independent* is not at all what the narrator ostensibly calls it, yet the vehement hatred and cynical hypocrisy of Barnes and the righteous malevolence of his father are very real and very clearly shown to us. Recalling this scene and their implacable wish to punish those who oppose them, we can later sense, when the Colonel is tempted by the *Independent* to take sides against Barnes in an election, that the results will be widely destructive. Finally, the additional passage also shows us for the first time Ethel together in a family scene with her father and brother; if we see a notable combination of courage and tact in her asserting independent views in a context of such oppressive sentiments, we also observe that her independence is limited by her need to secure the permission of her father for her proposed visit to Mrs. Mason. That mingled independence and dependence is precisely the keynote of Ethel's situation for much of the novel and we see it here epitomized for the first time in this significant added passage.

Seven cuts of five words or more were made in chapter 15, all of which removed minor information or redundant commentary. Two long additions were also made in proof. First, Thackeray inserted two paragraphs, beginning "Having nothing whatever to do" (1:148), that provide us with details concerning the Colonel's visit to Mrs. Mason, together with her reactions and those of her fellow townspeople. The narrator's stated purpose is to show us the "facts and opinions" that, "doubtless, inspired the eloquent pen of 'Peeping Tom,'" when he indited the sarcastic epistle to the *Newcome Independent*, which we perused over Sir Brian Newcome's shoulder in the last chapter" (1:149). The second addition shows how the Colonel responded to Ethel in the context of his memory of Leonore: beginning, "There was no point of resemblance, and yet a something" (1:151), and ending, "Ethel takes her place quite naturally beside him during his visit" (1:152). We now see that Ethel's hand becomes for him a "talisman" (1:152) that reveals the eternality of a passion, and we understand the immediate, deep response to the girl that, three pages later, leads him to think of her as a wife for Clive. So too, we note the characteristically Thackerayan break in the vision, bringing him and us back to the prosaic, intractable, everyday world where passions are not rediscovered so much as destructiveness, imperfection, and misunderstanding are revealed: whether the breaking of a "Chayny jar," Miss Honeyman's recollection of the Colonel's very much less than ideal wife, or the isolation of the Colonel's thoughts from those of his grateful hostess. This long insertion is all of a piece, however much the narrator's tone and ostensible subject shift within it, and it unmistakably reveals Thackeray's triumphant attention to his art.

As such analysis implies, Percival Leigh did not insert into this monthly installment the three leaves written by Thackeray in January 1854 for number six that Leigh mistakenly thought were intended for number five. The manuscript of number five, which is numbered consecutively in its two portions, does not contain three inserted leaves. If such an addition had been made in press, it could be readily identified. In fact, as we have seen, three passages have been inserted, one at the end of chapter 14 and two in the middle of chapter 15; they constitute the only substantial additions to number five and total almost three and one-half printed pages (160 printed lines). Because of their peculiar nature and their relation to the texts in which they are imbedded, however, it is clearly apparent that they cannot have been intended for anywhere other than their present location; the reaction of Sir Brian and Barnes to Peeping Tom (1:144–45), the narrative of the Colonel's movements in Newcome and the response to him by Mrs. Mason and the community (1:148–49), and the account of the Colonel's love for Ethel at Miss Honeyman's (1:151–52) are not transferable from an installment about Clive's career as an art student in London, the odd types who frequent his father's house there, the Colonel's increasing estrangement from everyone but Ethel, and the hostility of Barnes and Lady Kew to the Colonel and his son.

Just as chapter 15 began with several lines in Thackeray's own hand, so does 16, which is not formally marked off as a separate chapter. Although the manuscript consists of twenty-five leaves in Anne's writing, the printed chapter comes to only five pages, for here in the last chapter of the monthly installment the chief cuts were at last made. Besides the omission of the chapter initial, there were fourteen cuts of over five words each, making a total deletion of more than 1,500 words; the additions totalled six words. One of the deletions (fol. 34) removed an ironic use of the metaphor of electioneering and buying votes that further thought deemed inappropriate to the Colonel and to the situation, for his taking Lady Ann's children to Astley's, like all of his other instinctive responses to children, has nothing about it of calculation— an overtone that would have persisted along with the irony of the metaphor. The second major cut (fols. 35–37) occurred immediately after the contrast between Barnes and the Colonel, who can sit with his nieces and nephews in a public box for four or five hours and, "with perfect satisfaction," "eat an orange in the face of the audience" (1:156). At this point a long passage was deleted in proof; it narrated the return to Park Lane, Miss Quigley's moderately infatuated response to the Colonel's behavior to her that day, and—most extensively of all—Ethel's love for him, which takes the form of fond looks, affectionate gestures, and the undertaking of "ornamental feminine works in order to make him presents" (fol. 37): from bookmarkers, watch cords, and antimacassars, to netted purses.[10] Thackeray could cut the whole passage for two main reasons: a number of these details could be sacrificed because he needed to reduce the length of his narrative, and others could be omitted because they are repeated elsewhere. Ethel at this point is still a young girl who, having not yet "come out," has not developed the worldliness she will later display. Thackeray wanted to show this fundamentally loving aspect of her character—the root of her actions in the novel after the death of Lady Kew—but he decided that the moment after the ride home from Astley's was not the best time to emphasize this side of Ethel's character. Consequently, the novelist used a number of these details later, especially in number seven. There, if we see a somewhat less effusive Ethel, we still find a very fond one, hear of her constant riding out with the Colonel (1:187–88), again learn of the "purses, guard-chains, antimacassars, and the like beautiful and useful articles" (1:191), and discover that Miss Quigley has become so fond of the Colonel that she does four-fifths of Ethel's work for her.

Several considerable cuts were made in the lengthy narrative of Mrs. Hobson Newcome offering warning, chastising the Colonel, allegedly not concerning herself with Park Lane, and thinking herself perfectly virtuous; these are always the chief characteristics of her behavior and remain so in the portion that was retained (1:157–58). Aside from the omission of several rather insignificant matters like the mention of Binnie's library-retreat or a comment about knowing Sherrick's father, most of the remaining deletions originally concerned minor details of how the Colonel met Sherrick and came to rent the house in Fitzroy Square from him or, more important, what qualities the house possessed. The evocation of lingering traces of Madame Latour's school, which formerly occupied the house but went bankrupt, is ominously significant, but it could be removed because it is also mentioned elsewhere in the chapter. The longest, and penultimate, cut removed a description of the house which, although one would hesitate to regard it as essential to the novel, was nevertheless the most functional of all the omitted passages, beginning as it did with a foreboding description of how a new coat of paint, "like Madame Latours rouge in her latter days," not only failed to change the gloomy aspect of the house but indeed made it "look more g[ha]stly" (fol. 54). We also see, however, that the Colonel feels only cheerfulness, not gloom, and we observe that, for all the melancholy appearance of the house, furnishing it brings comfort and joyful spirits to others as well as to himself. As the last omitted line of the passage tells us, 120 Fitzroy Square is a "queer house So dreary so dingy so comfortless so pleasant" (fol. 56). There may have been regrets that the passage was deleted, for its elaboration and emphasis are significant, but such a decision could also be defended as necessary and appropriate. The passage had a further fate, as we shall see; but with the last two cuts, chapter 16 could be squeezed in and the monthly number, which began with a chapter carried over from the previous installment, was thereby completed.[11]

The manuscript of the sixth monthly installment is again separately numbered, beginning with fol. 1 and continuing through fol. 35. The handwriting of Thackeray alternates with that of Anne: Thackeray writing fols. 1–2, 7–9, 13*v*, 14–15, 19–20, and 27–35; Anne writing fols. 3–6, 10–12, 16–17, and 21–25; and both writing on fols. 13, 18, and 26. Though the opening chapter is not marked off as such except for its numbering, it begins with an evocation of Soho that obviously introduces a hitherto untouched subject: a London art school. It appears that the first two leaves may have been inserted by Thackeray ahead of dictated or copied manuscript, but it is certain that he interpolated fols. 7–9 between fols. 6 and 10—all before numbering—since he crossed out the phrase "numberless victims of Mr. Smee" from the top of what is now fol. 10 and squeezed it in at the bottom of what is now fol. 6. As a result, we have the wonderful description of the visit to Gandish's house (1:164–68). He wrote the interpolated section in his slanting hand on Bedford Hotel stationery, as he did fols. 1–2, and he left fol. 9 partly blank, as he did fol. 2. It is also clear that what is now the account of the evening parties that came to be given by the Colonel at 120 Fitzroy Square (fol. 19; 1:177) was originally a direct continuation from the earlier mention of the entertainments given by his son (fol. 13; 1:170), for in the first version, in slanted hand on green paper, the last two sentences describing Clive's parties were crossed out from the top of what is now fol. 19 and rewritten, in upright hand and with revision, on the verso of what is now fol. 13, which is also green. What we know as chapter 18, which is entirely on white paper, was therefore an insertion made in the original manuscript to introduce Clive's acquaintances at Gandish's, Barker's, and Lundy's, especially the comical but ominous Bobby Moss; chapter 19, the only one in this installment to be expressly marked off as a chapter in the manuscript, carries forward the narrative of Colonel Newcome's entertainments in his new house; while chapter 20 shows his growing isolation from members of his family, with the exception of Lady Ann and Ethel, and the increase of familial opposition to Clive as a possible suitor for Ethel.

As Thackeray's letter of 25 February 1854 indicates, the manuscript of number six produced a printed text that came to "25 pages and a bit." In Thackeray's absence, Leigh set about filling the rest of the installment with the assistance of the printer and Doyle. The printer made two contributions that extended the length of what we now know as chapter 17: first, he set up an unusually depressed chapter heading that took up the equivalent of fifteen lines instead of the usual twelve, and, second, he set up nine short pages—eight of forty-six lines each [12] instead of forty-seven, and one of only forty-five. He thereby stretched the chapter by the equivalent of thirteen lines. Doyle also made two contributions. He drew a chapter initial larger than usual (larger than all previous initials and larger than all but a few others in the entire novel), which took up the equivalent of about twelve lines of text. [13] He also drew for insertion in the text three wood-engravings that took up the equivalent of sixty-seven more lines. [14] As a result of all these efforts, the text, which represented approximately seven pages, was augmented by the equivalent of over two pages, so that it came to occupy the initial ten pages of the monthly installment.

Chapter 18 was apparently created by Leigh as a separate unit, for the only chapter marked off as such in the manuscript (it was, typically, unnumbered) came later, at the end of what we now know as 18. By taking the preceding portion and dividing it into two separate chapters, Leigh stretched the installment by slightly more than an additional page. The manuscript of what is now chapter 18 represented about four and one-quarter pages in proof; printed in a regular manner of forty-seven lines to the page, together with a roughly normal chapter heading and a small wood-engraved initial, the chapter occupied five pages. Seventeen pages of the monthly number remained to be filled. The manuscript for what we now know as chapters 19 and 20 represented approximately five and one-half printed pages and almost eight printed pages, respectively; normal chapter headings and initials would increase these figures to six and eight and one-half. An internal wood-engraving for each chapter added the equivalent of twenty-eight and eighteen lines respectively, but the woodblock for chapter 19 was the more important of the two as an insertion, for it carried the text over to a new page, while the latter did not. The installment, however, still lacked one page.

A third device made up the remaining deficiency. Leigh apparently decided to take the long passage that had to be cut from the proofs at the end of number five and to insert it into chapter 19. Accordingly, this description of the Colonel's house, beginning: "It had received a coat of paint" (fol. 54), and ending: "so dingy so comfortless so pleasant" (fol. 56), was placed at the opening of chapter 19 with only a slight adjustment in its language and in the language of its new context, where the phrase, "Our good Colonel who was one of the most hospitable men alive" (fol. 19), was divided. The chapter now begins: "Our good Colonel's house had received a coat of paint" (1:176), and continues after the added passage: "He, who was one of the most hospitable men alive" (1:177). As a result of this decision, almost one full page was added, extending the installment to thirty-two pages. By all these means, then—the spacing out of the printed text, the strategic placing of suitably large wood-engravings, and the inserting of a passage omitted in proof from number five—the monthly number for March was filled out.

The printer, Doyle, and Leigh were Thackeray's collaborators in preparing number six for its appearance, but this potentially would have been true for the printer and Doyle even had Thackeray been there to read proof. Only Leigh had any degree of control over the text in Thackeray's absence, and he can be credited with modifying Thackeray's language in but one instance—when the long passage from number five was inserted. As a result, only three of Thackeray's words were changed: "Colonel" was altered to "Colonel's," "It" was replaced by "house," and the altered word "Colonel" was replaced by "He." [15] Thackeray's ability to return the corrected proofs for the first five numbers makes him responsible for their texts. Although Leigh may have cut a line or two at the end of number five, that matter cannot be substantiated with concrete evidence. What may be astounding, however, is that, with the exception of Leigh's addition and the three related verbal changes in number six, Thackeray is also responsible for the text of that installment. By extreme good fortune, Thackeray apparently did get the corrected proofs to London in time for the changes to be made before the publication of number six, for there are over three hundred instances of verbal changes between the manuscript and printed text, involving additions and cuts of from one to ninety-seven words—somewhat more than half of these changes being *deletions*. [16] It will be apparent that Leigh, whose most urgent responsibility was to fill out the number, would hardly have engaged in an extended activity that reduced the text. Actual examination of these changes, moreover, compels one to term them authorial, except for a small number of compositorial errors. [17] A few of Thackeray's changes may suffice for illustration; I choose examples from all four chapters:

his falling collar? Why should he not wear a hat like Guy Fawkes and a beard like the Saracen Snow Hill? Why should he deny himself velvet? It is only a sort of fustian wh. costs eighteen pence a yard. He cannot help himself: and breaks out into costume naturally as a bird sings or a bulb produces a tulip. (fol. 1)	his shirt-collar? Why should he deny himself his velvet? it is but a kind of fustian which costs him eighteen-pence a yard. He is naturally what he is, and breaks out into costume as spontaneously as a bird sings, or a bulb bears a tulip. (1:162)
as he sat arrayed in gold and scarlet (fol. 6)	as, arrayed in gold and scarlet, he sate (1:164)
said with (fol. 14)	said to him with (1:172)
lads (fol. 16)	boys (1:174)
a guinea (fol. 19)	a wager (1:178)
committees you know. He (fol. 23)	committees. He (1:180)
to caress (fol. 29)	to soothe (1:184)

| says Barnes (fol. 31) | simpered Barnes (1:186) |
| beauty, whom he worshipped chastely from the pit-benches: whose (fol. 32) | beauty: whose (1:188) |

As this evidence suggests, the elaborately corrected text that greeted his March readers offers compelling testimony of Thackeray's commitment to his art—a commitment different in circumstances but similar in nature to that which one finds in comparing the other portions of the Charterhouse manuscript of *The Newcomes* with the resultant texts of 1854–55.

Thackeray wrote number ten, the installment for July 1854, during part of the preceding February, completing it by the 28th of the month, when he was in Naples with his daughters (*Letters*, 3:673). It comprises chapters 30–32, that portion of the narrative extending from Clive's realization that he must leave Baden to the scene in which Ethel burns his drawings. The manuscript of this number indicates that after being set down by Anne it was then augmented by Thackeray in his own hand. Realizing that the already written material was insufficient to fill up the monthly installment, Thackeray had the choice of carrying the narrative beyond Ethel's burning of the drawings, or of expanding the material already set down; he chose the latter, deciding to develop more fully what we now know as chapter 31, "MADAME LA DUCHESSE."

The evolution of chapter 31 (fols. 18–29) is rather complicated but can be reconstructed, though the leaves were not numbered until their final order had been established. One can distinguish a compositional sequence of three stages in two hand-writings: (1) fols. 19–22, 26, a replaced leaf or leaves, and 29 (Anne); (2) fols. 18, 24, 27, and 28 (WMT); and (3) fols. 23 and 25 (WMT). Fols. 19–22 and fol. 26 form a consecutive narrative; the replaced leaf or leaves carried the narrative to the top of fol. 29; and the latter, which begins by bringing to a close a scene already underway involving Florac, Antoinette, and several spectators (1:311), concludes with Florac's warning that Kew should leave Baden (1:312). All six of these surviving leaves not only are written in Anne's hand and narratively linked (with the exception noted), but are also united by their uniform original reference—sometimes still uncorrected—to the Prince and Princesse de Montaign instead of to the Duc and Duchesse d'Ivry, the name given them by Thackeray only while he was composing fols. 23 and 25 of chapter 31.[18]

At the point in the narrative marked by the beginning of fol. 19, Clive and Belsize have departed from Baden, leaving behind in favored positions their rivals, Lord Kew and Barnes, whose marital arrangements are being overseen by Lady Kew. Not long before, Thackeray had provided clear accounts by Clive and Lord Kew of how Barnes had been embarrassed by a former liaison; now Thackeray was about to depict Kew's former mistress and to show how embarrassing she could be. Here, then, was a problem Lady Kew had not yet resolved. Accordingly, Thackeray began what Anne set down at the top of fol. 19 as follows:

> There were other difficulties besides the Clive perplexity & the Jack Belsize complication wh. the old plenipotentiary who has just packed our hero about his business was bent upon arranging at this Congress of Baden.
> In our modern pictures of life, I know there are certain figures scarcely admissable. That poor wretch seated on Sir Brian Newsomes door steps and crying for justice to her children has no doubt shocked more than one squeamish reader who would not have his or her daughters Eyes offended by the sight of a creature so odious, so disreputable, clamouring in foul language against her seducer. He who writes has children of his own before whom he would like to present no object that should shock their purity or sully maiden cheeks with uneasy blushes, but the purest must one day learn that the world is a sinful world[.][19]

The latter part of the cancelled passage manifests the satiric defensiveness towards his reading public that Thackeray exhibits from time to time in his fiction, but one can see that Thackeray might have been dissatisfied because of the latter part's uncertain irony, its rather flat ending, and the bluntness of its challenge to his readers on a sensitive subject. Even so, such dissatisfaction hardly explains why he cancelled the whole passage, including the sentence about further matters that were engaging Lady Kew's attention at Baden. As that sentence indicates, Thackeray was about to begin a discussion of Lord Kew's former liaison with the Princesse and of Lady Kew's wish to deal with the problem of the Frenchwoman's presence in Baden—material that now appears in number eleven. Instead of continuing such a line of development at this point and perhaps later doubling back in characteristic fashion to give an explanatory background, Thackeray cancelled the whole introductory passage; later, however, he would take up again what lay behind it.

After deciding to make a new start, Thackeray resumed with what is now the second sentence of the chapter's second paragraph, giving an account of the Montaign marriage, which had been arranged much as Lady Kew is arranging matters for Ethel, Lord Kew, Lady Clara, and Barnes: "France is the country where that sweet christian institution of marriages de convenance (wh. so many folks of the family about which this story treats are Engaged in arranging) is most in vogue" (fol. 19). The subject of marriages of convenience thereby takes a more prominent place, instead of a position subordinate to the subject of Lady Kew's difficulties, and as we read of the restless incompatibility that characterizes the French marriage, we see very clearly how this narrative, by mirroring the past, shows us what to expect of any such future relationship, especially one between Lady Clara and Barnes, which receives so much attention in the ensuing chapter.

Thackeray's account of the Princesse's marriage and failure to bear a son began with six paragraphs, from the phrase: "France is the country" (fol. 19; 1:303), to the words: "the Prince and Princess quarreled with one another like the most vulgar pair that Ever fought across a table" (fol. 22; see 1:305). It then continued with a long passage (fols. 22, 26), subsequently cancelled, recounting how their marital estrangement took political expression, she becoming a Philippist in opposition to his Royalist sympathies, and how the collapse of Royalist hopes and the apprehension of the Prince in a chimney completed his disappointments, leaving him resigned to his fate but unreconciled to his heir, Florac. Here ended the passage that was later cancelled. Thackeray then continued with the words, "There had been many quarrels between M. de Montaign and his next of kin" (fol. 26; see 1:308), giving an account of the old nobleman's hostility to Florac and friendship with the Kew family, especially Lady Kew, and carrying it through at least one intervening leaf to what was later numbered fol. 29, which shows us the Princesse in Baden and ends with the words that now conclude chapter 31: "Partez mon petit Kiou. Partez or Evil will come of it. Such was the advice wh. a friend of Lord Kew gave the young nobleman" (fol. 29; see 1:312).

After the completion of what is now chapter 32 (fols. 30–38), the second stage of composition ensued as Thackeray took the pen in his own hand, made small insertions and corrections, and wrote out lengthier additions on four leaves that were later numbered fols. 18, 24, 27, and 28; it seems impossible to discover very much, however, about the order in which they were written. Though in the first stage Thackeray had cancelled the passage (on fol. 19) which, by alluding to one former mistress and to an unresolved difficulty to be faced by Lady Kew, was leading to a mention of the former relationship between the Princesse and Lord Kew, he now wrote an opening (fol. 18) for chapter 31 which returned to that material in a way that would quickly begin to prepare the reader for the revelation in number eleven of their previous liaison. Now, already at the opening of the chapter, she is in Baden, where Lord Kew introduces her to Clive. The first thing we learn about her, moreover, is her past association with Kew and her fantastic, though short-lived, use of him and other figures in her romantic book of travels. As a result, we have a developed sense of her extravagant willfulness before we see her as a victim of a *mariage de convenance*, and we have an awareness of her former acquaintance with Kew.

From fol. 26 Thackeray copied onto a new leaf (fol. 24) the latter half of the earlier passage about how the marital difficulties of the Prince and Princesse took political form (fols. 22, 26). After completing this slightly revised version of the Prince's embarrassment in the chimney and his dislike of his heir, Thackeray wrote three additional paragraphs, beginning "That pretty figure and complexion," about the Princesse's endless changes of personal appearance, diet, and especially religion, ending with her adopting the guise of a Quaker (1: 306–7). Here was a prominent narrative change, for this account of the Princesse was cast in the words of Florac, who speaks from personal experience in focusing attention on the dangers she represents to young as well as old men. In these speeches, which culminate in a warning to Clive, preparation is being made for Florac's later admonition to Kew and for Kew's subsequent misfortune.

Since the exact relationship between fols. 27–28 and the leaf or leaves they replaced remains unknown, the insertion of fol. 27 ahead of fol. 28 tantalizes more than it informs; consequently, one can do little except examine any idiosyncrasy of the surviving leaves themselves. The most notable of these is Thackeray's handling of another reference to unpleasant facts that he has to place before his readers (fol. 27). The function of these two leaves is first to explain briefly how the friendship between the Prince and Lady Kew resulted in Lord Kew's being

placed under the worldly tutelage of the Prince and Princesse and then
to show us at some length the present spectacle of the Princesse and
the Kew family in Baden together. Although Thackeray had apparently decided to defer revealing until number eleven how apt a pupil Kew
had been under his French instructors, he felt he had now to suggest
something of Kew's unsavory past. The author was therefore in a position somewhat resembling that in which we saw him when he composed and then cancelled the passage about unpleasant realities and
squeamish readers (fol. 19). Once again he shifted to the first person
and addressed his readers on the same sensitive subject as before, but
this time he treated the subject more hesitantly and indirectly:

> I am trying to tell this story, not in a sermonizing tone, wh. is a bore in
> society: where the fable is acted before us, and the observer must point
> his own moral. Admit that the novel is a newspaper; where the Editor
> utters his opinions only in a small part of the journal, the rest being filled
> up with advertisements, accidents offences fashionable news &c, and
> where Lady Brilliants last nights party: the running at Doncaster yester-
> day, Jack Splitskulls execution and behaviour at the Old Bailey: the price
> of peas at Covent Garden: Captain Screwby's appearance at Bow Street
> for wrenching off knockers, and so forth are registered without comment.
> But now and then in the newspaper columns you must come on a dreadful
> story or two. Do your children not see it? You take them to the National
> Gallery; do they not look at the Hogarths? Was the painter wrong in
> depicting that last awful scene of the series—the[.][20]

Once again he was dissatisfied with what he had written and cancelled
it. The analogy between a newspaper and an artistic creation was in-
exact, especially for a novel so suffused with commentary as his own.
This time, however, with the mention of Hogarth he had found a satisfactory analogy: immediately below the cancelled passage, therefore,
he wrote a revised version that he let stand, one that made a very
pointed allusion—not just to "the Hogarths" or to *The Death of the
Countess*, but to a specific, tightly connected series:

> Have you taken your children to the National Gallery in London, and
> shown them the Mariage à la Mode? Was the artist exceeding the privi-
> lege of his calling in painting the catastrophe in wh. those guilty people
> all suffer? If this fable were not true: if many & many of your young men
> of pleasure had not acted it, and rued the moral, I would tear the page.
> You know that in our nursery tales there is commonly a Good Fairy to
> counsel, and a bad one to mislead the Young Prince—You perhaps feel
> that in your own life there is a Good Principle imploring you to come into

its kind bosom, and a bad Passion wh. tempts you into its arms. Be of easy minds, good natured people! Let us disdain surprizes and *coups-de-théatre* for once; and tell those good souls who are interested about him, that there is a Good Spirit coming to the rescue of our young Lord Kew. (fol. 27; see 1:309–10)

If one compares the three passages on fols. 19 and 27, he notices that the blunt directness of the first is followed by a hesitancy and indirectness in the second and then a precise allusiveness in the third. Thackeray's reference to *Marriage à la Mode*, his characterization of Hogarth's series as a "fable," and his use of the supplementary analogy of the fairy tale provide greater exactness and substance. They also establish links to earlier parts of the novel, from the beast fables that introduce it, to the fairy tale used in chapter 10 to characterize Kew's escape from the confinements of home—an act which led to his career as a "Mohock" (1:101), a disorderly aristocrat of Hogarth's time and place, one of whose characteristic acts (as the wood-engraved initial of chapter 10 reminds us) was wrenching off door knockers, like Captain Screwby. Finally, Thackeray's third passage also prepares us for the duel that is to come. By alluding to Hogarth's fable and affirming its validity, he tells us that the consequences of human disorderliness may realistically be expected to include violence (Hogarth's Count, we remember, was killed in sword-combat with his wife's lover), but that we should not look at violence melodramatically, even when those who are engaged in it do so; instead, we are told that Kew will be morally saved and we are thereby encouraged to view the intervening developments not for the excitements of plot but for the outlines of fable.

At the top of another leaf Thackeray carried forward Florac's account of the Princesse's vagaries: "the turn of the philosophers then came—the chemists the natural-historians, what know I? she made a laboratory in her Hotel: she spent hours in the Jardin des Plantes— Last year it was the chase and poor Kiou—Kiou chased the fox and she chased Kiou—And, admirable thing!—there are women in the world who part from their lovers and remain friends with them; this one casts off her friends and never pardons them for leaving her. O it was a fatal wife my poor uncle took there! I believe her virtuous. Yes. She ought to be virtuous she is so abominably wicked! She has only memory for her revenges. She forgets her caprices as easily as I forget my dinner of last year" (fol. 18v). Whether he had already written on the other side of the leaf and now discovered that fact or whether the leaf had no other writing on it as yet, Thackeray decided to copy the first part of this passage on a fresh leaf and to alter the rest considerably.

With the fulfillment of this decision, we enter stage three, in which Thackeray first wrote "Duc" and "Duchesse." On the upper half of the new leaf (fol. 25), he set down the two paragraphs that were later printed on 1:307–8. In this second version of the passage, Thackeray retained the first two sentences and omitted the rest: mention of Kew, her pursuit of him the previous year, her capricious casting off of friends, her vengefulness, and an ironic praise of her "virtue." In their place he introduced a sinister analogy to the poisonous Madame Brinvilliers and an extended account of how the Duchesse has cultivated more eagerly than before the role of Mary, Queen of Scots.[21] Thackeray thereby had Florac present the Duchesse through her own identification of herself with the morally ambiguous queen whose favorites all came to misfortune. He also added a more pointed warning to Clive from Florac that characterizes the Duchesse as a "haggard Syren," whose "cave is *jonché* with the bones of her victims" (fol. 25; see 1:307). The sexual conquests of the Duchesse are thereby hinted at yet more openly and further preparation is made for Florac's warning to Kew and Kew's misfortune.

One leaf remains to be discussed: fol. 23. We have seen that during the first stage Thackeray composed an account of how the marital discord of the French couple took a political form, and that during the second stage he copied and revised the last half of this passage (fol. 26), including the episode of the chimney. Now, cancelling a portion of the first half of the original passage (fol. 22) and the revision of the second half as well (fol. 24), he rewrote them both, beginning: "In this unhappy state of home affairs, Madame took to literature, Monsieur to politics" (fol. 23; 1:305). In keeping with a number of other insertions into this chapter, these two paragraphs concentrate upon her. We have had indications of her activity as an author; now we receive a long account of the Duchesse in her role as Muse. The Duc's role in the Royalist conspiracy is diminished and as a result of his wife's behavior he not only suffers embarrassment but, significantly, becomes involved in a duel. Thackeray was thereby making further preparation for events at Baden and Kehl. He also made a number of minor corrections and augmentations, thereby cómpleting his additions to the manuscript of number ten. In doing so, he had both produced copy that was sufficiently long to submit to the printer and, equally important, he had notably improved the installment's artistry by clarifying relationships within his narrative, establishing further links between portions of it, adding resonant allusions, and bringing out the emblematic potential of persons, places, and objects already created.

The passage of number ten through the press was a good bit less complicated. Various brief changes were made throughout the installment, but only two have a significance that requires commentary; both are found in chapter 30. Thackeray's last sentence on fol. 2 had lacked end punctuation and had been succeeded by a space at the bottom of the leaf, as if more were to be added. In fact, the sentence, which followed mention of how Clive responded to Ethel's beauty with the enthusiasm of a painter, formed a satisfactory grammatical unit but failed to complete the idea implied by its context: "As he looked at a great picture or statue, . . . his heart sang Hymns as it were, before these gracious altars" (fol. 2). To the printed version, therefore, Thackeray added the words: "and, somewhat as he worshipped these masterpieces of his art he admired the beauty of Ethel" (1:291). This addition thereby completes the thought by linking Clive's intuitive response as an appreciator and practitioner of art with his admiration for Ethel and it helps epitomize not only his ardent yet distant appreciation of her but also her essential inaccessibility.

A second insertion, also made in press, removes unintended ambiguity concerning Clive's comment to Barnes in a low voice: "I thought you only swore at women Barnes" (fol. 11). In the printed version, before the comment is made, the reader learns that "'We were standing apart from the ladies,' so Clive narrated, 'when Barnes and I had our little passage of arms'" (1:297). The insertion thereby removes any possibility of interpreting the remark as one indelicately made within the hearing of Barnes's mother, sister, and aunt; it also makes clear that Barnes's immediately ensuing retort—"It is you that say things before women" (1:297)—does not refer to Clive's angry taunt but to his meeting and associating with Ethel in Germany, which Barnes believes is evidence that Clive is trying to thwart her family's wishes and win her from their favored suitor, Lord Kew, by telling Ethel of his love for her.[22]

These two additions extended the length of chapter 30 by three printed lines—normally an insignificant number, but not in this case. Thackeray's calculations for the installment indicated that the text was

still a bit short, and therefore on 5 June 1854 he wrote to Richard
Doyle asking him to make "a tolerably large [wood]cut in the first
chapter: and, if possible, in all the others" (*Letters*, 3:372). Doyle
responded with drawings for three internal wood-engravings that
occupied the equivalent of twenty-six, nineteen, and twenty-four lines,
and three chapter initials that occupied the approximate equivalent of
fourteen, six, and seven lines. When allowance had also been made for
the space required by the three chapter headings (normally, the equivalent of twelve lines each), it became apparent that the monthly installment required more than thirty-two pages set up in the normal way
with a format of forty-seven lines per page. Here the printer provided
important assistance: taking the text of chapter 30, which had the
smallest number of extra lines, he set up ten pages of forty-eight lines;
as a result, chapter 30 was squeezed into the thirteen pages that were
not to be taken up by chapters 31 and 32, and number 10 could now be
printed on the thirty-two pages available for it.

As has been suggested earlier, *The Newcomes* is not a novel organized
by a regular system of elaborate parallels and contrasts within monthly numbers and between them. Although Thackeray did not entirely
abandon his earlier principle of organization, its considerably diminished presence in *The Newcomes* facilitated any change in the novel's
planned structure such as the deferral of Colonel Newcome's dinner
from number four to five. Before proceeding to the rest of the manuscript, therefore, we might well consider the structure of the first
dozen installments, which make up volume 1.

Parallel structure appears most clearly, perhaps, in numbers one
and two. The opening chapters of these two monthly parts begin with
passages that have no direct connection with each other, but the chapters soon come to be linked by their focus on the Colonel and Clive in
London and by their direct chronological sequence, for the intervening
chapters double back to deal with earlier matters. In chapter 1 the
narrative of Colonel Newcome and Clive joining Pendennis in the Cave
of Harmony, ending with the Colonel's abrupt departure with his son,
is followed in chapter 4 by their arrival at Pen's lodgings the next
morning to apologize for that departure. Throughout these scenes the
Colonel is simple, unaffectedly cordial and generous, but inflexible

when he feels a moral principle is involved, whether in the bawdry of Costigan's song and its receptive audience or in the impiety of Fielding and Gibbon.

Chapters 2 and 5 both deal with earlier matters of family history, the similarity lying in the pattern of familial relationships. Just as Thomas Newcome the elder was dominated by Sophia Alethea, so are his sons ruled by their wives as well as by their mother, though in all cases there is rebellion, especially against the formidable Sophia—severe and open rebellion by Tom, limited and covert by his step-brothers. The harshness with which Tom is brought up and his resistance then find a contrast in the gradual reconciliation between Tom and his family and their moderately receptive treatment of young Clive. Similarly, Tom's thwarted love and enforced departure for India are succeeded in the latter chapter by a narrative of Tom, now a colonel and widower, resisting further matrimonial appeals and, after thirty years, returning from India.

The six letters that make up chapter 3 predominantly reveal parasitism and concern themselves chiefly with money and banking, the main exceptions being Madame de Florac's and, to a lesser extent, Martha Honeyman's; chapter 6 establishes parallels and contrasts in the generous self-sacrifice of the Colonel and the coolness or concealed hostility of his banking step-brothers and nephew. The separation mentioned in Madame de Florac's letter and her continuing love find their lateral counterparts in the reunion of the Colonel with his son— these strong, loving attachments being the chief contrast to the money-relationships revealed by the other correspondence. The letters of Brian and Hobson directly prepare for the step-brothers' cool reception of the Colonel in chapter 6 and for Barnes's patronizing remarks, both to the Colonel and behind his back. Hobson's letter, with its mention of Sophia Alethea pointing to Orme's *Hindostan*, also prepares for the discovery of her letter in the copy of Orme much later in the final double installment; likewise, Barnes's willingness to belittle the Colonel in the presence of Sir Thomas de Boots and others points ahead not only to his insulting behavior at the Colonel's dinner, where Sir Thomas is again present, but to his entire treatment of the Colonel later in the novel. Much the same can be said of the response of the Newcome brothers in Threadneedle Street.

At the opening of chapter 7, which begins number three, Colonel Newcome makes a significant emblematic appearance between the boys and the pensioners of Greyfriars (1:65), partaking as he does of the childlike qualities of the former and destined as he is for the fate of the latter.[23] In chapter 7 we learn that Clive's schooldays end with the arrival of the Colonel, while in chapter 10 at the beginning of number four—as the narrator overtly contravenes his promise at the start of number two not to recount the childhood of any other characters—we see that Ethel has not even had the narrow advantages of formal schooling but has been subjected to a bewildering succession of governesses, and that her cousin, Lord Kew, has had a youth remarkable chiefly for its frivolity and dissipation. Clive now has the companionship of a morally responsible parent, but Ethel continues to have only the company of her scatterbrained, trivial mother, and her cousin's life both provides further evidence of the failure of moral education in the Kew family and reveals the baleful influence of Lady Kew.

During the family party in chapter 8, we see the Colonel very much alone amidst the profusion of parasites and hypocrites; the tender love he shows towards his son at the chapter's end provides the chief contrast to the feigning of those who attend Mrs. Hobson's party. Lazy, luxurious, and hypocritical Charles Honeyman serves as one connection with chapter 11, where he again appears but where we see him—in a passage added by Thackeray—as a debtor, in novelistic anticipation of his imprisonment five installments later. Binnie's analysis of Clive's character also has a lateral counterpart in the narrator's account of the yet more imaginative J. J. Ridley, with whom Clive will journey abroad as a fellow artist in number 9; and the Colonel's love for Clive (1:84) finds an analogue in Miss Cann's affectionate rescue of J.J. (1:116–18)—a passage that Thackeray lengthened and clarified, as we have seen.

The final unit of number three, chapter 9, shows how the intention of Clive's aunt, Miss Honeyman, to withhold dinner from Ethel's mother and to eject her from the house yields to her own human sympathy and to Ethel's warmth; the reconciliation is marked by her taking Ethel's hand, serving the dinner, and offering Lady Ann's servant some "of the famous Madeira which her Colonel sent her" (1:96). Thackeray's original ending for number four was intended, of course, as a thorough contrast to this carefully prepared event, for the Colonel was to provide a dinner that, together with his song, was disrupted by Barnes's hostile, drunken laughter and by Clive's heated throwing of the Colonel's wine into the face of Ethel's brother. The ending of number two, where Barnes's malice had first shown itself publicly, was also to be recalled, as was the opening of number one, where the Colonel had successfully performed his song and had himself interrupted a drunken performer. The first four numbers were thereby to a certain degree to be rounded off, and a significant reversal in the Colonel's position and in Clive's was to be given a structural emphasis. As a result of Thackeray's need to defer this scene to the beginning of the following installment, however, the new ending of number four—preparation for the dinner—floats free of any distinct structural mooring, while the dinner scene's new placement causes its connections with the endings of numbers two and three to be somewhat obscured and its connection with the beginning of number one to receive new emphasis. It also now seems less of a conclusive breakdown of relationships than a heightened continuation of a movement towards such a breakdown—a movement that comes to extend through the next four numbers and to reach its most decisive point of resolution, during this portion of the novel, in number eight, where the Colonel sees "that Barnes was his boy's enemy" and reacts furiously when "Hobson Brothers wrote to him to say that he had overdrawn his account" (1:228). This movement had clearly been under way in number two, where the Colonel was annoyed to discover that he "had overdrawn his little account. There was no . . . balance of affection in that bank of his brothers" (1:61). There the overdraft was metaphorical; now it is literal and prepares for the eventual repudiation. In number eight he takes a new banker and returns to India to rebuild his finances, but later in number twenty, when Hobson Brothers refuse to accept B.B.C. bills, the damage is an immediate prelude to the Colonel's permanent ruin. Even more than earlier, therefore, we must look less for regular rhythmic patterns of development than for larger outlines.

After the catastrophic dinner, Barnes's hostility to the Colonel and especially to Clive expresses itself regularly during the next four installments and beyond, as Barnes's chief informant, Lady Kew, comes more and more to see them as threats to the marriage she is promoting between Ethel and her grandson.[24] The possibilities of an attraction between Clive and Ethel had first appeared in number four, where Lady Kew was told how Ethel had left Lord Kew's carriage following his inability to control it—itself an emblematic foreshadowing of events in number twelve—and how she then joined Clive in a congenial tableau. Ethel's fondness for Clive's father initially expressed itself in the first added passage of number five, where she replied to Barnes's reading of "Peeping Tom" with spirited praise of the Colonel. This fondness is then immediately explained by a retrospective account of their meeting and intimate association in Brighton, where the Colonel first speculates about a possible match between Clive and Ethel, having responded to the girl, as another inserted passage showed us, in the context of his memory of Leonore. The formulation of this possibility is succeeded in number 6 by an ironic structural parallel, however: the narrator's revelation that, unknown to Clive's familial enemies, he does not love Ethel. The attacks by Barnes on Clive in numbers five and six as "young pothouse" (1:142), who drinks with ineligible acquaintances and promises to be an "honour" to the family (1:175), provide another of the few direct links between the two installments, which end as Clive lovingly terms his father an honor not only to his family but to the human race and as Lady Kew, acting upon Barnes's comments, puts down Colonel Newcome and especially his son. The latter event, however, looks back not so much to the conclusion of number five as to number two, where Barnes had belittled the Colonel, and to Barnes's behavior ever since the dinner. It also looks directly ahead to the two succeeding installments.

Numbers seven and eight are also constructed in looser, broader terms more than in parallel sequence. Their opening chapters, 21 and 24, both develop the subject of a match between Ethel and Clive, an idea originally conceived by the Colonel in the middle of number 5. Mrs. Mason mentions it in chapter 21, leading Barnes to quarrel with Ethel and causing Lady Ann to arrange Ethel's absence during the Colonel's and Clive's Christmas visit to Newcome. At the beginning of chapter 24, reference to this absence acquaints us with the fact that Lady Kew's direct control over Ethel has been established and that the Colonel has explained to Lady Ann his hopes for Clive and Ethel, only to be told that the family has quite different plans for her. Other links between the two numbers are slender. In the middle of number seven, Clive's announcing himself in love with Venus and not Ethel/Diana connects not with the lateral portion of number eight but rather with the end of number six, where he becomes interested in a succession of actresses, and with the beginning of number seven. His visit to Paris in the middle of number seven anticipates his future trips to the Continent much more than does the immediately succeeding monthly part; a similar authorial purpose underlies the machinations of Mrs.

Mackenzie at the end of number seven. The events of number eight also tend to look ahead rather than backwards, as we can see, for example, when the Colonel returns with Pendennis and Clive to Greyfriars and sits in the room of one of the Poor Brothers (1:253); the chief exception, though only a partial one, is the departure of the relatively impoverished Colonel Newcome for India at its close, which not only foreshadows his ultimate ruin, but also completes an important stage of his life and that of his son and represents the culminating failure of his early attempts to establish himself as the chief companion in his son's life. Thackeray thereby concludes the first third of his novel and gives it a distinct structural identity.

The next four installments center around Baden, the first two drawing together more closely. Number nine begins in triumph as Clive sells his first sketches, holds a celebratory dinner, leaves for the Continent with J.J., takes in fresh and intoxicating sights, and begins a happy association with Ethel. Contrastingly, number ten begins as he sees that the holiday is over, surveys the dregs of the latest feast, and decides to leave Baden for Rome. The three weeks of growing attachment to Ethel, which have lasted for only one installment, are now over, having been terminated by the arrival of Barnes and the unsuccessful Belsize—Clive's exaggerated counterpart. The delights of the fresh new world through which Clive travels and the pleasure of his growing intimacy with his cousin are ironically paralleled in number ten by Lord Kew's dampening speech about the way of the world (1:295–96), as is Clive's arrival in Baden at the end of chapter 27 by his farewell and departure at the end of chapter 30. The narrator's account of the Vicomte de Florac, his *mariage de convenance*, and his flighty mode of life in chapter 28 also finds its parallel in the narrative of his cousin, the Duc d'Ivry, his *mariage de convenance*, and his wife's flighty mode of life in chapter 31. Ethel's wearing of the green ticket and Belsize's passion for Lady Clara in the former chapter have no structural counterparts in the latter but serve as preparations for future developments; they also dramatize the major theme of both these chapters, which end as Lady Clara faints on seeing Belsize at Baden (28) and as this news is avidly seized on by the Duchesse d'Ivry's circle (31). The two monthly parts end with narratives of "BARNES . . . A WOOING" and of "BARNES'S COURTSHIP." Both of these concluding chapters are marked by a variety of rages and battles, rebellions and acceptances. In chapter 29, Barnes fumes about

Clive and Belsize, Ethel taunts him, and Lord Kew puts him down; the major tumult results from Belsize's entanglement with Lady Clara, but he is at last calmed by Florac, Kew, Clive, and too much drink. In chapter 32, we see largely contrasting actions: how Lady Clara learns to reject Belsize and accept Barnes, who makes unusual efforts to be pleasant, and how Ethel battles Barnes and Lady Kew but burns Clive's drawings to demonstrate her lack of attachment to him. Ethel, in fact, rebels against the idea of being sold—as Lady Clara does not— but delights in the possibilities of the position for which she is being offered.

Numbers eleven and twelve, which trace the dispersal of "The Congress of Baden" and its consequences, have fewer lateral connections, being tied together more by the conflict running through them between Lady Kew and the Duchesse d'Ivry—a conflict that serves as a keynote for the opening of number eleven, where the battle is joined. In that number, Lady Kew is outdone by her opponent, the Duchesse, who has her greatest triumphs: her letter to Ethel causes the break with Kew and her instructions to Castillonnes result in the duel in which Kew is wounded. The reverse is true in number twelve, where Kew recovers, the Duc d'Ivry arrives in Baden to take control of his wife, and Lady Kew resolves to set out for Kehl to arrange a reconciliation between Kew and Ethel.

The end of number eleven, with its narrative of Clive and J.J. in Rome, carries on from the beginning of number ten and looks ahead to number thirteen; it has no significant linkage with the end of number twelve. The latter, which shows Lady Kew's failure to mend the relationship between Kew and Ethel, connects instead with the end of number 10. There Ethel had attacked the sordidness of her class, only to be told by her grandmother that she belongs to her belongings; now she again objects to being offered for sale but meets only stubborn coaxing from Lady Kew. Similarly, at the conclusion of number ten Ethel had replied to her grandmother by burning Clive's sketches; here, at the conclusion of number twelve, she responds by burning Kew's letter in "the same fire-place at which Clive's sketches had been burned" (1:380). Her essential ambivalence is thereby given a prominent structural emphasis at the end of the novel's first volume.

5
The Newcomes

Installments 14–15, 17–20, 22, 23–24

The next portion of the Charterhouse manuscript is number fourteen for November 1854, written entirely in Thackeray's own hand between 9 and 24 July in Paris, Boulogne, Brussels, and Spa (*Letters*, 3:676). Comprising chapters 4–6 of the second volume, the installment begins with Clive's letter to his father from Brighton and extends to Rosey's perception that Miss Sherrick loves Charles Honeyman. Again there were a number of important insertions in the manuscript. They seem to have been made early in the process of composition rather than late, but they necessitated further changes as the installment was passing through the press. During Thackeray's opening stints he apparently recounted Clive's news for his father, Clive's scolding by Miss Honeyman, his morning walks with his cousins and meeting with Lady Ann and Ethel, his return to Miss Honeyman's with them, and his scene with Farintosh, who has been ignoring him (fols. 1–8).[1] Shifting the scene to London, Thackeray then began a new section on a leaf that was originally numbered fol. 9: "In his communications with certain friends who approached nearer to his own time of life, Mr. Clive was much more eloquent and rhapsodical than in the letters wh. he wrote to his father, regarding this passion for Miss Ethel" (see 2:46). On five leaves originally numbered fols. 9–13, he wrote of Clive's celebration of Ethel with pencil and pen, his boredom with the Mackenzies, Bayham's news of J.J.'s progress, Clive's difficulty in meeting Ethel, and his association with a number of Guardsmen (see 2:46–52).

Thackeray, however, was not yet finished with the Brighton episode. He had already written a brief version of Clive's scene with Lady Ann, Ethel, and Farintosh, following the last phrase on fol. 8, where Farintosh first addresses Clive: "In the army I suppose?"

> I'm an artist says Clive turning very red.
> Oh really I didn't know! cries the nobleman: and my lord bursting out laughing presently as he was engaged in a conversation with Miss Ethel on the balcony; Clive thought, very likely with justice, 'He is making fun

of my mustachios, confound him! I should like to pitch him over into the street.' But this was only a kind wish on Mr. Newcome's part not followed out by any fullfilment—only a sulky nod when he quitted his aunt's room. (fol. 8*v*)

This passage then stimulated Thackeray to further invention, for the brief interchange in which Farintosh keenly touches Clive's sensitive pride led Thackeray to bring Clive back after his walk and to show his social disadvantage and his resultant jealousy and rage at greater length. Accordingly, he copied the above passage, omitted the last ten words, and went on for two leaves with a narrative of Farintosh's disinclination to leave, Clive's walk in Brighton and Hove, his return for dinner to find Farintosh still there, the fashionable conversation from which he is unintentionally but naturally excluded, his aggressive introduction of his tart-making aunt into the conversation, Ethel's decision to ignore him, and the young men's finally rising together to depart (2:40–42). The earlier portion of this scene had shown Farintosh's denseness and Clive's ability to caricature Ethel's (and his own) ancestor for their joint amusement and it had apparently ended with Ethel's ability to introduce Clive to Farintosh and his world; the addition then revealed the limits of that potential by finely dramatizing the social differences between Clive and Ethel and by showing both his inability to compete for her on Farintosh's level and the alienation from Ethel that his inability produced. The two new leaves on which it was written were numbered fols. 9 and 10, the five leaves they were now to precede being renumbered fols. 11–15.

Thackeray then made several more additions. First, he wrote another leaf (fol. 10a) to augment even more the dinner scene in Brighton. Apparently starting at the bottom of fol. 10, where the departing Farintosh begins to offer his compliments for the dinner, Thackeray carried the narrative to what we know as the end of chapter 4, where Lady Ann rules out Ethel's return to London with either young man, Clive and Ethel exchange thrusts on the subject of constancy, and Clive refuses to stay when Ethel motions him to do so (2:42–43). Second, Thackeray composed two further leaves containing a scene that he marked as the opening of a new chapter (2:44–46). As in the passage written on what was originally fol. 9, he shifted to London and moved across a gap of time. In this case, however, Thackeray began with a scene that grew directly out of the Brighton episode, especially its newly elaborated ending. Here we learn that Farintosh's question about Clive's mustachios and Ethel's subsequent laughter have caused the hypersensitive Clive to shave them off the very next morning, that just before his departure from Brighton he once again has refused to respond to a gesture of Ethel's, and that Clive's attempt to embarrass her with the tarts has only shown him the disparity between Ethel and himself—an insight emphatically endorsed by Pendennis. With this passage, Thackeray also illustrated in scenic form the narrative summary he had already written about the intensity of Clive's feelings towards Ethel—a summary that was now directly to follow this insertion. One more rearrangement of Thackeray's numbering system then ensued. As a result, fol. 10a, which ended chapter 4, became fol. 11; the two most recent additions became fols. 12–13, and the five leaves that had earlier been renumbered as fols. 11–15 received their present designation as fols. 14–18. A final addition completed chapter 5: the writing of fol. 15A, which recounted Pen's sly appeal to Mrs. Mackenzie's snobbery, Warrington's characterization of her as an old campaigner, and his denunciation of the marriage trade—a condemnation growing out of his response not only to Mrs. Mackenzie but also to the scene he has overheard between Clive and Pen (fols. 12–13). The manuscript suggests that the writing of chapter 6 had none of these complications; it seems to have proceeded directly along the lines of the present narrative, which recounts Honeyman's resurgence at Lady Whittlesea's Chapel, Sherrick's prosperous mentorship, and Miss Sherrick's love.[2]

In its published appearance the monthly installment contained three moderate-sized chapter initials and only two internal wood-engravings.[3] The manuscript nevertheless was considerably too long to print, partly because of the six inserted leaves, which not only brought artistically important additions to the installment but also necessitated cuts —on several occasions to remove abundant detail in the additions themselves. These cuts and a variety of small changes were introduced in press. Sixteen deletions of over five words net were made, removing over seven hundred words—the equivalent of approximately one and one-half pages of printed text. Half of the cuts, accounting for three-fourths of the total words, were made in chapter 4; all but one of the rest occurred in chapter 5. A number of them remove detail that is mentioned elsewhere or that is quite insignificant: how Martha Honeyman had long shown a spinsterish antipathy to rites of courtship (fol. 3); where the younger Newcome children stayed in Brighton (fol. 5);

the kind of Sunday meal that awaited them (fol. 6); how Clive amused himself on his afternoon walk and how he continued to be unable to pacify Miss Honeyman (fol. 9); the behavior of Lady Kew's footman and the appearance of Farintosh's cab horse (fol. 16). Though these cuts made in press are all artistically defensible, one would hesitate to call them necessary except to a novelist forced by the exigencies of serial publication to reduce the length of his text. Here, then, is an important question that must be faced by future editors of this and other serial novels: should such passages be reintroduced, and if so, on what basis shall they be chosen and in what manner shall they be printed?

A related problem is raised by the deletion of a passage containing materials that vary in their kind of relevance. The printed edition contains an abrupt and puzzling mention of Clive's meeting Miss Cann in Brighton and walking with her and the Newcome children on the Chain Pier—the same Miss Cann he has known in London living in Ridley's house, quite unacquainted with Lady Ann or her children: "So away went Clive to walk with his cousins, and then to see his old friend Miss Cann, with whom and the elder children he walked to church . . ." (2:37). The original passage, cancelled in press, had narrated matters much more clearly by telling us she had become their governess and describing the first walk in a way that clearly distinguished it from the second. In composing the latter portion of the narrative, however, Thackeray had been led into a certain elaboration of detail that presumably caused him later to delete almost the whole passage in which the detail was embedded. The passage originally read as follows:

> So away went Clive to walk with his cousins—who told him all their news and how they had got a new governess such a funny little kind old governess much nicer than Miss Quigley who knew Clive too, and her name was Miss Cann—And they all went forth on to the Chain Pier, and there some of them went below among the great pier-beams with the green waters tossing and shimmering below—a sight of pleasure and wonderment—and there Clive smokd that cigar wh. has been waiting all this while—and then he went to see his old friend Miss Cann with whom and the elder children he walked to church. . . . (fol. 5)

The inferences necessary to an understanding of the printed version can be made by the reader with a certain amount of effort; the change made in press nevertheless resembles the uncrossing of a "t."

If we find in this cancellation the kind of minor imperfection produced in part by the need to reduce a serial text to a printable length, we can also see a number of examples in which the author's need to scrutinize the text for possible deletions led him to tighten the narrative and subtly alter the nuance of character delineation. Mention of how Clive and Belsize groaned together for a month after leaving Baden and consoled each other after a fashion (fol. 2) is largely irrelevant in a narrative that concentrates on Clive and goes on immediately to reveal his ability to recover his appetite and spirits in Rome; as a result, it was removed and the narrative was given firmer coherence. Clive's comment that Miss Honeyman "has received me with a scolding on my return from abroad & is as sulky and angry and as proud as old Lady Kew" (fol. 2) inaccurately compresses two separate reponses of Miss Honeyman and creates an analogy whose comedy fails to overcome its inappropriateness; accordingly, the analogy was deleted. A gesture made by Ethel at the end of the dinner scene with Clive and Farintosh had already given Thackeray difficulty in manuscript stage, for he had added a second version, though without crossing out the first, describing her reaction when Farintosh again promises to do what she had earlier asked and get Clive an invitation to Lady Innishowan's party:

an askance look at Clive.
(Peuh! says Ethel with a shrug of her shoulder.) (fol. 11)

The gestures, especially the shrug, are too rude and too obvious for the dignified Ethel; moreover, they are also too simple and unqualified for a girl whom the scene shows as divided in impulse. This passage was also cancelled in press.

Two more deletions of this kind deserve mention—both from the scene in which Clive groans out to Pendennis his passion for Ethel. The first follows Pen's observation that Clive has shaved off his mustachios: "Farintosh asked me whether I was in the army, said Clive with another ingenuous blush, and she laughed. I thought I had best dock off the facial ornaments. Do you know old Gandish called upon me three days ago with a pair of mustachios, and yesterday I saw a little fellow by the name of Moss swaggering about Brighton pier with another pair? You remember Moss? O I would like to cut my head off as well as my hair!" (fols. 12–13). Thackeray's introduction of Gandish and Moss has partly obscured Clive's chief motive for shaving off the mustachios (the mortification that Farintosh's and Ethel's behavior have given his vanity) by adding to it the snobbish motive of consciously wishing to seem superior to Gandish and Moss—the latter being an impulse, furthermore, that has never characterized Clive, for he has always assumed his superiority. One could, of course, defend the revelation of such an impulse, but not so easily at this place in the narrative. Thackeray therefore made deletions in this passage that produced a much more pointed version of Clive's sensitive vulnerability. He also deleted the comment about Clive's blush, which is clearly implied by the context, and he refined upon the language: "'Farintosh asked me whether I was going in the army,' said Clive, 'and she laughed. I thought I had best dock them. O I would like to cut my head off as well as my hair!'" (2:45). Immediately thereafter Thackeray had originally gone on to give Clive one more utterance and to give a description of the physical signs of Clive's agitation: "I'm mad about this woman—mad about her! And he bit the backs of his hands, fired off twenty vollies of cigar-smoke: dashed the cigar into the fire place drank off tumbler after tumbler of water and gave other marks of distraction" (fol. 13). The vividness of the detail about biting the backs of his hands and the ensuing mild comedy of the passage might have argued for its retention, but the writing seems more appropriate for Thackeray's fiction of the 1840s than for this scene, which is marked by its high incidence of expressive dialogue rather than physical description, like a fair number of others in *The Newcomes*. Once again the cut, made in press, both improved the installment's artistry and helped make it printable in thirty-two pages. As a result of these various deletions, chapter 4 could be printed on eleven pages with five lines to spare, chapter 5 on nine pages with two lines to spare, and chapter 6 on the remaining twelve pages with an internal wood-engraving occupying the equivalent of twenty-two lines of printed text, and with three lines to spare on the installment's last page. The printed text was the longest in the novel, except for that of the final double number: the equivalent of 1398 lines.

Number fifteen for December 1854, comprising chapters 7–9, was written in Spa, Belgium, from the 25th through the 31st of July (*Letters*, 3:676–77). The manuscript—twenty-seven leaves in this instance—is again entirely in Thackeray's hand. It reveals no unusual difficulties of composition. Chapter 8 lacks a chapter heading to separate it from 7, and though chapter 9 has one, its squeezed appearance suggests that it may have been inserted later. Once again, the text was too long, and three major deletions totalling approximately twenty-eight printed lines—all in the same chapter—were made in press in order to free the necessary page. Although these twenty-eight lines could have been cut from the printed texts of either chapter 7 or 8, Thackeray chose to make them in the latter, "THE HÔTEL DE FLO-RAC," which also has the rather unusual distinction of lacking a chapter initial in its printed version.[4]

The first of these deletions (fol. 7) removes quite minor information relating how the generous Colonel had his booksellers regularly send copies of the *Pall Mall Gazette* to certain friends, including Madame de Florac, whose response to Bayham's paragraph about the alleged conversion of her son is the focus of the narrative at this point (2:73). The reader does not need to be told of the mechanism whereby she receives the publication; he already knows that she reads English journals (1:27) and has just been informed that "The Florac family read the 'Pall Mall Gazette,' knowing that Clive's friends were engaged in that periodical" (2:73). Therefore the passage could easily be cancelled.[5] The second omitted passage came in the midst of a narrative dealing with the Princesse de Moncontour (née Higg), whose new social prominence, marked especially by her presentation to the Queen, has attracted not only around her but around all her Manchester family a host of parasites, including the Hobson Newcomes. Mention of the Hobson Newcomes themselves being presented at Court, which now ends the paragraph, originally led to further narration of how Mrs. Mackenzie's urgent requests that she, Rosey, and Binnie also be presented were satirically rejected by Binnie (fol. 8). This bit of narration, plausible in itself but thoroughly digressive in the context of the Princesse's new life, was then cancelled.

The last deletion, which removed approximately nine printed lines, occurred in the chapter's final paragraph. Coming immediately after the question, "If Ethel had not wanted to see him, would she have come?" (fol. 13), it offered a brief explanation of Ethel's visits to the Hôtel de Florac to see Clive: "When Madame de Florac in her first talk with the young lady spoke to her with such special tenderness and kindness, told her how her uncle Thomas Newcome had spoken of her, and offered her friendship to the young girl: it may be that Miss New-come half divined what was in her new friend's heart, and that something respecting Clive was lurking there. She embraced this proffered friendship with such uncommon eagerness: she found that quiet old house and garden so exceedingly pleasant: that she was always going to see Madame de Préville" (fol. 13). It is difficult to identify any artistic necessity requiring the deletion of this passage; at most one can say that its omission removes mention of information that we are given elsewhere and also makes Ethel's visits seem a little less eager and less frequent. The reiteration of the two deleted sentences is minor, however, as is their somewhat greater degree of explicitness about Ethel's eagerness and the frequency of her visits; accordingly, their cancellation has a minimal artistic significance. Therefore, the chief reason for this deletion seems to have been Thackeray's need to cut sufficient material for the installment to be printed. With the removal of these lines from the final paragraph and the omission of a chapter initial, the text of chapter 8 could now be printed on nine pages, with two lines to spare; correspondingly, the entire installment now took up only thirty-two pages.[6]

Number seventeen for February 1855, which was composed during October of the previous year (*Letters*, 3:677), comprises chapters 14–16 of the second volume, extending from Barnes's visit to Lady Kew with news of the Colonel's unwelcome proposal for Clive, through Farintosh's entanglement, to the startling announcement of the sudden death of Lady Kew. It was written down entirely by Thackeray himself on twenty-nine leaves. The composition of the first and last chapters seems to have gone ahead rather straightforwardly, but such was not the case with chapter 15, "IN WHICH KINSMEN FALL OUT" (fols. 10–21). In composing this chapter Thackeray seems first to have written three leaves concerning the Colonel's negotiation for Ethel's hand and Barnes's bland assumption that his deceptive maneuvering was being done "very smartly and diplomatically" (fol. 12; 2:142). Thackeray seems either to have ended fol. 12 at that point, which marks the end of a paragraph, or to have continued a bit further—perhaps to Crackenthorpe's assertion near the bottom of the leaf: "Those private theatricals at Fallowfield have done Farintosh's business." Thackeray then apparently wrote Madame de Florac's letter to the Colonel, which takes up the whole of what is now fol. 15, and later went back to write or to extend the paragraph giving Crackenthorpe's news that Farintosh had finally succumbed to Ethel. Specific examples of Farintosh's behavior make Crackenthorpe's account more convincing and thus better prepare for Madame de Florac's news of the engagement; the addition ended with seven and one-half lines on the verso of fol. 12 that help prepare for Clive's challenge to Barnes by telling us that Clive's melancholy has made him not more lackadaisical but more fierce. Thackeray also felt that his narrative required a further revelation of Farintosh's complaisant pleasure in being pursued and of his condescending readiness "to give a Marchioness of Farintosh to the English nation" (2:144). Consequently, Thackeray wrote fols. 13–14, which contain the six paragraphs beginning: "A pauper child in London" (2:142–44).

Madame de Florac's letter was originally followed by what is now fol. 16a (then numbered 16), which began with a passage that was later revised: "The receipt of this letter only confirmed the suspicion under wh. Thomas Newcome had been labouring ever since the luckless day when Barnes thought proper to—to give a wrong address for Lady Kew. He sent a letter to Ethel and Lady Ann Newcome briefly congratulating them on the choice wh. he had heard Miss Newcome had made" (see 2:148). The chapter then continued with the narrative of the Colonel's receipt of Ethel's reply, his confrontation with Barnes, Barnes's response, Clive's reply to that, the Colonel's return home, and a scene there with Clive, Pen, and Warrington (fols. 17–21). Thackeray was about to continue the scene with Clive showing his father Barnes's reply to the challenge—"Here's Barnes letter said Clive taking out a crumpled paper full of tobacco from the ledge of his easel. The note said" (fol. 21)—but he crossed out the words and decided to end the chapter instead with the embrace he had already described (2:154). Taking up the cancelled line from the bottom of fol. 21, he then wrote a new chapter, marked as such, which began: "Clive presently answered the question wh. his father put to him in the last chapter, by producing from the ledge of his easel, a crumpled paper full of Cavendish now, but on wh. was written Sir Barnes Newcome's reply to his cousins polite invitation" (fol. 22). The final chapter (fols. 22–26) was then apparently composed quite straightforwardly, with the minor exception of a short paragraph concerning Sam Newcome added on the verso of fol. 24 (2:158). After completion of the chapter with the death of Lady Kew, the twenty-six leaves were numbered consecutively and the first major stage of composition was completed. Suitably augmented with wood-engravings, this text could have been printed as it stood. Instead, however, Thackeray made two major additions—both to chapter 15.

One was the insertion of fol. 14a. As the manuscript stood, the narrative made an abrupt leap from Farintosh's condescending acceptance of Ethel to Madame de Florac's letter informing Colonel Newcome of the engagement. Further thought caused Thackeray to write a brief transitional paragraph, beginning, "Miss Newcome has been compared ere this to the statue of Huntress Diana at the Louvre," and ending, "Here is the letter preserved by him along with all that he ever received from the same hand" (fol. 14a; see 2:144–45). As a result, the reader is given a narrative bridge between the two passages on fols. 14 and 15 and he is informed, in terms of the earlier huntress metaphor, that Farintosh only imagined the decision to marry was chiefly his: "at last he was brought to bay & taken by his resolute pursuers" (fol. 14a). With this significant narrative reorientation, which was followed by an overt identification of the letter writer and its recipient, Thackeray's insertion was complete.

Another addition, which immediately followed Madame de Florac's letter and preceded the Colonel's letter of congratulation, added two leaves to the manuscript. Thackeray began the addition by showing us that the Colonel's first concern would, of course, be for his son. We now see how the Colonel, uncertain about how best to inform Clive of Ethel's engagement, wanders about the streets and ends by seeing Maria, who gives important confirmation from Lady Ann of Madame de Florac's news (fol. 15a). As a result, the Colonel has fully authoritative grounds for believing it and walks home to tell Clive directly. On a second leaf Thackeray wrote a brief account of that conversation and then began a short transition to the narrative on fol. 16 of Colonel Newcome's anger at Barnes: "Clives father did not tell his son of his own bootless negociation with Barnes Newcome. There was no need to recal that now; but the Colonels wrath against his nephew exploded in conversation with me, who was the confidant of father and son in this business. Ever since that luckless day when Barnes thought proper to —to give a wrong address for Lady Kew, Thomas Newcome's anger had been growing. He smothered it yet for a while, sent a letter to

Lady[.]" Numbering this leaf fol. 16, he crossed out the earlier version of these lines from the top of the following leaf, which he redesignated 16a. This rather long manuscript subsequently went to press and appeared with its full text, because the monthly installment lacked any internal wood-engravings.[7]

Thackeray's progress with number eighteen for March 1855 was hindered by illness and other impediments. By the end of 1854, however, after the passage of two months spent mostly in England, he had finished the three chapters (17–19) that make up the installment (*Letters*, 3:407). Chapter 17 (fols. 1–13), contains a leaf in his hand (fol. 1), six in Anne's (fols. 2 and 4–8), and one shared by them (fol. 3). He himself wrote the next five leaves and all of chapter 18 (fols. 14–19). The first eleven leaves of chapter 19 are also in his hand, as is the last (fols. 20–30, 41); nine are in Anne's hand (fols. 31–39), and one is shared (fol. 40). The manuscript contains no evidence of compositional difficulties, but there were a few notable revisions.

In chapter 17 Thackeray deleted from the end of the long second paragraph, which offers a sardonic elegy for Lady Kew, the following sentence: "I turn away from the contemplation of a subject rather befitting the solemn remarks of a severe Divine like Charles Honeyman, than of the present writers worldly page" (fol. 2). Here the irony cuts partly against the narrator himself, but such a device seems more suited for the end of a discourse than for the middle, and since the narrator goes on to deliver some very earnest statements on the same subject of Lady Kew's funeral and death in general, Thackeray may have felt the comment inappropriate for its particular place. The same chapter, "BARNES'S SKELETON CLOSET," also shows Thackeray's defensiveness towards his reading public on the subject of sexual immorality, specifically Lady Clara's approaching decision to run off with Highgate. As he had done earlier in the novel, here again Thackeray justified his narrative on the basis of its truth and let most of his language stand, but on fol. 10 he made several interesting changes. Addressing the "Worthy mammas of families" in his audience who do not like to have their daughters informed about certain matters, he hinted that Lady Clara's decision illustrates the truth that marital mistreat-

ment can make "women forget the oaths wh. they have been made to
swear—if you will not hear of this, ladies, say the book is immoral and
send for some other. But, as surely as the writer has children of his
own, whose character is as dear to him as the very fairest of your ladyships—So surely must he speak the truth in his calling." However,
Thackeray, who mentioned elsewhere that irony is a dangerous device,
must have come to feel that he had given away too much to imperceptive readers with the word "immoral." Accordingly, he altered the
manuscript clause to read, "close the book and send for some other,"
and immediately added a further sentence that drew on the newspaper
for an example of a daily source of sometimes unpleasant actuality:
"Banish the newspaper out of your houses; and shut your eyes to the
truth, the awful truth of life and sin." He also cancelled the sentence
about his own children and his profession ("But . . . calling"), presumably because it distracted attention from the real issue: the actuality
that exists independently of his narrative and is reflected in it. As the
sentence he had already written, following the one about his children,
rhetorically asked: is the world of actuality made up only of children or
also of adults and adult passions? "Is the world made of Jennies and
Jessamies; and passion the play of school-boys and school-girls, scribbling valentines and interchanging lollipops?" (2:165).

Chapter 18 is, rather unusually, already entitled in the manuscript:
"ROSA QUO LOCORUM SERA MORATUR" (fol. 14). This Horatian allusion
to the last rose of summer was originally followed by another on the
same leaf—"The fable concerns thee, o worthy reader!" (*mutato
nomine de te fabula*)—but the latter was deleted from its context,
which was a printed question more than a "fable": "Whether is it the
more mortifying to us, to feel that we are disliked or liked undeserved-
ly?" (2:170). Chapter 18 was also shorter than it now is, for a new
chapter had been marked off at the top of fol. 18 above the words that
now begin chapter 18's final section in the printed version: "Our stay
with our friends at Brussells could not be prolonged beyond a month,
for at the end of that period we were under an engagement to other
friends in England" (2:173). It appears that Thackeray marked off this
division before writing the section but, when finished composing the
section one and two-thirds leaves later, changed his mind without cancelling the word "Chap." from the top of fol. 18. He appropriately
decided to include in chapter 18 this discussion between Pen and Laura

concerning the pressures for a marriage between Clive and Rosey. Chapter 19, which is also marked off in the manuscript and which begins, "The friends to whom we were engaged in England were Florac and his wife" (fol. 20), deals with quite other matters: "ROSEBURY AND NEWCOME."

As in the case of installment seventeen, the text of number eighteen was rather long. Chapter 17 required nine pages in print; chapter 18 required seven; and chapter 19, augmented by two internal wood-engravings that extended the text by the equivalent of a full printed page, required seventeen, for a total of thirty-three—one too many. Since the installment could most easily be reduced by making a cut in chapter 17, which required the deletion of only four lines instead of sixteen or forty-one, and since Thackeray made the installment's only substantial deletion in press from that chapter, it is likely that he made it in response to the requirements of serial publication. The omission can be termed an improvement, however, though it is a rather minor one. With a focus on Laura's refusal to answer Pen's question about why she disliked receiving invitations from Lady Clara, Thackeray had reintroduced the reader to the town of Newcome by reminding him that only inhabitants "concerned in the affairs of the family" (fol. 9) have hitherto been mentioned: Sarah Mason, Bulders, Vidler, Puff, Potts, and Batters—"persons with whom our friends have had already or will be found presently to have, some connection" (fol. 10). A new paragraph then began: "And it is from persons even more humble than these that we must get the meaning of that 'why?' wh. Mrs. Laura did not choose to interpret. We must suborn kitchen-maids forsooth. We must converse with Ladies' maids: we must interrogate Doctors' boys: and then we shall arrive at some particulars regarding the Newcome family, wh. will show us that they have a skeleton or two in *their* closets, as well as their neighbours" (fol. 10). Though Thackeray was faced with a need to delete only about four lines, in press he cancelled most of this paragraph as unnecessary: inquisitive, gossipy inhabitants of Newcome like Puff, Potts, and Batters were quite adequate as acknowledged sources of such information. Hence the passage's opening and closing words were retained and added to the previous paragraph, thereby being made applicable to Batters and his ilk: "And it is from these that we shall arrive at some particulars regarding the Newcome family, which will show us that they have a skeleton or two in *their* closets, as well as their neighbours" (2:165). Chapter 17 was thus fitted into eight pages and the installment could now appear, its artistry enhanced by Thackeray's response to the needs of serialization.

Information concerning the writing of the last six installments is rather scanty, and as a result one cannot say with very much precision when and where Thackeray composed number nineteen for April 1855. The sequence of composition, however, seems to have been as follows: the first two-thirds of chapter 20, "'ONE MORE UNFORTUNATE'" (fols. 1–5), chapter 21, "IN WHICH ACHILLES LOSES BRISEIS" (fols. 6–24), chapter 22, "IN WHICH WE WRITE TO THE COLONEL" (fols. 24–28), chapter 23, "IN WHICH WE ARE INTRODUCED TO A NEW NEWCOME" (fols. 28–30), and the final one-third of chapter 20 (a second sequence of leaves numbered 1–3, which I will designate fols. 1*a*, 2*a*, and 3*a*). Except for fols. 6–8, which were set down by Anne, all were in the author's hand.

Thackeray's account of Barnes's last quarrel with his wife, her interview with Highgate, and Barnes's meeting with the latter in chapter 20 took up fols. 1–3 and the five and one-half lines on fol. 4. The next leaf, which is the verso of an excerpt from the *Maidstone and Kentish Journal* of 19 September 1854, begins the narrative of Barnes's divorce proceedings, carrying it not quite to the bottom of the leaf and ending with the ironic aftermath of Serjeant Rowland's histrionic speech in the Court of Queen's Bench: "But when on the next day Serjeant Rowland was requested to call witnesses to prove that connubial happiness wh. he had depicted so pathetically, he had none at hand" (fol. 5). Thackeray apparently stopped at this point and went on with the rest of the installment, presumably intending to complete the account of the divorce later. In London on 7 March 1855 he made a point of reading "the trial of Norton v. Melbourne having a crim-con affair coming on in the Newcomes—but there will only be a page about it" (*Letters*, 3:428). The further account of the Newcome trial and the subsequent history of Lady Clara was then written on fols. 1*a*–3*a*, which completed chapter 20.[8] Originally this addition began, "Rowland QC. had his innings" (fol. 1*a*) and continued with two instances of the reversed use of Rowland and Oliver before an uncorrected use that is consistent with their roles as Serjeant and Q.C., respectively. Corrections were made at the top of the leaf, the results yielding the present reading: "Oliver, Q.C., now had his innings" (2:197). It seems, therefore, that the addition was begun separately but soon in the process of composition was compared with the manuscript into which it was being inserted.

Two interesting cancellations were made in the manuscript. Fol. 2 had completed the account of Barnes's physical assault on Lady Clara that resulted in the mutiny of servants and had begun the narrative of his public meeting with Highgate in Newcome. On its verso, Thackeray had later written for Pendennis the following commentary: "What food for observation we all are gentlemen for ourselves & others; what subjects for satire; what themes for leading articles, what morals for fables, what points for moralists what figures for caricaturists, what pregnant texts for sermons! I think perforce of my own career & contrast it with yours &c"; breaking off in mid-sentence, he ended Pen's interjection of himself, which threatened to become pompously self-righteous and which was susceptible to misinterpretation as an authorial statement. The rest of the passage was also cancelled because it was inappropriate, though in a different way. Aside from a certain awkwardness that would have been produced by the words that were to follow it, which point out Pen's ignorance "of all that was occurring" (fol. 2), the passage was inappropriate because it emphasized how notoriety provides a text for public sermonizing instead of showing how a wrongful act produces devastating moral consequences for the individual himself. The text for that sermon was to be supplied not by the meeting of Barnes and Highgate but by the misery of Lady Clara after she leaves with Highgate.

The second cancelled passage had been written on fol. 1a:

With the new name wh. she took, the poor lady passes out of the history of the Newcomes. If Barness children meet her, do they know her? If her once-husband thinks upon the unhappy young creature whom his cruelty drove from him, does his conscience affect his sleep at nights? Why should Sir Barnes Newcome's conscience be more squeamish than his country's, wh. has put money in his pocket for having trampled upon the poor weak young thing, and scorned her, and driven her to ruin? When the whole ⟨of the⟩ accounts of this wretched bankruptcy are brought up for final Audit, wh. of the unhappy parties will be shown to ⟨be the⟩ most guilty? Does the Bishop who did the benedictory business at St. George's repent in secret?

Unlike the former passage, this was cancelled not because of its in-appropriateness but because Thackeray decided to insert ahead of it a long paragraph that would show the moral effects which Lady Clara's decision to leave with Highgate brought upon her—a decision that meant not only the repudiating of her husband but also the abandoning of her children. Hence the exposition of her moral isolation, even from Highgate, "her sorrow and doubt and misery" (fol. 2a), culminating in the desperation with which she clings to her child by Highgate. At this point Thackeray reintroduced a slightly modified version of the can-celled passage, beginning—"but she no more belongs to our story: with the new name wh. she has taken, the poor lady passes out of the his-tory of the Newcomes." The first "her" (fol. 1a) gives place to the words "yonder solitary lady" (fol. 2a) and "the Bishop who did the benedictory business at St. George's" becomes "the Right Reverend Prelate who did the benedictory business for Barnes and Clara his wife" (fol. 3a), but otherwise the passage reappears essentially as it was first written. Now, however, as the chapter ends, the rhetorical question is overtly answered as Thackeray develops allusive implica-tions of the church in Hanover Square: "O Hymen Hymenæe! the Bishops beadles clergy pew-openers and other officers of the temple dedicated to Heaven under the invocation of St. George will officiate in the same place at scores and scores more of such marriages. And St. George of England may behold virgin after virgin offered up to the devouring monster Mammon—(with many most respectable female-dragons looking on)—may see virgin after virgin given away, just as in the Soldan of Babylons time—but with never a Champion to come to the rescue!" (fol. 3a; see 2:198).

Like the seventeenth installment, number nineteen has no internal wood-engravings. Even so, the text was too long to be printed, but in this case the excess was minimal. Chapter 20, after its augmentation, required three lines more than six pages; as a result, the printer added a forty-eighth line of text to 2:196–98 so that the chapter took up exactly six pages and the monthly installment could appear with its normal complement of thirty-two pages. Significant changes were nev-ertheless made in press. Chapter 22 took up almost all the available space on its four pages, but chapters 21 and 23 had room for the addi-tion of approximately forty and thirty lines respectively, and Thacker-ay took advantage of that space to make six fairly substantial additions —three to each chapter.

The first and longest of these additions in press shows how Farintosh has been able to dominate over his mother—by a course of sexual and other dissipations that she is unwilling to discuss with him—and it more fully prepares for ensuing references to his toadies by showing them in their roles as willing Figaros to his Count Almaviva (2:199). The second offers an amusing and important comment on the naïveté of Ethel's ambitions, as Pen's and Laura's laughter at Ethel's disdain towards the Misses Burr for pursuing Farintosh attracts the attention of their hostess, Madame de Moncontour: "We did not tell our hostess that poor Ethel and her grandmother had been accused of doing the very same thing, for which she found fault with the Misses Burr. Miss Newcome thought *herself* quite innocent, or how should she have cried out at the naughty behaviour of other people?" (2:209). Thackeray rightly saw that it is important for us to recognize this naïveté lest we overestimate the extent of Ethel's worldliness—especially in a chapter where she makes her most significant moral choice: the rejection of Farintosh. Hence Thackeray added the commentary that focuses our attention on the reason for Pen's and Laura's laughter and emphasizes the contrast between Ethel, who rejects a marriage of convenience, and the Princesse de Moncontour, née Higg. The last of these additions to chapter 21 provides a further example of Farintosh's inadequacy; it occurs just before Ethel's overt statement of rejection and exemplifies the differences in their moral nature. In the manuscript Thackeray had originally written that Farintosh did not quite understand "the train of ideas in his companion's mind" (fol. 22); now he added: "And I've given up every thing—everything—and have broken off with my old habits and—and things you know—and intend to lead a regular life—and will never go to Tattersall's again; nor bet a shilling; nor touch another cigar if you like—that is, if you don't like; for I love you so, Ethel —I do, with all my heart I do!" (2:214). This time we see not only that he fails to understand her but that he cannot understand her, for he is unable to make moral distinctions: his debaucheries, his expenditures, and his personal habits like the use of tobacco are all one. He can only choose a new form of indulgence: the momentary belief that he "loves" her.

These three passages added in press augmented chapter 21 by twenty-eight printed lines; the last three increased the text of chapter 23 by eight lines. In the manuscript, Thackeray had indicated that the Colonel was not in Brussels to receive Laura's letter about Ethel but

was in London, where he had dined with Warrington. Now, in preparation for the news of Clive's marriage to Rosey, Laura learns that the
two men dined together "and that the Colonel seemed to be in the
highest spirits. High spirits about what?" (2:220). A second insertion
added a further ironic indication of the Colonel's joyful hopes, for his
letter to Sarah Mason now reveals a man who not only feels well and
happy, but "who proposes to be *happier still* before any very long
time is over" (2:223). The longest of the three is also ironic, though in
a different way, for it adds the hopes of Madame de Moncontour for
Clive and Ethel: "She whispered to me in her kind way that she would
give a guinea, that she would, to see a certain couple made happy together; that they were born for one a[n]other, that they were; she was
for having me go off to fetch Clive: but who was I to act as Hymen's
messenger; or to interpose in such delicate family affairs" (2:222).
With these and a variety of minor alterations, the installment was complete. On the one hand, Thackeray's reluctance to curtail a satisfactory
text that had only three extra lines apparently caused the printer to
set up several pages of forty-eight lines each for the first time since the
tenth installment.[9] Conversely, Thackeray's wish to improve the artistry of his manuscript continued to reflect itself in his various corrections and augmentations.

Number twenty for May 1855 is in the hand of Anne, except for the last
two leaves (fols. 79–80), which were set down by Thackeray himself.
Chapters 24, "Mr. and Mrs. Clive Newcome" (fols. 1–21), and 25,
"Mrs. Clive at Home" (fols. 22–40), seem to have been copied and
perhaps composed as one long narrative, for there is no space at the
bottom of fol. 21 and no chapter marking at the top of fol. 22. A break
comes on fol. 40, the lower half of which is blank, and on fol. 45, which
leaves space for about four lines between the words "the Bundle cund
banking company of India" and "The news came like a thunderclap"
(see 2:243), but thereafter the narrative proceeds, as before, without
interruption. There are no chapter markings, for what is now chapter
26, "Absit Omen," ends near the top of fol. 56, at which point begins
what we know as chapter 27, "In Which Mrs. Clive Comes into
Her Fortune."

In its printed form, the installment lacks internal wood-engravings,

like numbers nine, eleven, twelve, seventeen, and nineteen and all
subsequent monthly parts. The text of the installment was too short to
be printed without augmentation, however, and as a result three significant additions were made—two in chapter 25 and one in 27. The
first passage added Bayham's speech at the testimonial dinner when
Rosey was presented with the amazing silver cocoanut tree, beginning, "as well as to Fred. Bayham's noble speech," and ending,
"Whilst F.B.'s speech went on" (2:236). The florid speech is a verbal
equivalent of that literal ornament of confused fantasy, and as such it
dramatically reveals as a human process the self-delusion that the
ornament represents in inert form—a process in which the elated Colonel and the cheering audience fully participate. The jumbled values
manifested in the testimonial ornament and in Bayham's speech epitomize the Colonel's domestic enterprise as well. This became the
second passage added in press: a description of the appalling gorgeousness that the Colonel inflicted upon the house he furnished for Clive,
Rosey, and himself. Beginning, "How different it was from the old
Fitzroy Square mansion" (2:236), and ending, "with all the new tunes
from Europe" (2:237), the passage evokes a decorative turmoil reflecting a confusion of values and a fantasy *manqué* not only similar to that
represented by the ornament and speech but directly correlative—
both in an economic and in a spiritual sense. As a result of these two
additions, the text of chapter 25 was lengthened from seven pages to
eight, and the artistry of the chapter was notably heightened.[10]

A final addition appears at the very end of the installment, where
four paragraphs that appear only in the printed version extend the
text of chapter 27 from nine pages to ten. Beginning, "Mrs. Pendennis
came away with rather a heavy heart from this party" (2:255), they
not only show her disturbance at the Colonel's vindictiveness but,
through J. J. Ridley, establish a positive value that provides a contrast
to the values of delusive materialism and confused ornament epitomized by the testimonial and by the Colonel's new house. For example,
instead of being associated with the East India Company cavalry and
howitzers that make possible the sequence of plough, bale, loom, and
company profits, J.J. is associated with chivalric enterprise:

> The palette on his arm was a great shield painted of many colours: he
> carried his maul-stick and a sheaf of brushes along with it, the weapons
> of his glorious but harmless war. With these he achieves conquests,
> wherein none are wounded save the envious: with that he shelters him

against how much idleness, ambition, temptation! Occupied over that
consoling work, idle thoughts cannot gain the mastery over him: selfish
wishes or desires are kept at bay. Art is truth: and truth is religion: and
its study and practice a daily work of pious duty. What are the world's
struggles, brawls, successes, to that calm recluse pursuing his calling?
(2:256)

By ending the chapter with Pen's encomium on the artist's dedicated
pursuit of truth, Thackeray not only establishes a contrast with Bayham's speech in honor of the Colonel but also shows us most strikingly
the considerable perversion of art and humanity that is represented by
Clive's caricature of Barnes and by the Colonel's vindictive glee:
"Capital! Capital! we'll have the picture printed by Jove Sir, show vice
its own image, and shame the Viper in his own nest Sir. That's what
we will!—" (fol. 80; see 2:255).

Here too, Thackeray extended the installment's length by one
printed page, thereby making it occupy its full complement. In no
other monthly part, however, were the additions more felicitous than
in number twenty, in which he responded to the challenges of preparing a serial for publication with a creativeness especially indicative of
his high abilities.

Numbers twenty-one and twenty-two are absent from the Charterhouse manuscript, but most of the latter is to be found in the Berg Collection on fifty-four leaves corrected by Thackeray but otherwise in the
hand of a secretary.[11] The installment consists of four chapters: 32,
"CHILTERN HUNDREDS" (fols. [1]–12), regarding the changed nature
of the Colonel's guests, the collapse of the B.B.C., the Colonel's bankruptcy, and, as the chapter title indicates, his failure to take his seat
in Parliament; 33, "IN WHICH MRS. CLIVE NEWCOME'S CARRIAGE IS
ORDERED" (fols. 13–31 [top]), narrating how the Colonel responded to
the bankruptcy and informed his household of the news, how Clive ordered Rosey to unpack her spoils, and how the household departed for
the Continent; 34, "BELISARIUS" (fols. 31 [bottom]–44), concerning
Pen's visit to the exiles in Boulogne; and 35, "IN WHICH BELISARIUS
RETURNS FROM EXILE" (fols. 45–[60]), recounting Pen's success in
bringing the Colonel and Clive back to London with him, away from
the terrible Mrs. Mackenzie.

The manuscript does not reveal much about its composition but it does help to identify, aside from a number of brief changes, four additions in press. The longest augmentation occurred in chapter 32; it was meant to illustrate more fully the change in the nature of the Colonel's guests and to emphasize the unpleasant implications of their presence. Previously the novelist had identified only two new guests: the "manager of the City branch of the B.B.C.," "an ominous-looking man" whose whispers, compliments, and continual presence made Clive very melancholy (2:290), and a "brisk little chattering attorney, very intimate with Sherrick" (2:291). Now, in press, Thackeray deftly indicated the presence of other figures, their dominance of the conversation, and their disturbing familiarity; one even seems to have gorged himself with money from the bank: "With the City manager came the City manager's friends, whose jokes passed gaily round, and who kept the conversation to themselves. Once I had the happiness to meet Mr. Ratray, who had returned, filled with rupees from the Indian bank; who told us many anecdotes of the splendour of Ram-un-Lal at Calcutta, who complimented the Colonel on his fine house and grand dinners with sinister good humour. Those compliments did not seem to please our poor friend, that familiarity choked him" (2:290–91). With these seven printed lines Thackeray also doubled the length of text on the chapter's last page.

In the case of chapter 33 Thackeray needed a minimum of four lines to extend the chapter onto a tenth page. He responded by making three separate insertions totalling fourteen printed lines. The first of these came in the middle of a sentence explaining how Clive obeyed his father's request that Rosey take away as few clothes as possible, leaving all the finery for the creditors. Originally Clive went upstairs to "his women's apartments," where he found the women busily packing up a host of "flounces, feathers, fal-lals, and finery." Now, in response to a need for more text, the novelist developed the implications of the phrase "his women's apartments" by focusing more clearly on the setting and by memorably evoking the past as well as present isolation of Clive, who enters the apartments, "looking with but little regret, I dare say, round those cheerless nuptial chambers with all their gaudy fittings; the fine looking-glasses, in which poor Rosey's little person had been reflected; the silken curtains under which he had lain by the poor child's side, wakeful and lonely" (2:303).

Another augmentation filled a minor gap between, on the one hand,

Clive's threat to kick off the lid of a box if the women did not unlock it and, on the other, the box's elaborately revealed contents: "Obeying this grim summons, the fluttering women produced the keys, and the black box was opened before him. The box was found to contain a number of objects which Clive pronounced to be by no means necessary to his wife's and child's existence" (2:304). Finally came a slightly longer addition that emphasized Clive's firmness in imposing his will upon the scavenging women, settled a few minor details of the plot having to do with servants, and mentioned not simply a change in residence but a journey as well: "Even the Campaigner could not make head against Clive's stern resolution; and the incipient insurrection of the maids and the mistresses was quelled by his spirit. The lady's maid, a flighty creature, received her wages and took her leave: but the nurse could not find it in her heart to quit her little nursling so suddenly, and accompanied Clive's household in the journey upon which those poor folks were bound" (2:304). The nurse remains faithful for a time, but when we next see the family—in Boulogne a chapter later—she is no longer with them. Even in such apparently mundane additions we can observe expressive detail.

The completion of the final double installment, number twenty-three–twenty-four for August, was dated by Thackeray on 28 June 1855 at Paris. Thackeray apparently returned corrected proof on 11 July from Strasbourg and at that time asked Percival Leigh to supply a few missing details: the Christian names of three minor characters and some lines from Peele's *Polyhymnia*, "to be quoted as by Warrington in the space left for him" (*Letters*, 3:462). The first fifteen leaves—if there were exactly that many—are missing from the Charterhouse manuscript, which begins on fol. 16 with the title of chapter 40: "In wh. the Author goes on a pleasant errand." This chapter (fols. 16–21), its title, and the title of the next one are in Thackeray's hand; all of chapter 41 except its last leaf (fol. 51) is in Anne's; and the final chapter was shared between them—one leaf being in Thackeray's hand (fol. 52 and 52*v*), two and one-half leaves in Anne's (fols. 53–55) with two and one-half lines added by Thackeray at the end of fol. 55, and the last seven leaves in Thackeray's (fols. 1*a*–7*a*).[12]

Thackeray made several notable additions and changes in the manuscript, the first two occurring in chapter 41. Not surprisingly, he did
not know Orme's *History* as well as the Colonel did and therefore he
had Anne leave a space for a later insertion in his own hand of the Colonel's quotation from Orme (fol. 38; see 2:361).[13] On the next leaf we
can see that Anne set down in blue ink the following passage concerning Clive and the Colonel: "He turned to his Father who still sat lost in
his meditations, You need never go back to Grey Friars Father he
cried out, Except to pack your things & to come back, and live with me
& Boy, and he told Colonel Newcome rapidly the story of the Legacy"
(fol. 39). Later, however, possibly after having composed the novel's
last scene, Thackeray returned to this passage and in black ink added
a final "e" and comma to "sat," an exclamation mark after the second
"Father," a period after "out," and an immediately ensuing speech:
"Not go back Clivey? must go back boy, to say *Adsum* when my name
is called—Newcome! Adsum! Hey! that is what we used to say—we
used to say!" Thackeray also struck out the final twenty-six words of
the original passage and recopied them with slight modification.

The final chapter seems originally to have been somewhat longer, for
the leaves set down by Anne were numbered fols. 58–60 before they
received their present designation as fols. 53–55. The opening leaf,
therefore, may well be an insertion that abridged an earlier dictated
passage.[14] Fol. 52, which now begins the chapter, carries the narrative
to Dr. Quackenboss's characterization of Mrs. Mackenzie as "a lady of
impetuous temper who expresses herself very strongly—too strongly
I own" (fols. 58–58v), the account on the verso continuing to the conclusion of his speech and Pen's reply: "Cannot Mrs. Mackenzie leave
the house Sir? I asked" (see 2:368). Multiple numbering also appears
on the four last leaves and helps reveal a complex of errors that Thackeray never fully detected. He originally wrote a sequence of leaves
that carried his postscript to a conclusion on what are now fols. 5 and 7.
Deciding to augment this ending, however, he copied the text of fol. 5
with a variety of changes and additions onto what is now fol. 6 and
completed this revision by turning what is now fol. 7 upside down,
writing sixteen new lines, and cancelling those on what was now the
bottom of the leaf. He failed, however, to cancel and remove fol. 5.
After misnumbering fols. 4, 5, 6, and 7 as 3, 4, 7, and 6, he corrected
the misdesignation but still did not detect the mistaken presence of the

uncancelled but superseded fol. 5. As a result, the compositor set up
type from fol. 5, then apparently noticed the seeming duplication on
fol. 6, and wrongly concluded that the two leaves were identical except
for the obvious introduction of new material in the final paragraph of
fol. 6 (which belonged to a new compositorial stint). The last half-dozen
or so lines of type were then presumably modified by the compositor
to incorporate identified changes made by the final paragraph of fol. 6.
Consequently the printed version of Thackeray's postscript contains
two-thirds of a page (2:374) that was wrongly set up from the original
version of copy instead of from the later version, which minutely revised the text throughout. This error extends through the first three
printed lines of the final paragraph ("What about Sir Barnes Newcome
. . . to keep that money which"), the printed text afterwards following
fol. 6. Any future edition of *The Newcomes*, therefore, should base the
appropriate portion of its text upon the segment of manuscript passed
over in the printer's workshop—the first twenty-four lines of fol. 6,
which read as follows:

one above mentioned. How could Pendennis have got all that information
about Ethels goings on at Baden & with Lord Kew, unless she had told
somebody—her husband for instance who, having made Pendennis an
early confidant in his amour, gave him the whole story? Clive, Pendennis
writes expressly, is travelling abroad with his wife. Who *is* that wife?
By a most monstrous blunder Mr. Pendennis kills Lady Glenlivat, at page
( ) and brings her to life again page ( )—but Rosey, who is so lately
consigned to Kensal Green, it is surely not with *her* that Clive is travelling, for then Mrs. Mackenzie would be with them to a live certainty,
& the tour would be by no means pleasant. Again, how could Pendennis
have got all those private letters &c, unless the Colonel had kept them in
a teak-box wh. Clive inherited & handed over to his friend? My belief is
then, that Clive & Ethel are living most comfortably together; that she is
immensely fond of his little boy; and a great deal happier now than they
would have been had they married at first when they took a liking to each
other as young people, and when she was a mere young lady of fashion.
That picture by J.J. of 'Mrs Clive Newcome' in the Crystal Palace Exhibi-
tion in Fableland, is certainly not in the least like Rosey who we read was
fair: but it represents a tall handsome dark lady, who must be Mrs. Ethel.
Nor can we judge much of her likeness by Mr. Doyles etchings in the
present volumes, for where the Heroine has been introduced, our provoking English Timanthes has turned her face away, and only shown the
public a head of hair.
    Some would like to know from Mr. Pendennis why he introduced JJ
with such a flourish? giving us as it were an overture & no piece to follow

it. JJ's history let me confidentially state has been revealed to me likewise, & may be told some of these fine summer months or Christmas
evenings when the kind reader has leisure to hear

What about Barnes Newcome, ultimately? My impression is that he is
married again & my hope that his present wife bullies him. Mrs. Mackenzie cannot have the face to keep that money wh. . . . .

By following fol. 5, the printed texts of 1855 give uncorrected readings such as these selected examples: "Lady Farintosh's mother" (an
obvious error) for "Lady Glenlivat"; "not surely" for "surely not";
"probably . . . to a live certainty" ("probably" was cancelled on fol. 5
though not very clearly) for "to a live certainty"; "but that the Colonel
kept" for "unless the Colonel had kept"; "made over" for "handed
over"; "in Fable-land somewhere Ethel and Clive" for "Clive and
Ethel"; "people." for "people, and when she was a mere young lady of
fashion"; and "Sir Barnes" for "Barnes." As usual, however, Thackeray did not read proof against copy and the major error along with its
subsidiary ones remained undetected.

A number of changes were made in press, however, two of which
stand out. The manuscript account of the Colonel's mental wandering
contains the words: "He talked louder: he gave the word of command
and murmured Threes about and Charge—" (fol. 3). The printed version removes the idea of a command leading to battle and bloodshed,
however, replacing it with a more general kind of communication: "He
talked louder; he gave the word of command, spoke Hindostanee as if
to his men" (2:372). Finally, a reference to Doyle's general tendency
not to depict Ethel's face in his etchings was also deleted in press—
perhaps both because it implied a criticism and because it was not
strictly true: we had been shown her face in over nine of them.[15]

In composing the second half of his novel, Thackeray tended to provide rather full copy. All of number nineteen was printed because no
internal wood-engravings were included; minor deletions were required in number eighteen. A longer cut seems to have been made in
the final double number prior to its being delivered to the printer, but
this remains an uncertain matter. Faced with the necessity of reducing
the length of numbers fourteen and fifteen, the novelist was led to
identify and omit weaker passages but also to delete material that need
not otherwise have been cancelled, thereby raising a special kind of
editorial problem for the future. On two occasions, those of numbers
eighteen and twenty-two, the original texts were too short; as was

usual in such cases, he chose the nature and placement of his additions carefully and frequently heightened the effect of his narrative with them.

To further our understanding of these compositional processes, we might finally turn to the larger context of their development as a part of volume 2. Its first installment, number thirteen, extends the previous narrative of Clive and J.J. in Rome and of Clive's continuing absorption in thoughts of Ethel. The latter theme, which dominates numbers thirteen through sixteen even more than it did numbers nine through twelve, furnishes the chief unity of this portion of the novel, though sporadic parallel linkages between adjacent monthly installments continue. At the opening of number thirteen Clive delights in Rome but, after travelling to Naples and Pompeii, excavates his heart and hurriedly returns to London and Ethel. Calling at Lamb Court the morning after his arrival, he soon makes Pen the confidant of his tormenting desire for Ethel, whom he alternately baits and pursues as she is carried by Lady Kew from entertainment to entertainment. The number ends as he manages a ride to Brighton with Ethel that culminates in a moment of considerable intimacy and a responsive return of pressure as he takes her hand (2:32). In number fourteen, however, after he has written to his father about the return from Italy and his renewed passion, the presence of Farintosh disrupts Clive's next meeting with Ethel—a passage expanded in manuscript—and Clive frustratedly returns to London, again seeking out Pen as a confidant. Subsequently Clive continues to pursue and berate Ethel at parties, but more forlornly than before. The installment ends as Clive, feeling attracted this time to Rosey, once again finds himself in a carriage holding a hand that responds to his (2:63). Meanwhile, several other developments are underway: formation of the Bundlecund Banking Company and the oppressiveness of Mrs. Mackenzie in number thirteen, who begins to afflict Binnie in that installment and receives from Warrington—in another passage added to the manuscript—her indelible characterization as "The Campaigner" in the following serial part.

Apparently, before Thackeray composed the first installment of volume 2, he set down a brief outline of chronological events that is now in the Berg Collection (see note 6). From its rather selective nature and its organization one gathers that Thackeray intended it primarily as a means of keeping a time-scheme in mind rather than as an outline of planned narrative sequence. This chronological pattern, which begins with the Colonel's departure for India in August 1841 (number eight), continues with Clive's departure for Rome in October (number ten) and his return to England in the middle of the following year— though in July rather than June (number thirteen; 2:13). After indicating on the outline that Clive meets Ethel at Paris the year after that (number fifteen; 2:71ff.) and possibly after indicating that Sir Brian dies in June of 1843 (number sixteen; 2:98), Thackeray inserted into the outline two chronologically earlier events: the deaths of Lord Highgate and Lord Dorking, which are reported in number fifteen (2:88) and number sixteen (2:102), respectively. The outline concluded with a focus on Pendennis, who marries in September 1843 and learns about the B.B.C. and its shareholders (instead of actually meeting them on a specific occasion, as the outline seems to have indicated) on his return to London the following year—events that came to occur in number sixteen (2:99–100).

As number fifteen begins, Lady Kew has failed to bring about Lord Farintosh's proposal by the end of the first season but continues her pursuit of him to Paris, where he has become entangled with a French courtesan and where Clive also arrives. This period of their lives ends at the beginning of number sixteen, where Lady Kew's willingness to forgive Farintosh's vices and her continuing pursuit of him are defeated once again—now by the death of Sir Brian, which calls Ethel home and restricts her social engagements. The success of the B.B.C. also gets recurring mention. The middle portions of these installments —chapters 8 and 11–12—go on to show us two ill-sorted couples, all four members of which are following their own selfish purposes: Florac, who has reached a "philosophical" resolution with his newly wealthy wife; Florac's wife, who has been agreeable because of his newly inherited title of Prince; the newly titled Sir Barnes, who has bought his aristocratic wife and who becomes a great social entertainer for commercial and political purposes; and Lady Clara, who has agreed to be sold but who comes to seek increasing refuge in the company of her former lover. We hear the worldly analysis and advice of two old mentors, Lady Kew and Major Pendennis, and we notice two contrasting characters: the dowager Madame de Florac and Laura Pendennis, who have the rare ability to be perceptive and selfless. So too, we see them offering Clive and Ethel a home in which to meet privately. In the concluding chapter of number fifteen we see Clive tell Ethel he loves her, while she speaks of the restrictions under which she lives, especially her duties to various members of her family; in the final chapter of number sixteen the Colonel, who has just returned from India, proposes a marriage between Clive and Ethel to Sir Barnes, who also talks of the restrictions under which she lives and who secretly visits Clive's other chief enemy, Lady Kew, to inform her of the proposal. As the first third of the novel ended, the Colonel found that the state of his finances required a return to India; during the next third, as he prospered, Clive followed his own career as an artist and then neglected it in his unsuccessful pursuit of Ethel; at the two-thirds point, the Colonel has returned and tried to assist Clive once again, but with the earlier failures of both men in our memory, along with clear knowledge of Sir Barnes's and Lady Kew's purposes, we are permitted only gloomy forebodings.

The Colonel's return and his proposal concerning Ethel and Clive were the first incidents included on an outline set down by Thackeray —this time a sketch of planned narrative sequence for the novel's chief remaining events:

> XVI. The Colonel comes back, and proposes to
> Barnes for Ethel for Clive.
>
> Rupture between the Colonel & Barnes—
> XVII. Announcement of her engagement to Lord Farintosh.
> death of Lady Kew.

XVIII.   Clives marriage. Binnies Nunc Dimittis.

  XIX   Elopement of Lady Clara. Ethel's revolt.

   XX   The Election. Height of Clives prosperity. Bitterness at home.

  XXI.   Failure of the B.B. Mrs. Mack comes to live with the young people.

 XXII.   Retreat of the Colonel before her. His resolve and its execution.

XXIII.IV. Orme's History of India. Too late. The Colonels Euthanasia.[16]

As these details suggest, Thackeray was sketching the final curve of his narrative, not outlining the structure of individual installments. In fact, as he came actually to write the monthly numbers, he departed from this sketch by arranging some of the events in a new sequence and by giving many of them an embodiment that was both less regularly spaced and also closer to the end of the novel.

In setting down the outline, Thackeray had indicated that the announcement of Ethel's engagement and the death of Lady Kew were to occur in number seventeen, but he had then remembered or decided that the rupture between the Colonel and Sir Barnes was to precede these two events; accordingly, the novelist inserted it into the outline ahead of the announcement, thereby seeming to indicate that number seventeen was to include all three events. Number eighteen was to narrate Clive's marriage and Binnie's *nunc dimittis*; only later, in number nineteen, was Lady Clara to elope and Ethel to revolt. Further thought altered this disposition of events, however, for in writing number seventeen Thackeray decided to show the Colonel discovering repeated evidence of Sir Barnes's deceits and lies but not actually exposing his nephew until after the engagement had been announced. The rupture does not finally take place until the Colonel decides that a letter from Ethel proves Sir Barnes has not only lied but even misappropriated a letter from Thomas Newcome to his niece—at which point the Colonel confronts and publicly denounces him. The death of Lady Kew then ensues, in accordance with the planned sequence. Again in number eighteen, however, Thackeray departs from his outline. Clive's marriage is announced only at the end of the following installment and does not take place until number twenty. Binnie indicates his readiness to sing *nunc dimittis* in number eighteen but his death does not occur until two installments later as well. Number twenty accommodates both these developments, together with two of the three subjects indicated on the outline: the momentary height of Clive's prosperity, as his father showers him with a wife and a gorgeous house (emphasized in an added passage) but cannot make him happy—a failure that produces domestic bitterness. The election was another matter and was deferred by Thackeray, who thereby strengthened the novelistic connections between the marriage, the prosperity, and the bitterness.

Thackeray's composition proceeded laterally as well as in immediate narrative sequence, of course, as we can see from the relationships among numbers seventeen through twenty, which are loosely united by a number of parallel connections, several of them across installments as well as between adjacent ones. The opening of number seventeen, though it shows a coughing and trembling Lady Kew, is not connected so closely to the beginning of number eighteen, with its account of her funeral, as it is to the beginning of number nineteen, for both of these installments open with extended news of Lady Clara: her mistreatment by Sir Barnes, her resistance, the changes it has brought about in her, and the varied concern of Lady Kew, Highgate, and Ethel in number seventeen; her continued mistreatment, her resistance, the changes in her, and the varied concern of her servants, Florac, Pendennis, and Highgate in number nineteen. In the former, Lady Kew and Ethel give Sir Barnes good advice about his treatment of Lady Clara. His inability to take the advice, especially Ethel's, is responsible for his finding himself physically assaulted by Highgate in the latter. As these three chapters conclude, Lady Clara finds herself alone and unhappy in number seventeen, blighted by the influence of Sir Barnes and her life of hypocrisy in number eighteen, and isolated from all, even Highgate, after her demoralized flight from home with her lover in number nineteen.

In the middle portion of number seventeen Clive's first attack of love for Ethel, his cure, and his relapse are recapitulated by the narrator at the opening of chapter 15, while at the beginning of chapter 18, in the middle of installment eighteen, we learn how he has resolutely endured the news of the Ethel-Farintosh engagement and his own defeat, in contrast to his father, who becomes further enraged at the Newcome family. The next link involves number nineteen, for the apprehensiveness of Farintosh's retinue of toadies at the possibility of his marriage in chapter 15 is developed in chapter 21 after his refusal to break off from Ethel in spite of the scandal about her sister-in-law. Also in chapter 15 the Colonel reacts to news of the engagement and to Sir Barnes's deception by publicly denouncing Barnes and withdrawing his account, while in chapter 18 the father tries to arrange a compensatory marriage between his son and Rosey. A link between chapters 15 and 22 is later established when Ethel tells Farintosh the truth and when Highgate and Farintosh withdraw their accounts after Highgate's elopement with Lady Clara and Ethel's refusal of Farintosh.

In the concluding chapter of number seventeen we see Lady Clara's family reestablished in Park Lane, while the end of number eighteen finds Florac established for the first time at his wife's home of Rosebury. In the former, Lady Kew triumphantly completes arrangements for Ethel's marriage, but all the while disruptive arrangements are emerging between Lady Clara and Highgate. In the latter chapter, Thackeray contrasts the simple triumph of Florac with the fatality Florac perceives in Newcome, Lady Clara, and Highgate. The sudden death of Lady Kew at the end of number seventeen, before Ethel's marriage, does not connect with the final portion of number eighteen, but it does have an ironic counterpart at the end of number nineteen, where—although the chief antagonist of Clive's marriage to Ethel is now dead—we hear the unfortunate news that Clive is to be married to Rosey.

The opening of number nineteen, as we have seen, recalls the opening of number seventeen, where Sir Barnes rejected advice concerning his treatment of Lady Clara. Here that treatment receives its climactic response in her flight with Highgate, which results in her ultimate isolation from everyone, even her new husband. Number twenty begins by drawing on the opening chapters of the two previous monthly installments, for the death of Lady Kew causes an important delay in Ethel's marriage plans and the flight of Lady Clara completes the revolt in Ethel that puts a stop to the marriage plans altogether. At the opening of number twenty we see the positive effects, as Ethel matures, educates herself, and devotes herself to others. The flight, divorce, and unhappy marriage of Lady Clara with Highgate have now occurred, but the widespread practice of worldly, perjured marriages, the narrator reminds us, continues. This observation is verified in number twenty-one, where we see another marriage undertaken upon inadequate grounds: Clive's decision to please the Colonel and Binnie and to settle the marriage question once and for all by marrying the insipidly sweet Rosey.

In the two middle chapters of number twenty we are first reminded of the Colonel's repudiation of Sir Barnes and withdrawal of his personal account in the middle of number seventeen, together with his failure to transfer the B.B.C. account at the same time; we are then shown the outcome when Sir Barnes has Hobson Brothers reject the B.B.C. bills, with very damaging results. Whereas we had seen Ethel and Highgate meditating wrongful actions at the end of numbers seventeen and eighteen, respectively, and had learned at the end of number nineteen how the Colonel had judged Ethel wrongly and succeeded in persuading Clive to marry Rosey, by the end of number twenty we have witnessed a moral decline in Colonel Newcome, who is consumed by suspicion and resentment, even towards his son, and by hatred. The result is misery for those who love him, especially for Clive, whom the Colonel has cut off from his painting and from Ethel: "In place of Art the Colonel brings him a ledger; and in lieu of first love, shows him Rosey" (2:256).

Thackeray's brief outline proposed the B.B.C.'s failure and the descent of Mrs. Mackenzie upon Clive and Rosey for number twenty-one, Colonel Newcome's retreat, his resolution to enter Greyfriars, and its execution for number twenty-two, and the belated discovery of Orme and the Colonel's death for the final double installment. Since composition of the four preceding installments had led Thackeray to defer treating the election, however, he now had to devote attention to that subject, which took up much of number 21, leaving no room for the failure of the B.B.C. and space for only brief mention of Mrs. Mackenzie's coming to stay with Rosey and Clive—a subject that did not lead to the Colonel's retreat before her until Thackeray reintroduced it after the bankruptcy. As a result of the collapse of the B.B.C. in the opening chapter of number twenty-two, the Colonel comes to be not only financially but also emotionally debilitated—a submissive victim of Mrs. Mackenzie, who assumes full control of the exiled household in Boulogne. Pen's success in getting Clive and the Colonel away from her at the end of the installment therefore serves as only a brief remission of her tyranny.

The final double installment treats all the remaining deferred subjects, beginning with Mrs. Mackenzie, who in chapter 37 comes to London and makes her last and most oppressive descent upon her victims. The Colonel retreats immediately and by the end of the same chapter has already become a pensioner at Greyfriars. The first half of the installment then ends with the discovery of Sophia Alethea's letter in Orme—years too late. Thackeray thereby left himself the second half of the installment to complete a number of other developments before ending the novel with the quiet death of Colonel Newcome.

These developments had often been lateral and came to span several installments instead of being confined to immediately adjacent numbers; the linkages also came to range freely beyond parallelism. Thus Ethel's maturing, educating herself, and devoting herself to others at the beginning of number twenty not only contrasts with Rosey's naïve and destructive self-absorption at the beginning of number twenty-one but also leads directly to Ethel's discovery of the letter in the Colonel's beloved Orme at the end of the first half of the final installment—precisely because of her mature impulse to enter the feelings of others in loving sympathy. The injustice of the Colonel towards Ethel early in number twenty reappears early in the following installment as he distantly bows and passes her without speaking, but the coolness of his son undergoes modification in the same number as he sees her on the occasion of Sir Barnes's lecture on the affections and feels a sad longing even though she seems hopelessly separated from him. Only in the second half of the final double installment is this separation bridged, as Ethel arranges to give Clive and the Colonel financial help and as she is reconciled to the Colonel as well as to his son.

The subject of art provides connections at the beginnings of numbers twenty-one and twenty-two and of the two halves of the final installment as Rosey's complaints about Clive's painting and his furtive pursuit of it in chapter 28 are followed by the ominous presence of the Colonel's creditors in chapter 32, by Clive's refusal of charitable commissions from his friends and humble acceptance of his ability to earn an income by selling drawings of mail coaches and charging cavalry in chapter 36, and by his continuing support of himself in chapter 40. Rosey's parturitions make another link as she loses a son in the middle of number twenty, gives birth to one near the end of number twenty-one, and dies after unsuccessfully bearing another son near the novel's end, being buried in the same cemetery as Lady Kew, who had died at the end of number seventeen. Lady Kew's destructive counterpart, Mrs. Mackenzie, is implicated in Rosey's death, as recurring instances of the woman's enervating influence have led us to expect—notably at the end of number twenty-two, where the girl sits "under Mrs. Mackenzie as a bird before a boa-constrictor, doomed—fluttering—fascinated—scared and fawning as a whipt spaniel before a keeper" (2:319). Especially, of course, it is the process of the Colonel's decline and purification that we witness in these final installments, from his overt appearance as Don Quixote and his admission of wrong in seeking to punish Sir Barnes, to his successive reappearances as Belisarius, beadsman, and transfigured child. Finally, however, at the end of this vast and complex design, Thackeray drew a memorable line that ended all connections and that left any further links, such as marriage between Clive and Ethel, to be the ambiguous responsibility of his readers.[17]

6

The Virginians

Installments 1–10

The origin of *The Virginians* lies, of course, in *Henry Esmond*, especially the preface, written last and set down in 1852 under the signature of Rachel Esmond Warrington. Before Thackeray's departure for America later that year, he evidently had discussed the possibility of a continuation with George Smith, who had published *Esmond*, for in a letter of 7 December 1852, written to Smith from New York on hearing that *Esmond* was going into a second edition, Thackeray alluded to the sequel: "And now, Dont you think we may do the Warringtons of Virginia?"[1] In another letter to Smith on 22 September 1855, Thackeray indicated that its appearance "in 3 vols. or 20 numbers" would "depend on the size to which that book goes" (*Letters*, 3:471). By mid-1856, after Thackeray's return from his second American trip, he had settled upon its format and publisher, for in advertisements appearing with volume 3 of his *Miscellanies*, Bradbury and Evans announced Thackeray's new serial novel. By September the artist felt himself "haunted by No. I of Mr. Thackeray's new serial, wh. won't leave me alone wh. follows me about in all my walks, wakes me up at night, prevents me from hearing what is said at the play, and yet seems farther off than ever." He tells his correspondent, "in fact this very sheet of paper was pulled out for the purpose of writing a page" (*Letters*, 3:616–17). By mid-October he confided that he had "burned 2 or 3 beginnings . . . the other day" (*Letters*, 3:620). Lecturing took up a good deal of his time, however, and on 16 February 1857, writing to George Smith from Sheffield, he indicated: "My idea for the forthcoming (?) Serial for B & E is that novel expanded into 20 or 24 numbers wh. was to have been the continuation of Esmond—embracing the American War, Dr. Johnson, Wilkes & Liberty the deuce knows what—In the Summer I tried 3 or 4 months in vain at a Modern Story finding that I repeated my self, and beginning to suspect that my vein is worked out" (NLS). It was not until 14 May 1857 that Thackeray mentioned he was about to begin writing *The Virginians* (*Letters*,

4:44–45). On 10 October he sent Dr. John Brown "a tracing of the design of the paper cover of the monthly numbers," commenting: "Sir, this is the best part of *The Virginians* which is done as yet. I have been working hard and don't like what I have done."[2]

Shortly after the appearance of the first installment at the end of that month, he mentioned that the novel "has taken me an immense deal of trouble" (*Letters*, 4:56). Any idea of beginning publication with a substantial amount of manuscript in his desk would have had to be abandoned, for a number of other matters, including his unsettled health, claimed his attention during the latter half of 1857. By the beginning of the following year he acknowledged that he was writing against an immediately forthcoming deadline: number four for February was still incomplete (*Letters*, 4:64). In general, his compositional difficulties grew especially out of the need to do historical research and to give the results of this research a fictional embodiment, but the "trouble" mentioned in November can be presumed to refer also to his difficulties in shaping the first two installments. Here, as elsewhere, the manuscript does not supply complete documentation, for it not only lacks whole installments but also fails to preserve the entire text of even a single monthly number; nevertheless, it does contain most of the novel's original text and offers a good deal of evidence.

The Morgan manuscript of number one for November 1857, which consists of chapters 1–4, contains thirty-nine leaves: eighteen in Thackeray's hand (fols. 1–3, 10–17, 26–27, and 36–40) and the rest divided between his daughter Anne (fols. 18–25) and a secretary (fols. 4–9 and 28–34), though with additions by Thackeray; fol. 35 and about two final leaves are missing. It is impossible to reconstruct the earliest opening of the novel, but from the evidence available in the Morgan manuscript, one can see that an early opening began with fols. 1 and 1a (now fols. 1 and 2), containing the present five initial paragraphs, and led to a sequence consisting of fol. 1b (which survives as a partly obscured portion of what is now fol. 26), fols. 1c, 1d, 2–7 (now fols. 27–34), a now missing leaf (then presumably fol. 8, later renumbered fol. 35), fols. 9–11 (now fols. 36, 39, and 40), and probably one additional leaf, now also missing, numbered 12 (later 41). This sequence, which may have followed another opening or an earlier version of the present one, summarized the fortunes of Colonel Henry Esmond, his daughter, and his two grandsons, and it provided, among other matters, the account we now receive in chapter 3 and the first portion of chapter 4,

ending with Colonel Esmond's "maxim that we can't change disposi-
tions by meddling, and only make hypocrites of our children by commanding them over much" (fol. 36; see 1:25). In a passage later
cancelled in part, what is now fol. 39 completed this sentence and went
on to explain how after his death Colonel Esmond's daughter rapidly
assumed control over the management of the estate (1:28). What is
now fol. 40 subsequently brought the narrative to the point at which
Esmond's daughter stopped the construction going on at Castlewood,
which drew on such costly materials (1:30). This account, ending at the
bottom of the leaf in mid-sentence, most likely continued on an additional leaf (probably fol. [⟨12⟩ 41]), presumably to the end of the ensuing scene, in which Harry sits in church "with his arm round his
brother's neck" (1:31); it then apparently continued on fols. [13]–
[20] (now missing) and 21–23 (now 51–53), to "'one day will come when
he *wont* go away,' groaned Mountain" (fol. 53)—thereby developing
further American material that now appears in the second installment.

The most notable fact about this whole sequence is its concentration
upon the Virginian family; Thackeray's shifting of the scene to England (fols. 3–25; 1:2–19) was therefore a later addition that made the
Virginian portion into a flashback narrated to the Baroness Bernstein
by Harry Warrington. Subsequently, Thackeray added four other passages, deferred some of the Virginian narrative, and renumbered fols.
1b–11. One addition, which was pasted over the top fifth of fol. 1b (the
composite leaf now constituting fol. 26), provided the opening for a
new chapter, from: "Colonel Henry Esmond, an officer who had served
with some distinction during the wars of Queen Anne's reign" to:
"county of Hants; and it" (fol. 26; see 1:20). A second addition recounted the death of Esmond, beginning, "At length the time came"
and ending, "weeping cherubs" (fol. 37; 1:25–26). A third, ending,
"would she have listened to him?" (fol. 38; 1:27–28), opened chapter
4 by giving an extended and emphatic account of Castlewood and the
entire neighborhood under the full influence of his daughter's will to
domineer—which is to be a recurrent and important force in the novel,
especially in its early chapters. The fourth addition concluded the installment by bringing the reader out of the flashback with a brief narrative of how Madame Bernstein delighted in Harry's tale and how she
identified herself to him as the former Beatrix Esmond (presumably
fol. [42]; 1:31–32). The result of this altered perspective is familiar to
readers of *Vanity Fair*, *Pendennis*, *The Newcomes*, and to a degree

Henry Esmond: a novel that opens with a dramatic action and then doubles back to provide background material with an extended narrative. One should also observe that a further result was Thackeray's providing his English readers with a novel fundamentally set in England, not one that concentrated for several numbers exclusively on scenes set in what they thought of not even as a colony but as a foreign country. The whole subsequent history of the novel's composition, furthermore, involved his giving it an increasingly greater English emphasis.

Thackeray also made further additions, deletions, and substitutions in manuscript; all are of considerably lesser magnitude, but several concerning Madam Esmond deserve mention. Thackeray's surviving account of Castlewood, in the hand of a secretary, began as follows: "After a score of years residence upon his great Virginian estate, affairs prospered so well with the worthy proprietor that he determined to build a mansion much nobler & more durable than the plain wooden Edifice In which he had been content to live, & leave his heirs a habitation worthy of their noble name." The narrative then continued: "About this name to say truth Colonel Esmond of Castlewood was not especially proud or anxious, but his daughter had a very high opinion of the merit & antiquity of her lineage; and her sire, growing exquisitly calm & good-natured in his serene declining years, humoured his childs peculiarities." Later, however, Thackeray decided to give the initiative to Esmond's daughter. Hence he made a number of changes in his own hand, so that the text read, for example: Esmond "acquiesced in his daughter's plans for the building of" a mansion; "Several of Madam Warringtons neighbours had built handsome houses for themselves, perhaps it was her ambition to take rank in the country, wh. inspired this desire for improved quarters"; and Colonel Esmond of Castlewood "neither cared for quarters nor for quarterings" (fol. 28; see 1:22). These changes thereby brought the Colonel and his daughter more into accord with the figures whom we see at the end of *Esmond* and in its subsequently written Preface.

Thackeray, moreover, made other alterations in the manuscript of the first installment that caused her to seem more pompous and domineering. Now she no longer "occasionally" but "frequently" (fol. 30; 1:23) acted as though the marquis' patent from King James still existed. Upon Colonel Esmond's death she now no longer "in her fond grave way transferred her fealty to her eldest son . . ., henceforth the chief of the house," but "in great state proclaimed her eldest son George her successor and heir of the estate" (fols. 31–32; see 1:23). From the middle of another clause in the hand of the secretary, Thackeray later cancelled language terming her one who was "the most humane of women and who of her own will would inflict no pain upon any mortal"; the remaining words of the clause, therefore, now read: "his mother was inflexible" (fol. 34; see 1:24). In a change involving the substitution of seven words for eleven, and concerning a quarrel with her son, the most notable alteration was the replacement of "fond mother" simply by "mother" (fol. 34; 1:24). Similarly, while first composing fol. 39, Thackeray inserted another mention of her assuming the name of Esmond instead of Warrington and of her alluding to the marquisate—thereby giving additional emphasis to her irrepressible vanity. A further insertion concerning her emphatic nature came as George, who originally had given his opinion when the matter of the London lawyer's decision was referred to him, now had additional pressure exerted upon him: "and his mother vehemently insisted that he should declare himself" (fol. 40; 1:30). Thus, by these changes Thackeray made Madam Esmond consistently relentless and imperious.

The first installment's passage through the press brought a considerable number of further changes—over sixty-five of them substantive.[3] Besides altering several names, Thackeray refined various words and phrases, like "thrusting" (1:4) for "sticking" (fol. 4); "servant, who at length issued" (1:10) for "lazy servants who issued" (fol. 13); "ask for a dish of bacon and eggs" (1:11) for "order a rasher of bacon & eggs" (fol. 13); "*won't*" (1:15) for "wont" (fol. 17); "Dutch traders" (1:21) for "Dutch boors" (fol. 26); "mansion much grander" (1:22) for "mansion much nobler" (fol. 28); "the rightful king" (1:23) for "the King" (fol. 31); and "an ancient name" (1:27) for "a noble name" (fol. 38). A reference to time was changed, "at the close of King William's reign" (1:21) replacing "in the first years of the 17th. Century" (fol. 26), the opening sentence of chapter 2 was added (1:10), and the concluding sentence of chapter 3 received its final phrase: "and reciting an epitaph which for once did not tell any falsehoods" (1:26). The most substantial alteration, however, was the addition of a paragraph in chapter 4. Beginning, "A very early difference" (1:29), it concerned Madam Esmond's quarrel with George's tutor, Mr. Dempster, and was presumably inserted in order to prepare for the account of his replacement by Mr. Ward and of

Dempster's subsequent reinstatement—material from an early portion of number two that Thackeray had presumably already written by the time the first installment went to press. The former monthly part appeared in print divided into four chapters, with a full complement of chapter initials, an internal wood-engraving for each of the first two chapters, and space at the end of the four chapters representing the equivalent of two, thirteen, twenty-seven, and seven additional lines, respectively.[4]

The surviving Morgan manuscript of number two for December 1857 lacks approximately eight leaves representing the text of chapter 5 (presumably fols. [43]–[50]) and four from chapter 8 (fols. [77]–[80]). Twenty-nine leaves survive, one having writing and numbering on both sides (fol. 81, 82); eighteen are in Thackeray's hand (fols. 51–63, 70–71, 81, 82, and a second 63 and 64, which I shall designate 63a and 64a), six are in Anne's (fols. 64–69), and five are in a secretary's hand (fols. 72–76). The composition of the installment was not straightforward, but most of that development cannot seemingly be reconstructed. We can see, however, that the most prominent change involved the insertion of fols. 54–59 (originally numbered fols. 53a–53f) into the text ahead of a fol. 54 that was later removed—and perhaps replaced by the present fol. 60, which now ends chapter 6. As a result of the insertion of fols. 54–59, Thackeray added the historical narrative of English disputes with the French along the Ohio, especially as they were epitomized by Washington's journey of 1753, his skirmish with the French at Fort Necessity the following year, and his return to Virginia and Castlewood (1:47–49). At first, Thackeray's account of Washington's involvement with Madam Esmond and her sons ended with Mountain's comment to the jealous George Warrington that the day would come when Washington "*wont* go away" (fol. 53; see 1:46–47); an abrupt shift to an historical narrative then ensued at the top of the following leaf, which was then still unnumbered: "The convenient maxim of the old American settlers was that the possessors of the coast had a right to all the inland territory, so that . . ." (fol. 55). Thackeray later cancelled these initial words, however, and he inserted the present fol. 54 to provide more of a transition by explaining that in spite of Mountain's fears, Washington was in fact just about to depart for the western Virginia frontier, where there was conflict between the French and English over the matter of ownership, the English charters maintaining "that whoever possessed the coast had a right to all the territory inland as far as the Pacific . . ." (1:47).

A number of phrases are crossed out and revised on fols. 54–60, suggesting a certain difficulty in composition, but these revisions are relatively minor in nature and reflect Thackeray's wish to carry out his thoughts with greater fullness and precision rather than any problems in handling historical details. The chief cancellation furnishes a good example, for it shows that Thackeray realized he had proceeded too quickly in his handling of the jealousy produced by Washington's presence at Castlewood. After the narrative of Washington's return from Fort le Boeuf, Thackeray originally had written: "It was on his return from this mission wh. he had conducted with an heroic energy and simplicity that the young Mr. Washington created so much jealousy and admiration in our Virginian family" (fol. 56). Thackeray immediately cancelled this passage as premature, however, and at the top of the next leaf wrote a new passage—beginning, "Harry Warrington cursed his ill-fortune" (1:48)—which helps prepare for future jealousy by showing the increase of Madam Esmond's favor towards Washington but which soon leads to an account of historical developments, especially Washington's second departure to meet the French, rather than of developments in Washington's relations with the Warrington family. An increase in jealousy comes only at the end of the chapter, after Washington's return from the latter expedition (fol. 60; 1:50).[5]

Chapter 7, which is marked off in manuscript as the installment's third chapter, seems to have been composed with more difficulty, for the manuscript contains a number of cancelled and revised passages. After carrying his narrative to the point where Braddock arrived at Annapolis, called a council of governors, and sought aid from the colonies (fol. 63; 1:52). Thackeray suddenly tried to assure his readers that they were receiving a novelistic account of Harry and George Warrington, not an historical account of certain developments in the colonies, but he soon contradicted himself: "This veracious narrative contains the history not of Virginia or North America, but of a couple of Virginian gentlemen and so I am luckily spared from uttering the words of blame, wh. a historian and moralist must have uttered in this place on this subject—A hundred years ago there existed among the two millions of inhabitants of the British North American provinces some folks whose breed has fortunately died out and who were" (fol. 63). Halting at this point, he presumably realized that he had just begun an account not about two Virginian gentlemen at all but about colonial parsimony; dissatisfied also with the ironic tone of what he had written, he cancelled the passage and went on more straightforwardly:

> The efforts made by the provinces were not particularly energetic. In fact they seemed inclined to let the British Government fight their battle, fulfilled none of their engagements, and contributed neither men nor money nor horses nor beef. The British general broke up his congress of Governors in a fury. Maryland & Virginia on wh. he had counted for his conveyance and a great portion of his provision, brought him only twenty waggons and two hundred wretched horses. Pennsylvania was absolutely unprepared to give horses or men until Mr. Benjamin Franklin informed his fellow citizens that the General would take what he wanted by force, if he could not get it by fair payment on wh. the Pennsylvanian farmers found horses and wagons[.] (fol. 63)

He may well have carried this narrative forward to a new leaf; if so, he cancelled it, as he did this passage, and deferred treating the subject of colonial niggardliness until the final chapter of number three, except for a brief allusion on fol. 65 (1:53). Instead, he reverted to his original impulse to concentrate upon his two Virginians and to integrate his historical details more closely with his account of the Warrington family.

Beginning with the sentence, "The arrival of the Genl. & his little army caused a mighty Excitement all through the Provinces, & no where greater than at Castlewood" (fol. 64; see 1:52), he composed a narrative, set down by Anne, of how the two Warringtons became acquainted with Braddock and his officers. This account took up seven leaves, ending with mention of how George and his tutor, Dempster, again began to practice with foils, Dempster being reluctant to say where he had learned the art. Here too, there were second thoughts, but they came only after Thackeray had begun a further narrative, set down by a secretary, and they did not involve any changes in direction. The lengthiest alteration was that in which Thackeray himself recopied onto a new leaf (fol. 70), with a number of stylistic changes, the last leaf in Anne's hand, which never had been numbered and now was cancelled. He then turned the cancelled leaf over and began to write a passage (fol.

71) that was to lead into his previous account set down by the secretary. He intended it to begin a new chapter but later changed his mind, deciding to "break a line" (fol. 71) instead and to begin the chapter at the top of fol. 76, which was also in the secretary's hand.

It is impossible to tell how long the portion of narrative set down by the secretary (beginning fol. 72) continued, for fols. [77]–[80] are missing. Since what are now fols. 83–85 (in Thackeray's hand) were originally numbered fols. 78–80, however, it is possible that only fol. [77] (or a leaf it may have replaced) was a part of the original narrative. If this is so, then Thackeray would have had a manuscript of roughly thirty-eight leaves, representing approximately twenty-eight fully printed pages, that ended with the description of Braddock's arrival at Castlewood: "There was room for all at Castlewood when they came: there was meat drink and the best tobacco for His Majestys soldiers and laughing and jollity for the negroes and a plenteous welcome for their masters" (fol. ⟨80⟩ 85; see 1:68). Suitably augmented with chapter headings, initials, and an internal wood-engraving or two, such a text could have been printed as a monthly installment, but if this possibility was ever considered, it was not chosen. Instead, Thackeray inserted four leaves ahead of fols. 78–80, renumbered the latter as 83–85, and, marking off the beginning of a new chapter, carried his narrative to the point at which Washington took Madam Esmond's hand in his own (fol. 93). Thackeray may well have intended this incident as the climax of number two, for fol. 93 marks the end of the numbering system he had used until now. By the time he had developed the second half of this narrative, however, it was too long to print as a single installment.

Instead of making a number of cuts, Thackeray decided to postpone the narrative of Braddock's journey to Castlewood and his arrival there until the following number, where it now makes up the opening chapter (1:65–74). As a result of this decision, he had to augment the text of number two—and he did so not by inserting illustrations, for the monthly part has only chapter initials, but by writing additions to the text as the installment was going through the press. Thackeray's main changes in the text of the surviving manuscript chapters (5 is missing) occur in chapters 7 and 8. The chief alteration in the former came as he revised and extended part of Mrs. Mountain's scene with George; the relevant portion of the manuscript reads as follows: "But the fire burnt low, and before the flame could reach it. The housekeeper had once more possession of the paper. You should thank your stars, child, that I saved the letter! cried she 'and not call me names, and fly into a passion with me. See! Here are his own words . . ." (fol. 74). Prompted at least in part by the need to lengthen his text, Thackeray came to realize that this particular scene took place too rapidly: George had scarcely flung the letter into the fireplace with passionate disdain before he was reading it with a certain amount of willingness.

Beginning, therefore, with the words "I could not help it, George" (1:57), Thackeray had Mountain offer a justifying explanation that caused George to reply no longer with vehement scorn but with a transitional emotion of grim humor; Mountain then completed her partly successful attempt to manipulate George's feelings by trying to make him feel guilty for upbraiding her and for refusing to read the letter. Thereafter the narrator himself entered with hints of explanation: "Perhaps George was absorbed in his dismal thoughts; perhaps his jealousy overpowered him, for he did not resist any further when she stooped down and picked up the paper." Thackeray then was ready to complete the augmented passage: "'You should thank your stars, child, that I saved the letter,' cried she. 'See! here are his own words . . .'" (1:58). As a result of the addition, Thackeray both improved this portion of the narrative and lengthened it by about twenty-four printed lines. Since only twenty-three lines occupy the chapter's final page, we can see that his revision significantly extended the chapter by carrying the text over onto an eighth page (1:51–58).

The changes made in press to the text of chapter 8 are more difficult to discuss, since four early leaves are missing (fols. [77]–[80]). We can see, however, that the text of the chapter's opening leaf (fol. 76) was considerably modified upon its appearance in print. Thackeray made a minor cut of about one printed line in the first sentence concerning Castlewood's appearance for its guests, but immediately below he added the equivalent of twelve printed lines. This leaf, which survives in the Arents Collection, was designated fol. C by Thackeray and inserted in page proof at the same time as the above addition (presumably written on fols. [A] and [B]), for he indicated that it was to be inserted "at 58"—that is, into what was then page 58 but is now page 59 because of the text added by fols. [A] and [B].[6] Whereas in the manuscript Washington had arrived and immediately announced that Braddock was not far distant, in the augmented version Washington and Madam Esmond have a leisurely and cordial conversation before Washington's announcement:

> The widow received him in the covered gallery before the house: He dismounted at the steps and his servants led away his horses to the well-known quarters. No young gentleman in the Colony was better mounted or a better horseman than Mr. Washington[7]
>
> For a while ere the Major retired to divest himself of his riding boots he and his hostess paced the gallery in talk. She had much to say to him; she had to hear from him a confirmation of his own appointment as aide-de-camp to General Braddock, and to speak of her sons approaching departure. The negroe-servants bearing dishes for the approaching feast were passing perpetually as they talked—They descended the steps down to the rough lawn in front of the house—whence the broad gleaming waters of the Potomac were visible, and here the pair paced awhile in the shade. (fol. C; see 1:59–60)

Washington then announced Braddock's arrival with Franklin, and a further change occurred in the printed text. The manuscript read as follows:

> Mrs Esmond thought the Major was a great deal too liberally disposed towards this gentleman. She had heard stories about him she would not particularise but there were and indeed he has owned so himself subsequently
>
> The young Virginian officer might know but did not choose to own or remember these petty tales of scandal [.] (fol. 76)[8]

The Madam Esmond we have met, however, is more of a snob than a prude, and Thackeray must have recognized that Franklin's plebeian background would have been sufficiently objectionable to her, for upon the installment's appearance this passage was considerably different. Madam Esmond's mention of scandal about Franklin had disappeared and been replaced by Washington's defense of him as "a most ingenious, useful, and meritorious man." Washington's reluctance to repeat gossip had also been given a new context—Madam Esmond's pleasure that her son will not be associating with tradesmen but with English military gentlemen of honor and fashion: "Mr. Washington had seen the gentlemen of honour and fashion over their cups, and perhaps thought that all their sayings and doings were not precisely such as would tend to instruct or edify a young man on his entrance into life; but he wisely chose to tell no tales out of school . . ." (1:60). Here, one feels, Thackeray detected a slight aberration in his narrative and responded by providing greater clarity and fullness of detail. A some-what similar change a few pages later removed an uncharacteristic wish of Madam Esmond's to have neither of her sons respond to the call of duty and honor. Hence, the words "Why need either go? she asked—Have I not often asked why" (fol. 82) were replaced in the printed text with "She knew not from which she would like to part" (1:63).

Even with these additions, however, the text of the installment would have carried only to a point about nine lines from the bottom of 1:63, thereby requiring an illustration or more letterpress. Thackeray chose to write an additional passage on two small leaves—after he had seen revised page proof, for he numbered them fols. 63 and 64 (not 82a and 82b), beginning with 63 because it was the number of the printed page on which the addition was to start.[9] With these last two leaves, beginning: "George performed ever so many trills and quavers," Thackeray brought his installment to a striking conclusion, for instead of ending with Washington's puzzlement at George's calling "Malbrouk s'en va-t-en guerre" (a song unknown to him) "God save the King,"[10] Thackeray has George's performance swiftly lead to increasingly vivid developments: Washington's somewhat disdainful wonder prompts his wish to retire, which causes George's rude comment about Washington's knowing his way, Madam Esmond's angry decision to conduct him to his room herself, and George's dramatic revelation to Harry and to the reader of the contents of Washington's letter.

In early December 1857 Thackeray was at Brighton to "get a little ahead with The Virginians."[11] He already had a chapter made up of the last manuscript leaves numbered under the old system: fols. 83–93, all written in his own hand (84.85 being a single leaf), and by 11 December he saw himself within a week of finishing number three for January 1858.[12] By the 21st he had done so, for on that day he wrote John Blackwood: "I got through the number in a dreadful nervous way and want if I can to do another number this month."[13] The surviving manuscript (fol. [89] is missing) reveals no notable difficulties of composition, the lengthiest cancellation being a passage of just over five handwritten lines made up of a redundant sentence about Castlewood's special appearance on the day of Braddock's arrival and a similar sentence about Braddock's train that began what was originally marked off as a new chapter (fol. 86). The rest of the installment had a fresh numbering system and apparently comprised twenty-five leaves, though only fols. 3–24 survive. Here too the composition seems to have been straightforward.

If the manuscript alterations were rather minor, so too were the changes made in press. Since chapter 10 was to end with Washington's "taking the widow's hand very tenderly in his" (1:74), and since his fond regard for her had been shown quite amply, Thackeray deleted a needless mention towards the chapter's end that "Mr. Washington took the lady's hand and respectfully kissed it" (fol. 93). At the conclusion of the same chapter two brief additions were made: an incomplete reference to a song performed after dinner by Braddock's aide became "the latest ditty from Marybone Gardens" and George's final outburst was given fuller expression by his angry cry to Harry: "They were billing and cooing this morning; they are billing and cooing now before going to roost" (1:74). Only a few individual words were altered in the following chapter, the regiment of the two drunken recruiting officers becoming Halkett's (1:79–80, 82) instead of "St. Clair's" (fols. 6–7, 9; various spellings), for example, and an expletive uttered by one of them becoming "hang me" (1:81) instead of "dammy" (fol. 7). In the last two chapters of the installment, which had very full texts, Thackeray made a few more brief alterations, one of which included the changing of Mrs. Mountain's reference to Washington's future wife from "Mrs. Martha Custis" (fol. 16) to "that little widow Custis" (1:88).[14] A few historical details were also modified; for example, the report of Braddock's death arrives in Virginia not "Two days afterwards" (fol. 24), but "Four days afterwards" (1:96)—that is, on July 14th, which is early even for a rumor but impossible for an actual report, since Braddock in fact died only on the previous evening.[15] The speediness of the report of his death, however, is quite in keeping with the rapidity with which other reports are received, for Thackeray has news of the battle arrive throughout Virginia on "the 10th of July" (1:96)—the day after it was fought. These corrections having been made, the monthly number appeared, its last two chapters containing full concluding pages of forty-seven lines each.

By 2 January 1858, if indeed not earlier, Thackeray was "grappling with No. IV" for February (*Letters*, 4:64), which he finished on 22 January, berating himself for "getting more disgustingly lazy every day. I *can't* do the work until it's wanted. And yet with all these attacks of illness wh. I have, I ought" (*Letters*, 4:66).[16] The manuscript is entirely in his own hand and lacks only two leaves: fols. 13–14. Consisting of chapters 13–16, from Harry Warrington's unsuccessful search for his brother to Baroness Bernstein's lack of success in persuading Harry to leave Castlewood with her for Tunbridge Wells, its evolution was somewhat complicated but is largely discernible. One can see that in the writing of chapter 13, for example, Thackeray made three major changes. Before numbering the leaves, he apparently inserted ahead of what is now fol. 6 the present fol. 5, beginning: "now. Never mind my Harry" (see 1:99), and ending three-quarters of the way down the leaf: "Mother, and if our George" (see 1:100). Since fol. 6 lacks its topmost portion, however, one must be guarded in commenting on the significance of the interpolated leaf. Because of the manuscript hiatus one cannot be sure whether or not fol. 5, by showing Madam Esmond's confidence in George's eventual return and her illogical belief in Washington's responsibility for his death, added new material or simply a new elaboration of it. One *can* see, however, that fol. 5 contains the first mention of Madam Esmond's consoling dream and of the irrationally vengeful feelings that her grief has produced. As a result of the addition, therefore, we are—at the least—given fuller and partly comic preparation for what follows, especially her chilling reception of Washington.

This reception, which ended with an embarrassed Washington standing "dumb on the floor" (fol. 7; 1:101), once marked the end of the American narrative, for after a break of a line, Thackeray had gone on to write: "I cannot tell how it has come said Harry as he brought the story to an end wh. we have told through the last two numbers, and wh. he confided to his new found English relative Madame de Bernstein—but since, since that fatal day of July last year, and my return home my mother has never been the same woman." In this climactic speech, Harry then went on to explain that Madam Esmond's gloom spread throughout the house, affecting everyone in it, isolating one from another, and even apparently taking a physical form as well as a psychological one in his case: "I was again and again struck down

by the fever and all the Jesuits Bark in Canada would not cure me"
(fol. 7). The ultimate aim of the passage seems to have been to show
how his sickness and alienation from his mother led to his taking the
voyage to England that opened the novel. Thackeray decided, however, that this climactic speech needed more adequate preparation;
accordingly, he cancelled the passage, which seems to have continued
on another leaf that presumably was replaced, and made his second
major addition by continuing on fols. 8, 9, and the top of 10 Harry's
account of the effect upon Castlewood House of the news of George's
apparent death.[17] In this new portion, Thackeray illustrated the extent of Madam Esmond's illogical scorn for Washington and furnished
examples that showed exactly how her fierce grief and hope oppressed
the people around her. He thereby illustrated the phenomena that
Harry had summarized in the cancelled passage and so prepared for
the final step in this process—the passage's reappearance, in only
slightly modified form, on fol. 10. A portion of the manuscript may
have been removed as well, however, for the single leaf numbered 1.2
possibly replaced two leaves that originally opened the installment. As
a result of these alterations, the manuscript of chapter 13 emerged in
the form of nine leaves numbered from 1.2 to 10, two final lines of text
being written on the verso of fol. 10.

Only two-thirds of the manuscript of chapter 14 survives (fols.
11–12, 15–16), no notable changes appearing in it. On the first leaf of
the following chapter, however, Thackeray cancelled a brief passage
concerning Parson Sampson's sermon. "A SUNDAY AT CASTLEWOOD"
begins with Harry, seated in the family pew near the kneeling stone
effigy of his ancestor, listening to the parson, who "preached a brisk
sermon wh. did not last a quarter of an hour containing many sensible
remarks wh. might serve the congregation in this world if it did not
advance their knowledge of the next" (fol. 17). Thackeray struck out
these words, for the account he went on to write was not intended to
demonstrate the worldliness of the sermon so much as the worldliness
and theatricality of the preacher. Parson Sampson's brief discourse
might indeed serve the congregation in this world, but its chief force in
the narrative comes from our subsequent discovery of the ironic discrepancy between the overt content of the sermon and the actual character of the man preaching it, the slaying of the Philistines being in his
case a mere rhetorical exercise undertaken while he is fully in thrall to

pleasure. It seems, therefore, that Thackeray suddenly saw how by communicating to us Sampson's sermon at some length he could give greater emphasis to Sampson's subsequent unwitting demonstration of the prudence of his formal maxims, for the cancelled sentence was succeeded by language that evoked not only the clergyman's histrionic ability but also the specific vices against which he is "generously indignant" (fol. 18)—especially drinking, card-playing, cockfighting, and horseracing.[18] No other changes worthy of mention occur in the manuscript of this chapter. The final chapter of the monthly number, which already has its title, also seems to have been composed with ease, the only anomaly in the manuscript being the absence of most of the last sentence on its final leaf, which ends at the very bottom with the words, "So all the little knot of people at Castlewood House" (fol. 30; see 1:127).

Although the net result of these changes was a fuller monthly number, it was too short to print. Thackeray responded in part by making his first two chapter initials quite large—the equivalent of about nineteen and twenty printed lines, respectively, compared with thirteen and eight for the last two. He also added internal wood-engravings to chapters 14 and 15—the last internal wood-engravings in the entire novel—that took up the space of thirty and twenty-nine printed lines. Even so, the four chapters occupied only approximately seven, six, nine, and eight pages, for a total of thirty. Accordingly, Thackeray was prompted to make a number of additions in press. One passage lengthened chapter 13 by only seven lines; although it was not enough to extend the text onto another page, it answered an unresolved question: what happened to George's servant after Braddock's disaster? "A fortnight after the defeat, when Harry was absent on his quest, George's servant, Sady, reappeared wounded and maimed at Castlewood. But he could give no coherent account of the battle, only of his flight from the centre, where he was with the baggage. He had no news of his master since the morning of the action. For many days Sady lurked in the negro quarters away from the sight of Madam Esmond, whose anger he did not dare to face" (1:101). Another passage added eight lines to the account in chapter 15 of Parson Sampson's Sunday tales of fashionable London life. The manuscript had explained how he poured out his spicy gossip "to the amused ladies and the delighted young provincial until the chapel bell clinking for afternoon service summoned his Reverence away for half an hour" (fol. 22). Now, however, Thackeray somewhat qualified Harry's pleasure and added a half-ironic historical justification for the benefit of squeamish nineteenth-century female readers: "seasoning his conversation with such plain terms and lively jokes as made Harry stare, who was newly arrived from the Colonies, and unused to the elegances of London life. The ladies, old and young, laughed quite cheerfully at the lively jokes. Do not be frightened, ye fair readers of the present day! We are not going to outrage your sweet modesties, or call blushes on your maiden cheeks. But 'tis certain that their ladyships at Castlewood never once thought of being shocked, but sate listening to the parson's funny tales" (1:117). As a result of this insertion and of printing one line less than normal on 1:117, the chapter's text now occupied an additional page containing nine lines.

Thackeray also made two substantial additions in press to the first and last chapters—insertions that have survived in manuscript form (fols. A, B, and fols. C1, C2, C3).[19] The first of these interpolations contains a text that added thirty-six printed lines to the end of chapter 13 and hence extended it by a page.[20] It begins in Thackeray's upright hand with instructions to the printer—"Break a line and insert at 103" —and follows the conclusion of the long speech Thackeray had earlier deferred and revised in which Harry concludes his narrative to Madame Bernstein by explaining how he came to put on mourning and take ship for England. Now Thackeray wrote three additional paragraphs in which the narrator enters in his own voice to provide his own conclusion by focusing on Madam Esmond in Virginia, succinctly characterizing her behavior, commenting on philosophical issues that it illuminates, and ending with a brief account of her move from the loneliness of Castlewood to the partly consoling social life of her house in Richmond. Thackeray thereby provides a neat, aesthetically satisfying conclusion to the chapter, but one whose importance derives more from its contribution in filling out the installment than from any other artistic function.[21]

Thackeray's numbered manuscript concluded, as we saw, on fol. 30 in the middle of a sentence: "So all the little knot of people at Castlewood House"; after sending this manuscript to the printer in its unfinished form, he completed the sentence on the page proof (p. 126) by adding a comma and then going on: "and from these the people in Castlewood village and from thence the people in the whole county, chose

to imagine that Mr. Harry Esmond Warrington was the heir of im-
mence wealth and a gentleman of very great importance, because his
negro valet told lies about him in the Servants Hall" (see 1:127). The
final long insertion in press then came, adding sixty-one lines to the
last chapter by providing it with a new ending. Written entirely in
Thackeray's upright hand, it covers the upper third of fol. C1 (from
"Harry's aunt" to "her benefit" [1:127]), the half-leaf C2 (to "Tunbridge" [1:128]),[22] and the upper half of fol. C3. Since the page proof
only went to page 126, the top of C1 has that numeral to inform the
printer where the insertion was to be made. As a consequence of this
change, the chapter and number did not end with the narrator's explanation of how Harry's English relatives came to believe that he was a
great heir but with a striking scene in which Madame Bernstein, having resolved to remove Harry from their subtle meshes, especially
Maria's, asks him to accompany her to Tunbridge Wells, only to have
him startlingly refuse—as a result of which Madame Bernstein furiously leaves the room and the Esmonds look at one another with wonder,
except for Maria, who "never lifted up her eyes from her tambour-
frame" (fol. C3; 1:128). In prompting Thackeray to write additional
material, therefore, the need to fill out his number led not only to narratively as well as quantitatively useful augmentations but also to the
creation of a scene that is superlative in its dramatic artistry and stun-
ningly effective as an ending.

Thackeray finished number five for March 1858 early on the morning of
Friday, 19 February, and was waiting that evening for the proofs—or
at least a portion of them (Letters, 4:68).[23] The manuscript, in Thackeray's hand except for a portion set down by Anne (fols. 30–34), survives in thirty-five leaves: fols. 1–20, 23–34, and 1a–3a, the latter
bringing chapter 20 to a conclusion.[24] The first chapter, which ends on
fol. 7v, reveals no substantial changes during composition, nor does
chapter 18 (fols. 8–15), but chapter 19 (fols. 16–20) seems to have one
inserted leaf, fol. 18, which contains space for several more lines at the
bottom of the leaf and which is followed by two leaves originally
marked as fols. 18 and 19, but redesignated fols. 19 and 20. Beginning:
"Harry Warrington hoped" (1:147) and ending: "at his cousin's taste"
(1:148), fol. 18 provides a needed indication of Harry's delighted re-

sponse to his aunt's assertion that he will accompany her and Maria to Tunbridge; as such it establishes a transition between Madame Bernstein's brief but significant announcement and the following scene, in which an elated Harry wins yet more from Will and Sampson. The surviving leaves of the final chapter include two that are three-quarters and two-thirds blank respectively (fols. 27 and 29), but it is not clear that they are inserted rather than, say, recopied leaves. The only obvious idiosyncrasy is the lack of continuity between the bottom of fol. 34 (the last leaf set down by Anne) and the top of the following leaf: the textual equivalent of five printed lines that close the middle paragraph on 1:158 is missing, beginning with the words, "rich young American." Even with these lines, however, the installment lacked a recognizable ending. Thackeray therefore provided one on fols. 1*a*–3*a*, presumably giving them a new numbering system because he had already sent the first thirty-four (or thirty-five) leaves to the printer but had not yet received proof. The only other notable change made to chapter 20 in manuscript was the deletion of a phrase indicating how Sampson quoted Hamlet "with an excellent imitation of Mr. Garrick" (fol. 27).[25]

In press, several significant alterations were made—chiefly, but not exclusively, in chapter 20. The first, in chapter 17, corrected a historical reference and changed some of the language. One of Will Esmond's original examples of an attraction of age to youth was Lady Suffolk's falling in love with "Tom Berkeley, and isn't the old woman languishing after him? 'tis the common talk of the town" (fol. 4). In press, however, Berkeley received his proper name and the event was moved into the past, no longer a subject of current gossip; now Will rhetorically asked whether Lady Suffolk did not fall in love with "George Berkeley, and marry him when she was ever so old?" (1:133).[26] Another error that Thackeray tried to remove—though with incomplete success—concerned the horses wagered by Sampson and Will. In the manuscript, Sampson staked his "⟨bay⟩ brown mare," while Will cried: "I have my bay Comus—I will back Comus against you." Ten minutes afterwards, "Comus & the bay mare had both changed owners" (fol. 20). Three leaves later, Thackeray wrote of Harry's pleasure at having won "Will's bay horse" and explained both that Sampson sent over his "little black horse" (fol. 23) and that Will gave Harry not the "brown horse, Prince William," but the "bay horse Cato" (fol. 25) —which Will called "the horse" (fol. 23) that Harry had won. In press,

Thackeray tried to harmonize the earlier details with the later ones and with Sampson's statement that "the colour of the horse was not mentioned" (fol. 26; 1:155). Therefore he deleted mention of "my bay Comus . . . Comus . . . Comus" and replaced it with more reticent language: "my horse . . . my horse . . . the horse" (1:149). He also changed "Will's bay horse" to "Will's brown horse" and Sampson's "little black horse" to "little black mare" (1:152). The early references to Sampson's "brown mare" and to "the bay mare" (1:149) escaped Thackeray's notice, however—readings that future editors, acting on the basis of manuscript evidence and a concept of "ideal copy," may wish to remove through emendation that would parallel Thackeray's own alterations.

Other noteworthy changes were prompted by a need to reduce a monthly number whose text required more than thirty-two pages to be printed. The chapter with the fewest number of lines on its last page was chapter 17, with thirteen lines; if the text of the missing three fols. of chapter 20 already existed in its present form, however, then that chapter offered Thackeray an almost equal opportunity, quantitatively speaking, for it would have had about fourteen lines for its final page. Once again, therefore, Thackeray seems to have made his decision on qualitative grounds, choosing chapter 20 and making four separate deletions in the text of fols. 24–3a, all of which removed relatively inconsequential material. In the first instance, a description of the two carriages carrying the Baroness Bernstein to Tunbridge gave rise to the observation that her baggage train was as nothing compared to that of a nineteenth-century lady's (1:153); the two following sentences were then deleted: "It was no uncommon thing for a gala gown to last a whole life and to be transmitted from mother to daughter. Think of the superior civilization of our own days, when three ladies going on a week's visit to a country house, will take two and forty dresses between them, with hoops as big as any wh. our grandmothers wore!" (fol. 24). The result was a brief rather than a somewhat extended contrast between this feature of the two ages. In a second case, concerning Harry's departure with the Baroness, Thackeray removed a short descriptive phrase that pictured the Castlewood villagers not only cheering Harry but even "lingering about the green to witness and salute his departure. All the people of the village liked the lad" (fol. 28); the cheers remained, but the following nineteen words became simply: "they all liked the lad" (1:156).

The remaining two of these four deletions, like the first, removed historical asides. After Harry told Maria that Venus herself could not induce him to leave her (1:157), Thackeray had originally gone on to make the following comment, set down by Anne: "(The Heathen Gods & Goddesses were not as yet deposed from their places in poetry, school-boy Exercises, & lovers rappsodies)" (fol. 31). Such an explanation was expendable under pressure of the need to reduce his text, however, as was one in a later paragraph that followed a remark about Maria's and the Baroness's ready ability to enjoy a dinner (1:158): "Remember, this was the time when a fine lady, being pressed to drink more, artlessly said, 'If I do, I shall be *muckibus*! A hundred years ago The honest creatures did not disdain to clear the platter and drain the glass" (fol. 1*a*).[27] This too could be sacrificed to the need to curtail chapter 20, and as a result of these deletions, which removed the equivalent of about fourteen printed lines, the installment could be printed on thirty-two pages, its chapters containing final pages with thirteen, twenty (in effect), forty-five, and forty-seven lines each. Future editors will have to decide whether or not to reprint these and similar passages, and if so, in what format.

Shortly before finishing his February installment, Thackeray wrote to Macready: "I am behind hand with my work in consequence of repeated fits of illness with wh. of late I have been knocked over and want to try and make a rally next month & get a couple of numbers ahead of the world. Otherwise it is more than probable the present flourishing firm of the Virginians will have some day to stop payment."[28] By 3 March he could write of number six for April 1858: "The Novel gets on pooty well—well, I think the last week *very* well" (*Letters*, 4:71). The installment survives in manuscript on thirty-three of what apparently were thirty-four leaves numbered fols. [1]–31, 1*a*–3*a*, of which fol. [1] is missing.[29] Again there are four chapters, this time dealing with Harry's adventures among "SAMARITANS" (fols. [1]–8), "IN HOSPITAL" (fols. 9–18), on "HOLYDAYS" (fols. 19–24), and among friends who come "FROM OAKHURST to TUNBRIDGE" (fols. 25–31, 1*a*–3*a*). The second and fourth chapters already contain their titles. All leaves are in Thackeray's own hand, including a portion of fols. 12–13 that was written in pencil on what appears to have been a very unsteady surface, with a corresponding distortion of the script. The composition of the first three chapters seems to have been rather forthright; though the first originally began with Mrs. Lambert's letter to Madam Esmond (initially fols. 1–3), Thackeray soon decided to insert a prefatory leaf (fol. [1]) and redesignate the other three.

A number of changes appear in the final chapter, however, which originally began: "Mrs. Lambert and her daughters continued to watch the departing travellers until such time as a tree-clumped corner of the road hid the riders from view" (fol. 26v). Though these lines were not literally cancelled, Thackeray put the leaf aside, took up a new one, wrote a revised version of this opening (fol. 25), and continued with his narrative. He then picked up the discarded leaf and on the verso extended Colonel Lambert's remarks to Harry about James Wolfe. Here, too, came a change, for Thackeray decided to cancel part of a final sentence in which Lambert observed that Wolfe was "scarce thirty years old" (1:186), "though his father and mine and your good grandsire were at Blenheim and Malplaquet under the Duke—and both served in Kingsley's in wh. you know your father and I were ensigns together" (fol. 26).[30] From this point, composition went on for five more leaves, ending with Baroness Bernstein's words to Harry: "Those three individuals have the most active tongues in the Wells— They will trumpet your good qualities in every company where they go" (fol. 31; see 1:190). Presumably Thackeray sent these thirty-one leaves to the printer and then concluded the installment by writing three more (fols. 1a–3a), in which he had the Baroness explain to Harry the advantages of a reputation for wealth, warn him against Castlewood, and, misled by her worldliness, mistakenly think Harry in love with one of the Lambert girls.

As usual, various alterations were made in press; in this case, however, they were brief stylistic changes or slight modifications of detail. Only a few are worthy of mention. One was an inaccurate or at best misleadingly generic characterization of Katharine Lowther, whom Wolfe was courting; "his Amelia" (fol. 30) therefore was emended to "his mistress" (1:189). Another involved the alteration of the narrator's reference to a phrase used "some five and twenty lines back" (fol. 21); this became "some five-and-thirty lines back" (1:180), thereby reflecting both the altered disposition of words on the printed page and Thackeray's attempt while correcting proof to achieve greater accuracy of detail.

In a letter of 2 April to his mother, Thackeray mentioned that "though I am writing to you I am thinking about No VII—can't help myself— and am very happy thinking about No VII after all—only silent and solitary. Tomorrow I am going into hospital at Thompsons for a couple of days: and hope I shall come out all the better for the discipline. Meanwhile out with you No VII!—let us see if we can do a page or two" (*Letters*, 4:77). On 9 April he wrote: "Am pretty well on with my work this month, and have found it go easier: am better in general health too I think" (*Letters*, 4:78). He concluded:

> Come let us get to
>
> > Chapter
>
> These feats of agility being over, the four gentlemen quitted the Bowling Green and
> The rest is no VII, page 16 of The Virginians by
>
> > W. M. Thackeray. (*Letters*, 4:79)[31]

On 10 April, however, he revealed that two attacks of illness in late March and early April had delayed him to such an extent that he had only written "3 pages" (*Letters*, 4:79) of his approximately half-finished number during the first part of April. Almost two weeks later, on Friday, 23 April, he wrote: "on Friday night after awful trouble, I only got my number done, just in time to send it by post to Liverpool & America" (*Letters*, 4:80). Since "Friday night" meant 16 April, as the rest of the letter also makes clear, the phrase "just in time" refers to the sailing deadline of the *Arabia*, which left Liverpool for New York with the Royal Mail on Saturday, 17 April. A sister ship, the *Europa*, on which Thackeray himself had sailed in 1853, left for Halifax and Boston a week later, and another sister ship departed for New York on 1 May (see issues of the *Times* for April), but Thackeray apparently felt he could not wait another week or two for a subsequent sailing of the British and North American Royal Mail Steam Ships. Since this is the earliest monthly date recorded for his sending proof of *The Virginians* to Harper, one suspects something of a compulsive need to meet a partly arbitrary, self-imposed deadline.[32] At the same time, it seems clear that *two* weeks would have meant too long a delay.[33]

A good deal of the original manuscript of number seven is missing: all of chapter 25, most of 26, and all of 27. Five leaves set down by a secretary survive from chapter 26, providing fifty-two lines of printed text; the secretary apparently first numbered them fols. 1–5 in pencil, and then redesignated them fols. 1a–5a in ink. All of chapter 28—its title, "The way of the world," already given in manuscript—also survives (fols. 1–8 and [9]–[15], the last seven leaves being unnumbered). Thackeray appears to have started this chapter with a passage, in Anne's hand, beginning: "After a fortnight of Tunbridge Mr. Harry had become quite a personage" (fol. 3; see 1:219), but later, on the only leaves written in his own hand (fols. 1–2), he composed the present opening, which ends on the upper one-third of fol. 2. As a result, we receive an explanation of how and why Harry had become such a personage and how he responded to his new acquaintances and popularity.

Thackeray made brief changes on the great majority of the surviving leaves (though not on fols. [9]–[15])[34] and also made a few in press. Of the latter, one of the most notable was the change of "bear" (fol. 2a) to "care"—"She would not care to read the volumes, over which her pretty actresses wept and thrilled a hundred years ago" (1:207)—for by making this emendation Thackeray was probably distracted from seeing an error in the same sentence, one that constitutes the chief "point" mentioned in booksellers' catalogues today: the erroneous reading "actresses," which was mistakenly set up by the compositor from the manuscript reading of "ancestresses." Thackeray also inserted in press the letter that now closes chapter 27—either to embody a fresh thought or to fill a gap consciously passed over during the composition of the now missing manuscript leaves, for the sentence that the letter follows and that may have existed in the missing manuscript already contains an introduction: "The end of the day's, and some succeeding days', sport may be gathered from the following letter, which was never delivered to the person to whom it was addressed, but found its way to America in the papers of Mr. Henry Warrington" (1:216). The five leaves on which the letter was written were set down by a secretary and then were numbered by Thackeray, starting with the page number on which the insertion was to begin: fols. 216, 217, 218 (originally 217), a second 218, and 219.[35] This letter lengthened chapter 27 by a page and thereby enabled the installment to fill its complement, but the letter also nicely ended the chapter by counterpoising against Harry's naïve success at cards the ominous intention of the worldly Lord March to reverse that good fortune.

In the case of the next three installments, our information concerning their composition essentially comes only from the evidence of the manuscript itself; here too there is considerable incompleteness. The first two and one-half chapters of number eight for June 1858 (chapters 29–33) survive in the Morgan manuscript, but the difficulties of following all the renumbering of their constituent leaves are such that one must be content with discussing the composition chiefly in terms of three portions of material: fols. 1, 1a, 1b, 2–4; fols. 5–10; and fols. 12–20. The previous installment had ended with Harry caught up in the way of the world at Tunbridge: playing, feasting, and drinking. Thackeray then apparently opened number eight with an account of how Harry met Sampson at an ordinary and established a new relationship with the parasitical clergyman by giving him shelter, gifts, and the nominal position of tutor (1:229–31). This narrative began on fol. 1b (originally fol. 1), first in Thackeray's hand and then in Anne's; it continued in her hand on what are now fols. 2–4 (the latter previously numbered fol. 3). Later Thackeray preceded it with additional material that gave a further account of Harry's pleasures at Tunbridge, together with news of how Colonel Wolfe told the Lamberts of the conversation he had had with Harry (in chapter 28) and how Colonel Lambert immediately planned a visit to the Wells with his family (1:225–28). Written down by Thackeray on what are now fols. 1 and 1a (earlier fols. 4, 5 and also 5, 6, 2), this became a separate chapter, the extremely short chapter 29.

The second portion, entirely in Thackeray's hand, showed Madame Bernstein's reception of Sampson, the splendor of Harry's mode of living, and the contrasting letters Harry sent home to his mother and to Mountain; this narrative took up fols. 5–6 (originally 4–5), 7–8, 9 (earlier 3, 7), and 10 (originally 4), becoming the last two-thirds of chapter 30 (1:231–36). The final portion was set down by Anne and then modified in two ways. First, the initial leaf or leaves, the text of which apparently ended with the first three syllables of the word "unobservant," was replaced by a leaf about two-thirds full in Thackeray's own hand (fol. 12).[36] Second, at the point where this narrative shifted from a discussion of aging and gradually less observant female dragons (fol. 14; 1:238) to an account of the amorous Duc de Lauzun, who failed to make a single conquest in America (fols. 17–18 [originally 15–16]; 1:239), Anne set down two leaves concerning the contrasting responses of the Lambert family and the Baroness Bernstein to Harry's bad reputation. These Thackeray numbered fols. 15 and 16, thereby necessitating the renumbering of the next two leaves as 17–18. After Anne had set down fol. 19 and most of 20, Thackeray wrote the final ten lines of the latter leaf himself and continued on fols. 21, presumably [22] (which is missing), and 23. The rest of chapter 31 is missing, as is all of chapter 32.[37]

The relatively few verbal changes made in manuscript are not particularly worthy of mention, except perhaps for the statement that Harry decorated his room "with pictures from Ovids Metamorphoses wh. would have made Madam Esmond open her eyes" (fols. 5–6)—a passage that was deleted, presumably because it was out of keeping with Harry's nature, and perhaps his mother's. In press, however, Thackeray made a number of significant alterations. Four additions were made to the text of chapter 29—not surprisingly, considering its extreme brevity. The first of them extended the account of Harry's response to the importuning mother of Cattarina, the opera-house siren. Originally, the hysterical mother had called upon Harry to tell him that a cruel bailiff had impounded all Cattarina's goods "for debt. Harry left softer people than himself to pay the debt: and ordered Gumbo to mark the old lady well, and never admit her into his lodgings again" (fol. 1a). Further thought gave this terse narrative needed fullness, however, for the scene had clearly been intended not to summarize so much as to illustrate the positive qualities of Harry's character: "for showing of what stuff he was made" (1:226). The mother now explained that Cattarina's goods were locked up for debt

and that her venerable father was at present languishing in a London gaol. Harry declared that between himself and the bailiff there could be no dealings, and that because he had had the good fortune to become known to Mademoiselle Cattarina, and to gratify her caprices by presenting her with various trinkets and knickknacks for which she had a fancy, he was not bound to pay the past debts of her family, and must decline being bail for her papa in London, or settling her outstanding accounts at Tunbridge. The Cattarina's mother first called him a monster and an ingrate, and then asked him, with a veteran smirk, why he did not take pay for the services he had rendered to the young person? At first, Mr. Warrington could not understand what the nature of the payment might be: but when that matter was explained by the old woman, the honest lad rose up in horror, to think that a woman should traffic in her child's dishonour, told her that he came from a country where the very savages would recoil from such a bargain; and, having bowed the old lady ceremoniously to the door, ordered Gumbo to mark her well, and never admit her to his lodgings again. No doubt she retired breathing vengeance against the Iroquois: no Turk or Persian, she declared, would treat a lady so: and she and her daughter retreated to London as soon as their anxious landlord would let them. (1:226–27)

This account is much more convincing, both because it shows Harry finally learning the nature of these people with whom he has been associating and because in place of Harry's abrupt dismissal of the woman we are shown more characteristic behavior—in this case, a thoroughly courteous disinclination to pay extortionate demands and an instinctive refusal to collect from an impoverished, if loose, woman the only payment she can make. He is quite ready to collect from a non-paying male card-player, however, and to prepare a little more clearly and fully for that immediately ensuing episode, Thackeray continued his addition: "Then Harry had his perils of gaming, as well as his perils of gallantry. A man who plays at bowls, as the phrase is, must expect to meet with rubbers." The ensuing phrase, "After dinner at the ordinary" (1:227), completed Thackeray's addition, following which Harry refused to play any further with Captain Batts, who then left town as soon as possible—like the ladies. As a consequence of this entire modification, the chapter was augmented by twenty-two printed lines.

In a second instance, two lines were added. Originally, upon finding that a calumny concerning himself and the opera-dancer had been repeated by Mr. Hector Buckler, Harry "publicly informed Mr. Buckler that the story was a falsehood" (fol. 1a). Now, however, he is given a specific justifying occasion as well: "Mr. Warrington stepped up to Mr. Buckler in the pump-room, where the latter was regaling a number of water-drinkers with the very calumny, and publicly informed Mr. Buckler that the story was a falsehood" (1:227). Two final examples added specific human actions that also give the narrative greater concreteness, first as Mrs. Lambert not only verbally acquiesced in her husband's suggestion of the Tunbridge visit but warmly responded to him and his motives for making it by "taking her husband's hand and pressing it" (1:228), and, second, as Thackeray ended the installment not with Lambert's speech agreeing to have a bottle of wine for supper, but with the note of the family actually gathering round their table together (1:228). Totalling twenty-six printed lines, these four additions extended the text of chapter 29 onto a fourth page, which now came to have twenty-three lines.

Two new passages also augmented chapters 30 and 31 in press, the former carrying the text of the chapter onto a new page. The middle of chapter 30 had explained how Harry took up Sampson and bounteously provided for him; a paragraph concerning Harry's opulent style of life at the Wells then followed (1:231–32), after which Thackeray made a somewhat abrupt shift to a sentence introducing Sampson's and Harry's letter to Madam Esmond: "And now from the following letter wh. is preserved in the Warrington correspondence it will be seen that Mr. Harry not only had dancing & fencing masters but likewise a tutor chaplain and secretary" (fol. 6). In press, Thackeray inserted ahead of this sentence a transitional passage that took up twenty-eight printed lines (1:232–33). He thereby not only extended the text of the chapter onto a new page that now has twenty-eight lines, but also gave a pointed account of Sampson's behavior as a toad-eater and provided suitably ironic narrative commentary on the pleasures of such "exceedingly fragrant, wholesome, and savoury eating" (1:233)—pleasures no longer enjoyed, for "no doubt there are no such people left in the world now" (1:232). Then, lest he be accused of inconsistency by imperceptive readers coming upon remarks in chapter 31 contrasting eighteenth- and nineteenth-century sycophancy, Thackeray added the following sentence in the latter chapter: "That was but satire just now, when we said there were no toad-eaters left in the world" (1:241). As a result of seeing this close link between the two passages, we can understand not only how Thackeray attempted to harmonize them but also how the latter gave rise to the former, which in turn led to a modification in the original passage. The effect is not so much repetitious as developmental, however, for we see from reading the two passages in sequence that Sampson's sycophancy is not only continued but varied, and that it is motivated not only by a life-long devotion to the profession of toad-eating but by a particular manipulative purpose that also goes well beyond what Harry can perceive.[38]

Only about the first half of the manuscript of number 9 for July 1858, all in Thackeray's hand, survives: chapter 33, "CONTAINS A SOLILO-QUY BY HESTER" (fols. 1–5); 34, "IN WHICH MR. WARRINGTON TREATS THE COMPANY WITH TEA AND A BALL" (fols. 6–10); and the opening portion of 35, "ENTANGLEMENTS" (fols. 11, 12, and the un-numbered lower half of [14]); the latter chapter is designated "Chap III." and given no title in manuscript, unlike its two predecessors. No notable difficulties or modifications appear in the manuscript, but sev-eral significant additions were made in press. A passage of thirty-nine lines (not counting slight modifications made to accommodate it) was inserted on 1:261–62; beginning, "but invited them for the next day" (1:261), and ending, "Miss Hester must proceed to make" (1:262), it showed Hetty's sharp-tongued comments to Harry about the boredom of dancing and Harry's hurt response to her impoliteness. By drama-tizing what had only been reported in the manuscript version—that when Harry came to drink tea, "Hetty was so curt, cruel, and snappish with him" (fol. 4)—Thackeray added another page to the text of chap-ter 33, which now has twenty-eight lines on its last page.

In chapter 34 a descriptive passage was cut in press after mention of the fact that minuets were called and performed by two or three couples: "the rest of the company sitting round and looking on, under the twilight illumination of a few sconces on the walls, and an iron hoop of wax-candles pendent from the centre of the dancing" (fol. 6). Thack-eray removed it, presumably because it interrupted his narrative, which immediately continued with a further account of the dancing. He also deleted a comment that inappropriately made Harry's aunt seem less acute and verbally agile than the particular circumstances re-vealed her to be: "says Madame de Bernstein, who saw but could not parry or comprehend some mischief in the other woman's counte-nance" (fol. 7). He evidently needed to lengthen his chapter consider-ably, however, for he added five passages in press. The first came after mention of the Countess of Yarmouth-Walmoden, whom George II "delighted to honour" (fol. 6; 1:265). At this point, Thackeray added a little over six lines relating how the Countess had earlier that day met Harry and invited him to play cards with her when she visited his entertainment that evening; beginning, "She had met Harry Warring-ton in the walks that morning," the passage concluded by mentioning how everyone congratulated Harry on his receiving this invitation.

Soon afterwards, Thackeray added sixty-one lines, beginning: "Harry's bow had been no lower than hospitality required" (1:266), and ending: "You are as bad as the rest" (1:267), that showed a variety of further responses to the Countess—notably Harry's—and included a brief scene in which Hetty, having chosen to be angry with Harry's politeness towards the Countess, tormented and infuriated him. A good deal had already been made in the manuscript account of people's comportment towards Madame Walmoden, conduct that helps provide us with a means for judging them; hence it became important to show us Harry's behavior. As a result of this addition we now see that he alone treated the Countess with courtesy devoid of flattery or insult and thus acted in a manner that attractively contrasts on the one hand with the servility of almost all his guests, and on the other hand with the rudeness of Hetty and the Duchess of Queensberry. Both of the latter angrily over-respond—Hetty with unbecoming sarcasm, and the Duchess with giggles and affected laughter that Thackeray introduced with this addition to qualify our admiration of her tough-minded frankness.[39] With artistic appropriateness, therefore, the augmented depiction of this portion of Harry's entertainment gave greater prominence to Harry by showing his behavior and by relating the events of that evening more closely to him.

In making his third addition, Thackeray expanded a portion of a scene involving Harry, the Baroness Bernstein, and the Duchess of Queensberry, where the latter welcomes Harry's statement that there are two or three other non-flatterers in the room and tells him: "Bring 'em to me, my dear Iroquois! Let us have a game of four—of honest men and women. I am sorry you cant play, my good Bernstein!" (fol. 7). After deleting the last sentence, presumably because it was too suddenly rude, Thackeray then expanded the exchange: "'that is to say, if we can find a couple more partners, Mr. Warrington!' 'Here are we three,' says the Baroness Bernstein, with a forced laugh; 'let us play a dummy.' 'Pray, madam, where is the third?' asks the old Duchess, looking round" (1:267–68).

The next augmentation provided dialogue that gave the title of one of the number's two steel etchings, "A VICE-QUEEN" (opposite 1:271), as Thackeray added four lines: "'If her ladyship were a queen, people could scarcely be more respectful to her,' says the Chaplain. 'Let us call her a vice-queen, parson,' says the Colonel, with a twinkle of his eye." Here Harry too was made to participate in the joke, for the manuscript reading of "She pocketted forty of my guineas at Quadrille" (fol. 10) became, "Her majesty pocketed forty of my guineas at quadrille" (1:271).

The final addition concluded chapter 34, for instead of ending with Lambert's bidding Harry farewell: "Mind that Sir—And herewith saluting the Chaplain and squeezing Harry very heartily by the hand the Colonel left him" (fol. 10), Thackeray deleted the last sentence and wrote the portion that now brings the chapter to a close by having Harry explain to Colonel Lambert his unwilling bondage to Maria, express his misogyny to Parson Sampson, and tantalizingly allude to his missing property. These sixty-two lines, together with the four previous additions, increased the chapter's length by almost three full pages.

A number of smaller changes were also made in press, of which the following may serve as examples. In chapter 33 Colonel Lambert's allusion to a journey by way of Prester John's country, or "Africa" (originally "China" [fol. 2]), became "Persia" (1:258), and "pained" (fol. 4) became "still farther pained" (1:262), in keeping with the second major addition (1:261–62), which includes Hetty's tart remarks to Harry. A phrase concerning Hetty's pain—"there will that Care be tearing at her little heart, who has given . . . respite" (fol. 5)—was repositioned to tighten the syntax: "there, tearing at her little heart, will that Care be, which has given . . . respite" (1:263). In chapter 34 an erroneous reading, "and all" (fol. 6), was changed to "for all" (1:264), and in a reply of the Baroness Bernstein to the Duchess of Queensberry, the somewhat excited expression "to attack" (fol. 7) was replaced by the more controlled "to doubt" (1:268). In chapter 35 Thackeray's contempt for Edmund Yates expressed itself with greater effectiveness: "my gallant glorious young Grubstreet!" (fol. 11) became the more urbanely ironic "my eminent young Grubstreet!" (1:274) and, similarly, "Dear accomplished youth!" (fol. 11) was deleted. So too, "Harry is too modest or too indifferent to discover it for himself. He regards her as a child, a wilful little sister, and plays and prattles with her" (fol. 12) became simply, "Harry is too much preoccupied to discover it for himself" (1:274). Two sentences later the idea was extended as Thackeray added a few words: "He has, perhaps, a care of his own" (1:274). Correspondingly, in the following paragraph, Thackeray altered "drinks his bottle with his usual appetite & gaiety" (fol. 12) to "calls fiercely for his bottle" (1:275), thereby showing the continuing effect of the inner disturbance that had been openly revealed by Harry's declaration of misogyny in the scene added in press to the end of the previous chapter (1:271–72). Even more than usual, therefore, Thackeray's modifications of number 9 were both extensive and carefully minute.

The manuscript of number ten for August 1858—the last surviving manuscript portion of volume 1—contains most of the text of the installment's first three chapters, 37–39, but several misnumberings and lacunae in each of these chapters make it somewhat difficult to discuss. Seven leaves survive from chapter 37, "IN WHICH VARIOUS MATCHES ARE FOUGHT": fols. 2 (WMT), 3 and 5 (a secretary, fol. 5 continuing from 3 in mid-sentence without any break), and 6–9 (WMT). Presumably because he needed to do historical research before he composed the account of the Figg-Sutton fight, Thackeray seems to have begun the chapter on fol. 6 (earlier fol. 1): "Harry pronounced this indeed to be something like sport" (see 1:291). After that narrative had been set down, Thackeray added in his own hand the last three lines on fol. 5, which connect with his previously composed account of Harry's departure at the end of the fight. Chapter 38, "SAMPSON AND THE PHILISTINES," which already has its title in the manuscript, and 39, "HARRY TO THE RESCUE," were each written down by Thackeray essentially in their present state. The former was apparently composed on seven leaves, of which five survive: fols. 10–13 and [14], the latter having been misnumbered "15" in pencil by someone—perhaps the printer—who also erroneously added "14" to the already numbered fol. 13. Fols. 17–19 and 23–24 survive from the final chapter and conclude the manuscript. The bottom of fol. 18 and all of fols. 20–22 are missing, as is the entire last chapter.

A number of brief changes were made in press, the most substantial of which were three additions of from three to seventeen lines. The first occurred in chapter 37 just after Lord March had dismissed the news about Lady Maria's imprisonment and taken up his cards again; it extended Betty's plea to Harry and gave a little more point to Lord

March's subsequent cry that she hold her tongue (fol. 8): "O, Mr. Harry! you won't be a going on with your cards, when my lady calls out to you to come and help her! Your honour used to come quick enough when my lady used to send me to fetch you at Castlewood!" (1:294). The last two additions were made to chapter 38. In the first of these instances, Thackeray had originally discussed arrangements for the sermon that Sampson was to preach before the company at Tunbridge that was to include Lady Yarmouth: "and so we may be sure that Mr. Sampson prepared his very best discourse for her hearing" (fol. 11). Thackeray then went on: "Sampson was the domestic chaplain of Madame Bernstein's nephew. The two ladies of the Esmond family patronized the preacher. On the day of the sermon the Baroness had a little breakfast in his honour, at wh. Sampson made his appearance. rosy & handsome, with a fresh flowered wig, and a smart rustling new cassock, wh. he had on credit from some church-admiring mercer at the Wells" (fol. 12). Urged by the necessity of extending the chapter and apparently aware of the usefulness of a transition between the account of Sampson's preparations and of the sermon day itself, Thackeray inserted a passage of seventeen lines that also served a significant new artistic function. After mention of Sampson's preparations for Lady Yarmouth's hearing, there now came the analogy of Trotter the curate, also hoping for advancement from a member of his audience, whose efforts to be impressive are suddenly dashed by the sound of "the Right Honourable Lord Naseby, snoring in the pew by the fire! And poor Trotter's visionary mitre disappears with the music" (1:299). The passage not only lengthened Thackeray's narrative and helped bridge two portions of it but also provided an amusing prefiguration of what was to be Sampson's own interrupted and doomed glory, the unappreciative audience in his case being the bailiffs.

The final addition concerned the attempts of Betty and Lady Maria to find sufficient means for the maid to seek Harry in London. In manuscript, the account read simply: "Mrs. Betty came over to console her mistress: and I suppose they found money enough between them to pay for the hire of a post-chaise in wh. Mrs. Betty whisked up to London" (fol. 15). In press, however, Thackeray crossed out the words following "I suppose" and substituted instead: "the two poor women cast about for money enough to provide a horse and chaise for Mrs. Betty" (1:302). At this point he also added several sentences concerning the actual means by which Lady Maria was enabled to help Betty obtain money, thereby explaining how a woman incarcerated for debt could yet provide for her maid's journey. Thackeray used the passage to tie a minor loose knot, but its chief significance came from its providing eleven more printed lines; hence, with the seventeen lines of the chapter's other addition, it extended the text onto a ninth page that finally contained twenty lines of print.

Pausing to consider larger aspects of structure in volume 1, one finds evidence not only in the text itself but also in two documents that happen to have survived from among the "notes" that Anne Thackeray Ritchie tells us "my father used to make . . . for his work, not only in writing, but with his brush and pencil." She quotes the first of these notes, which contains five thematic statements concerning the novel's opening portion:

> Madam Esmond tries to dominate.
> Her idea that people are in love with her.
> Her respect for her elder.
> Her passionate love for her younger son.
> Her heroism during the siege.
>   (Centenary Biographical Edn., 16: xxxiv, xxxviii)

In the actual novel, the first four of these motifs appear in the two opening installments, while Madam Esmond's heroism during the siege, which had been briefly mentioned in the preface to *Esmond* as the occasion on which she lost her husband, remained undeveloped. As Thackeray gave novelistic embodiment to these statements, he showed us at first not Madam Esmond *trying* to dominate, but actually doing so: "She wrote herself Esmond Warrington, but was universally called, Madam Esmond of Castlewood, when after her father's decease she came to rule over that domain" (1:23). "The truth is, little Madam Esmond never came near man or woman, but she tried to domineer over them" (1:28). These are the keynotes of the early American narrative and are sounded as we observe her conduct with her neighbors, her servants, and especially her sons. Although she successfully carries through her early purposes of punishing Gumbo (1:24) and unjustly denouncing Mr. Draper (1:30), her high-handedness produces alienation from George and noticeable partiality for Harry. When we eventually see her actually trying to dominate, by reasserting her authority through the boy's tutor, Thackeray uses the occasion to reveal the limits of her power, for here George successfully defies her and thereby prompts her admiration (1:33–42)—the third of Thackeray's outlined themes, which he later restates in language much like that in his note: "She admired and respected the elder, but she felt that she loved the younger boy with all the passion of her heart" (1:54). Previously her respect for George has been for his position as the "elder" twin, but here in the chapter, "FAMILY JARS," she discovers her respect for him as a human individual. Finally, we see that Thackeray transforms the second theme, for in the novel she does not so much believe people are in love with her as she feels that all their admiration is mere justice: "There was no amount of compliment which she would not graciously receive and take as her due. Her little foible was so well known that the wags used to practise upon it" (1:35).

After devoting the latter half of number one and the opening portion of the next serial installment to Madam Esmond's dominance and attempted dominance, Thackeray went on in numbers two and three to develop George's jealousy of Washington and to place the boys' lives in a historical context that included Quebec, Washington's military career, and Braddock's defeat—the latter event resulting in George's disappearance and Harry's temporary emergence as heir of the Virginian estate. As we saw, moreover, Thackeray placed the whole American narrative (chapters 3–13) in a further context by offering it as a summary of Harry's account to the Baroness Bernstein on his arrival at the English Castlewood. The plot dealing with Harry's adventures in England thereby becomes primary, beginning the first installment and then continuing in number four, where the American narrative ends and Harry comes to be entangled not only with Will Esmond but with Sampson, Lord Castlewood, and especially Lady Maria.

Amid a thematic counterpoise of continuity and discontinuity in the first four installments, relatives battle with each other as they both acknowledge and reject kinship. At first Harry finds a cold reception in England, but by the end of number one he has discovered a new relative: a half-aunt whom he had been unable to identify from her youthful portrait because she both is and is not Beatrix Esmond. As His Majesty's troops receive an ambiguous reception in the colonies, George rejects throughout number two what he mistakenly sees as the proposed foster-fatherhood of Washington, concluding with the ironic cry to Harry: "Let us upstairs at once, kneel down as becomes us, and say, 'Dear papa, welcome to your house of Castlewood'" (1:64). In number three, George's firmly purposed duel with Washington is aborted and his determined accompaniment of Braddock in place of Harry leads at the close of the installment not only to another abortive ending but to another illusion: the apparent death of George and the substitution of Harry as heir. In the following installment, as a result of George's disappearance and Madam Esmond's even more oppressive dominance at Castlewood, Harry reluctantly puts on his suit of mourning but willingly parts from his mother. He soon becomes the protégé of his English half-aunt and then, as the peaceful weapon of the long-bow is brought into play by Gumbo, Harry finds increasing favor with the Castlewood family, which sets about preparing metaphorical ambuscades for him. Whereas number three had concluded with news of Braddock's defeat and the reported death of George, number four ends with an equally striking *coup de théâtre* when we suddenly discover Harry's infatuation with Lady Maria, as his unwillingness to leave her causes him to anger his new-found half-aunt by declining to accompany the Baroness Bernstein to Tunbridge, and as Maria conceals her joy by demurely embroidering—an action that figuratively embodies her successful contriving. By the end of the first four installments, then, Thackeray has brought Harry to England, completed his retrospective American narrative, and entangled him in the meshes of the Castlewood family, especially Maria's.

As one moves on to consider the structure of the remaining eight installments of volume 1, especially numbers five through ten, which appeared between March and August 1858, several supplementary documents become relevant. While at work in November 1858 upon number fourteen, in which Harry finally gets free from Maria, Thackeray wrote to a friend that his novel "ought to have been at its present stage of the story at No. X. I dawdled fatally between V. and X" (*Letters*, 4:115). In March 1859 he felt he had "dawdled so that the American part wh. was to have been in 12 numbers now has dwindled to 6" (*Letters*, 4:135). In September 1859 he said "About the 4th. number, . . . I got all my people into a fatal groove through wh. I was obliged to see them."[40] Although his meaning is not entirely clear, he seems to be suggesting that the material from about six installments (five through ten) ought to have been condensed into two so that the four subsequent installments (eleven through fourteen) would have filled up the space saved. This suggests what the "fatal groove" was, but a recently discovered outline offers further evidence. Another of Thackeray's "notes," it is written in his upright hand on the upper three-quarters of a leaf and reads as follows:

Harry agitated by pangs of remorse determines to marry Maria.

He leads a great life in London & spends his own & his brothers patrimony there, the luck turning against him.

⟨———⟩

The young Rachel is lost in her voyage from America with Captain Franks on board

———

Franks was bringing the news of GEORGES return.

George arrives suddenly (having quarreled with his mother at home) in the midst of some grand scrape of Harry's—rescues him, shows his spirit.

Has probably to work ⟨and⟩ his way by his wits—meets with these latter—toils and struggles to get on—to keep his brother & family. Gumbo & Sady probably sell themselves to benefit their masters.. Warrington relations die & bring relief.

In the midst of his struggles, he loves Fanny. Maria deserts ⟨George⟩ Harry ⟨fond⟩ when he has lost his money—Fanny almost likes George—but parson Sampson who has received an injury from the family, produces Maria's intercepted letters in wh. her sisters shameful intrigues with *an august personage* are laid bare.

⟨George has previously ⟨⟨and⟩⟩ been intimate with his Warrington relations, may be entering parliament &c.⟩

⟨Harry enters the army & sails for Quebec wh. ought to end Vol 1.⟩

Harry enters the army, and the Siege of Quebec ends the volume.

———

Georges affair with Fanny may commence after Harrys departure for Quebec. and with the 2d. volume.[41]

We cannot positively identify the nature of this outline, nor date it with certainty. It might be a continuation of an outline begun on another leaf for the entire first volume, or a replacement for the latter portion of an earlier outline for much or all of the volume, or a supplement to an earlier outline for the initial installments. It might, furthermore, have been set down either before or during composition of the first volume. Amid these uncertainties, what chiefly strikes one is a number of discrepancies between this sketch and what finally emerged from the long process of composition—discrepancies resulting from a change in the planned sequence of events, in the actual nature of the events themselves, and especially in their position in the novel, for many of them occur in the second volume instead of the first. Before taking up the discrepancies, however, one might attempt to understand what Thackeray had in mind when he wrote out this sketch.

Unfortunately, we do not have grounds for knowing why Harry is to be agitated by pangs of remorse, nor even where he is when he feels these pangs and determines to marry Maria. Is it at Castlewood or at Tunbridge? Is there, in fact, even to be a visit to Tunbridge, or is Harry to proceed from Castlewood directly to London? We can see only that he suffers remorse—presumably at having felt or shown a cooling of his ardor for Maria—and that he resolves to remove the cause of his remorse by marrying her. A narrative of the young greenhorn's "great life" in London is then to follow, marked at first by profuse expenditure and very likely by success in gaining fashionable associates and in experiencing the pleasures of gaming, but then by dissipation of both George's and his own patrimony through his opulent, impulsive style of living and the inevitable turn of the luck against him. News of George's survival, escape from Fort Duquesne, and return home is to be sent from Virginia, but not to reach Harry because of the loss of the ship carrying it, the *Young Rachel*. Accordingly, Harry is not to learn of his brother's survival until George, having quarreled with Madam Esmond, suddenly arrives in England to rescue Harry from a "grand scrape," the nature of which Thackeray leaves notably unspecified. In short, Thackeray seems to be sketching the outlines of plot developments, not a detailed narrative sequence. There is no indication that the reader is to learn of George's survival before Harry does—only that Harry is to be in a "grand scrape" and that George is to show "his spirit"—in rescuing Harry, or afterwards, or both; the lack of a clearly defined "scrape" inhibits further specificity.

Thackeray's tentativeness at this point appears again in the following phrases, where the word "probably" occurs twice. Because Harry has spent George's patrimony as well as his own and because George has quarreled with his mother, he has to support himself by his wits, to toil and struggle in order "to get on." Here we see that Thackeray clearly intends to center his narrative on George after the latter's arrival in England but is not sure of the main direction of George's life and the kind of activity that will characterize it. But what does Thackeray mean by "meets with these latter"? The word "these" presumably indicates either his toils and struggles, or his wits, or both—that is, the successful expression, which the struggles have called forth, of this defining quality of his character. George's difficulties are to provide him with the means of discovering what he is made of and what he can do in the world. One can readily understand that George labors to provide subsistence for Harry and himself, but the phrase "& family" is puzzling. Neither George or Harry has a family at this point and it is difficult to picture Madam Esmond needing support, even after the loss of the *Young Rachel*. One can only infer that Thackeray's mind is leaping ahead to George's own subsequent marriage and that the novelist is projecting a whole strand of plot connected with George rather than indicating his intention to narrate the events of this plot in immediate sequence. One might even feel that "latter" could be a misspelling for "later." However we interpret this word, we can see that Thackeray follows out developments of George's struggle before turning back to events that are to take place earlier in time and probably earlier in narrative sequence. As the financial straits become more serious, Gumbo and Sady "probably sell themselves to benefit their masters." Then, after a certain period of time, the "Warrington relations die & bring relief"—as George undoubtedly inherits the title and property.

At this point, Thackeray again drops back in time, on this occasion to take up George's romantic life and to tie up a strand concerning Harry's involvement with Maria (though the novelist momentarily confuses George's name with Harry's, as he does in the novel's manuscript): "In the midst of his struggles, he loves Fanny. Maria deserts ⟨George⟩ Harry ⟨fond⟩ when he has lost his money." Harry is therefore to be saved from Maria (who may now be able to afford emotion) by a combination of his own naïveté and extravagance, together with outer circumstances that follow as a consequence of these qualities, while George is to be saved from Fanny by the fortuitous intervention of Sampson, who has not only opportunely quarreled with the Castlewood family but also come into fortunate possession of letters detailing Fanny's incriminating behavior with a great personage, somewhat in the manner of Beatrix Esmond. Thackeray then drops back in time once more to sketch a possible career for George by mentioning his previous intimacy with his Warrington relations, thereby creating the possibility that George "may be" going to take a seat in Parliament, "&c."—whatever that tantalizing *etcetera* may mean. After cancelling these two phrases concerning George, however, Thackeray returns to Harry, indicating that Harry will enter the army, sail for Canada, and be present at Wolfe's siege of Quebec, which is to end the twelfth installment and the first volume. Finally, Thackeray decides that George's involvement with Fanny will not take place in the first volume but will instead begin in the second. We thereby see again that this outline served the novelist as a means both of working out various separate plots of the novel and also of deciding how certain sequences from different plots would follow each other in narrative order. On the whole, however, the sketch served less as a tracing of narrative sequence than as a means of discovering some of the larger patterns of plot development.

As we compare this outline with the rest of volume 1, we may recall that already in the second installment Thackeray has provided a potential future wife for Harry in the figure of little Fanny Mountain, who is introduced in a manner that connects her with Harry, as she delightedly crows at his satirical mimicry of Mr. Ward and laughs at a subsequent joke in which Harry participates. She is mentioned three times in the next installment, once as Harry bowdlerizes on her behalf a passage of a letter he is reading aloud in her presence (1:93). In addition, Thackeray mentions her twice in number four—the same installment in which Fanny Esmond's incipient flirtation with Harry is firmly quashed by Lady Castlewood (1:108–10), thereby inadvertently clearing the path for Maria, who sets to work immediately after Gumbo begins to exaggerate Harry's wealth. The possibilities of the Harry–Fanny Mountain relationship are further extended in number five, where he sends her a kiss (1:143–44); in eight, where he does so again (1:235); in eleven, where the Warrington daughter who most resembles Fanny becomes his especial favorite (1:339); and in twelve, where he speculates about possible marriage to Fanny (1:371). This is all in possible keeping with Thackeray's intentions when he set down the outline, as is Lady Castlewood's putting an end to her daughter Fanny's flirtation with Harry in number four, since Fanny Esmond is thereby potentially available for George. So too is Madame Bernstein's neat undermining in the next installment of Harry's infatuation for Maria, by which Thackeray establishes a basis for Harry's subsequent feelings of guilt.

At the same time, however, we notice that in number five Thackeray initiates developments that take him away from the events and sequences of the outline—especially by sending Harry upon the journey to Tunbridge after all, and even more by giving him into the care of people not even mentioned in the outline: the Lamberts (see "WEL-COME," opposite 1:160, which depicts in the foreground Martin Lambert and a female figure—probably Mrs. Lambert—and in the background the outline of another female figure). In fact, of all the discrepancies between the outline and the published novel, the omission of the Lambert family is the most striking. This strongly suggests that the outline was set down before the composition of number five, which took place during February 1858. A second omission, almost as striking, is the lack of any mention of events at Tunbridge, for which Harry sets out at the end of number five and where he remains from the end of number six until almost the end of number ten. It very much appears, therefore, that during these five and one-half installments—one-fifth of the novel—Thackeray to a large extent diverged significantly from his outline and progressed slowly through the new "groove."

His reasons for doing so seem clear. First we have to learn of the actual courtship and its reasons, which we do from some of Thackeray's finest writing and one of his most telling illustrations, "GATHER YE ROSEBUDS WHILE YE MAY," where he wittily shows Harry literally gathering his rosebud while Maria metaphorically gathers hers. As the novelist explains his inability to write a new story because Harry and Maria are acting in the age-old way of infatuation and encouragement, Thackeray reaffirms the continuing experiential reality of the "OLD STORY" (1:137). Increasingly at Castlewood, Harry is the subject of intrigue, not only as Maria entangles him, but also as Lord Castlewood maneuvers to promote the marriage, as Sampson enlists in the cause, as the Baroness Bernstein attempts to subvert it, and as Will (anticipating Lord Castlewood's later behavior) cheats Harry—on this occasion by substituting a broken-down horse that soon flings its victim to the ground in front of Lambert's door. This is Harry's first fall, which foreshadows his second, at the end of number eleven, after he is fleeced by Will's brother. On both occasions, moreover, Lambert is present to take him up and on both occasions Harry immediately enters the Lambert house—the second time with George, who there finds his future wife, Theo.

Number six hovers about Oakhurst before completing the movement to Tunbridge. In contrast to the Castlewoods, and later to Sir Miles Warrington's family, Thackeray created the Lambert family, whose members are close-knit by love and therefore essentially self-reliant in their dealings with the world. The girls offer Harry, and later, George, spritely and warm personal relationships; Mrs. Lambert offers a motherly responsiveness that notably contrasts with Madam Esmond's behavior; and Colonel Lambert offers a benevolent fatherliness and a figure for partial emulation that the boys have never had, George especially having fiercely rejected two earlier approximations of such a figure: Mr. Ward and Mr. Washington. As a soldier, Lambert also serves to introduce Harry to military men like Wolfe, whom Harry will accompany to Quebec.

Almost as soon as Harry is taken into this household, warm-hearted efforts at match-making are begun by Mrs. Lambert and are benevolently mocked by Lambert comically playing Orgon to Theo's Mariane, as he addresses her concerning marriage to their guest—who, though not Tartuffe, is yet an imposter unwittingly standing in place of his brother, Theo's future husband. Indeed, in retrospect we can sense here Thackeray's intention to marry George to Theo, for the novelist both shows us her disappointment in Harry and tells us that she is someone of whom we will see a great deal (1:174). But Harry's brief stay at Oakhurst is significant for himself as well as for George, since his experience here is deeply educative. Having escaped from his narrow Virginian atmosphere and the threatening confinements of the English Castlewood, he finds himself "in the midst of a circle where everything about him was incomparably gayer, brighter, and more free" (1:182), and he finds the basis for a new continuity: "Perhaps he had never, since his grandfather's death, been in such good company" (1:181). What he has not yet discovered is the contrast at Tunbridge and London that will confirm this experience and fully reveal its meaning. In leaving Oakhurst, Harry in fact goes off as if to school (1:184). The meeting with Wolfe establishes the basis for a future career, but meanwhile Harry arrives in Tunbridge, where, in the Baroness Bernstein's house, he is in the opposite of Oakhurst (1:192).

During numbers seven and eight, most of nine, and part of ten, Harry remains at the fashionable spa. Tunbridge offers an easily accessible microcosm of life—especially fashionable life—from the King's mistress to inferior hangers-on like Jack Morris and Cattarina. In this place of resort, Harry not only serves as the center around whom considerable intrigue takes place, and makes his entrance into a thronging

English public world, but also meets a number of characters who will function later in the novel, like Madame Walmoden and Lord March of the fashionable world, and Samuel Johnson, who will come to figure in the literary life of Harry's brother. In Tunbridge, as the Fortunate Youth, Harry will not only enjoy the misleading success of a lucky novice but will gain entry to the great world of London, where he and later his brother will experience not only the good fortune that can be provided by luck and friendly patrons but, even more, the fundamental intractability of life. The Tunbridge installments also provide Thackeray with an opportunity of showing in a usefully extended way Harry's positive qualities—especially his courage, his forthright integrity, and his charming good nature—before exhibiting his foolish and moody collapse in London. For all this and more, these five installments provide significant embodiment and preparation.

Even if one considers only the pattern of major incidents in this portion of the novel, it is difficult to imagine how Thackeray could satisfactorily have compressed into two serial parts such significant events as the following: Madame Bernstein's maneuvering, Harry's courtship of Maria, the settling of Harry's accounts with Will and Sampson, and Harry's disenchantment with Maria (number five); his stay at Oakhurst, where he meets the Lambert family and wins their affection, his departure from Oakhurst, his meeting with Wolfe, his arrival at Tunbridge, and his gaining a reputation as a man of wealth (number six); his making new acquaintances at Tunbridge, plunging into fashionable dissipation, and winning the name of the Fortunate Youth (number seven); his renewal of acquaintance with Sampson and the Lamberts, his unhappy reaffirmation of his commitment to Maria, and Hetty's unintentional acknowledgement of her love for him (number eight); Hetty's unhappiness, Harry's acquaintance with Madame Walmoden, his aunt's battle with Lady Maria over Harry, her unsuccessful attempts to steal Harry's letter proposing marriage, and her dispatch of Harry to London (number nine); Madame Bernstein's retrieval of Harry's letter from Maria, Harry's refusal to retract his promise, his final departure from Tunbridge, his quarrel with Will, and his immersion in London pleasures (number ten). No doubt some tightening of the whole narrative was theoretically possible, but nothing approaching the amount implied by Thackeray's impatient comments. When he made them, the novelist appears to have been not only too harsh but also too much attached to his original outline to consider in detail the contributions made by the Oakhurst and Tunbridge installments and the implications of curtailing them so severely.

Nowhere in this portion of the published novel does Harry remorsefully determine to marry Maria. He refuses to repudiate her, but he also decides to put off the marriage indefinitely. The only remorse he feels comes from his recognition that his proposal to Maria has been a mistake. As he sets out alone on an excursion to London in the ninth installment, he is "very gay and happy, if it must be owned, to be rid of his elderly attachment. Yes. There was no help for it. At Castlewood, on one unlucky evening, he had made an offer of his heart and himself to his mature cousin, and she had accepted the foolish lad's offer. But the marriage now was out of the question. He must consult his mother. She was the mistress for life of the Virginian property. Of course, she would refuse her consent to such a union. The thought of it was deferred to a late period. Meanwhile, it hung like a weight round the young man's neck, and caused him no small remorse and disquiet" (1:285).

The excursion is only a brief one, however, for Harry must soon return to Tunbridge to rescue Maria (1:295), accompany her back to Castlewood, and settle accounts with Will Esmond (1:314–17), thereby concluding Thackeray's lengthy divergence from his outline. The novelist still had not brought Harry to the point of a remorseful decision to marry Maria, but after establishing an affectionate relationship between the Lamberts and Harry, and after introducing Harry at Tunbridge to the "OTIUM SINE DIGNITATE" (1:225) of fashionable English life, Thackeray was ready at the end of number ten to carry out his intention of plunging Harry into the dissipations of a great life in London:

> By the time he reached London again, almost all the four-and-forty pounds which we have seen that he possessed at Tunbridge had slipped out of his pocket, and farther supplies were necessary. Regarding these he made himself presently easy. There were the two sums of £5000 in his own and his brother's name, of which he was the master. He would take up a little money, and with a run or two of good luck at play he could easily replace it. Meantime he must live in a manner becoming his station. . . . He sought out proper lodgings at the court end of the town, and fixed on some apartments in Bond Street, where he and Gumbo installed themselves, his horses standing at a neighbouring livery stable. And now

tailors, mercers, and shoemakers were put in requisition. . . . He figured in the Ring in his phaeton. Reports of his great wealth had long since preceded him to London, and not a little curiosity was excited about the fortunate Virginian. (1:317–18)

An economy of narrative similar to what is found in this passage follows in number eleven (1:321–52), which shows not only Harry's rise but also his fall. Harry's life in London now comes to represent the culmination of his life at Castlewood, where he was cheated, and at Tunbridge, where his idle apprenticeship to life (1:211) was fully begun, for now he reaps the fruits of the seeds sown by the fool who committed himself to "THE WAY OF THE WORLD" (1:218). After "RAKE'S PROGRESS" (1:321), "FORTUNATUS NIMIUM" (1:329), and "IN WHICH HARRY FLIES HIGH" (1:335), there follows "WHAT MIGHT, PERHAPS, HAVE BEEN EXPECTED" (1:343). In accordance with the outline, Harry's luck turns, but—the novel here departing from the outline— he runs through only his own patrimony (2:155). Then, after being cheated in London by Castlewood, Harry is taken by the very same bailiffs who had apprehended Maria in Tunbridge. Similarly, as Harry had earlier rescued Maria from the bailiffs at Tunbridge, so in number twelve George arrives to free him from confinement. The general formulation of the outline for Harry's rescue in London had helped Thackeray to create specific events for Tunbridge, but these in turn helped the novelist to decide upon the exact nature of Harry's "grand scrape."

Other influences of the outline upon Thackeray's composition of the Tunbridge installments can also be detected—several in modified form, as one might expect. The *Young Rachel* is not lost, but another Virginia ship, the *Lovely Sally*, has "been taken in sight of port by a French privateer" (1:288)—together, perhaps, with the letter carrying news of George's escape (2:2). A more notable modification concerns Sampson and Maria's intercepted letters. In the outline, George frees Harry, struggles to support himself and his brother, and—after Harry's departure for Canada—falls in love with Fanny Esmond, only to be saved by Sampson, "who has received an injury from the family" and who "produces Maria's intercepted letters in wh. her sisters shameful intrigues with *an august personage* are laid bare." By introducing the Lambert girls into the novel, however, Thackeray not only provided a tart relationship for Harry in young Hetty, but also a future wife for George in Theo. Hetty, of course, contrasts with Maria Esmond, for though Maria has full respect only for Harry's alleged wealth and can feel for him merely a limited, if genuine, fondness, Hetty does not sufficiently respect Harry himself; therefore, though she falls in love with him she resolves to suppress her love. The way is thereby kept open by Thackeray for a marriage between Harry and Fanny Mountain. Moreover, with the creation of Theo as a wife for George, Thackeray did not need to develop the character of Fanny Esmond. Hence Fanny's intrigues are never specifically identified; it is now Maria who is mentioned as having been "*au mieux* with the late Prince of Wales," the gossip being retailed not in one of Maria's letters, naturally, but in Walpole's (1:320).[42]

Thackeray carried out his intention of having Maria write incriminating letters, but he had her incriminate not only Fanny (1:308) but the whole family (1:276), and he had Maria send the letters to Harry rather than to some other correspondent, as may seem implied by the outline. The intercepting takes place at Tunbridge, moreover, when Sampson—far from having received an injury from the family—is acting as Lord Castlewood's agent, and through his theft of the letters is protecting the family from public exposure of its secrets. In the published novel, furthermore, Thackeray carries the intrigue several delightfully comic steps forward. The really damaging letter appears for a time to be Harry's proposal to Maria, who urgently guards it in a little bag under her stays. The Baroness Bernstein then becomes the chief interceptor, for she not only arranges to have Maria's letters purloined from Sampson but also sets the bailiffs against her own niece and chortlingly seizes the bag herself from the prostrate Maria. This riotous and ironic sequence then ends in typically Thackerayan fashion as the novelist empties the melodrama of all its content by having Harry honorably reaffirm his pledge—making it worth more than the paper it is written on and confounding his aunt's machinations. Maria has her own secrets, of course, like Fanny and the rest of the family, but although both Sampson (1:246) and the Baroness Bernstein (1:281–82) know these secrets, Harry refuses to listen (1:311) when the Baroness threatens to reveal them.

Influences of the outline are also apparent in numbers eleven and twelve of the published novel. The first instance reflects preparation for George's inheritance of the baronetcy, as Sir Miles tells Harry in number eleven that if young Miles were to die, the title would descend to Harry (1:339), and as George's arrival in number twelve again es-

tablishes his own priority. Secondly, Thackeray has Harry look ahead
to future service in the army, though at this point Harry can only
despairingly see a role as a recruit (1:349). Taking up the suggestion
that Gumbo and Sady might sell themselves to benefit their masters
during George's later struggles to support himself and Harry—a melodramatic event that Thackeray ultimately rejected—the novelist introduces the subject earlier, during Harry's confinement: "Gumbo
. . . flung himself, roaring with grief, at Harry's feet: and with a thousand vows of fidelity, expressed himself ready to die, to sell himself
into slavery over again, to do anything to rescue his beloved Master
Harry from this calamitous position. Harry was touched with the lad's
expressions of affection, and told him to get up from the ground where
he was grovelling on his knees, embracing his master's. 'All you have
to do, sir, is to give me my clothes to dress, and to hold your tongue
about this business. Mind you, not a word, sir, about it to anybody!'
says Mr. Warrington, severely" (1:361). Thackeray thereby makes
the suggestion a comically melodramatic aspect of Gumbo's character,
as well as a sign of his affection, rather than an event of the plot, and
the novelist adds the further comic perspective of Harry's apprehensiveness at the social embarrassment that such an act would cause him.

In the volume's last installment, estrangement finally develops between Sampson and the Castlewood family (1:350), as Castlewood,
who has just won a large sum from Harry, claims he has no money to
pay Sampson his three years' salary, even at a time of pressing need,
nor to free the imprisoned Harry, Sampson's benefactor. Though
Sampson continues in the family's service for a time, the alienation
produced in number twelve eventually leads to an open break. Finally,
Harry's remorseful determination to marry Maria seems at last to
occur. Harry is ashamed that he has let her deliberately entrap him
and take "unfair advantage of him, as her brother had at play" (1:378),
but when she comes to his place of confinement, feigning love by following her brother's strategic advice and returning with elaborate protestations of affection Harry's gifts to her (which cannot possibly pay
his debts but which she hopes will revitalize her chances for the Virginia establishment), Harry succumbs to her melodramatic artifice.
Even here, however, Harry's remorse at his inner alienation must be
inferred by readers, for we are told only that the largely deluded
Harry is "strangely agitated and immensely touched," and that he in-
articulately expresses "his gratitude, his affection, his emotion"

(1:379). So too, the outline's phrase, "determines to marry Maria," is fulfilled only to the extent that he promises to inform his mother "of all her goodness" (1:379) and, after Maria has left, cries out to himself— not without a touch of staginess—"'What? Shall she trust me, and I desert her?' says Harry, stalking up and down his room in his flowing, rustling brocade. 'Dear, faithful, generous woman! If I lie in prison for years, I'll be true to her'" (1:381). After all the comical posturings and all the inflated rages, sobs, and raptures uttered in this installment, especially in its final chapter, the arrival of George comes as a sardonically appropriate revelation and relief.

Although the Tunbridge installments made often lively and significant contributions to his novel, Thackeray's decision to devote so much space to them inevitably resulted in a volume with a structure considerably different from the one sketched on the outline. Hence, instead of ending with Harry's participation in the victory of Wolfe at the siege of Quebec, it concluded with George's arrival to rescue Harry from confinement for debt—an event that seems more appropriate to the typical mock-heroic diminishments of a Thackerayan novel. As a consequence of Thackeray's departure from the outline, he had to use a portion of volume 2 for matters that he had not yet been able to narrate. These included Harry's escape from Maria, his entrance into the army, and his participation in the siege of Quebec, as well as George's struggles, his love affair, and his inheritance of the baronetcy—as we shall see.

7

The Virginians

Installments 13, 17–18, 20–24

In composing number thirteen of *The Virginians*, the installment for November 1858, Thackeray was reasonably ahead of his deadline. After having finished the previous installment by 16 September in Paris (*Letters*, 4:394), he plunged ahead into number thirteen and by the 20th of the month wrote, "I have done more work in a week than I do in 2 months at home" (*Letters*, 4:111). On 26 September he consulted the Virginian novelist, John Pendleton Kennedy, then on a visit to Paris, about the subject of the installment's last chapter: George Warrington's escape from Fort Duquesne (*Letters*, 4:111n). Thackeray apparently suggested in joking exasperation that Kennedy write the chapter because he knew the topography: "'Now you know all that ground,' he says to me, 'and I want you to write a chapter for me to describe how he got off and what travel he made.'"[1] Although Kennedy was about to leave Paris and had little time at his disposal, he gave Thackeray a few oral "hints for the description" and supplemented them with "a rough map of illustration" and "a sketch for [the] chapter"—a sketch, Kennedy said, that Thackeray "partially incorporated . . . in the book." When Thackeray wrote out the chapter, however, its few topographical details were confined to the chapter's last page and included the erroneous mention that sap from sugar maples was obtained in the autumn.[2]

Most of the manuscript (thirty leaves, all in Thackeray's hand) survives in the case of number thirteen, which has four chapters: chapter 1, "FRIENDS IN NEED" (fols. [1]–4); chapter 2, "CONTAINS A GREAT DEAL OF THE FINEST MORALITY" (fols. 5–7 and A–D); chapter 3, "CONTICUERE OMNES" (fols. G–H, 9, 11–13, 10, 14–16, 16a, and 17–18)—the latter having in manuscript the title later given to chapter 4: "Intentique Ora tenebant" (fol. G)—and chapter 4 (fols. 1a–2a and 24–27). As these designations indicate, the composition was somewhat complicated, except for the first and last chapters. On fol. 5, Thackeray marked chapter 2 "(not complete)"—presumably for the benefit of the printer, to whom he evidently later sent fols. A–D. Originally he had planned to end chapter 2 with George Warrington preparing to tell his tale, the setting for this narration presumably having been indicated on a fol. [8] that was later replaced. Thackeray then began "Chap III" with George's first words: "I remember, at the table of our general, how the little Philadelphia agent, whose wit & shrewdness we had remarked at home, made the very objections to the conduct of the campaign of wh. its disastrous issue showed the justice" (fol. 9; see 2:19). After ending the second paragraph of George's narrative at the bottom of the leaf ("force as our's"), Thackeray then, at the top of a new leaf, took up the narrative after an obvious gap at the point where "Florac's rough application stopped the bleeding of [George's] leg" (fol. 10; 2:22). Clearly, the novelist intended to go back and fill this gap with an historical account of the onslaught against Braddock's column; this he did on three small leaves that he misnumbered fols. 11–13—presumably because they were written just after fol. 10, even though they were to precede it narratively.

After George had explained how he had been rescued by Florac, brought into the fort, and laid in Florac's own bed (upper half of fol. 10), George went on with his account, beginning: "Next day I was in a high fever, wh. continued I know not how long. When I awoke to my senses my dear Florac was gone." After continuing with this narrative, however—possibly to the bottom of an additional leaf that later became fol. 16—Thackeray decided to insert after the first of these sentences a new passage; written on the verso of fol. 10, it concerned Indian savagery after the battle. Following a note for the printer— "Insert after 'I know not how long'"—the new passage went on: "Happy for me was my insensibility. I had been brought into the fort as a wounded French soldier of the garrison. I heard afterward, that, during my delirium, the few prisoners, who had been taken on the day of our disaster, had been brought in under the walls of the fort by their Indian captors; & there savagely burned, tortured, and butchered by the Indians under the eyes of the garrison" (fol. 10v). Afterwards, following cancellation of the sentence about George's fever, beginning: "Next day," the bottom portion of fol. 10 was neatly removed and the passage to be inserted was copied with revisions onto a new half-leaf, where it was followed by over a half-dozen additional lines that included a historical detail concerning the white man's savagery.[3] These lines also, for the first time after the beginning of George's narrative,

revealed the presence of the Lamberts and showed the contrasting reactions of several members of George's audience to his tale: Theo's
affectionate alarm, Harry's vehement anger, and Mr. Lambert's playful detachment.[4] The passage on the verso was cancelled and the new
half-leaf was joined with the upper portion of fol. 10. In turn, the former lower portion of fol. 10 was pasted onto a new leaf and given a brief
new introduction: "'I know not how long I lay in my fever,' George
resumed." Because of the existence of fols. 11–13, this latter leaf
was marked as fol. 14, even though it followed fol. 10 in the narrative
sequence.

George's account continued from the bottom of fol. 10, which became
fol. 14 ("the other *canaille* of *Rosbifs*"), to what is now fol. 16 ("had
deservedly met with."), and then went on:

> The Commandant of the fort, an old Lieutenant too, one Monsieur
> Blaireau, who knew that according to the exclusive system of the French
> service, wh. gives all the promotion to the *noblesse*, he never wd. ad-
> vance in rank, had made free with my guineas. I suppose, as he had with
> my watch for I saw it one day on his chest when I was sitting with him
> in his quarter.
> At first we were pretty good friends. If I could be exchanged or sent
> home I told him my mother would pay liberally for my ransom—and I
> suppose this idea excited the cupidity of the commandant. . . .

Deciding to rewrite most of this passage, Thackeray copied on a fresh
leaf, fol. 15, the four words ("had deservedly met with.") that ended
the incomplete sentence at the bottom of fol. 14. He proceeded to write
a paragraph that added several historical details about the departure
of French and Indians from Fort Duquesne and explained that the
French commander, Contrecoeur, had left the fort in charge of an old
lieutenant named Fouin. Thackeray then composed a new opening for
the passage at the top of the following leaf, followed by a single vertical
line; he also made two brief syntactical modifications in the passage on
fol. 16 and cancelled its first one and three-quarters lines. Ultimately,
however, he continued to revise the text of fol. 16, thereby adding
about seven more lines of writing to the new leaf, as far as the words
"this idea" (2:23). Subsequently, he cancelled the corresponding five
and one-quarter lines on the older leaf, fol. 16. George's further dealings with Fouin, his escape, and the end of his story then continued on
fols. 17 and 18, which concluded the chapter.

One more major manuscript revision remained, for George's account of how Fouin became enraged to learn that his Indian mistress had developed a partiality for the young Virginian whom she was nursing back to health originally led to the following paragraph: "He forbade her, with a great deal of foul language to both of us, to see me except in his presence: but he was forced to admit of her seeing me from time to time, for she was especially skilful in the Indian way of treating fever, and when the fits came upon me, I suffered so severely that my gaoler thought he shd lose his prisoner and his ransom: and he trembled lest he should be superseded in his little command of the fort, before this opportunity of plunder could be realized" (fol. 16). Thackeray decided to cancel this passage, however, because he wished to dampen the romantic overtones of the Indian girl's attraction to George. The novelist also decided to have George interrupt the narrative with a deliberately reductive shift of perspective intended to curtail sentimental and melodramatic expectations in his audience. Accordingly, Thackeray wrote fol. 16a, which shows George comically breaking into his own tale in order to reduce the stature of his heroine by revealing her inordinate passion not for him but for the bottle (2:24–25). Thackeray then completed George's narrative in chapter 4, making a number of brief changes but composing the chapter with no apparent difficulty. Its only unusual feature is a direction to the printer concerning the wood-engraved initial: "The small W. to this chapter" (fol. 1a), the large W. being intended for chapter 2.[5]

One major addition was made in press, for Thackeray followed a brief portion of text that may have been provided by the now-missing fol. [8] with a lengthy passage written on eight leaves designated fols. A–H, of which [E] and [F] are now missing. Since his proofs showed him that the text of fols. [1]–7 and apparently [8] had produced ten printed pages, he marked fol. A: "to follow after page 10." Beginning, "I never never never wished," fols. A–[F] continue the discussion of Harry that is being carried on by members of Sir Miles Warrington's family. In this part of the augmentation (2:11–16), Thackeray begins by emphasizing the hypocrisy of the family, especially its female members, and shows us the quarrelsome jealousy of the two sisters for each other. The addition then becomes more pointed, for Sir Miles has no sooner denounced Harry than he finds Harry and George calling on him and, together with his wife and daughters, has to improvise an appropriate reception. This scene and the family's renewed quarreling and belittlement of the two visitors after their departure then serves nicely to emphasize by contrast the loving relationships among Colonel Lambert, his wife, and their two daughters, and the fond manner in which this family receives Harry and George—the latter material being set down on fols. G and H, which furnish a new opening for chapter 3. As we saw, Thackeray originally began chapter 3 with George's account of his adventures on Braddock's expedition (fol. 9; 2:19). Whether or not the novelist originally had intended to include the Lamberts among George's audience, he now decided to lead off the chapter by setting the scene at their house. The final result of this entire addition of eight leaves, therefore, is an extended and emphatic contrast between the two households and between their response to George and Harry Warrington.

A number of brief alterations were also made in press, but only a few deserve notice. The title of chapter 3 was shifted to 4, and two names were regularized: the sponging-house proprietor became "Amos" (2:3) instead of "Nathan" (fol. [2]), in accordance with the name given him on fol. 4, and "Fouin" (fol. 15 ff.)—originally "Blaireau"—became "Museau" (2:23 ff.). So too, "the Picardy regiment" (fol. 13) became "the Quebec Volunteers" (2:22), and George's wound resulted from a rifle ball that "struck" (2:21), rather than "broke" (fol. 11) his leg. Two short sentences concerning Colonel Lambert's affectionate response to Harry's defense of his brother were cut from the final page of chapter 3: "Martin Lambert put his hand on Harry's shoulder. 'No he couldn't fight a whole company, and we use all sorts of agents in war—Harry'" (fol. 18). As a result, the reader's attention concentrates entirely on the ensuing idea: "See the women how disappointed they are!" (fol. 18; see 2:26). This omission was not motivated by the necessity to reduce his text, for there was just sufficient room to accommodate the two deleted sentences of chapter 3. The text of chapter 4 was apparently about three lines too long, but none of the deletions was made solely out of a need to curtail the text. From the phrase, "they would drive the Rosbifs into the sea in another year and all America should be theirs from the Mississippi to Newfoundland" (fol. 1a; see 2:27), Thackeray removed "in another year" and thus saved one line, but those three words also may have struck him as reflecting an excessively optimistic hope, even for an enthusiastic Frenchman. The next cut also reduced the text by a line, for the phrase about Hetty and the subsequent "too" were deleted from: "You turn pale dear Miss Theo—and even Miss Hetty wishes to spare me? . . Well, I will have pity too, and will spare you the tortures wh. honest Fouin recounted in his pleasant way as likely to befal me" (fol. 1a; see 2:28). Undoubtedly, however, dissatisfaction with the repeated use of "spare" also bore significantly on his decision, as did, perhaps, the somewhat inappropriate distinction implied by "even" between two girls George hardly as yet knew. Deletion of a sentence's final words, "for a guide" (fol. 2a), freed another line but also improved the phrase from which they were cut, for emphasis now fell less on the man's specific function and more on the idea of his general trustworthiness: "'How do you know,' he asked, 'that this hunter will serve you?'" (2:29). A final reduction came from the replacement of "ere a while and at last" (fol. 26) by "ere long" (2:31), but here too the change brought a stylistic improvement. Therefore, although these four cuts—one more than was needed—enabled the installment to be printed in the allotted thirty-two pages, there seems little reason for future editors to restore them.

Number fourteen for December 1858 is missing from the Morgan manuscript, as are all but three leaves of the following installment. Number sixteen is also missing but most of number seventeen for March 1859 survives: chapter 16, "IN WHICH HARRY LIVES TO FIGHT ANOTHER DAY"—originally "Horrida Bella"—fols. 1, 1v, 2–6); chapter 17, "SOLDIER'S RETURN"—originally "VIRTUTIS FORTUNA COMES" —(fols. 7–9, 9v, A); chapter 18, "IN WHICH WE GO A-COURTING" (fols. 14–15, B, 16–19); and chapter 19, "IN WHICH A TRAGEDY IS ACTED, AND TWO MORE ARE BEGUN" (fols. 20–[22]).[6] The composition of chapter 16 was marked by only one addition: the present fol. 1, which was written and inserted after at least two other leaves had been completed and two had been numbered (fols. 2 and 3, originally 1 and 2).[7] It appears impossible to say whether or not the chapter had been completed before fol. 1 was written, but one can see that the text of fol. 1 harmonizes with the narrator's turn, in the chapter's final paragraph, from the subject of the army to a typically Thackerayan consideration of those who remain at home to suffer in its absence, for the narrative on fol. 1 (ending with three lines on its verso) focuses not on military affairs (fol. 2 ff.), but on those whom Harry has left behind him, especially Gumbo and Hetty (2:129–30).

One brief passage was cancelled in manuscript. Originally, in mentioning Gumbo's success with English servant girls and in contrasting European responsiveness to Negroes with the behavior in "a certain other respected Quarter" (fol. 1; 2:129)—obviously the United States —Thackeray had used Othello and the Chevalier de St. George as examples of "notorious favorites with the fair sex"; he then went on: "who love contrast doubtless, and who rebuke the haughtiness of the owner of the slave by their tenderness towards the poor Negro: They seem to say to his master, "Tyrant! this (coloured) gentleman is not only your Man, but he is your Brother! If you are harsh we will console him" (fol. 1). This was inadequate for a number of reasons, including its rather jumbled handling of Othello, the Chevalier, and a slave, and its inappropriate distortion of what the servant girls actually did feel towards Gumbo's master. Thackeray therefore immediately deleted the last fifty-one words, went on with a sentence providing a transition between the Chevalier and Gumbo, explained that the girls regarded Gumbo as "not only Mr. Harry's Man, but their Brother" (fol. 1; see 2:129), and then gave an account of Gumbo's partly comical sorrow at Harry's departure.

Chapter 17 had several brief, insignificant cancellations and one addition to the manuscript: in the middle of the final leaf, following the words, "reported highly of his behaviour" (fol. 9; 2:140), Thackeray inserted an "A," indicating a leaf that added to his narrative a long historical note concerning the warm public response to the returning soldiers, beginning: "Those volunteers and their actions were the theme of everybody's praise." Then, in an ensuing paragraph, he focused upon Harry:

> My Lord Howe was heard to speak in special praise of Mr. Warrington, and so he had a handsome share of the fashion and favor wh. the town now bestowed on the Volunteers. Doubtless there were thousands of men employed who were as good as they: but the English ever love their gentlemen, and love that they should distinguish themselves; and these Volunteers were voted Paladins and heroes by common accord. As our young noblemen will, they accepted their popularity very affably. White's and Almack's illuminated when they returned, and St. James's embraced its young knights. Harry was restored to full favor amongst them. (fol. A; see 2:140)

Earlier, there had been a rough shift from the favorable public reception of his brother volunteers to the similar behavior of the London

clubmen, marked by a pronoun, "Their," that had an incorrect antecedent—the brother volunteers instead of the frequenters of White's
and Almack's: "His brother volunteers when they came back to St.
James's Street reported highly of his behaviour. Their hands were
held out eagerly to him again" (fol. 9). Now, by means of his addition,
Thackeray set Harry's return to favor in a more detailed historical
framework than previously and made a more adequate transition between the larger public events and those of Harry's individual life.
Four leaves may have been cancelled shortly after this place in the
manuscript, for chapter 18 begins on fol. 14,[8] but fols. 14–19 reveal
nothing unusual about their composition, nor do the few surviving
leaves of chapter 19.

As was the general pattern, significant alteration was made in press.
Chapter 16 was lengthened by two additions, both dealing with Harry's letter to George.[9] Thackeray originally had Harry begin his letter:
"After a month the army is come back. We landed on the 6 at Cancalle
Bay, we saw a few dragons on a hill who rode away from us without
engaging" (fol. 3). In press, however, Thackeray cancelled the first
sentence and added eight new ones marked very much more by Harry's personality and spelling; in addition, they provide a quietly reductive Thackerayan attitude towards the expedition, culminating in the
judgment: "all I can say in truth is, that we have been to France and
come back again. Why, I don't think even *your tragick pen* could make
anything of such a campaign as ours has been" (2:132). Thackeray then
made a second insertion, a comical exchange between George, Hetty,
and Hetty's young brother that comes just after Harry's mention of
dragons; the effect here too is gently reductive. These qualitatively
significant changes also had an important quantitative dimension: since
they took up twenty-five additional lines, they thereby lengthened the
chapter from seven pages to eight, the final page now having only
twenty lines.

From the marking on fol. 9 and on fol. A itself—"to be inserted at
9"—it appears that fol. A was added to chapter 17 before the chapter
was set up in type. Chapter 18, however, was significantly augmented
in press by a passage deriving from two leaves or their equivalent (i.e.,
a margin of a proof sheet)—one of which apparently does not survive,
and one of which does (fol. B). The passage they combine to produce
augments the narrator's discussion of his reluctance to tell any secrets
about the increasing intimacy of George's association with Theo.

Thackeray evidently felt that he had to offer some details about
George's courtship, and therefore, presumably, he inserted the paragraph beginning: "Whilst Harry's love of battle has led him to smell
powder . . ., George has been pursuing an amusement much more
peaceful and delightful to him" (2:144). In a similar vein Thackeray
wrote fol. B, which supplies most of the next paragraph, with its account of the notes sent by means of Gumbo and Sady, the proposals
to visit Ranelagh, Hampstead, Vauxhall, and Marylebone Gardens,
and George's request that Theo copy his tragedy; it also includes the
narrator's circumspect allusions to the letters she wrote to George,
ending with the words, "In fine," which connect with his earlier text
from fol. 15: "You see we have said very little about it" (see 2:145).[10]
We can see that these thirty-four lines also added an extra page to
chapter 18, the last page now containing twenty-four printed lines, but
we cannot discern whether or not any such augmentations were made
in the final chapter during its passage through the press, for its manuscript is too fragmentary.

Number eighteen for April 1859 again had four chapters: chapter 20,
"IN WHICH HARRY GOES WESTWARD"; chapter 21, "A LITTLE IN-
NOCENT"; chapter 22, "IN WHICH CUPID PLAYS A CONSIDERABLE
PART"; and chapter 23, "WHITE FAVOURS." Much of the manuscript
is missing, however. Of chapter 20, only the last two leaves survive
(fols. 5–6), but there is one interesting manuscript change. George had
originally expressed his favorable opinion of the Earl of Castlewood by
saying that the nobleman would be good if he could: "only that Fate at
the commencement put him on a wrong way of life, from wh. he has
had no possibility of escaping since" (fol. 5). This line of argument,
however, was to be the basis of Castlewood's own defense of his conduct (fol. 8; 2:167–68)—a defense that was to turn on the word "Fate"
and was to become largely an excuse for not trying to change; hence,
with this later passage written or in view, Thackeray altered George's
vocabulary by removing the reference to "Fate" and modified George's
viewpoint towards Castlewood's amendment by making it seem only
improbable instead of impossible. Cancelling the words quoted above,
which were written in his slanted hand, Thackeray substituted in his

upright hand the following: "or rather he would have been once. He has been set on a wrong way of life from wh. tis now probably too late to rescue him. *O beati agricolae!*" (fol. 5; see 2:164).

Chapter 21 survives more fully than any other in this installment, fols. 7–14 apparently providing all of the text originally sent by Thackeray to the printer. They seem to have been written in succession, with no notable revisions. Thackeray then went on to chapter 22, only the first four leaves of which are to be found (fols. 15–18), again with no major changes. Chapter 23 may have been incomplete when it was sent to the printer, but Thackeray seems quickly to have sent him three final leaves numbered 1*a*–3*a*, which bring the installment to its climax with the announcement of Castlewood's marriage; only these three leaves have survived, not those that preceded them in the chapter.

Significant alterations were again made in press.[11] In addition to the lengthy cut made early in chapter 20 implied by the printer's markings on the manuscript, the chapter's last ten and one-half printed lines were apparently added in press, following the abrupt sentence in which the narrator broke off his quotation from George's letter to Harry: "Here follows a page of raptures, and quotations of verse wh. out of a regard for the reader, and the writers memory, the editor of the present pages declines to reprint" (fol. 6; see 2:165). Thackeray thereby concluded the chapter with three sentences that served a new artistic function, for he now did not simply imply that George was guilty of an insufficiently amusing absurdity; with the final three sentences the novelist implicated all his readers, both young and old, by assisting them to recall or imagine similar feelings of their own, and he identified them all as participants not only in a universal folly but also in a universal delight.

In chapter 21 Thackeray made a number of brief changes and supplied names omitted in the manuscript: Draper (2:170–73), Drabshaw (2:170), Trail (2:170), and Tubbs (2:173). More important, however, he added what are now the last 159 lines of the chapter's text, thereby extending its length by three pages. This material begins with a paragraph concerning Lydia's freedom and adaptability.[12] It then continues on one and one-half extant leaves: fols. A and [B], only the lower portion of the latter having survived. Beginning, "It was because she knew he was engaged" (2:174), fol. A carries the text to: "the eyes that were looking so gentle and" (2:176), while—after a hiatus of twenty-nine lines—the lower portion of fol. [B] provides the text for twenty-four printed lines, ending, "What mattered to him how often Kensington entertained Bloomsbury or Bloomsbury made its bow at Kensington?" (see 2:177). Most of the added passage on those pages dramatized Lydia Van den Bosch's flirtatiousness more clearly than ever before by showing her in a long, teasing tête-à-tête with George, but it also provided important information concerning Madame Bernstein's cultivation of Lydia as a match for Harry and concluded with the ironically revealing news—to us, though not to George—that Lydia has been secretly seeing the Castlewoods. Besides the text contained in the transitional paragraph and on fols. A and [B], Thackeray also added a final paragraph that provided a concluding generalization for the chapter.

Thackeray's insertion on fol. [B] ended with news of the double intrigue between Kensington and Bloomsbury, but he also (apparently on a missing fol. [C]) made a further addition—one that nicely connects with his addition to the previous chapter, for whereas that ended with the optimistic perspective of broadly imagined future love, here such a viewpoint is qualified by a perspective that turns universality into a mocking diminishment: "Have you not fancied that Lucinda's eyes beamed on you with a special tenderness, and presently become aware that she ogles your neighbour with the very same killing glances? Have you not exchanged exquisite whispers with Lalage at the dinner-table (sweet murmurs heard through the hum of the guests, and clatter of the banquet!) and then overheard her whispering the very same delicious phrases to old Surdus in the drawing-room? The sun shines for everybody; the flowers smell sweet for all noses; and the nightingale and Lalage warble for all ears—not your long ones only, good Brother!" (2:177).

Thackeray modified a number of words and phrases from chapter 22 in press but none of these alterations calls for special notice; several changes made at the end of the final one, chapter 23, however, require brief mention.[13] Though there is now space for five additional lines on the chapter's last page, six lines were removed from the final three pages—chiefly on artistic grounds but also, curiously, to an apparent degree on quantitative ones as well. The removal of the last six words of "in parley with a servant there, and wearing a very long face" (fol.

1*a*; see 2:190) saved a line by deleting a phrase that may or may not have seemed premature, for the servant only gives his bad news in the ensuing sentence—or perhaps repeats it there for George. The final four words of "the young men walked away—each crumpling his letter in his pocket, silent along the flags" (fol. 1*a*; see 2:190) seem even more clearly to have been cancelled chiefly to save a line, for stylistic considerations would seem to have required at most a shift in their position in the sentence rather than their outright removal. The deletion of the words "& attired in her very best" (fol. 1*a*; see 2:191) to describe Mrs. Lambert's arrival with her footman at Lydia's house did not save a line and seems to reflect a decision made entirely on artistic grounds, but the following cancellation of George's invitation to her following his announcement that there is no use in her going any farther—"Or at any rate better go no farther than my lodgings and take a dish of tea" (fol. 1*a*; see 2:191)—seems to have been made chiefly to remove another line—the third so far.

The final three omissions also reduced the text's length by three lines and came in Castlewood's letter announcing his marriage. Instead of indicating his hope of introducing to his family "a new and charming member—and to present you all to a Countess of Castlewood" (fol. 3*a*), he now merely conveys his hope to introduce to the family "a Countess of Castlewood" (2:192). So too, the second last paragraph of his letter now ends with Lydia's remembrances, without the comment, "She welcomes you to Castlewood *d'avance*," while the final sentence of the last paragraph merely mentions Castlewood's own "establishment, where you will ever be welcomed" (2:192), instead of going into the greater detail of his "establishment in London, where as at our house in the country you will ever be welcomed" (fol. 3*a*). Again in the last three alterations a mingling of motives appears to have operated on Thackeray's part: a wish to improve the texture of his narrative—here by purging it of a few slightly effusive details— and to reduce its length.

During the first part of 1859 Thackeray had apparently been concerning himself to a considerable degree with military history. On 22 January, for example, he wrote to Sir Henry Knight Storks: "I want you

very much to give me some military information for the Virginians"
(*Letters*, 4:126). By 29 March, after completing number eighteen for
April, he planned to devote the last six installments to "the American
part." Though upset at what he considered his dawdling, unable to
visit America for "a study of it *sur les lieux*," and obliged to describe
the military developments "in quite a difft way to that wh. I had first
intended," he was nevertheless partly glad not to be following the
original plan: "I should have got out of my depth in the military details" (*Letters*, 4:135). Though his treatment of such matters was now
to be different, he still seems assiduously to have sought out historical
evidence, thanking an acquaintance four days later, for example, for
assisting him in preparing for "My death of Wolfe" in the immediately
forthcoming installment: "I would gladly read any documents regarding Canada and Wolfe wh. might help me to give one or two touches of
reality to the little picture. If your friend will part with his papers I
will take good care of them" (*Letters*, 4:137). An unpublished letter of
March 1859, also reveals his interest in documents about Wolfe, for he
thanks his correspondent for lending him manuscripts of Wolfe's military orders.[14] In describing Wolfe's death, he drew "upon the authority . . . of a bystander who professed to have seen him wounded,
carried to the rear, and dying" and later he thanked a correspondent
for sending him a similar piece of evidence, though it arrived too late
for him to use (*Letters*, 4:140).

Number 19, in which George takes over the narrative, is missing,
but number twenty for June 1859 survives. Because Thackeray was ill
for eight days towards the end of May, he was enabled to finish it only
on 27 May and had to allow it to make its appearance without the customary steel etchings (*Letters*, 4:142); they came out with the next
installment, which therefore had four plates. Only the first three chapters survive in manuscript, all of them with lacunae. Chapter 28, originally "Contains what might have been foreseen" but then retitled in
manuscript "Informs us how Mr. Warrington jumped into a landau,"
exists on five leaves: fols. 1–5, the upper part of fol. [3] being missing.
Composition seems to have been quite uncomplicated, but less so in the
following chapter. Thackeray began the latter in his own hand with a
leaf that contained the present chapter opening to the point where
Hetty, delighting in the effects upon Theo of the secret meeting with
George, exclaims that all the doctor's medicine had not been so effec-

tive in restoring her sister to health: "the girls went home after their act of disobedience and did not think of concealing what they had done. I heard how it befel afterwards. The child came in from her" (fol. 6). Apparently Thackeray then inserted a period after "disobedience," cancelling the ensuing words, and on a new leaf began, "If I had a mind I could write twenty sentimental chapters"; instead, however, of writing even an explanation of why he was not going to dramatize "how it befel" at the Lambert home when Mr. Lambert learned the news, Thackeray also cancelled these eleven words and began the scene that took place on the following morning when the now enlightened and angry Lambert called on George. This portion of the narrative took up all of one leaf and most of another, which Thackeray numbered as fols. 7 (later renumbered 8) and 8.

He then decided to write the former scene after all, presumably to make fully understandable the confrontation between Lambert and George that he had just set down. Consequently, he showed at greater length and in a private scene with Lambert's family the General's grief as well as anger. This passage, which may originally have occupied a single leaf in Thackeray's hand (fol. [7], thereby necessitating the renumbering of fol. 7 as 8), now takes up six leaves in Anne's hand with corrections by Thackeray (fols. 7–10, 10½, and 11), beginning, "I gave up the place" (fol. 7; 2:232), and ending, "It was all my doing" (see 2:233).[15] After redesignating the original fols. 7 (already renumbered 8) and 8 as fols. 13 and 14, Thackeray then seems to have sent a number of leaves to the printer, including fol. 13 but not fol. 14, which he now completed in his own hand along with the rest of the chapter (fols. 15–18). By the time he sent these last five leaves to the printer, he had received proof, for he wrote at the top of fol. 14: "to follow ⟨after page⟩ at page 11"; in its published version, the passage begins in the middle of the seventh line on 2:235, the eleventh page of the monthly installment.

Chapter 30, "Pyramus & Thisbe," begins with nine leaves in Anne's hand (fols. 1a–9a) that end in mid-sentence: "on my account or her" (2:242). On a new leaf (fol. 1b) Thackeray completed the sentence, and eventually he set down the two other surviving leaves (fols. 2b–3b). These last three leaves, introduced with the words "(in continuation of Chapter III)" (fol. 1b), were then sent to the printer. Relatively few changes were made to the text of the surviving leaves on their passage through the press; this fact, plus the absence from the manuscript of the ending of chapter 30 and of the installment's entire last chapter essentially preclude discussion of that aspect of composition.

Number twenty-one for July 1859 was completed "on Saturday night," June 25th, "after a fearful struggle" (*Letters*, 4:144)—especially, it would appear, towards the end of the installment, though we may never know exactly how "fearful," since the final leaves have disappeared. The first three chapters all have their titles given in manuscript: "POCAHONTAS," "RES ANGUSTA DOMI," and "MILES'S MOIDORE"; they also have a common numbering system and hereby, too, differ from the final chapter: 35, "TROUBLES AND CONSOLATIONS." Chapter 32 originally began by recounting the failure of George's play, "Pocahontas," beginning: "With such ill omens preceding the day, what wonder that Pocahontas should have turned out not to to be a victory?" This leaf and the succeeding one were marked fols. 1 and 2; both were later designated fols. 4 and 5, after Thackeray wrote and inserted the present fols. 1–3. The new leaves began with an account of how George attempted to improve the chances of his play by means of the "ground-bait" verses that Sampson had proposed be published in a newspaper so as to help attract an audience for the drama (fol. 1). The "ground-bait" verses took up fol. 2 and were followed by a paragraph concerning "Pocahontas," beginning: "I need not describe at length the plot of my tragedy" (fol. 3; 2:259). On the same leaf, Thackeray then set down a new opening for the paragraph already written on what is now fol. 4 and cancelled the first nine words of its previous version, thereby producing the following: "But I have mentioned the ill-omens wh. preceded the day: the difficulties wh. a peevish and jealous and timid management threw in the way of the piece, and the violent prejudice wh. was felt against it in *certain high quarters*. What wonder then I ask" (fol. 3; see 2:259). As a result, Thackeray had George supply the reader with the basic elements of the play and a delightfully ambiguous indication of its possible appeal—George's estimation and his wife's loyal support contrasting with the somnolent reaction of his unintellectual son and of the parson. So too, in the rewritten beginning of the ensuing paragraph about the play's actual failure, we are not simply told again that it faced difficulties but are specifically reminded what those difficulties were. The augmentation, then, provided us with fuller as well as clearer understanding. So far as one can judge from the manuscript, composition of the rest of the chapter seems to have followed without any complications.

The first portion of chapter 33 (fols. 10–18) is in Anne's handwriting, with corrections and additions by Thackeray, including the chapter title and a footnote by the Editor (fol. 14; 2:266). At the bottom of fol. 18, Thackeray himself took up the pen, but a secretary's writing begins on fol. 22 and seems to have continued for at least five more leaves, one of which is now missing: fols. 23–25, [26], and 29 (originally 27). This latter portion of the chapter concludes the narrative of Lady Castlewood's visit to George and Theo's lodgings in Lambeth, and of the failure of Lord Castlewood and Sir Miles to help them (2:270–71). The missing fol. [26] apparently concluded the account of the pharisaical behavior of George's English relatives and then began to show his attempt to secure money through the help of his friend "Mr. Johnson & he procured me a little work from the booksellers" (fol. ⟨27⟩ 29). After receiving these leaves from the secretary and perhaps after adding some further lines in his own hand to the last leaf, which was still numbered fol. 27, Thackeray wrote and inserted two leaves (fols. 27–28) that showed the kindness of Johnson and the vestigial action of George's pride, which caused him to walk out of the first bookseller's shop. A somewhat rapidly handled narrative thereby received fuller treatment, the added incident being significant enough to become the subject of one of the installment's two steel etchings: "THE PATRON" (opposite 2:272).

The final lines on fol. 29 and its verso, which were written down by Thackeray himself, also constitute a significant addition. The account in the secretary's hand had ended as George explained how the sight of several magazine articles written during a time of great poverty and desperate labor "awaken in me the keenest pangs of bitter remembrance," make him recall the "doubts & fears which agitated me," and "see the dear wife nursing her infant and looking up into my face with hypocritical smiles that vainly try to mask her alarm"; in short, "the struggles of pride are fought over again." To these words, written either immediately before or after the composition of fols. 27 and 28, Thackeray himself added the following: "the wounds, under wh. I smarted, reopen. There are some acts of injustice committed against me wh. I dont know how to forgive: and wh., whenever I think of them, awaken in me the same feelings of revolt and indignation."

Hence, Thackeray wanted to end on the note not of Theo's alarm but of George's bitter resentment, for the novelist then went on to write a footnote explaining more than George was willing to admit: how his unremitting anguish prompted him to prepare a book into which he pasted not "two or three magasine-articles," as George had claimed, but "various extracts from Reviews and Newspaper[s]"[16]—a book into which was pasted his own bookplate and which was "lettered without *Les Chaines de l'Esclavage*" (fol. 29; 2:273). In a further ironic addition Thackeray made this emblem of bitterness both survive into the present age and also disappear. He then concluded the footnote with three sentences that introduce further ironies by pointing out how George's words contradict his claim at the beginning of the chapter that he has transcended bitterness, and by making clear that although physical emblems of human bitterness and pride may eventually disappear, the human phenomenon—"The same [m]anner of forgiving our enemies"—persists down to "the present century" (fol. 29v).

Almost all of the brief chapter 34 exists in Anne's writing, perhaps originally on either seven or eight leaves, of which six survive: fols. 31–[34] and 37–38. The numeral 30 apparently was inadvertently passed over, and the same thing may have happened with either 35 or 36; if not, then material was cancelled, for the text of only twelve and one-half printed lines—the equivalent of one of the adjacent leaves —is unaccounted for between the bottom of fol. [34] and the top of fol. 37.[17] Thackeray's chief addition came at the chapter's end, where he himself wrote down its final paragraph, which shifts attention from how Theo permanently keeps Miles's moidore to the eventual agreement even of Madam Esmond concerning the choice of his name for her grandson, and which concludes with a note of affectionate mockery as George refers to "our Miles Gloriosus of Pall Mall, Valenciennes, Almack's, Brighton" (fol. 38; 2:276).

The final chapter is marked in three numerically self-contained sequences, of which the following leaves survive: fols. 1a–4a, 1b–3b, both in Thackeray's writing, and fols. 1c–4c and 6c, this final portion being in the secretary's hand. The top of fol. [2a] and at least one concluding leaf are missing from the first sequence; fol. [5c] and a number of final leaves are absent from the last. The first of these sequences carried over into the next, for fol. 1*b* begins by completing a word and sentence evidently begun at the bottom of the missing previous one: "ly when I saw her" (2:281). The second ended with an inch or so of space at the bottom of its last leaf, but it seems unlikely to have been intended as the installment's ending: "He had been looking into Mr. Miles's crib, as the child lay asleep; and, when the parson went away, I found the money in the baby's little rosy hand. Yes, Love is best of all. I have many such benefactions registered in my heart, precious welcome fountains springing up in desert places, kind friendly lights cheering our despondency and gloom" (fol. 3*b*; see 2:284). The third sequence shifted attention from Sampson to the Baroness Bernstein, whose death scene now began. The manuscript breaks off after only the upper third of fol. 6*c* had been covered, however—in the very middle of that great narrative, just as she awakens and those around her see that "her speech was changed and one arm & side were paralyzed—" (fol. 6*c*; see 2:286). The two paragraphs completing that scene and the final section of the chapter (2:286–88) are missing.[18]

In press Thackeray considerably altered and expanded the opening paragraph of chapter 32, which had originally begun with an account of how Sampson promoted George's tragedy and proposed the use of "ground-bait" verses. It then went on as follows: "In brave Captain Smith's life as narrated by himself, I dont read of any such tremendous battle with the Red Indians as that in wh. I took the liberty to make him prisoner: but he had fought in many brilliant actions, and notably cut off three blackamoors heads in a battle with the Turks on the Danube, (wh. heads truncated he wore afterwards in his shield of arms*) and I thought we might make him perform some similar exploit on the banks of our Potowmac or James River. Our 'ground-bait' verses ran thus" (fol. 1). Deciding to modify and augment this portion of his narrative instead of inserting a footnote after "arms," Thackeray wrote out two additional leaves, fols. A and B.

Fol. A, which is bound with the Morgan Library's portion of the *Denis Duval* manuscript, begins: "I made acquaintance with brave Captain Smith, as a boy in my grandfathers library at home" (see 2:257), and explained how George's grandfather drew pictures for him of Smith's exploits against the Turks, and how George especially delighted in the battle between Smith and Bonny Molgro (2:257–58). Fol. B, which was marked "Chap 32 page 258," apparently by the printer, introduced a quotation from Harry's favorite old book with the following words, later cancelled: "Bonny Molgro. They fell to with their battle axes, when the." The quotation itself then began with three words ("whose piercing bills") that were later also cancelled, presumably because they had been replaced by an introductory passage written at the bottom of fol. A.[19] Following the quotation, George now concluded: "Disdaining time and place (with that daring wh. is the privilege of poets, in my tragedy Smith is made to perform similar exploits on the banks of our Potowmac and Jamess River. Our 'groundbait' verses ran thus" (fol. B; see 2:258). As a result of the entire addition, Thackeray gave the reader a much livelier sense of the charmingly naïve enthusiasm out of which the young man's tragedy was written and provided a hint of how George's bias distorts his account of why the play failed on the stage. Even more, by linking Esmond and George with "Smith's travels, sufferings, captivities, escapes, not only in America but Europe" (2:257), he brought out the analogical implications of Smith's life. Additionally, the novelist lengthened his chapter by about twenty-three printed lines—an additional page, for the text on its final page now takes up the space of fourteen lines.

Though the surviving manuscript helps reveal no significant alterations made in press to the final two chapters, we can see that a few brief additions were made in press to chapter 33, one of which provided a necessary link. In the manuscript George had overheard a bookseller say to an employee who has brought word that George has come: "O its Pocahontas is it? Let him wait" (fol. 28). But it had remained a private conversation into which George had intruded with his reply. Hence in press Thackeray inserted the intervening words: "And he told his boy to say as much to me" (2:272). The most important addition, however, was the chapter's final sentence. In manuscript Thackeray had taken the pen in his own hand to write how George's recollections of past difficulties reopen wounds and awaken the same feelings of revolt and indignation" (fol. 29). Thackeray also wrote the footnote that reveals George's bitterness and that emphasizes how it causes him to contradict himself. Though such bitterness recurs, however, it does not prevail; hence Thackeray added in press a further final sentence that shows the resolving action of even more powerful memories and emotions: "The gloom and darkness gather over me— till they are relieved by a reminiscence of that love and tenderness which through all gloom and darkness have been my light and consolation" (2:273). Here we see the characteristic tone of George's narrative reasserting itself—with all the ambiguity that normally attends his rationalizations.[20]

Number twenty-two for August 1859 was completed sometime after 24 July (*Letters*, 4:146). Containing only three instead of the usual four chapters, the surviving manuscript of the installment was set down entirely by Thackeray himself, who made a variety of interesting modifications. The manuscript of chapter 36, "IN WHICH HARRY SUBMITS TO THE COMMON LOT," reveals a number of cancellations, two of which deserve mention. In the first instance, Thackeray wrote down, almost entirely in his slanted hand, most of the initial paragraph of Harry's letter to George about his love for Fanny Mountain. Later Thackeray cancelled these lines and wrote out a new version immediately below in his upright hand. The initial changes were few, but in the last half of the paragraph he made more, the most significant of which give a new emphasis to Harry's subjugation, in keeping with the theme that was to be announced by the chapter initial, for example, which shows Hercules with a distaff; thus Harry's reference to Fanny as "my dictionary" became "my pretty Dictionary," and his claim that she makes no spelling errors became a belief that she neither makes mistakes in spelling "nor *in anything* else I know of: being of opinion that she is *perfection*" (fol. 5; 2:293).

In a second instance, Thackeray cancelled a paragraph of five and one-half lines concerning Harry's purchase of Tom Diggle's property: "This estate, being to be sold, our mother said she would give her savings—and brought no less than £1760 towards the purchase. Here where money is scarce, 'twould have been dear and difficult to get the rest on mortgage: and we thought we shd. lose the property, wh. our new relation Mr. Van den Bosch bid for, when, my aunt's legacy coming in, we were enabled to complete the purchase over him; and now I am owner of a good house & negroes, and I daresay shall be called to the house of Burgesses" (fol. 6). In its place, Thackeray composed a longer passage that significantly rearranged and added some details. Madam Esmond now comments on the possibility of purchasing the estate, calling it not only an "opportunity . . . such as never might again befal," but—as the result of a further striking change made by Thackeray to his revision—"a second opportunity . . ." (fol. 7), thereby recalling to the reader the earlier occasion and the persistently bitter influence of her first major quarrel with Harry: when she unsuccessfully tried, years before, to appropriate some of George's property for Harry's benefit and Harry refused to agree that she had the right to do so. In the revision, reference is now made to his aunt's legacy coming "most opportunely," the consequence being an even more forceful revelation of Harry's dependence upon women.

The domesticity of his feelings also came in for development as his delight in ownership is immediately succeeded in the revised passage by a characteristic loving "hope to see my dearest brother and family under my own roof-tree," but also by the somewhat surprising statement, reminiscent of one made by Wolfe (1:189): "To sit at my own fireside, to ride my own horses to my own hounds, is better than going a-soldiering." Thackeray inserted additional words into his revision to explain Harry's views—"now war is over, and there are no French to fight"—but the whole sequence of phrases culminates in two sentences that firmly emphasize the whole ironic context of determined female purpose that undercuts Harry's remarks and comically reveals the naïveté of his claims to "ownership": "Indeed, Madam Esmond made a condition that I should leave the army & live at home, when she brought me her 1750 £ of savings. She had lost one son, she said, who chose to write play-books, and live in England: let the other stay with her at home." Here Thackeray added only slight additional emphasis with the insertion of an introductory "Indeed" (fol. 7; see 2:294).

The third cancellation occurs on a leaf (fol. 8) that seems to have been inserted into the manuscript, presumably as a substitute for a leaf that originally completed the unfinished sentence on the bottom of fol. 7 ("I found her crying one day in her mothers room, where the two ladies") and introduced the scene in which Madam Esmond discovers Harry and Fanny together. In the version on fol. 8, Madam Esmond began a harsh attack upon Fanny: "For shame Miss! *You* engaged to Mr. Lintot, and making eyes at Mr. Warrington! Go to your apothecary and your pestle and mortar Miss; and dont dare to look at my son! Do you suppose that he is going to"; ending in mid-sentence, Thackeray cancelled most of this language, removing any mention of an engagement and having Madam Esmond allude to Harry's military rank:

"For shame Miss! What would Mr. Lintot say, if he saw you making eyes at the Captain?" Drawing a vertical line down through half of the space remaining, Thackeray left the rest of the leaf bare.

Chapter 37, its title ("INVENI PORTUM") already given in manuscript, originally took up probably seven leaves, beginning with a misnumbering that was never corrected: fols. 12*a*–[⟨18⟩].[21] Recounting how the long estrangement between George and his mother continued and how his succession to the baronetcy resulted only in dissatisfaction with his role and in unpopularity with his neighbors (2:300–303), George explained how "Harry ought to have been Squire. His letters from home" (fol. 15), we learn on a new leaf, "were full of gaiety and good spirits. . . . Had Hal been master of Warrington manor house in my place, he would have been beloved through the whole county." Continuing on this leaf, fol. ⟨16⟩, George's account went on to explain how Harry differed from his mother in politics as well as in his choice of a wife (fols. ⟨16⟩–⟨17⟩) and—in preparation for George's return to Virginia—how correspondence was reestablished between George and his mother (fol. ⟨17⟩), who continued to maintain her fierce consistency in matters medicinal as well as moral, endlessly dosing those round her, "both infants and adults, white and coloured" (fol. [⟨18⟩]). Deciding to augment the narrative of George's dissatisfaction, however, Thackeray cancelled from the bottom of fol. 15 the last ten words characterizing Harry as a more suitable squire, and had George go on: "I know the theory and practice" (fol. 18; 2:304). Continuing with this long discourse on the theme of secret cares, Thackeray had George explain how his catalogue of complaints to his doctor resulted in an instant and definitive diagnosis: "his inheritance has been his ruin: and a little poverty and a great deal of occupation would do him all the good in life" (fol. 19; see 2:305).

The partial inconsistency of George's account perhaps helped stimulate Thackeray to make a further insertion ahead of this one, for, prior to numbering these two leaves and renumbering fols. ⟨16⟩–[⟨18⟩], he wrote another leaf and a half, beginning: "What admission is this I am making?" (fol. 16; 2:303) and ending: "Here 3 pages are torn out of Sir George Warringtons M.S book for wh. the Editor is sincerely sorry * * * I know" (fol. 17; see 2:304). Now George both admits he has secrets from his wife, then denies that he does, then apparently goes on to "make a clean breast of it" (fol. 17)—on three pages that disappear from his manuscript notebook (a work which itself is a fiction of Thackeray's, through which he himself is presumably making and concealing his own personal revelations). The effect of this careful multiplication of ambiguities, of course, is a dramatic increase in the reader's awareness of the novel's ironic texture, which distances us from the narrative and forces us to notice the succession of perspectives that reveals the infinitude of experience itself and the severe limitations of each individual perceiver. The addition of this whole insertion (fols. 16–19), therefore, considerably enriches the chapter and does so in a characteristically Thackerayan way.

The novelist then renumbered the earlier fols. ⟨16⟩–[⟨18⟩] as fols. 20–[22] and completed the chapter with a brilliantly effective change of the perspective from which we are permitted to view Madam Esmond. Though he had just had her report to us her brutally callous and insufferably righteous response to Mrs. Mountain's dying wish for a reconciliation between them, now at the top of fol. 23 Thackeray wrote for Madam Esmond a final paragraph (though not printed as such) in which he makes the reader see in her the ability to love that renders her both human and pitiable: she is sentimental as well as arrogant, but here—even as she engages in emotional blackmail—she is, above all, loving and vulnerable:

> I send my grandson an Indian bow and arrows. Shall these old eyes never behold him at Castlewood, I wonder, and is Sir George so busy with his books and his politics that he can't afford a few months to his mother in Virginia? I am much alone now. My son's chamber is just as he left it: the same books are in the presses: his little hanger and fowling-piece over the bed, and my fathers picture over the mantlepiece. I never allow any thing to be altered in his room or his brother's. I fancy the children playing near me sometimes, and that I can see my dear father's head as he dozes in his chair. Mine is growing almost as white as my father's. Am I never to behold my children ere I go hence? The Lord's will be done.

It is a splendid conclusion, since it not only makes a powerful appeal to George and Theo but also, by calling forth our sympathy for her, it suddenly demonstrates to us what we have most probably been withholding from her throughout the novel—thereby unconsciously emulating the harshness of Madam Esmond herself.

Chapter 38, now designated "Chap. III. At Home" in manuscript (fol. 1*a*), originally began: "Some two years after our establishment at the Manor, our dear General returned" (fol. 2*a*). The final paragraph of chapter 37, however, required a response from George and Theo; consequently Thackeray wrote a few lines on a fresh leaf that constituted an opening for chapter 38: "Such an appeal as this of our mother would have softened hearts much less obdurate than our's, and we talked of a speedy visit to Virginia, and of hiring all the Young Rachels cabbin accommodation: but our child must fall ill, for whom the voyage would be dangerous, and from whom the mother of course could not part; and the Young Rachel made her voyage without us that year— Another year there was another difficulty, in my worship's first attack of the gout (wh. occupied me a good deal, and afterwards certainly cleared my wits, and enlivened my spirits) and now came another much sadder cause for delay in the sad news we received from Jamaica" (fol. 1a). The first three leaves (fols. 1a–3a), which carried the narrative to the moment of arrival at Castlewood, when Theo knelt down to receive Madam Esmond's blessing, may have preceded the final leaves to the printer. All of the latter are now missing except two and one-half leaves: fols. 1b, 2b, and what appears to be the bottom of fol. [4b], fol. 1b having been inscribed in pencil: "ch 38. p. 312," which accurately indicates its present position as the first new paragraph on that page.

Few substantial changes were made in press, so far as one can detect. The lengthiest was a paragraph of two relatively short sentences added to the rather empty final page of chapter 36 that showed George's and Theo's reaction to Harry's letter, especially its surreptitious last paragraph, and that placed his uxoriousness in an allusive context that develops the implications of the chapter initial: "The conclusion to which we came on the perusal of this document was, that the ladies had superintended the style and spelling of my poor Hal's letter, but that the postscript was added without their knowledge. And I am afraid we argued that the Virginian Squire was under female domination—as Hercules, Samson, and *fortes multi* had been before him" (2:299). The allusions convey both George's comic attempt to excuse Harry (and no doubt himself) and—through mention of Samson, especially—Thackeray's wish to reiterate one of this novel's most prominent themes. In the case of the last two chapters, only an occasional word was changed or added in press, the most notable alteration concerning the name of Lambert's son, Jack, who was incorrectly called "Tom" nine times in manuscript (fols. 2a–3a) and twice in print

(2:310–11).[22] Because the final portion of the manuscript is missing, however, one cannot say whether anything was added in press to the end of the installment.

As late as 24 July 1859, Thackeray had hoped to conclude *The Virginians* with the customary double number (*Letters*, 4:146), but he had to give up that plan; even so, on 23 August he still had "12 pages to do" (*Letters*, 4:149) on number twenty-three for September, which appeared in thirty-two pages. In addition to fols. 4 and 5, which are in the Huntington Library, the first and last leaves of chapter 39: "THE LAST OF GOD SAVE THE KING," survive (fols. 1 and 6). All four were written down by Thackeray himself, but a cancelled passage on the verso of fol. 9, in Anne's hand, appears to be an earlier version of the first two lines at the top of fol. 6, which deal with the watch given young Miles by Madam Esmond on his departure for England, and the cakes she caused to be stowed in his cabin. The sentence reads: "Where Sir, is the Tompean Watch ur. grandmother gave you & how did you survive the ton of cakes wh. she caused to be stowed in yr. cabin?" (see 2:326).

Another cancelled passage at the bottom of fol. 1 in Thackeray's hand reappears at a later stage in the printed text and helps provide evidence of an insertion into the text. Following Madam Esmond's refusal to attend a ball given by "rebels" and her unsuccessfully provocative public cry of "God save the King" (fol. 1; 2:322), Thackeray had gone on to explain that in those days everyone uttered the cry: "Militia was drilled bullets were cast supplies of ammunition got ready, cunning plans for disappointing the royal ordinances devised and carried out but God save the King to be sure was the cry everywhere: and, in reply to my objections to"; Thackeray deleted this passage, however, made a new beginning—"On the night of the"—and added a note to the printer: "(1a, 1b, 1c to follow)." The interpolated passage, therefore, seems to be his account of the ball that Washington attends but Madam Esmond does not, and perhaps of her own entertainment, where Washington intervenes to disperse a mob that she has incited to disorderliness because of her provocative singing of "Britons, strike home!" (2:322–23), the latter passage, especially, furnishing an even more effective example of her fiercely stubborn pride.

The brief chapter 40, "YANKEE DOODLE COMES TO TOWN," is now entirely in Thackeray's handwriting (fols. 7–9), but the verso of fol. 11 contains two lines in Anne's hand that represent an earlier version of chapter 40's second paragraph: "Nor was Maria the only member of our family to whom America was to afford a shelter." The present fols. 7–9 reveal no significant alterations. The manuscript of chapter 41, "A COLONEL WITHOUT A REGIMENT," contains two leaves written down by Thackeray (fols. 10–11) and eleven by Anne (fols. 12–17, [17a], 18–21).[23] Whether the first two leaves were inserted or whether they replaced an earlier passage set down by Anne, they became a part of the chapter before renumbering took place, and they open the chapter as we now know it. The manuscript shows no significant difficulties of composition but reveals one substantial addition in press concerning "the Castlewood or Westmoreland Defenders." Originally we were to learn only that this was a unit of which George "had the honor to be appointed Colonel. Friend Hagan eagerly came forward to offer himself as chaplain" (fol. 11).

In press, however, Thackeray cancelled the words "Castlewood or" and added a passage to the first sentence that expressed George's sense of self-importance but qualified his success as a military figure, in keeping with the chapter title, which was also added in press: "and which I was to command when it appeared in the field. And that fortunate event must straightway take place, so soon as the county knew that a gentleman of my station and name would take the command of the force. The announcement was duly made in the Government Gazette, and we filled in our officers readily enough; but the recruits, it must be owned, were slow to come in, and quick to disappear. Nevertheless, friend Hagan eagerly came forward . . ." (2:335–36). In keeping with this change, Thackeray made another later in the chapter where George's command, which in the original version "dwindled considerably Especially after the outrageous conduct of his chief" (fol. 22), now "dwindled utterly away" (2:339) after the Governor's behavior. The manuscript for chapter 42, "IN WHICH WE BOTH FIGHT AND RUN AWAY," is missing.

Thackeray finished writing number 24 for October 1859 early on the morning of 7 September (*Letters*, 4:149) and apparently completed

correcting and revising proof by the 10th or thereabout (*Letters*,
4:151n). Its two chapters took up only twenty-four printed pages, but
the surviving manuscript is quite fragmentary and permits only a limited discussion. The two remaining leaves of chapter 43 (fols. 1 and 2)
may have been inserted into the manuscript, for after one and one-half
leaves of text in Anne's hand, Thackeray himself added seven and one-
half lines, of which he cancelled the last two and then drew a vertical
line down through the blank portion remaining on the page. These
seven lines offer the chief interest, for they show Thackeray taking
great pains to refine George's description of Wolfe at Quebec, whom he
contrasts with Howe at Philadelphia. The text in Anne's hand had concluded: "Ah! think of Eighteen years before and the fiery young War-
rior whom England had sent out to fight her adversary on the american
Continent," at which point Thackeray wrote: "for every prowling
round the wall behind wh. the foe lies sheltered, by night and by day
sleepless and eager; losing all rest in his hunger for battle, and never
closing his eye so intent is it in watching the prey." This portion of the
sentence, which promised to become even longer or perhaps already
continued at some length, was divided in two after the word "Continent," while the word "alike" was added after "day." The words
"Fancy him" were also added, and the words "prowling" and "wall"
were replaced: "Fancy him for ever pacing round the defenses." The
phrase "losing all rest in his hunger for battle" became "consuming
away in his longing his," then ". . . fierce longing after," and finally
". . . wrath and longing." Thackeray also deleted "the prey," so that
Wolfe's intensity centered in the single word, "watching."

The animal metaphor was then reworked as Thackeray cancelled an
earlier reading: "now here now there snuffing" became "winding the
track with untiring scent that pants and hungers for blood & battle,"
and the word "prowling" reappeared in "prowling through midnight
forests." The ensuing phrase, "or climbing slippery peaks, where he
may watch and watch, till his great heart is almost worn out," became
"or climbing silent over precipices before dawn; and watching till his
great heart is almost worn out." So, too, "bounds down and grapples"
became "springs on him and grapples." Thackeray originally concluded: "Think of Wolfe at Quebec, and hearken to Howe's fiddles, as
he sits smiling amongst the dancers and lights at Philadelphia!" He
then drew a vertical line through the remaining blank space at the bottom of the leaf. Subsequently, however, he went on with a new para-

graph: "Th[ink of]²⁴ those lights, and that splendor and merriment and good cheer; and the gay commander and amidst his ladies: and the jolly Captains tossing beakers and throwing dice:—and yonder lamp, the only one in the still huts of Valley Forge" (fol. 2; see 2:354). However, Thackeray decided to cancel the last sentence, along with the interpolated words ("and lights") from the previous one, for he decided not to develop a new contrast at this point between Howe at Philadelphia and Washington at Valley Forge but to narrate instead the failure of Burgoyne.

Three brief portions of the manuscript of the final chapter remain: fols. 6–10, in the secretary's hand; fols. 12–16, in Thackeray's; and fols. 3*a*, 4*a*, and the top of 5*a*, in Anne's.²⁵ The chapter's beginning and end are missing, as are the three intervening portions; altogether they contain something more than five-eighths of the chapter's text. Even in what survives, however, there are interesting changes. After mention of Washington's difficulty with Gates (2:363), Harry originally began his passionate outburst: "And it was at this time says Harry with tears in his eyes and many passionate exclamations indicating his rage with himself and his admiration of his leader when by heavens the glorious Chief was oppressed by troubles enough to drive ten thousand men mad" (fol. 9). Thackeray decided to defer this passage, however, and therefore cancelled it in order to give a further example of Washington's troubles: the Conway cabal (fols. 9–10; 2:363–64), after which he dictated a revised and extended version of Harry's outburst (fol. 10) and an account of Harry's scene with Washington.²⁶

The surviving manuscript reveals no other such lengthy revisions but it does show a number of deletions made from Chapter 44 in press. George's account of the Castlewoods, now beginning: "Since my accession" (fol. 3*a*; 2:369) was originally preceded by a sentence at the very top of that leaf: "Many of the Whigs in England were as fierce & Eager in support of American independence as any native American patriot who spoke in Congress, or wore the blue & buff in Camp." For some reason this sentence was cancelled in press, perhaps because Thackeray feared offending American super-patriots. A cancellation in press made a few lines below, concerning Lord Castlewood's disappointed hope for a place at Court, is perhaps more understandable, for the words "It is said that the place had actually been promised to him but that the most august Person in the Realm had flatly refused" (fol. 3) became more plausible and ironic: "It is said that the most August

Person in the realm had flatly refused" (2:370)—thereby making the possibility of a position entirely Castlewood's own illusion. The final major deletion occurred in the text supplied by fol. 4*a* immediately after mention of Madam Esmond's suspicion that Van den Bosch had been maneuvering "'to keep his Virginian property safe what Ever side should win'; and as this property was not inconsiderable and my brother & I had been accused of taking different sides for the very same mercenary motive, we laughed and thought no more of the matter. and indeed my wife called to mind how in her conversations with Lady Castlewood at the spa her Ladyship Expressed her gratitude to her Father for promising to provide for her second son." This rather confused passage was deleted and the focus was thereby kept entirely on Van den Bosch and his subsequent success in America. With these and other presumed revisions, Thackeray's labors on this massive, complex serial were over.[27]

A summary of these labors may be useful at this point, especially if we consider at the same time how the novelist was enacting larger patterns—partly, as before, by developing and modifying the projections of his earlier outline. In number 13 we see Thackeray revising his narrative so as to provide it with a richer historical texture, to curtail romantic overtones of George's account of his experiences as a prisoner, and to place that account in a context of varied perspectives that are intended to keep the reader at a certain ironic distance from the tale of adventure. As the installment moved through the press, the novelist completed it by adding a considerable portion of narrative in which he dramatized extensively the hypocritical, unsamaritan behavior of Sir Miles Warrington's family towards their young American relatives, and in which he contrasted such behavior with that of the audience at whose house George relates his adventures: the loving, open, sympathetic Lambert family, to which George will eventually ally himself by marriage. Significantly, then, Thackeray opened the second volume not only by freeing Harry from imprisonment and having him share narrative attention with George, but also by emblematically enacting George's turn from America to an English context that will provide him with future definition as the husband of an English wife and the successor to an English title—a wife from among the very family listening to the tale, and the very title now held by his reluctant kinsman, Sir Miles.

George has arrived in England not only because of his quarrel "with his mother at home" (*outline*) but also because of the Baroness Bernstein's letter to Madam Esmond about Harry's entanglement with Maria (1:326–28, 2:2). So too, George "shows his spirit" (*outline*) not only in rescuing Harry at the end of the thirteenth installment but, even more, in freeing Harry from Maria at the end of the fourteenth— thereby completing Harry's liberation from English confinement. George's love for Harry and financial support of his brother would have kept Maria interested; hence, after having George give his long retrospective narrative in number thirteen, Thackeray went on in the following serial part to create for George an additional occasion for showing his spirit: the fine scene with Lord Castlewood, when George, "with a sardonical, inward· laughter" (2:60), tells Castlewood in grave and forceful terms that Harry will be a penniless dependent for the rest of his life. On learning this news, Maria of course frees Harry and, now that marriage is out of the question, can afford to feel and express a genuine fondness for him (2:64). One might also note that the idea in Thackeray's cancelled outline notation—that George "may be entering parliament &c."—appears to have reflected itself in number fourteen when Castlewood asks George, "Have you ever thought of public life?," and George replies, "Of course I have thought of public life like every man of my station—every man, that is, who cares for something beyond a dice-box or a stable" (2:61). Eight installments later comes a final ironic development: on inheriting his uncle's title and property, George thinks he may also "perhaps succeed to my uncle's seat in Parliament . . .; but I . . . would not bribe. I would not coerce my own tenants to vote for me in the election of '68. A gentleman came down from Whitehall with a pocket-book full of bank notes; and I found that I had no chance against my competitor" (2:303).

Although Thackeray cancelled from the outline his statement about George's previous (and apparently lapsed) intimacy with his Warrington relations, in actually writing the novel he decided to develop at least one side of this relationship. In number fifteen, therefore, after continuing to show Harry out of favor with his relatives but warmly received by the Lambert family, the novelist centered this contrast on the obsequious Sir Miles and the newly promoted General Lambert. The former presents George to an indifferent king, while the latter presents him to the king's responsive son, the Duke of Cumberland, to whom Harry has been introduced in number eleven by Lambert's friend and fellow-officer, Wolfe. Whereas George had earlier refused to allow Harry to accompany Braddock in his place, now he shows a mature indifference to worldly advancement by declining the Duke of Cumberland's invitation to join his staff and by making the unworldly but sensible proposal of Harry as a substitute. By the end of the installment, George's refusal of the Duke's offer has ended for George the possibility of one form of public life, has failed to help Harry, and has further alienated Sir Miles—until he learns of Cumberland's subsequent disgrace, which is narrated in number sixteen, together with George's magnificent courtesy towards the humbled Duke. The latter occasion is probably George's finest moment. These two installments also mark the beginning and the progress of George's love affair with Theo, the readying of George's play, *Carpezan*, for dramatic presentation, and the beginning of George's studies in the Temple, which are undertaken in preparation "for the magisterial and civil duties which, in the course of nature, he would be called to fulfil" (2:100)—though in England, not America. As George grows closer to Theo, Hetty becomes more sharp with Harry, her taunts and his own moody dissatisfaction at his way of life finally prompting him in number sixteen to fulfill the intention of Thackeray's outline by joining the army (2:128).

In number seventeen Thackeray's main compositional change was to add greater definition with historical detail and to clarify the social effects of Harry's return from action against the French. During its passage through the press, he made two extensive augmentations: in one chapter, by giving Harry's letter about his military adventures a greater impress of personality, historical detail, and steadily reductive irony; in another chapter, by providing a contrasting account of George's peacetime pursuit of Theo. By the end of number seventeen, George has asked permission to marry Theo, has been denied financial support by his mother, and therefore has resolved to earn a living by his pen, being encouraged to do so by the reception given to *Carpezan*; so too, Harry has been set in motion for Quebec, as Wolfe invites him to join the expedition to Canada (2:158–60). George's love affair, then, does not "commence after Harrys departure for Quebec" (*outline*), but before it, and before George's struggles to earn a living rather than in the midst of them.

With the departure of Harry at the beginning of number eighteen,

George comes to be the center of the narrative. He optimistically sets about writing a second tragedy, but even as he is doing so, the increasing intimacy between Lady Maria and Hagan is helping to create an obstacle to the successful production of his play and to the fulfillment of his financial hopes. Against Lady Maria's silly, if unworldly marriage, Thackeray then counterpoints her brother's prudent, worldly union with Lydia Van den Bosch, whose flirtatious appeals George has rejected out of imprudent but wise devotion to Theo. The two chief identifiable changes to this installment were additions made in press that emphasized these ironic developments and broadened their scope. With several sentences of universalizing commentary, the first change provided a more satisfactory ending for one chapter, while the second added several pages at the end of another by supplementing narrative commentary with a scene between Lydia Van den Bosch and George in which she dramatically reveals her quick succession of moods, her jealousy, and her general flirtatiousness. Thackeray concluded this change by subjoining information about her association with the Castlewoods that George does not understand but that we do because of the narrator's added hints and ironic universalizing commentary that again serves as the chapter's final resting point.

Number nineteen marks George's permanent assumption of the narrative, as he looks from the perspective of a long-achieved maturity in recounting the progress of his courtship. More than ever, personal relationships metaphorically express political and historical ones— notably when Lydia's handling of the imperious Baroness is rendered by the phrase, "America had revolted, and conquered the mother country" (2:209). Harry's brief career in the British army reaches its climax as the long-delayed narrative of victory at Quebec occurs but also as Harry's patron, the commanding general, dies. At the same time, George's engagement is disrupted by the meddling of his English relatives and the interference of the loyalist Madam Esmond, who withdraws even the grudging acceptance given two installments earlier. Even so, however, at the conclusion of the serial number Hetty's visit to George marks the end of his isolation from Theo and the approach of his climactic rebellion from his mother.

After Lambert has been persuaded to change his mind and George has married Theo in number twenty, George's estrangement from Sir Miles Warrington is complete and George's financial struggles, which had been mentioned in the outline, begin in earnest. In spite of the

family's rejection, young Miles is friendly and the Baroness capricious-
ly becomes fond of Theo, but the installment ends with an inauspicious
omen for the success of George's forthcoming play. Back in number
fifteen at the performance of Home's *Douglas*, Thackeray had epitomized the two basic ways of viewing histrionic behavior: as true or
false representation, and hence touching or ridiculous. Analogously, he
had shown false and true marriages: first Lady Maria's silly union with
an actor, then the marriage of convenience between Castlewood and
Lydia Van den Bosch, and finally George's marriage to Theo. What
George can achieve in a personal relationship, however, he cannot sus-
tain as a playwright, for the success of *Carpezan* in number seventeen is followed by the failure of *Pocahontas* in number twenty-one,
partly because the play is too closely related to actual experience that
challenges the audience's social predilections—whether the costuming
of Pocahontas or the marital status of the chief actor. In contrast to
such behavior, Thackeray shows us the responsiveness of young Miles.
In number thirteen the latter had announced to his unresponsive family his willingness to assist the impoverished Harry; now, in number
twenty-one he disobeys them to visit George and Theo upon the birth
of their first-born child, a son. In contrast to the false artifice of the
Baroness's coverlet and Lydia's moldy jelly, he brings for the baby his
own whistle and coral, and for the impoverished George a gold moidore
that becomes unspendable precisely because young Miles's love has
endowed it with a more precious value, thereby making it into an artifice full of touching meaning. In number seventeen young Miles had
sent Harry the first game he shot; now, as he accidentally shoots himself, he opens for George the prospect of a whole new life. At the end
of this decisive twenty-first installment, then, the death of the Baroness reveals Harry as her heir, and the death of young Miles makes
George inheritor of the baronetcy. Beginning with the rescue of John
Smith, the predecessor and analogue of Henry Esmond, as Thackeray's addition in press had emphasized, the serial number concludes
with the rescue of two other analogous figures—Harry and especially
George.

Number twenty-two begins by showing how Harry establishes himself through buying Virginian property with his aunt's legacy, and
then how George actually comes into his English inheritance upon the
death of Sir Miles, the latter event completing novelistic embodiment
of all details mentioned in Thackeray's early outline. Inevitably, how-

ever, counter-movements immediately set in, for Harry comes under the domination first of his mother and then of Fanny Mountain—as Thackeray's revisions emphasized—and George fails to gain popularity among his neighbors or to find personal satisfaction in his new role, as another authorial change had underlined. In the installment's final chapter, George responds to his mother's appeal and, with his wife and children, returns to the Virginia he had left ten installments before and which is still "HOME" (2:309) to him. As the chapter and serial part end, the Boston Tea Party has taken place and the verbal conflict between Fanny and Madam Esmond comically epitomizes the approaching revolutionary war. Number twenty-three narrates the inability of George, his fellow loyalists, and English troops to subdue the rebels. At the installment's conclusion George anticipates his return to England—an event that takes place in the final serial number, where George thwarts another attempt by his English relatives to cheat the American branch of the family. Finally, formal separation of the two homes and countries is achieved, peace is restored, and the last fires are put out (2:376). For Thackeray, too, the novel's completion marked the end of a stage in his career. *The Virginians* was the longest of his serial novels, if only barely, and the one that most extensively integrated personal history with political events; it was also the last of his serials to be published in separate monthly numbers. Henceforth he was to write shorter novels in shorter installments for monthly publication in *The Cornhill Magazine*, of which he was about to become the first editor.

8
Lovel the Widower

The predecessor of *Lovel*—Thackeray's comedy, *The Wolves and the Lamb*—appears to have been completed between December 1854 and March 1855, when he unsuccessfully tried to have it produced (*Letters*, 3:429–30; *Wisdom*, pp. 234–35). We next hear of it on 23 August 1859, when Thackeray indicated that he was "going to turn the Comedy into a story in 6 numbers" (*Letters*, 4:148) for *The Cornhill Magazine*.[1] We have very little information about its stages of composition, however, beyond a letter to George Smith during early March in which the novelist says, "I am getting on with Lovel and hope to astonish you by its speedy completion" (*Letters*, 4:178).

Since he was writing for serial publication in a magazine instead of for regular thirty-two-page part issues, Thackeray had greater latitude. As editor of the *Cornhill*, he had to produce a text of 128 pages for each magazine issue, but the length of the individual pieces that made up each periodical issue became a matter of secondary, though still important, significance. In the first six issues Trollope's installments of *Framley Parsonage*, for example, varied slightly in length: twenty-four pages in May, twenty-five in January, February, and June, and twenty-six in March and April. G. H. Lewes's series of "Studies in Animal Life" varied more widely: nine in June, ten in February, April, and May, thirteen in March, and fourteen in January, as did G. A. Sala's series on Hogarth: seventeen in February, nineteen in March, twenty-one in April and May, and twenty in June. Individual essays in these six issues ranged from five to twenty-six pages and poems from one-half to four pages. If an issue was too short, Thackeray could add a poem or replace an article with a longer one; if the issue was too long, he could have the author cut a piece slightly or, if the piece was an essay or poem, could defer it until the next issue and replace it with something shorter. He also generally had two pieces of his own that he could alter—an installment of *Lovel* and a Roundabout paper—and he eventually came to conclude each number with one of the latter, at least partly, one assumes, because they were admirably suited to the making of last-minute changes in length. He seems to have intended to write *Lovel* in installments of about sixteen pages each,[2] for it took up seventeen, fifteen, sixteen, eighteen, fifteen, and seventeen pages, respectively—for an average of sixteen and one-third.

What is apparently the first compositional unit of *Lovel the Widower* was written in Thackeray's slanted hand and originally extended from the words, "Who shall be the hero of this little story?" (fol. 1; see *CM* 1:44), to, "And so I intend to show up *other* women and *other* men who have offended me" (fol. 3; *CM* 1:46). Consisting of one long paragraph, the passage introduces the novel's characters: an over-bearing dowager, a flawed heroine, and the principal personage—a "muff" (fol. 1). Moving easily between the worlds of fiction and actuality, the narrator posits the interchangeability of these two worlds and the omnipresence of "muffs." (The latter assumption was also to be illustrated by the chapter initial.) He then begins to tell us about his friend Lovel and about Lovel's domineering wife and mother-in-law, concluding with an assertion of the narrator's wish to "show up" in his narrative those who have offended him in life—not only Cecilia and her mother, but other people as well. On these leaves we see earlier versions of two names: what appear to have been "Agnew" and "Lady Denby," which were later crossed out and replaced in the upright hand by "Lovel" and "Lady Baker." Although at the top of fol. 1 there is a cancelled number "15," no other evidence of renumbering helps us to interpret it; therefore, it may well be an error. One wonders whether, as in the case of *The Newcomes* and *The Virginians*, the present opening was inserted ahead of an earlier beginning; if it was, the portion that follows in the present narrative sequence now exists only in a later, revised, and recopied version, for fols. 4–10, written in Thackeray's upright hand on different paper, contain the names "Lovel" and "Lady Baker" solely in their final forms.

It appears more likely that these two portions were composed in their present sequence, even though fol. 5 has a number "2" written and cancelled in ink in its upper left corner. On the first two of fols. 4–10, the narrator makes some necessary further remarks, "Before entering upon the present narrative" (fol. 4; *CM* 1:46). In this portion, he touches on the ambivalent relationship of his narrative to actuality ("though it is all true, there is not a word of truth in it"), overtly reveals some of his inconsistency (especially his timidity in showing up people), tells us that Lovel is now married to a wife named Elizabeth, and then, on the bottom portion of fol. 5, begins his narrative proper with an account of his own former days on Beak Street with Mr. Prior, Mrs. Prior, and their daughter, Elizabeth—especially the latter, who began as a poor dancer but later rode in her own carriage (*CM* 1:47–51). While writing fols. 1–3, Thackeray made a number of minor revisions in his slanting hand. Later he made alterations in ink in his upright hand, including the change of names and the addition of a final sentence that emphasizes the partiality of his narrator: "Is one to be subject to slights and scorn, and not have revenge?" (fol. 3). Subsequently, Thackeray took up a pencil and made further changes on fols. 2–10, the most substantial being the addition of yet another sentence at the bottom of fol. 3 that establishes the narrator's ironic tone even more clearly and continues to do so partly at his own expense: "Kindnesses are easily forgotten: but injuries?—what worthy man does not keep *those* in mind?" (see *CM* 1:46). Thackeray also numbered fols. 4–10, the latter of which has a text covering only about two-thirds of a leaf, and, still in pencil, wrote the upper portion of fol. 11, beginning, "Nothing dear friend escapes your penetration" (*CM* 1:51), and ending with three questions regarding Mr. and Mrs. Prior's concealment of Elizabeth's profession that were to be answered towards the end of the chapter.

In the text beginning at the bottom of fol. 11, where Thackeray again reverts to pen and ink, attention centers on the narrator himself as we see that he willingly submits to Mrs. Prior's petty thefts, even of his brandy—much as Pendennis permitted Mrs. Flanagan's tippling in Lamb Court. In fact, at this point, where reference is made to "Mr. Warrington" (fol. 12), and a little thereafter, Thackeray thought of Pendennis as the narrator, for a cancelled passage at the bottom of fol. 16 (originally fol. 15) overtly identifies him. That leaf began as the narrator took up the subject of his relationship with Lovel: "In my third year at college, there came to St. Boniface a young gentleman who was one of the few gentleman-pensioners of our society" (fol. ⟨15⟩ 16; see *CM* 1:55). This account continued through the rest of the paragraph that we now know and then went on to a new paragraph that identified Pendennis as the narrator and Lovel as his great admirer: "I then, a young man myself, was affable and kind to this young fellow; and it is possible that he administered to me something sweeter than the sweetest jam omelette more exhilarating than the most frisky champaign—flattery, namely, to wh. of course most persons are quite superior. Mr. Lovel adored his present biographer: he repeated Mr. Pendennis's jokes: he never wearied of Mr. P's company: he copied my verses into dainty albums (he treated his books to the most prodigious fine coats, gilding" (fol. ⟨15⟩ 16).

Thackeray presumably continued this sentence and paragraph on a new leaf but soon decided to discard it and to cancel the portion at the bottom of fol. ⟨15⟩ 16, for he now fully discovered his need to assign qualities and experiences to the narrator that increasingly conflicted with the publicly established attributes of Pendennis and the circumstances of Pendennis's life. Already on fol. 14, Thackeray had decided that his narrator would have to be not only middle-aged, but still a bachelor because he had never recovered from being jilted by a girl now married to a judge in the West Indies.[3] The narrator had slowly been emerging as a character in his own right, who would not be a distant observer, like Captain Touchit in the play, or Pendennis, but a timid, emotionally disabled, yet emotionally involved, participant. Fols. 13 and 14 had recounted his extorted "loan" to Mrs. Prior, his hypochondria, and his attraction for the adolescent Elizabeth, the latter revealing detail helping to conclude the narrative of how he came to stay in Beak Street. Deciding to cancel the passage about Pendennis and to develop instead the emerging qualities of the narrator's quite different character, Thackeray wrote a new fol. 15 (first numbered 16 and 1) and, in the paragraph contained on that leaf, gave his narrator an overt new identity signified by his permanently unmarried state: "Batchelor." Beginning, "Though I am now a steady a *confirmed* old bachelor" (see *CM* 1:54), the paragraph conveyed information about his former infatuation,[4] a small independency of his own that he supplemented by taking pupils, his inheritance of a legacy that provided a further small income, the end of his university career, and his arrival in London. The paragraph ended roughly halfway down the leaf as the first four words ("In my third year") of fol. ⟨15⟩ 16 were cancelled and replaced by "Now in my third year" (fol. ⟨16⟩ ⟨1⟩ 15). Thackeray then continued the narrator's account of Lovel and himself, explaining how Lovel rescued him from the bailiff's house, recalling his former reference to pupils (fol. 17), and again alluding to his deceased relative (fols. 17–18; *CM* 1:56)—though inaccurately, for earlier he had said he had a small independency *before* receiving the bequest of his relative (fol. ⟨16⟩ ⟨1⟩ 15; CM 1:54–55).

After brief mention of Lovel's intention to travel and of his finding consolation for an unspecified grief, the narrator posed four questions concerning Mrs. Prior, Mrs. Lovel, and Lovel that he immediately proceeded to answer (fols. 18–19; *CM* 1:58–59), thereby ultimately explaining how Lovel found himself married to Cecilia and how Batchelor "gave up going to Shrublands" (fol. 19). Thackeray seems to have gone on from this point to an account of the ensuing eight years (*CM* 1:59–60), an account that began at the top of what is now fol. 21 and ended on fol. 22 with the revelation that Miss Prior is now the governess of the widowed Lovel's children. Thackeray then apparently inserted a paragraph concerning Lady Baker's forced departure from Shrublands. At the chapter's end young Popham rudely surmised that his grandmother and mother had fought; now, Thackeray went back to indicate that such had been the case and to explain the battle's consequences. Beginning with two lines at the bottom of fol. 19 ("So too did my lady Baker"), he completed the paragraph on a new leaf, which he numbered fol. 20; he then gave designations to the two unnumbered final leaves (fols. 21–22).

Composition of the chapter was still not completed, however, for Thackeray also inserted four additional leaves (fols. 1a–[4a]) that were set down by Harriet Thackeray and then completed by the novelist, who started his continuation in the middle of fol. 3a. Harriet's handwriting on fol. 1a originally began, "My college friends," but these words were replaced by two lines in Thackeray's hand that were squeezed in at the top of the leaf: "You must know that when I was at Oxbridge and for some brief subsequent period I had strong literary tastes. I got the Prize Essay one year at Boniface, and plead guilty to having written Essays Poems & a tragedy. My college friends" (fol. 1a; see *CM* 1:56). Fols. 1a–3a, which contain a few brief pencilled additions by Thackeray, concern two matters: the narrator's ownership of a newspaper, the *Museum*, and his acquaintance with Bedford, the printer's boy. A passage on fol. 5 had originally identified the narrator as "one of the Editors of The Asterisk Weekly Paper," but Thackeray cancelled this reading. Later, on fol. 17 (see *CM* 1:56), the narrator had been termed a contributor to a "Literary Periodical," who imposed on the Editor as a good classical scholar. A few lines further, however, he had been identified as a contributor of articles to "the paper of wh. I was part proprietor for several years" (fol. 18). Its name was not the *Museum* but, in a now cancelled reading, "The [one or two words illegible] Review." Thackeray then developed this assertion on fols. 1*a* and 2*a* by explaining how the narrator came to own the paper, thereby becoming an innocent victim of its previous owners, Honeyman and Sherrick, and how he conducted the paper with wonderful naïveté. On the following leaf Thackeray explained how Slumly, who had previously been termed "Editor of 'the Swell,' a newspaper then published" (fol. 6; see *CM* 1:48), "wrote for a paper printed at our office" (fol. 3*a*), and received proofs from the same boy as the narrator: Dick Bedford, with whom the narrator enjoyed sharing his breakfast. At this point Thackeray took up the pen himself and continued the narrative of young Bedford's reception at the Prior's and his grand gesture of engaging a cab and escorting Elizabeth home from the theatre. Fol. 3*a* carries the text to the words: "I chanced to be coming" (*CM* 1:58), at which point Thackeray made his customary mark calling attention to writing on the verso: "(T.O.)" He crossed it out, however, and instead of writing on the verso presumably completed the paragraph on a fresh leaf, now missing: fol. [4*a*], representing the equivalent of the final eight printed lines.[5] By means of this addition, therefore, Thackeray further revealed the narrator's literary ambitions, together with his ineptitude, and prepared for Bedford's later infatuation with Elizabeth.

These four leaves apparently were sent to the printer after the earlier portion had been set up in galley proof. Thackeray received and corrected this first galley proof, a set of which survives at Yale and will be referred to as Yale A (YA). He then received a subsequent set of galley proof that prints his corrections and concludes with the text of fols. 1*a*–[4*a*]. Two sets of this later proof survive, one at Yale (YB) and one at the Huntington Library (H), the latter containing further corrections in Thackeray's hand, including a direction to the printer to insert the text derived from fols. 1*a*–[4*a*] after the words, "success in their day" (galley 8; *CM* 1:56), which had completed the first sentence on fol. 18.[6] Thackeray also made a number of later alterations in press, including over twenty-five substantive changes. The unusual survival of these proofs makes it possible for us to see something of the complexity involved in the passage of a *Cornhill* installment through the press, for they show that Thackeray made corrections during at least three separate stages, which we can examine in detail.

First, stage one. Earlier, in manuscript, Thackeray had made two overt allusions to himself: first, "a certain writer's good women are, you know, so *very* insipid" (fol. 1); and then, "my good women are all insipid" (fol. 3). In manuscript he had changed the first to read, "certain writers' . . . ," but he had left the second, which appears in Yale A (gal. 2). Now, in the first stage of press corrections, he altered the latter to read, "all good women in novels are insipid"—the text that appears in the Huntington and Yale B proofs (gal. 2). He also changed his second reference to "muffs"—"a contrivance made of ermine or sable" (fol. 5; YA, gal. 3)—to read, "that before-named sable or ermine contrivance" (H & YB, gal. 3), thereby connecting this reference to the preceding one. An additional change removed a stylistic awkwardness and added a tinge of subjectivity, for Batchelor's statement concerning Prior's death—"There were two people in the world were sorry for him" (fol. 6; YA, gal. 3)—became, "I think two people in the world were sorry for him" (H & YB, gal. 3). A more significant alteration in this tale of female dominance made Elizabeth give her weekly earnings to her "mother" (H & YB, gal. 4) instead of her "Papa" (fol. 7; "papa" YA, gal. 4).

Of the two most substantial alterations, the first involved the addition of a long paragraph totalling thirty-one printed lines, beginning, "Once or twice the captain succeeded in intercepting that piece of gold" (H & YB, gal. 4; *CM* 1:49). In it we receive important evidence both of Elizabeth's constant charities to her brothers and sisters and also of Batchelor's good-natured kindness and his incapacity to act or even to make a convincing threat to act. At this point we clearly see that these are several of his chief characteristics, and we therefore have the basis for anticipating his ensuing pattern of behavior in the novel. In writing this paragraph, Thackeray partly drew on material already set down but from a later portion of the narrative, concerning Mrs. Prior's thievery and her ability to extort "loans" from Batchelor; consequently, by modifying the later reference, Thackeray linked it to the first and made apparent Batchelor's awareness that he is introducing for the second time the subject of Mrs. Prior's acquisitiveness: "and yet, as I have said, my groceries were consumed with remarkable rapidity" (H & YB, gal. 6). Thackeray thereby also gave us an increased sense of Batchelor's self-conscious relationship to his narrative. In the long added paragraph, what is now the first reference to Mrs. Prior's thievery is immediately understandable: "my jam-pots were poached, and my brandy bottles leaked." Batchelor's allusion to "those money transactions" (H & YB, gal. 4), however, depending as it almost entirely does on ensuing information, becomes oblique and leads the reader to seek a fuller understanding of the phrase. Thackeray's second substantial alteration, though shorter than the first, replaced Batchelor's statement that he knew it was not the maid who ate his jam, and it preceded his claim, "I know. I dont care who the culprit was" (fol. 12; "I know I don't . . . was" YA, gal. 5), with an allusive addition: "I have seen the *Gazza Ladra*, and know that poor little maids are sometimes wrongfully accused; and besides, in my own particular case, I own" (H & YB, gal. 6; see *CM* 1:52).[7]

Aside from the minor alteration of the now-widowed Lovel's invitation to Batchelor coming "months" (H & YB, gal. 9) after the death of his wife, rather than "two months" (fol. 21; YA, gal. 9), the remainder of the substantive changes were brief stylistic modifications. Thus "after all" (fol. 2; YA, gal. 2) became "assuredly" (H & YB, gal. 2), "remember" (fol. 10; YA, gal. 5) became "recollect" (H & YB, gal. 5), and "clink" (fol. 12; YA, gal. 6) became "ring" (H & YB, gal. 6). A missing word was supplied as "great" (fol. 20; YA, gal. 9) became "great battle" (H & YB, gal. 9). A repeated word was omitted (H & YB, gal. 10) as the first instance of its use was deleted from "whose harp now dimly muffled in leather stood dimly in the corner of the room" (fol. 22; YA, gal. 9). And finally the syntax of a long sentence was tightened as Thackeray changed "will any one" (fol. 2; "will anyone" YA, gal. 2) to "has anyone" (H & YB, gal. 2).

Stage two is represented by the alterations made by Thackeray on the Huntington proofs. These included the following changes of accidentals:

professors (gal. 4)	Professor (*CM* 1:50)
youth; up (gal. 5)	~. Up
name); she	~). She (*CM* 1:51)
about;	~:
splendour;	~:

pebble;	~:
in,	~:—
cupobard (gal. 6)	cupboard (*CM* 1:52)
lock.	~! (*CM* 1:53)
entrés (gal. 8)	*entrées* (*CM* 1:55)
sprung	sprang
juventâ:	~;
bosoms:	~;
Gandish; she (gal. 9)	~. She (*CM* 1:59)
being (gal. 10)	Being (*CM* 1:57)

Stylistic changes also, of course, extended to substantives: "some ladies" (gal. 1) for "some" (fol. 1; YA, gal. 1); "Fanny's" (gal. 1) for "Jones's" (fol. 2; YA, gal. 1); "partner in" (gal. 9) for "partner of " (fol. 19; YA, gal. 8); "began" (gal. 10) for "burst out" (fol. 1*a*); and the addition of "Henchman" (gal. 8) to the phrase "that abominable sneak & toady" (fol. 16; "that . . . and toady" YA, gal. 7). More important, Thackeray removed a final allusion to himself. Already in manuscript, we remember, he had changed "a certain writer's good women are, you know, so *very* insipid" to "certain writers' good women . . . " (fol. 1), but he was still too clearly pointing to himself; therefore, he now had Batchelor say, "many writers' good women are, you know, so *very* insipid" (gal. 1).

Because the text of Thackeray's major manuscript insertion (fols. 1*a*–[4*a*]) had been received by the printer after the rest of the manuscript had been set up in type and the first set of galleys (Yale A) had been pulled, the text of fols. 1*a*–[4*a*] appeared at the end of the second (H & YB) galleys. Consequently, Thackeray indicated on the Huntington galleys exactly where this text, which he referred to as insertion "A," had to go: "†A at page [i.e., galley] 10, 11 to be inserted here" (gal. 8). At the same time, he wrote two short new transitional passages. Hence, "Indeed at Oxbridge, if I did not obtain university honours at least I showed literary tastes" replaced, "You must know that when I was at Oxbridge, and for some brief subsequent period, I had strong literary tastes" (gal. 10) as insertion "A's" first sentence, and "I revert to my friend Lovel" was added as the beginning of the newly paragraphed text that followed the insertion (gal. 8). Another alteration seems to have been made in harmony with the change from the journalistic employee, Pendennis, to the journalistic entrepreneur, Batchelor, for "I contributed articles to a literary periodical" gave way to "I became connected with a literary periodical," the narrator no longer imposing upon the editor with his classical learning but "upon the public" (gal. 8).

Two final changes are still more notable. In the first, Thackeray had Batchelor take up an apparent error in his narrative: the aged Miss Montanville's present occupation as a box-keeper, which contrasts so strikingly with her former occupation in the theatre and with the splendid appearance of a former acquaintance, presumably Elizabeth Lovel, who has now become a patron of the drama. The contrasts are quintessentially Thackerayan, and he kept them by turning the error into a complex joke of Batchelor's that again raises the question of his authority and of the relationship between actuality and his narrative: "I am told there are *no* lady box-keepers in the English Theatres. This, I submit, is a proof of my consummate care and artifice in rescuing from a prurient curiosity the individual personages from whom the characters of the present story are taken. Montanville is *not* a box opener. She *may* under another name keep a trinket shop in the Burlington Arcade for what you know: but this secret no torture shall induce me to divulge" (gal. 5). The paragraph then concludes, as before, with Batchelor giving his fictive account of a meeting with Montanville in the theatre where she is a box-keeper. He thereby, in the new context, reasserts the validity of his narrative.

Perhaps most important of all, Thackeray altered the opening of his novel, for now he immediately focuses our attention not on the "hero" or on the nominal subject matter but on the narrator and on his role. Hence the initial question, "Who shall be the hero of this story?" (originally "little story" [fol. 1]), is immediately succeeded by the succinct characterization of the Thackerayan narrator, made with typically ironic self-belittlement: "Not I who write it. I am but the Chorus of the play. I make remarks on the conduct of the characters: I narrate their simple story" (gal. 1). (Accordingly, the first sentence was modified to read: "Who shall be the hero of this tale?" [gal. 1].) Such a narrator, in short, though not a "hero," is yet a major character and a very self-conscious one, who not only provides the narrative of his personages and comments on their behavior but also remarks on his own conduct—both as a character in his tale and as the teller of the tale. The addition thus provides an incisive, essential introduction to Batchelor and one that he immediately fulfills, especially in the intriguing narrative complexities of the first chapter.

Stage three was presumably represented by a missing set or sets of page proof on which were made a variety of further changes that appear in the published *Cornhill* text (gal. 11 is marked "Revises as soon as possible. paged." in the hand of Thackeray's secretary, Samuel Langley).[8] These changes—chiefly in accidentals—are not important so much for their individual nature as for the quality revealed by them together: meticulousness. By a careful, minute series of adjustments, words are capitalized or have their capitals removed, commas are inserted or deleted, dashes replace commas or are replaced by them, commas become semicolons and semicolons become periods, titles are italicized and exclamation points are added. In a number of instances, accidentals deriving from the manuscript are replaced, but we also see Thackeray returning to original readings, while a few substantive changes also appear: the correction of "the par" (gal. 2) to "the pas" (*CM* 1:46, as in fol. 3); "Cacadozes" (gal. 3) to "Cacadores" (*CM* 1:48, as in fol. 6); "three little mysteries" (gal. 8) to "some little mysteries" (*CM* 1:58); and "her [i.e., Cecilia's] guests" (fal. 9) to "his [i.e., Lovel's] guests" (*CM* 1:59). After all these separate instances of revision, then, chapter 1 at last appeared in print. As a result of the three additions made in stages one and two, thirty-nine printed lines were added to the installment, thereby extending its length from sixteen pages to seventeen, for the last page now has only thirty lines.

The February installment, which consists of seventeen leaves, all in Thackeray's hand, originally began, after a chapter marking, on what is now fol. 5: "The lady, into whose hands Papa & Grandmamma threatened to consign rude children, was, as you will have divined, my friend Miss Prior of the last chapter. She was Miss Prior of Beak Street no longer. A landlord (not unjustly indignant) quickly handed over the mansion in Beak Street to other tenants." Composition then probably continued on the rest of fol. 5 and on fol. 6, which is the only other leaf of exactly the same size, with Batchelor's continuing victimization by Mrs. Prior, an account that took up two paragraphs and ended at the bottom of fol. 6 and on its verso: "and from this I opine"

(fol. 6) "that there are sly-boots in other Communions besides that of Rome" (fol. 6*v*; see *CM* 1:239).

At this point he composed fols. 1–4 and replaced the text at the top of fol. 5 with the present reading: "You understand that she was no longer Miss Prior of Beak Street, and that mansion, even at the time of wh. I write, had been long handed over to other tenants. The Captain dead his widow with many tears pressed me to remain with her, and I did, never having been able to resist that kind of appeal. Her statements regarding her affairs were not strictly correct; are women often correct about money matters?" (fol. 5; see *CM* 1:237). By this time Thackeray had fully discovered his essential narrative requirement in composing this chapter: the need to devote the first two-thirds to retrospective narration. The discovery also reflects itself in the chapter title he wrote on fol. 1—"In wh. Miss Prior is kept at the door" —and in the witty chapter initial, which shows a bespectacled man who resembles Thackeray brusquely preventing Time's forward progress.[9]

Fols. 1–4 began, "Of course we all know who she was, the Miss Prior of Shrublands" (fol. 1), and went on to explain how the Beak Street lodgings had gotten new tenants in the intervening years, and to comment on "how long we have been keeping [Elizabeth] waiting!" Elizabeth, we are told, "means a history to me" (fol. 2; *CM* 1:234), and therefore we must watch the impingement of memory upon Batchelor, following his sight of her at Shrublands, before the narrative can proceed in the present tense. Consequently we learn of the "strange intimacy" (fol. 2) that grew up between them as she became his confidante (his earlier audience), seemed to sympathize with him (fol. 3), and inadvertently revealed her own disappointed interest in the departed Bombay officer (fol. 4). Thackeray then ended the inserted portion with another reminder of the deferred scene at Shrublands: "Elizabeth is waiting all this time, shall she come in? No not yet I have still a little more to say about the Priors" (fol. 4; see *CM* 1:237).

Presumably after making corrections on fols. 5 and 6, Thackeray then continued composition on fol. 7, "⟨I fear that⟩ Now Mamma Prior had not been unaware of the love passages between her daughter & the fugitive Bombay Captain,"[10] and he explained how Mrs. Prior and Elizabeth then turned to a new victim—himself: "I did not see at the time, but *now* I know that her artful mother was egging that artful child on" (fol. 8; see *CM* 1:240). An account of Batchelor's success in getting Elizabeth a position as governess for her cousins then follows (fols. 9–12), and the retrospection at length ends as Batchelor bids her enter his narrative in her present role as a governess at Shrublands: "Come fellow sufferer! Come child of misfortune come hither!"—and as she does so—"I protest here is Miss Prior coming into the room at last" (fol. 12). The leaf ended with several rather abrupt lines as Batchelor is finally alone with her and the children—Lovel and his mother-in-law having left the room to dress for dinner. The last stage of composition then ensued as Thackeray wrote the final five leaves, which he numbered fols. 1–5, but which were renumbered fols. 13–17 in pencil by someone else; I shall designate them fols. 1*a*–5*a*. They present the scene that closes the chapter and installment as preparations are made for dinner, as Batchelor and Miss Prior exchange a few private words, and as Bedford leads Batchelor to his room.

In press a number of corrections and other changes were made, as usual, including the substitution of "Are not women sometimes incorrect about money matters?" (*CM* 1:237) for "are women often correct about money matters?" (fol. 5). After supplying a new ending for the chapter that included mention of Batchelor's journey to Putney on top of a bus, Thackeray deleted the following sentence, which also provided that information and which got Lady Baker and Lovel out of the room a bit too quickly: "I had come down in my evening dress on the top of the Putney omnibus; so I staid in the drawing room with the children whilst the Widower and his mother in law retired to prepare for the evening meal" (fol. 12). Thackeray also revised the next sentence, "It always takes Grandmamma a precious long time to dress for dinner! cries Pop" (fol. 1*a*), so as to make Popham reply to Bedford's question: "'Yes, the first bell has rung, and grandmamma must go, for it always takes her a precious long time to dress for dinner!' cries Pop" (*CM* 1:244).[11]

The most extensive and significant change in press, however, was the addition of the last twenty-three lines. The final leaf had ended with the entrance of Mr. and Mrs. Bonnington. Now Thackeray added a few final touches, making Mrs. Prior take upon herself "to do the honours of the house" in greeting the Bonningtons, and showing at greater length the fond relationship between Batchelor and Bedford, who is now overtly termed "my young printer's boy of former days."

Their relationship occupies the greater part of the addition, and as a result the installment now ends not with the arrival of two new characters but with an ironic generalization on human nature: "What a queer fellow! I had not only been kind to him, but he was grateful" (*CM* 1:247). Though the addition did not extend the text onto a new page, it did fill out the page more substantially and conclude the number more adequately, providing a more satisfactory ending by turning our attention to a matter of considerable importance in this novel: the continuing action of the past on the present.

The manuscript of chapter 3 for March 1860 reveals no complexities of composition or any notable cancelled readings. So too, although a number of minor changes were made in press, all were brief and none call for attention.[12] Chapter 4, however, offers somewhat more material for discussion. Fols. 1–12 exist in the Huntington Library, fol. 13 is in the Fales Library, five and one-half leaves survive in the Morgan manuscript (numbered 1–6, the bottom of 6 being missing), and one is in the Berg Collection (numbered 7)—all in Thackeray's hand. For the sake of clarity I shall designate the Morgan and Berg fols. 1a–7a. The opening portion ended with the dramatic moment when Lovel orders the drunken Captain Baker taken up to bed and the combative inebriate goes reeling out, insulting Lovel as a sugar-baker. Thackeray apparently sent this portion to the printer but, needing a longer installment, went on to compose the lengthy addition of seven more leaves (fols. 1a–7a).

In press the chief alterations occurred after the full text was set up in page proof.[13] They mostly served to curtail the text's length by one page. A phrase indicating that Bessy not only made the tea (*CM* 1:399) but also "served the breakfast" (fol. 1a; YC, p. 399) was deleted in press, presumably because the latter action was inappropriate for her; its deletion also reduced the number of printed lines, however. On the other hand, the phrase, "What could he have been about to say?" (fol. 2a; YC, p. 400), became: "What was he about to say?" (*CM* 1:399) for no other apparent reason than to save a line. For a similar objective, one assumes, "*I* know what Pa means well enough" (fol. 2a; no italic, YC, p. 400) became "I know what Pa means!" (*CM* 1:399). So too, in a later paragraph, two brief changes together saved a line as "of quitting Shrublands" and "squared accounts with them" (fol. 3*a*; YC, p. 400) became "of going" and "squared accounts" (*CM* 1:400). Similarly, two other lines were saved, one by each of the following substitutions: "Pray," (*CM* 1:400) for "I should like to know" (fol. 3*a*; YC, p. 400), and "She says meekly" (*CM* 1:400) for "The grey eye nearest me looked over its spectacle" (fol. 4*a*; YC, p. 401; also desirable on stylistic grounds). A sixth line was saved by a combination of three changes in a subsequent paragraph: "sadly" (*CM* 1:401) for "sadly in the face" (fol. 4*a*; YC, p. 401); "me" and "end" (*CM* 1:401) for "me by her meekness" and "end of the chapter" (fol. 5*a*; YC, p. 401). The text was shortened by a seventh line with the removal of a stage direction that was appropriate but awkwardly expressed and expendable under pressure of a need to reduce space; hence, "I gasp with a beating heart, and grasp the firm hand" (fol. 5*a*; "I gasp, . . . hand" YC, p. 402) became "I gasp, with a beating heart" (*CM* 1:401). A final cut came as Batchelor's "four hundred and twenty pounds" (fol. 5*a*; YC, p. 402) became "four hundred" (*CM* 1:402).[14] As a result of these deletions and changes, one page was saved, for *CM* 1:402 now had space for only three additional lines. Even with this reduction, however, the eighteen-page installment remains the longest in *Lovel*.

Chapter 5 for May 1860, "IN WHICH I AM STUNG BY A SERPENT," seems originally to have been begun on a number of long leaves presumably containing Batchelor's narrative of Captain Baker's confrontation with Miss Prior, together with the ensuing appearance of Bedford and Bulkeley. Thackeray then seems to have shifted to an account of Drencher's arrival and departure (the present fol. 9) before making his first insertion: the present fols. 7 and 8, the latter of which is one-third blank, detailing Batchelor's sight of Mrs. Bonnington and her children, which leads to a dismaying vision of what life with Elizabeth Prior would be like. Thackeray then apparently went on from what is now fol. 9 with Batchelor's alternative view of himself as a happy paterfamilias with half a dozen little Batchelors frisking over the grass of Red Lion Square (fol. 10; *CM* 1:591–92). After having apparently written eight leaves, all of roughly similar size, Thackeray then seems to have begun to reread, correct, and number them—going as far with his numbering as fol. 3 before deciding to substitute an expanded opening for the chapter. This he apparently did on four shorter leaves that replaced the original first two leaves and concluded with four words already written at the top of fol. 3, which he now renumbered fol. 5: "filled the room with"—a description of the cloud that arose when Bedford knocked the cap off Bulkeley's powdered head (*CM* 1:586). In this augmented opening, Batchelor's self-incriminating protests were presumably extended. So too may have been the description of his hiding-place, for it originally may have been simply the "confounded lilac bush" mentioned on fol. 5 that refers to a detail presumably recopied from a replaced original leaf onto fol. 2: "a blue lilac bush." Therefore, Batchelor's bumping into "a marble urn frothing over with scarlet geraniums" (fol. 3) may have been a detail added in Thackeray's modification of the opening. In either event, it was itself to be modified, as we shall see. Meanwhile, Thackeray seems to have completed his chapter on fols. 11–16 in reasonably straightforward fashion. Thackeray also made various brief modifications of the manuscript text, one of which stands out, for it serves pointedly to underline Batchelor's jealousy. In Batchelor's scene with Captain Baker concerning Elizabeth, the novelist added the phrase, "The jealous demon writhed within me and rent me" (fol. 6; *CM* 1:588)—an allusion already prepared for on fol. 5 by Batchelor's allusion to fiends and hellish torments.

Thackeray's alterations in press occurred in at least two stages, as the survival of two identical sets of publisher's page proof (pp. 1–15) at Yale and Texas reveals. Thackeray first made a number of minor adjustments like "Jove" (pp. 1–2) for "Jingo" (fols. 1–2), but most came during a subsequent stage. His major change in press was adding the emblematic bronze of the lion and snake that he now placed in Lovel's garden, used as the chapter initial, and employed in the chapter title, where Batchelor sees an actual bite in the combat between lion and snake.[15] Originally Batchelor had said that at the sight of Captain Baker recognizing Elizabeth as Bessie Bellenden, "a keen arrow of jealousy shot whizzing through my heart." He then ran against an urn and paused: "and then the Lion was up in my breast again," causing him to prepare "to *rush* forward from behind the urn where I had stood for a moment with thumping heart" (fol. 3). This metaphor of his heart as a wounded but only partly disabled lion then led in press to the emblematic lion and serpent. Now, instead of running against "a marble urn frothing over with scarlet geraniums" (fol. 3), Batchelor bumps up against "a bronze group in the gardens. The group represented a lion stung by a serpent. *I* was a lion stung by a serpent too" (*CM* 1:585). Thackeray retained the earlier mention of the arrow and overlooked the second reference to the urn (*CM* 1:585)—which must seem puzzling to readers unacquainted with the manuscript—but he altered a later reference, as "Behind the Geranium urn" (fol. 4) became "Behind the lion and snake" (*CM* 1:586). Similarly, "behind that confounded lilac bush" (fol. 5) became "behind that confounded statue" (*CM* 1:587). Thus, although the change was not made with entire neatness, it provided a pointedly ironic emblem for the chapter.

Thackeray also introduced a number of minor alterations, perhaps the most striking of which made an allusion to Bessie more effective by comparing the bones under her velvet glove not to "iron" (fol. 11) but to "cold steel" (*CM* 1:593). Thackeray had a bit of trouble with the amusing fact that Lovel's children were the niece and nephew of their contemporaries, Mrs. Bonnington's children by her second marriage, for he had to change "uncle and aunt" (fol. 7) and "aunt and uncle" [twice] (fol. 11) to their correct designations (*CM* 1:589 and 592) but failed to notice another, reverse, instance of the error; hence "nephews and nieces" (fol. 11; *CM* 1:592) remained unaltered until the book publication of 1861. He was also unsure about the proper dose of laudanum for Bedford to give Captain Baker and hence left a space in the manuscript for the number of drops (fol. 15), which became "forty" in press (*CM* 1:597).

Thackeray's frequent practice of folding the leaves of his manuscript in half and carrying them about in his coat evidently helped produce a certain disintegration in the manuscript of the concluding installment, chapter 6 for June 1860; much of it consists of half-leaves that have separated from each other. The separate lower halves, consequently, have usually been given half-numbers in pencil by another person—perhaps the printer. Thus fols. 7½–10½ and [15½] are not intervening leaves but separate lower halves of what were once full leaves numbered by Thackeray. Fols. 1–6 and 11–13 are still full leaves, although fol. 13 contains writing only on its lower half. The half-leaf fol. [14½] is missing, as is fol. [16½], which presumably contained at least some of the novel's last four paragraphs. As usual, few of the leaves were exactly of the same size. Fol. 1 is unique in size and bluish color, but it seems impossible to say whether it contains the original opening or a rewritten version of it. From this point on, however, there is no evidence to suggest anything but straightforward composition. Fols. 2–4 carry the narrative from the middle of an aside by Batchelor—"disgusting carrots!" (*CM* 1:653)—to the middle of a sentence dealing with his recollections of Phoenix Park: "there was the bench on wh." (see *CM* 1:655). After extending his narrative on nine leaves of a somewhat larger size (fols. 5–13),[16] Thackeray then completed it or all but completed it on three additional leaves of a still larger size (fols. 14–16).

Thackeray made a number of minor changes in press, but none of them call for comment.[17] Several undetected compositorial errors, however, each by a different compositor, deserve notice. Thus Batchelor's remark, "when I *do* lie, I promise you, I do it boldly & well" (fol. 6), appears without the expressive italics in the printed version (*CM* 1:657),[18] as does the word "your" in Captain Baker's cry to Bedford: "Pray Who told you to put *your* oar in [?]" (fol. 8; see *CM* 1:659). A compositor also overlooked Thackeray's insertion of an "h" into Baker's drunken assertion: "You're s†h†peakin loud enough—though blesht if I hear two sh-shyllables" (fol. 7; see *CM* 1:658). The most important error, however, involved the improper assignment of a speech, due to mispunctuation. Here is an example of the kind and degree of error that can result when an author submits an insufficiently punctuated manuscript to a printer, expecting him to supply omissions and corrections, and not reading proof against the manuscript. As was frequently his practice with quotation marks, Thackeray had omitted them around the following line of dialogue: "Silence ⟨woman⟩ I say. Have you a word against her. Have you, pray, Baker" (fol. 11). The compositor set it up as follows: "'Silence!' I say. 'Have you a word against her—have you, pray, Baker?'" (*CM* 1:662) As a result of this compositorial decision, the speech was assigned to Batchelor, the "I" of the novel. The context makes sufficiently clear, however, that the speech should be assigned to Lovel, for *he* conducts the questioning in this scene, and "I say" is a dialogue substitution for "woman." Therefore, the speech should, in future editions, read: "'Silence, I say. Have you a word against her? Have you, pray, Baker?'"

By turning his comedy into a short novel, Thackeray inevitably created a new form. *The Wolves and the Lamb* opens as Miss Prior's cool
sense of superiority to the butler contrasts with his silent love for her
and his cool acceptance of the maid's love for him, but in *Lovel the
Widower* we first meet the narrator, whose personality and musings
fill the entire first installment and the first half of the second. In "THE
BACHELOR OF BEAK STREET," we hear the choric voice of Batchelor
and discover that the primary dramatic sequence is the unfolding of his
consciousness—an unfolding that is not linear but, because of its richly
digressive nature, spiral. Beginning with his awareness of his relationship to the narrative and of his full participation in the common humanity of a world made up chiefly of muffs, we spiral in and out of
Beak Street, Shrublands, the theatre, Dublin, Boniface, Shackell's,
the *Museum*, and other memories—emerging briefly at the end of the
chapter to anticipate, with Batchelor, the meeting with Miss Prior as
governess at Shrublands.

Elizabeth is kept waiting at the door for much of the second installment as we move through other memories of Batchelor, especially his
intimacy with her at Beak Street. Finally the sequence becomes linear
as Batchelor recalls her entrance into the drawing-room at Shrublands
and traces the ensuing events and conversation, ending with his being
conducted to his room by his old friend, Dick Bedford. In the third installment, in which Batchelor plays the spy, especially from his vantage point in the snug apartment just off the drawing-room, we again
follow the spiral rhythm of Batchelor's unfolding consciousness as he
recalls the behavior of Shrubland's inhabitants and visitors. Gradually
his memories take the form of reported scenes—Bedford and the ador-
ing maid, Bedford and the scavenging Mrs. Prior, the diners, Bedford
and Batchelor, Elizabeth and Batchelor, and a further meal culminating in the anticipated arrival of Captain Baker. The narrator's consciousness remains the fundamental source of unity, though by now it
has receded into the background, yielding more and more to the linear
scenic intervals.

The last half of *Lovel* continues generally in the manner of the third
installment, beginning with "A BLACK SHEEP." Here Batchelor narrates the hostility of Bedford for Bulkeley and touches on Lady Baker's
unwillingness to leave, Bedford's confidences concerning her son, the
ghostly presence of Cecilia's harp, and Fitz-Boodle's confidences con-

cerning Captain Baker, before recounting the actual arrival and behavior of the black sheep—the latter action occurring in a number of
scenes linked by Batchelor's commentary. The most striking event in
this portion of the chapter is the drunken shrieking of Captain Baker,
ending with his being led off to bed calling out, "Come on, old sh-sh-
shugarbaker!" (*CM* 1:399), but, as we saw, Thackeray did not conclude the installment with this outcry. Instead, the novelist went on to
have Batchelor narrate several more scenes, including his proposal to
Elizabeth, before telling us of the counterpart to Captain Baker's
muddled recognition of the night before: his sober outcry, *"Bessie
Bellenden, by Jove!"* Even here, however, the chapter ends not with
the recognition itself but with Batchelor's brief reassertion of his own
primacy: "what happened I shall tell in the ensuing chapter" (*CM*
1:402).

It is Batchelor who is kept waiting at the beginning of chapter 5, "IN
WHICH I AM STUNG BY A SERPENT," as we follow his spiralling account of his own timidity and jealousy, which keep him from intervening to assist Elizabeth. The vigorous entry of Bedford then leads
to an extended dramatic sequence, including a confrontation with
Bulkeley and decisions by Bedford and Elizabeth to leave Shrublands
permanently. Against this series of events, Thackeray rhythmically
counterpoises Batchelor's churning emotions, as he happily muses on
the good fortune of his discrediting nonintervention, then inconsistent-
ly hopes Elizabeth will accept him, but subsequently feels chills as he
contemplates the cool perfection of her role-playing, and finally receives the tantalizing intercepted note in which, he has been told, she
writes disparagingly of him. "CECILIA'S SUCCESSOR" is, of course, the
Elizabeth mentioned as Lovel's wife in chapter 1, where the primacy
of Batchelor's consciousness and memory were established. Again we
begin with his musings, now as he responds to the letter, first writhing
at having been called a muff and then accepting it—for the moment, at
least. He recedes before the dramatic immediacy of Captain Baker's
final drunken revelation, the outrage of the matrons, Lovel's proposal,
Elizabeth's acceptance, Mrs. Prior's triumph, and Elizabeth's quiet
assumption of control, but intermittently Batchelor reasserts the
primacy of his inner being. Finally he dismisses not only his audience
but also the fellow actors of his consciousness: *"Valete et plaudite*, you
good people, who have witnessed the little comedy. Down with the

curtain; cover up the boxes; pop out the gas-lights. Ho! cab. Take us home, and let us have some tea, and go to bed. Good night, my little players. We have been merry together, and we part with soft hearts and somewhat rueful countenances, don't we?" (*CM* 1:668). It is a more subtle, because more internalized, version of the ending to *Vanity Fair*.

9

The Adventures of Philip

Installments 1–10

On 29 March 1859, Thackeray told a friend, "for next year, I am engaged to write a story in 16 numbers" (*Letters*, 4:136). As we know, however, *Lovel* was written instead. After the appearance of its last installment in the number for June 1860, Thackeray also published *The Four Georges*, ending with the issue for October 1860. Writing to Charles Lever on 15 October, Thackeray said that *Lovel* had not "hit" the public, but announced his intention to remedy matters with *Philip*: "I begin a Serial in January in the Cornhill Magazine: and must make it as strong as I can to fetch up the ground wh. I have—not lost, I trust, but only barely kept. I sang purposely small: wishing to keep my strongest for a later day, and give Trollope all the honors of *violino primo* [for his *Framley Parsonage*]. Now I must go to work and with a vengeance: and there's not room for *two of our size* in my magazine." [1]

The first number of *The Adventures of Philip on his way through the World; shewing who robbed him, who helped him, and who passed him by* finally appeared on 22 December 1860, with publication announced in *The Examiner* and elsewhere. We do not know when Thackeray began to compose the first number, but unusual surviving evidence gives us an insight into his procedure at this time. Thackeray sent the three chapters of the installment with his secretary to Smith on Tuesday, 27 November, and returned the final revise to the printer on Saturday, 1 December. The following Monday, Thackeray's secretary went to the printer and checked to see that the author's corrections had been carried out. The secretary then went to Smith with a specimen of the long title for *Philip*. [2] By the time the new novel began to appear, Thackeray had completed or almost completed the following serial part, for on Christmas day he was already into the first chapter of the third installment (*Letters*, 4:214), with which the Huntington manuscript begins.

Although only ten of approximately thirty leaves of number one are known to exist, a brief discussion of some aspects of this installment is possible.³ Fols. [2]–[6] of the initial chapter's nine leaves are missing, but there is evidence to suggest that fols. 7 and 8 may have been an insertion. If so, the narrative continued from an account of the Grey Friars dinner and its aftermath (ending, "and I a fifth-form boy at school" [*CM* 3:7]), to the following, now cancelled, passage at the top of fol. 9:

> Firmin and his present biographer 'knew each other at home' as the school phrase went. Our fathers had been at college together—The Doctor attended me in all juvenile illness I had at school and carried me safely through the malady. I had an uncle Major Pendennis, well known in society in those days, who used to dine at the Doctor's grand dinners. He used not to 'tip' young Phil when he came to see us at school but always asked very affectionately after him—and was in the habit of speaking of his mother as a sweet creature a great beauty when Firmin married her, and of one of the best families in England—Then he used to sigh and shake his old head and hint to me that Dr. Firmin had made a runaway match with this lady, Philip Ringwood's daughter who was killed at Busaco, and niece of the great Earl of Ringwood of the North.'

The opening sentence of a new paragraph went on to question the actual fact of Mrs. Firmin's beauty and raised the subject of her apparently flattering portrait. Thackeray deleted all this material, however, apparently in order to replace it with fols. 7 and 8, which provide a good deal of exposition by mentioning the friendship of Doctors Pendennis and Firmin, Phil's illness at school, Dr. Firmin's invitation to Major Pendennis and young Pen, Phil's forthrightness, Pen's identification of Phil's father as "Doctor Fell" (the chapter's title [fol. 1]), Mrs. Firmin's mindless chatter about herself and her background (including a father lost at Busaco), and finally Major Pendennis's private comments to Pen about her and her beauty. With the creation of this new material, ending with a transitional comment about her portrait, Thackeray drew a line down through the empty space at the bottom of fol. 8 and cancelled the upper portion of what was now to be fol. 9.

Only the last leaf of the earlier version of chapter 2 is known to exist (fol. 20); it reveals nothing of particular significance. The three surviving leaves of chapter 3, however, contain two matters of some interest. First, the chapter was originally called "We all know what was in the cupboard," but Thackeray cancelled this phrase and substituted "A CONSULTATION" (fol. 21), which refers to the chapter's and installment's climax—the occasion when Dr. Goodenough, attending Phil, discovers the skeleton in Dr. Firmin's past. Second, the fact that fol. 21's text contains an uninserted allusion to a poem in the December *Cornhill* about a skull[4] indicates that in late November Thackeray either first composed this or partly reworked an earlier manuscript shortly before the appearance of his first installment, for he wrote: "What skeleton was there in the closet? In our last month's Magazine you may remember there were some verses about a portion of a skeleton: and did you remark how the past and present proprietor of the Human Skull' at once settled the sex of it, and determined off-hand that it must have belonged to a woman? Such skulls are locked up in many gentlemen's hearts and memories. . . . *We* know what is inside."

The ten leaves of number one reveal that Thackeray made several changes in press, notably by adding further material to the first chapter. A proofreader's mark on fol. 9 indicating the beginning of page 9 now coincides with the beginning of the sixteenth line on that page. Missing leaves prevent us from identifying all fifteen lines, but the first leaf helps identify twelve of them. Most were added in a single passage, which was inserted just before Major Pendennis comments upon Mrs. Firmin's delicate nature and just after Dr. Goodenough has told Mrs. Pendennis that she would chop off her head to make broth for Pen if the young man were hungry:

> "*Potage à la bonne femme*," says Mr. Pendennis. "Mother, we have it at the club. You would be done with milk, eggs, and a quantity of vegetables. You would be put to simmer for many hours in an earthen pan, and———"
>
> "Don't be horrible, Arthur!" cries a young lady, who was my mother's companion of those happy days.
>
> "And people when they knew you would like you very much."
>
> My uncle looked as if he did not understand the allegory.
>
> "What is this you are talking about? *potage à la*—what d'ye call 'em?" says he. "I thought we were speaking of Mrs. Firmin, of Old Parr Street." (*CM* 3:2)

The insertion served both to create an amusing transition and to extend the chapter's length on its final page, the latter purpose also being served by respacing the text so as to create two new paragraphs, beginning "And my uncle" and "Stuff! nonsense," on the same page.

Another addition in press is represented by the text of fols. A and B, which was inserted into the page proof of chapter 2, the former leaf being marked by Thackeray for placement "at 14." Just ahead of this insertion Pendennis had briefly mentioned Old Parr Street and then gone on to emphasize the dismal changes that had overtaken London since early Georgian times, as he mused extendedly on the city's bustling, fashionable past. He had then made a quick transition to Dr. Firmin's house: "In that building there were stables once, doubtless occupied by great Flemish horses and rumbling gold coaches of Walpole's time; but a celebrated surgeon, when he took possession of the house, made a lecture-room of the premises" (*CM* 3:16). The text of fols. A and B was written to precede this sentence, however, and to make a more adequate transition, beginning by a greater concentration on the destructive action of time upon Old Parr Street itself, and especially by emphasizing Pendennis's memories from his youthful past of visits to the house and the secret pleasures he enjoyed during those visits (from "I choose" to "the shilling" [*CM* 3:14–15]). Looking over a further set of proof, Thackeray also made a number of minor changes in this passage, and presumably in others.[5]

Although the entire manuscript of number two for February 1861, mentioned in an unpublished letter to Smith of 19 December 1860 as "all but done" (NLS), is missing, the Arents Collection of the New York Public Library contains corrected author's page proof for the installment, with printed numbers 1–23 and inked designations by the printer in accordance with their eventual *Cornhill* numbers: 166–89. On the first of these pages all words of the long title and subtitle have been deleted save "Philip," which was underlined and eventually printed in slightly larger type than on the proof. In ink Thackeray identified the full-page wood-engraving ("For the *large cut* Mr. Frog requests the honor of *Prince Ox's company at dinner*") and the initial ("The Jack daw here"), space for which had not been provided, thereby necessitating the resetting of the first paragraph. Beginning in ink a square to indicate the necessity of that space, he completed the square in pencil, which he used to add a chapter title ("A GENTEEL FAMILY"), and to make more than twenty corrections of spelling, punctuation, and language. The major change in chapter 4 was the addition of fol. A, a portion of a leaf written in ink that replaced on proof page 3 the following portion of Lord Ringwood's harsh speech to the Twysden ladies: "'No husband, yet, for the girls, Maria?' he would say. 'I suspect the men must know what devilish bad tempers you have got, girls.'" In its place, fol. A provided the following passage, which followed the French governess's characterization of Lord Ringwood's behavior ("When milor come, he vip you, and you kneel down and kiss de rod"):

> They certainly knelt & took their whipping with the most exemplary fortitude. Sometimes the lash fell on Papa's back sometimes on Mammas, now it stung Agnes and now it lighted on Blanche's pretty shoulders. But I think it was on the heir of the house, young Ringwood Twysden that my lord loved best to operate. Ring's vanity was very thin skinned his selfishness easily wounded, and his contortions under punishment amused the old tormentor.
>
> As my lords brougham drives up—the modest little brown brougham, with the noble horses, the lord chancellor of a coach man and the ineffable footman—the ladies who know the whirr of the wheels and may be quarreling in the drawing-room call a truce to the fight, and smooth down their ruffled tempers and raiment. Mamma is writing at her table in that beautiful clear hand wh. we all admire: Blanche is at her book; Agnes is rising from the piano quite naturally—A quarrel between those gentle smiling delicate creatures? Impossible! About your most common piece of hypocrisy how men will blush and bungle: how easily, how gracefully, how consummately women will perform it.
>
> 'Well,' growls my lord, 'you are all in such pretty attitudes, I make no doubt you have been sparring. I suspect Maria the men must know what devilish bad tempers the girls have got.' (see *CM* 3:169)

The addition validates the governess's judgment of the Twysden women and also shows us that old Ringwood is not simply a cowardly abuser of women; he operates upon the Twysden men as well, his favorite victim in fact being Ringwood Twysden. The Earl's ensuing speech to the women is further justified, so to speak, by the view we are now given of their quarrelsome and hypocritical nature—which is precisely what draws the verbal lashing of the old man. One might also note that, together with the large chapter initial, this addition extended the chapter more fully onto its final page.

Chapter 5 already had its title, "THE NOBLE KINSMAN," in the Arents proof but again had neither a chapter initial nor designated space for it. Accordingly, Thackeray pencilled in the margin a sketch of a robed figure wearing a coronet shaped to form the initial letter of "We have had to mention" (proof page 11). Again the novelist made a number of brief verbal changes as well as those of punctuation and word form—just under a dozen and a half in all. Thackeray then apparently requested another set of proof and made further changes on it.

In this case the text was slightly reduced so as to occupy the usual twenty-four pages, the printer assisting by rejustifying some of the type to save a few lines. The most prominent alteration was Thackeray's substitution of a different initial for the second chapter, which required slightly new wording at the beginning of the first sentence: "Having had occasion to mention" (*CM* 3:177). An additional dozen and a half changes, both substantives and accidentals, were made in the installment—aside from two dozen changes in accidentals that attended the setting up in type of fol. A. Here, then, we have considerable evidence of minute care in the preparation of Thackeray's final printed text. Although the novelist obviously expected the compositors to supply needed punctuation—especially quotation marks and commas—he scrutinized their work on successive occasions after a proofreader had already done so, and he corrected it.[6]

Beginning with number three for March 1861, we have substantial manuscript evidence. The manuscript of "Chapter VI. BRANDON'S" (fol. 1), which is entirely in Thackeray's hand, reveals one major revision and one substantial deletion. The former is especially interesting, for it appears at a point immediately adjacent to a passage quoted in one of his letters. When Thackeray wrote to the Baxters on 25 December 1860, he announced: "I am hard at work trying to get the new story on a head. I have been quill-driving all the morning." He transcribed for them "the very last sentence" (*Letters*, 4:212) he had written: "When I was a girl I used always to be reading novels, she said but la! they're mostly nonsense! There's Mr. Pendennis, I wonder how a married man can go on writing about love and all that stuff!" Then he went on to the Baxters, apparently in his own voice: "And indeed it is rather absurd for elderly fingers to be still twanging Don Cupid's toy bow & arrows. Yesterday is gone, yes—but very well remembered. And we think of it the more now we know that Tomorrow is not going to bring us much." Thackeray ended: "Goodbye my dear Yesterdays. And believe me affectionately yours" (*Letters*, 4:214).

After completing his letter, Thackeray apparently continued composition in the middle of fol. 3 of his manuscript after the word "stuff." Eventually, however, he seems to have decided to remove the lower half of fol. 3 and to insert fol. A (a half leaf) in its place. Written on a leaf of Garrick Club stationery, fol. A began, "Into Mrs. Brandon's parlor Mr. Ridley's old father would sometimes enter of evenings," and continued to "provided for him" (see *CM* 3:273) at the end of the paragraph. As a result, when we first learn of the relationship between Ridley, Senior, and Captain Brandon, we see that they not only met at the "Admiral Byng" but also at Brandon's, over the supper tray and at "a solemn game at Cribbage," where "the little Sister would make a jug of something good for the two oldsters" (fol. A). Even more, the passage added to the narrative a characteristically Thackerayan reminder of the passage of time in the tone of *ubi sunt*: "The homely little meal has almost vanished out of our life now, but in former days it assembled many a family round its kindly board.—A little modest supper tray—a little quiet prattle—a little kindly glass that cheered and never inebriated—I can see friendly faces smiling round such a meal at a period not far gone but how distant! I wonder whether there are any old folks now in old quarters of old country towns who come to each others houses in Sedan chairs at six o'clock, and play at quadrille until suppertray time?"

It appears that after Thackeray began this paragraph, and possibly after he composed it, he took the fourth, third, and second last sentences of what he had written to the Baxters ("And indeed . . . much") and inserted them into the manuscript of his novel, squeezing them in at the bottom of what remained of fol. 3 and at the top of fol. A. Thackeray thereby provided another ending for the paragraph immediately preceding the new one on fol. A and made a transition to it by commenting upon how the very diminishment of hope that is brought by advancing age leads to the cherished exercise of memory (*CM* 3:273). If it is rather absurd for elderly figures to twang Cupid's bow, nevertheless it is understandable and inevitable that they should attempt to keep alive what will never recur.[7]

The major deletion from chapter 6 came when a paragraph at the very end was removed. After originally writing, "Suppose to day to day is feast day; may not tears and repentance come tomorrow? Such times are in store for Master Phil, ah so please to let him have rest and comfort during a single chapter" (see *CM* 3:280). Thackeray then went on in a new paragraph: "That is what the little Sister always said as she looked at him, or when people rebuked his idleness. 'Let him be happy whilst he can, poor dear fellow, I daresay there's troubles enough in store for him.' And she would gaze again and with a motherly tenderness on her spoilt child. Dont tell me, she wd. say. If I did not bring him into the world, I kept him there. He was a going out of window that night he was so bad, at the school; if I had not been there to hold him back'" (fol. 10). The passage must have seemed anticlimactic, however, especially with its final emphasis on the Little Sister's love for Philip and her success in saving him. Because a more effective ending would have concentrated on the hint of Philip's coming sorrow, and possibly because the narrator could make the ominous prediction about coming chapters more authoritatively than the Little Sister, the final manuscript passage was crossed out in pencil and the end of the previous sentence was altered to read: "rest and comfort for a chapter or two."

Thackeray originally intended only to "break a line" before going on to compose a brief account of Philip's "merry time" (fol. 11), especially at the Haunt; this the novelist may well have ended several inches from the bottom of fol. 11 with the words, "Law Mr. Philup how you do go on, to be sure!" (see *CM* 3:282). Then on another leaf, numbered fol. 1, he started a new chapter, entitled "In [word illeg.] Buildings," which began: "At Philip Firmin's call-dinner we were assembled, a dozen of his friends. There was . . . ." Subsequently, however, Thackeray cancelled the phrase "break a line" on fol. 11, added the words "Chap. 7 IMPLETUR VETERIS BACCHI," changed the number of the following leaf by replacing 1 with 12, cancelled its title and first line (from "At" to "There"), and added the connecting word "There" at the bottom of fol. 11. By this time he had set down the final paragraph on fol. 11, beginning, "A little more gossip about his merry days, and we have done." Only after having written these words, however, did he squeeze in the resonant *ubi sunt?* that now concludes the previous paragraph: "Where is the Haunt now, and where are the merry men all who there assembled: The sign is down: the song is silent: the sand is swept from the floor: the pipes are broken & the ashes are scattered" (fol. 11; see *CM* 3:282).

Thackeray was now underway in his narrative of Philip's call-dinner, but rather complex stages of composition were to ensue. After mentioning the guests—Burroughs, Stackpole, Pinkerton, Rosebury, Dale, Macbride, Haythorn, Raby, and Maynard—Thackeray continued at the bottom of fol. 12 and top of what was originally fol. 13 with a portion of narrative that was later cancelled. Following the words, "the affection of their old friends" (fol. 12; *CM* 3:282), he went on:

There were three or four more, old school or college or chance friends of Philip Firmin, among whom the kind reader may fancy himself seated —And there was Phil's cousin—Philip Ringwood, and Phil's father Doctor Firmin of Old Parr Street.

Several of the guests present were members of the Inn of Court (the Upper Temple) wh. had just conferred upon Phil the degree of Barrister at Law. He had dined in his wig and gown (Blackmore's wig and gown) in the Inn Hall that day in company with other members of the Inn; and, dinner over, we had adjourned to Phils Chambers in Parchment Buildings where a dessert was served to wh. Mr. Firmin's friends were convoked.

We had speeches wh. need not be reported. Some one of course proposed Phils health and success to him at the bar, and Phil stammered a reply. Lord Ascot, a young nobleman of much familiar humour proposed Phil's father, his health & song." (fols. 12–⟨13⟩)

After this passage Thackeray gave an account of the Doctor's neat, theatrical reply and Buffers's derisive thumps, which were mentioned at the very bottom of fol. ⟨13⟩. Subsequently, Thackeray cancelled most of the above passage about Philip's dinner (from "There were," to "at the bar, and"), but before doing so he continued on three unnumbered leaves. The first leaf (later replaced) presumably detailed Dr. Firmin's departure, Philip's relief at his going, and Lord Ascot's ironical comment on the doctor's appearance. The second began with what seems to have been the initial mention of Tufton Hunt: "We might also have been easily consoled, if the Doctor had taken away with him an elderly companion whom he had introduced to Phil's feast. This was a pale-faced, red-eyed gentleman in black, whom Philip addressed as Mr. Hunt when he spoke to him, and who could not have been very welcome to our host, for Philip scowled at his guest, and whispered 'Hang Hunt' to his neighbour." "'Hang Hunt'—the Reverend Tufton Hunt we afterwards learned was his name was in no wise disconcerted by the coolness of his reception." This leaf then gave an account of Hunt's familiar conversation, which continued on the third leaf; the conversation included mention of his recognizing the wine as having come from Dr. Firmin's cellar and Hunt's explanation of his presence at the party: "And when your father said he was coming to your party—I said I'd come too."

Thackeray decided, however, to augment this narrative and to change its structure, beginning with the replacement of the passage from fols. 12 and ⟨13⟩ quoted above. In its stead he inserted a lengthy passage written on three new leaves (fols. 13–15); he renumbered fol.

⟨13⟩ as 16; he included Ascot's name in the paragraph that originally listed the guests—"There was my lord Ascot, Lord Egham's noble son"; and he added two final sentences to that paragraph: "Most of these must be mute personages in our little drama. Could any chronicler remember the talk of all of them?" (fol. 12; *CM* 3:282). The lengthy new passage began with a slightly revised version of the two superseded sentences at the top of fol. ⟨13⟩ 16, from "Several of the guests present" to "friends were convoked" (*CM* 3:282). Thackeray now prepared for Hunt's recognition of the wine by making it clear that "The wines came from Dr. Firmin's cellar" (fol. 13). The novelist also mentioned Twysden's early arrival and emphasized the oppressiveness of Dr. Firmin by showing us not merely the Doctor's presence but also Philip's nervous silence in anticipation of his father's arrival and then the Doctor's actual entrance—an event made all the more ominous, we can see in retrospect, by mention of his companion, Tufton Hunt (fol. 14; *CM* 3:283). So too, Thackeray prepared for Philip's comment of "Hang Hunt!" by having him barely suppress that observation now; the novelist also added a description of Hunt's somewhat disreputable appearance, cancelling mention of it on the third unnumbered leaf ("This was a pale-faced, red-eyed gentleman in black") and cancelling mention of the fact that the guests did not at first know his name. In this addition, Thackeray significantly emphasized the sinister relation between Dr. Firmin and Hunt, for Rosebury says with dark humor to Philip: "I should suggest that your father is in difficulties, and attended by an officer of the Sheriff of London, or perhaps subject to mental aberration, and placed under the control of a keeper" (fol. 15; see *CM* 3:284). Thackeray also added overt narrative commentary regarding the effect of the Doctor's presence on the younger guests: "The conversation, wh. had been pretty brisk until Dr. Firmin came, drooped a little after his appearance" (fol. 14). Philip explains to Pendennis that he and his father "had an awful row two days ago" and he grimly predicts the Doctor's contrived departure. Finally, Twysden's free-loading thirst now receives emphasis (fol. 14), and it is he to whom the novelist assigns the speech in honor of Philip (fol. 15) that had been mentioned in the superseded section at the top of the renumbered fol. 16. On the latter leaf, just beneath the cancelled passage, Thackeray then made a final adjustment: "Phil stammered a few words in reply to his uncles voluble compliments; and then Lord Ascot, a young nobleman of much familiar humour proposed Phil's father, his health &

song." At this point, apparently having sixteen numbered leaves and three unnumbered leaves, Thackeray presumably designated the latter, which I shall refer to as fols. [17], ⟨18⟩, and ⟨19⟩.

Fol. [17], as we saw, probably narrated Dr. Firmin's departure, Philip's relief, and Lord Ascot's ironic observation on the doctor's appearance. Thackeray now must have decided to begin an account of Philip's annoyance at Ascot's remark; he presumably did so at the very bottom of fol. [17], later discarded, and at the top of a new fol. 18, which I shall denote ⟨18a⟩: "Ascot! Your ancestors were sweeping counters when mine stood by their Sovereign in that righteous fight! bellowed Phill." After retracting his comments,[8] Philip ultimately sought refuge in a change of subject by taking up Ascot's earlier mention (fol. 16) of song: "A song. who spoke of a song? Warble us something Tom Dale—a song, a song, a song!" (fol. ⟨18a⟩; see *CM* 3:288). But here too the novelist decided to augment his narrative by developing it more thoroughly. For one thing, he decided to enlarge Twysden's role still further; for another, he resolved to increase Hunt's role and to make the exchange between Ascot and Philip grow out of Philip's anger at Hunt's extended remarks about the Firmin family. To achieve the former purpose, Thackeray presumably added at the bottom of fol. [17] a remark of Twysden's about wine and then inserted ahead of fol. ⟨18⟩ a leaf half covered with writing that told how the young men took out their cigars and how Ascot[9] gave the free-loading Twysden his comeuppance with a deadly powerful weed (*CM* 3:286); the novelist misnumbered this leaf fol. ⟨17⟩ because it was intended to precede fols. ⟨18⟩ and ⟨19⟩.[10] He then inserted ahead of it a further leaf, apparently by revising and adding to the text of fol. [17] on a larger size leaf that carried the narrative from the derisive thumps of Buffers, through Philip's renewed prediction of his father's contrived departure, Ascot's satirical remark on the Doctor's appearance, Rosebury's wish that Dr. Firmin had taken Hunt and Twysden with him, Rosebury's ironic baiting of Twysden, and the latter's avuncular remarks about wine (*CM* 3:285–86). Thackeray designated this leaf fol. 17 and renumbered fols. ⟨17⟩–⟨19⟩ as 18–20.

The next portion of Thackeray's narrative, which also served the second purpose mentioned above, was written on fols. 21–22 and extended from Rosebury's reading of "bills, billiards, Boulogne, gambling houses in his noble lineaments" (see *CM* 3:287) through a revised version of the opening of the exchange concerning ancestors between

Ascot and Philip that Thackeray had originally written at the top of fol. ⟨18a⟩ and now partly cancelled on that leaf. He then renumbered fol. ⟨18a⟩ as 23 and went on to write the final portion of the present chapter without discernible complications,[11] concluding near the top of fol. 27. Only one manuscript alteration on these final leaves is worthy of mention. During the sharp exchange between Ascot and Philip, Thackeray's revised version read: "O—I say—If you are going to come King Richard III over us, continues my lord, and trot over Bosworth field." The novelist decided to shorten and intensify the utterance, however; consequently, he deleted "continues," added above it, "! . . . breaks out," and also cancelled his final five words alluding to Bosworth field. As a result he achieved his objective, but in doing so removed the antecedent of "that righteous fight" in Philip's ensuing retort: "Ascot, your ancestors were sweeping counters when mine stood by King Richard in that righteous fight! shouts Philip" (fol. 22; see *CM* 3:288). Several other modifications made in connection with this spirited interchange were more thoroughly successful, however.

In press further alterations were made, the sequence of which we can see with the help of several sets of page proof surviving in the Arents Collection and in the Humanities Research Center of the University of Texas at Austin.[12] The earlier sets of Arents and Texas page proof for chapter 6 contain three lines of heading and blank space that ultimately proved too large for the chapter initial; the Texas set, which includes the six pages missing from the Arents set, reveals that exact space was left for the initial of chapter 7—presumably because the woodblock had already been prepared. On the eleven pages of the Arents A set Thackeray added further corrections for chapter 6: twenty changes of punctuation and word-form and several verbal alterations. Thus Caroline was turned away not by her father and stepmother but by her father and mother, as the reference to Captain Brandon's rejecting Caroline while "married a second time, and under the dominion of a cruel & blundering woman" (fol. 1) was changed to his rejecting her while "under the domination of his wife, a cruel and blundering woman" (Arents A, 2; *CM* 3:271). The Captain now met his cronies at the "Admiral Byng" not "nightly" (fol. 2) but "frequently" (Arents A, 2; *CM* 3:271). Thackeray also added to his observation that the sight of "these two good fogies [Ridley Senior and Brandon] together was a spectacle for edification. Their elderly friendship brought comfort to themselves and their families" (fol. 4). Between these two sentences Thackeray inserted the humorous comment, "Their tumblers kissed each other on the table" (Arents A, 5; *CM* 3:274).[13] Somewhat later, "In the day's work must occur critical moments" (fol. 6) became "Each day there must occur critical moments" (Arents A, 7; *CM* 3:276), for the introductory phrase had already appeared two sentences earlier.

The major change in press to chapter 6, however, was the addition of the following passage towards the end of Philip's irate speech on the chapter's next to last page: "I have dangled about at fine parties, and danced at fashionable balls. I have seen mothers bring their virgin daughters up to battered old rakes, and ready to sacrifice their innocence for fortune or a title. The atmosphere of those polite drawing rooms stifles me. I cant bow the knee to the horrible old Mammon. I walk about in the crowds as lonely as if I was in a wilderness; and don't begin to breathe freely until I get some honest tobacco to clear the air" (Arents A, 10; see *CM* 3:279). Six and one-half printed lines were thereby added to the chapter and helped to extend the text on the final page to a point slightly below the half-way mark. One could not call it a necessary addition, but it did reduce the blank space on the final page and, more important, it added forcefulness and expressive length to Philip's outburst.

Two substantial additions were made to the earlier set of the Arents page proof of chapter 7, both of them towards the end of the chapter and installment. After the account of Tom Dale singing "Moonlight on the Tiles," Thackeray inserted two sentences beginning, "Then politeness demanded that our host should sing one of his songs" (Arents A, 20; *CM* 3:289), together with the song itself: "Doctor Luther," which was copied on the verso of a letter from George Smith dated 6 February 1861 and which contained Thackeray's instruction to the printer: "Space the song well out."[14] As a result, the text was extended by the equivalent of thirty-nine lines. The second addition, on a leaf or leaves now missing, provided three paragraphs at the end of the chapter's final page ("I may have been . . . the day before the eruption") that came to comprise fifty printed lines, for a combined total of just under two full pages.

The first of these three paragraphs begins by directing our attention away from Pendennis's sleeping wife and child to a more germane subject: the sinister relationship just revealed to us at the call dinner. Thackeray does so by having Pendennis narrate a subsequent conversation with Philip, beginning:

> I may have been encouraged in my suspicions of the dingy clergyman by Philip's own surmises regarding him, which were expressed with the speaker's usual candour. "The fellow calls for what he likes at the Firmin Arms," said poor Phil; "and when my father's bigwigs assemble, I hope the reverend gentleman dines with them. I should like to see him hobnobbing with old Bumpsher, or slapping the bishop on the back. He lives in Sligo Street, round the corner, so as to be close to our house and yet preserve his own elegant independence. Otherwise, I wonder he has not installed himself in Old Parr Street, where my poor mother's bedroom is vacant. The doctor does not care to use that room. I remember now how silent they were when together, and how terrified she always seemed before him. What has he done? I know of one affair in his early life. Does this Hunt know of any more? They have been accomplices in some conspiracy, sir." (B, 23; *CM* 3:292)

Here Thackeray not only refocuses the reader's attention on the central mystery of the chapter but provides a decisive hint of what underlies it: the connection between Hunt's power over Dr. Firmin, the Doctor's late wife, and a previous unsavory conspiracy between the two men.

Thackeray then has Philip link this matter, through mention of young Cinqbars, "the worthy son of the worthy Ringwood," to the whole subject of family involvement—indeed, possible complicity—in the guilt of Doctor Firmin:

> "I say, does wickedness run in the blood? My grandfathers, I have heard, were honest men. Perhaps they were only not found out; and the family taint will show in me some day. There are times when I feel the devil so strong within me, that I think some day he must have the mastery. It's not a jolly thing, Pendennis, to have such a father as mine. Don't humbug *me* with your charitable palliations and soothing surmises. You put me in mind of the world then, by Jove, you do! I laugh, and I drink, and I make merry, and sing, and smoke endless tobacco; and I tell you, I always feel as if a little sword was dangling over my skull which will fall some day and split it. Old Parr Street is mined, sir,—mined! and some morning we shall be blown into blazes—into blazes, sir; mark my words! That's why I'm so careless and so idle, for which you fellows are always bothering and scolding me. There's no use in settling down until the explosion is over, don't you see? *Incedo per ignes suppositori*, and, by George! sir, I feel my bootsoles already scorching. . . . Suppose there's no escape for me, and I inherit my doom, as another man does gout or consumption? Knowing this

fate, what is the use, then, of doing anything in particular? I tell you, sir, the whole edifice of our present life will crumble in and smash." (Here he flings his pipe to the ground with an awful shatter.) "And until the catastrophe comes, what on earth is the use of setting to work, as you call it? You might as well have told a fellow, at Pompeii, to select a profession the day before the eruption." (B, 23–24; see *CM* 3:292–93)

Here, then, we gain a dramatic sense of damaging family connectedness, of possible taint, of Philip's fearful sense of impending destruction, and the desperation of his resultant immersion in fleshpots. Thackeray thereby establishes a firm bond to the previous numbers and develops subjects raised there by giving us further insights into family guilt and the reasons underlying Philip's behavior.

In the later proof versions of the installment, chapter 6 contains its wood-engraved initial together with a rejustified opening text because the block proved smaller than the space left blank for it. Chapter 7 does not have its initial in the Arents set, though it has its headings, but in this instance exact space had been left for the woodblock that was ultimately inserted (Arents B, 12); Texas B contains the initial. Although these are publisher's sets, Thackeray himself evidently received a set, for further changes—a number of them clearly authorial—had been made when the installment appeared in the *Cornhill*. Aside from a number of brief alterations of substantives and accidentals, there were four longer additions, all to chapter 7. The first two consisted of eight words identifying the occasion of a comment made privately to Pendennis by Hunt ("on his part, when we came away together") and one hundred ten words describing Twysden's arrival home and parting from his less inebriated escorts ("A large butler . . . all that way home" [*CM* 3:291]). The third added a more explicit statement of Philip's fear at being some day mastered by a strong demon within him: "I'm not quite bad yet: but I tremble lest I should go. Suppose I were to drown, and go down?" (*CM* 3:292). Finally, Thackeray added two additional concluding paragraphs, for the chapter now ends with a tantalizing turn as Pendennis alludes to a possible escape and as Philip indicates a possible new resource and an alternative pattern of behavior:

"If you know that Vesuvius is going to burst over Pompeii," I said, somewhat alarmed, "why not go to Naples, or farther, if you will?"

"Were there not men in the sentry-boxes at the city gates," asked Philip, "who might have run, and yet remained to be burned there? Sup-

pose, after all, the doom isn't hanging over us,—and fear of it is only a
nervous terror of mine? Suppose it comes, and I survive it? The risk of
the game gives a zest to it, old boy. Besides, there is Honour: and some
One Else is in the case, from whom a man *could* not part in an hour of
danger." And here he blushed a fine red, heaved a great sigh, and emp-
tied a bumper of claret. (*CM* 3:293)

Philip has in mind Agnes Twysden but Thackeray is probably also
pointing ahead to Charlotte Baynes. If the first two of these augmentations supplied clarifying minor detail, the third added brief emphasis,
and the fourth, in conjunction with the previously inserted chapter
ending, decidedly strengthened Thackeray's narrative, both in content
and in structure.

On 10 March 1861, just after one of Thackeray's "attacks of illness wh.
are now so frequent," he "had to struggle to [his] unfinished months
work and get it done somehow or other" (*Letters*, 4:223–24). Although
often one cannot be sure whether he is referring only to initial composition or also to evolution in press, here he may mean the former.[15]
The month's installment, number four for April, consists of three chapters, 8–10, only the last two of which contain their titles in manuscript.
The former, "WILL BE PRONOUNCED TO BE CYNICAL BY THE BE-
NEVOLENT," has only Thackeray's word "Chap" and the numeral "8"
(fol. 1). The chapter consists of five leaves (fols. 1–5), but the top of fol.
[2], is missing—a portion containing space for about eight handwritten
lines. Fol. 1, which lacks its bottom, contains only ten lines instead of a
normal complement of about thirty. The roughly twenty-eight lines of
handwriting missing from fols. 1 and [2] represent approximately the
equivalent of the absent lines of printed text: from "No. Only I know"
to "her little tea-tray. And" (*CM* 3:386). Therefore it seems probable
that the missing text was a part of the original manuscript rather than
an addition made in press. No other notable complications appear in
the manuscript of the chapter.

  Chapter 9—"Contains one riddle wh. is solved, and perhaps some
more" (fol. 6)—was originally begun on fol. 7 as "Chap II" (i.e., the
installment's second chapter), with the same title. In the previous
chapter, Pendennis had hinted how Philip's courtship of Agnes had
been complicated by the presence of a wealthy rival. The chapter had

ended: "This is what is called cynicism, you know. Then I suppose my wife is a Cynic, who clutches her children to her pure heart, and prays gracious Heaven to guard them from selfishness, from worldliness, from heartlessness, from wicked greed" (fol. 5). In the voice of Pendennis, Thackeray then continued on a new leaf: "And yet, if a novelist may chronicle any passion, it's flames, it's raptures, it's whispers its assignations its sonnets, its quarrels, sulks, reconciliations and so on the history of such a love as this first of Phil's may be excusable in print because I dont believe it was a real love at all" (fol. 7). Later he decided to insert a new opening paragraph for chapter 9, where he makes a typically Thackerayan apology for not providing "a description of love-making," all the more because the "love-making" between Agnes and Philip is essentially just a charade of deception and self-deception. Even more, he provides a decisive orientation for the reader by inviting him to share the perspective of experience as metaphorically embodied in a pilgrim journeying towards his ultimate destination, far from the land of youth's bittersweet passions: "When we were young we too perhaps were taken in under Love's tent: we have eaten of his salt: and partaken of his bitter his delicious bread. * * Now we are padding the hoof lonely in the wilderness, we will not abuse our host, will we? We will couch under the stars; and think fondly of old times; and tomorrow resume the staff & the journey" (fol. 6). As a result, we are provided not merely with the ironic viewpoint of the second paragraph, but with an initial, broader perspective that deepens the irony with a consciousness of sad as well as fortunate loss. Thackeray then numbered the leaves of the chapter, no other notable complexities of composition being evident in the surviving manuscript (fols. 6–14, 14v).[16]

The final unit of the installment was designated "Chap.—IN WH. WE VISIT ADMIRAL BYNG" (fol. 1a); later, the numeral "10" was added. Approximately an inch is missing from fol. 1a, which is a leaf of blue Athenaeum Club paper, like fols. 2a and 3a; this missing portion presumably contained the opening of the chapter's second paragraph, from "How came she" to "and fever, and" (CM 3:401).[17] Otherwise the six leaves reveal nothing worthy of special comment.

In press, however, there were again interesting developments. By the time he forwarded the manuscript to the printer, Thackeray had sent off two woodblocks for chapter initials or the drawings for them, since he marked on fol. 1, "Leave Space for Initial the blocks," and on fol. 1*a*, "(The monk for a letter)"—one of his purposes being to determine as accurately as possible how much space he had filled and needed to fill, if any. Chapter 8 appeared with the usual number of minor changes, but there were major alterations in chapters 9 and 10. Since the text of chapter 8 required six pages to be printed, Thackeray theoretically had eighteen remaining for the last two chapters. He found, however, that it was necessary both to add and to delete significantly. The most extensive cut came in the text of chapter 9 and was apparently made in conjunction with an addition consisting of over 175 words. Pendennis had just asked the reader to imagine Mrs. Twysden having left Agnes and Philip alone together, and had commented: "(. . . but my poor dear little younger son of a Joseph, if you suppose she will leave the room and *you* alone in it—o my dear Joseph, you may just jump down the well at once!)" (fols. 10–11; see *CM* 3:395). At this point, after the words, "Mamma, I say" (fol. 11; *CM* 3:395), Pendennis originally continued:

confiding in her child (Fool, Fool, Fool I say. Thrice dubbed fool to think you can watch or count or describe or tell the doubles and artifices of a woman!). Mamma, I once more remark, leaves the room and her innocent to take care of her innocent self—and they begin—the daring young *roué*;—the reckless man of the world;—the wretch who smokes, plays billiards, and frequents man's Society—and the pure young being—who has but the experience of four or five years beside a dear mother's skirts —who has not been at more than fifteen hundred parties; who who has not waltzed with more than three thousand gentlemen, and heard their small talk; who has not listened (with tolerably shrewd ears) to more than five thousand young women's, private confidences, their scandal, the married scandal round about them, and the clack of their dowagers—I say, between such a young billiard-playing, cigar smoking reprobate as the boy, and such a well-educated and very well brought up Vestal as my spotless girl, is n't it absurd and ungenerous to ask wh. is to have the mastery?—the Hawk, or the Dove?

And pray, wh. is the Dove and wh. is the Hawk? or, stay—Have you ever read that fantastic pretty book of Michelet—'DE L'OISEAU'? whose aim it is to show that the female is always the better, the cleverer, and *the conquering bird*.

Now suppose Mamma is gone away and the young folks are alone. Mrs. Twysden is not a literary Mr. Twysden though a woman of very great shrewdness, prudence, and sense of humour. She has an album somewhere about the drawing room, a faded old green morocco thing with a ruptured lock, dim gilt edges, and poems written in faded brown ink (Talbot copied into it, as Clerk of the Powder and Queue Office, lines by

Walter Scott Byron &c.)—But I say, beyond this album, and a great deal of fun, and reading of Tom Jones and Humphrey Clinker when she was a girl at Whipham, she has done little in the way of literature except the Morning Post— . . . . In fine, you see, that if Phil were to begin to talk to his aunt about Tennyson's Poems, or Buckle, or what shall we say?— the Essays and Reviews—or Motleys Spanish Armada—or what you will, that lady would return a clever certainly, but still more certainly, a clever and bewildered answer. What did *she* know about books—except the decent outside of some: the babbling echo of genteel opinion founded (or not founded) on perusal or received as the dictum of the two or three admitted leaders of the literary monde of the time being, the casual peep into Reviews, the skim of the Skim? This sentence by the way is a Parenthesis. Rub it out. Snip it off. It has nothing earthly to do with this history, or yours, or mine. But, if you & I read a book, we say it is admirable, or it is stupid, or as you will. I have three books on the table before me, on each of wh. asked, my hand on my heart, I could give my own private opinion respecting its worth. But, my poor dear creature, in society, in the *monde, vous comprenez*, this is by no means the rightsome way of criticism. You say—'That is a very good book, (or a very dangerous, wicked, incendiary, improper moral, highly-religious, improving, book) because BIGGLEWIGGLE says so—or Lord BUNKY has expressed himself in high terms of it—and the man or lady in Society says Ha! Remarkable book. Remarkable man. Must be, if Bunky says so. Knows more about books than any man not of our party, Bunky does. More of literature. Sound man. Sound Scholar, Bunky is'—And the rest. And Mamma says 'Emily my love! What was that book wh. Faladdleson said Lord Bunky liked so much?—Popham on Ginger Beer was n't it?—Order Popham at Mudie's Emily! My dear friend if you wish to succeed in the world, don't think for yourself. Get a respectable, well *poséd* eminent person in Society, as certain what he thinks about men measures and books and think as he thinks for you.

Well. We have got Mamma out of the room at last . . . .. (fols. 11–12)

Thackeray certainly had Pendennis go astray here, especially in the paragraph about Mrs. Twysden's literary tastes: not only is the satire heavy-handed, but the discourse is quite prolix, errant, and indeed empty. What Pendennis himself says of one sentence could well be said of this whole passage, particularly its hallucinated, vacuous second half: "Rub it out. Snip it off. It has nothing earthly to do with this history, or yours, or mine." Thackeray wisely followed the advice. He deleted these paragraphs from the proofs, but retained the last four words, the sentence that concludes them, and the ensuing passage detailing Mrs. Twysden's activities below stairs while Agnes and Philip "are prattling in the drawing-room" (fol. 12; *CM* 3:396); ahead of "the room at last," he inserted "has left" (*CM* 3:395), thus connecting with the last words retained from fol. 11: "Mamma, I say."

Part of Thackeray's difficulty resulted from Pendennis's concentration on the young people, then his turn to Mrs. Twysden, and his subsequent return to Agnes and Philip. After deleting the first of these passages but retaining the second, Thackeray then inserted on fol. A a new, brief introduction to the third of the passages. Between the words "are prattling in the drawing-room" and "'As I came by Apsley House,' says he" (fol. 12) Thackeray added the text of fol. A (marked for insertion "at 397," but now, because of the above deletion, printed on *CM* 3:396):

> About what? About everything on wh. Philip chooses to talk—There is nobody to contradict him but himself, and then his pretty hearer vows and declares he has not been so very contradictory. He spouts his favorite poems—Delightful! Do, Philip, read us some Walter Scott—He is as you say the most fresh the most manly the most kindly of poetic writers—not of the first class certainly—in fact he has written most dreadful bosh as you call it so drolly—and so has Wordsworth though he is one of the greatest of men and has reached sometimes to the very greatest height and sublimity of poetry—but now you put it—I must confess he is often an old bore and I certainly should have gone to sleep during the Excursion, only you read it so nicely. You dont think the new composers as good as the old ones, and love Mammas old fashioned playing? Well Philip, it is delightful So ladylike so feminine! Or perhaps Philip has just come from Hyde Park and says 'As I passed[.]'[18]

Here the drivel does not flow for very long—and is, moreover, quite suited to the naïve cunning of the speaker.

Thackeray also added two other passages to the chapter in press. On fol. 13 he had gone on to indicate that if Mrs. Twysden went below, Agnes and Philip were not entirely alone, being with her sister, Blanche: "During Phil's visits the girls remain together, you understand: or Mamma is with the young people." The narrator's voice had then imperceptibly and somewhat confusingly shifted into the tone of Mrs. Twysden. In press, however, Thackeray added the following: "Female friends may come in to call on Mrs. Twysden, and the matrons whisper together, and glance at the cousins, and look knowing. 'Poor orphan boy!' mamma says to a sister matron. 'I am like a mother to him since my dear sister died. His own home is so blank, and ours so merry, so affectionate!'" (*CM* 3:398). As a result, besides a transition, we are given a dramatic insight into Mrs. Twysden's hypocrisy and a speech that effectively contrasts with a sister matron's ensuing utterance, delivered to her own daughter on coming away from the Twysden house: "and Isn't it monstrous, keeping that poor boy hanging on until Mr. Woolcombe has made up his mind about coming forward?" (fol. 14; see *CM* 3:398).

The final addition came at the very end of the chapter. In the manuscript, Thackeray had concluded the chapter by having Woolcomb repeat his simple riddle and then having the narrator comment: "And *Da capo*. And the family as he expounds this admirable rebus, gather round the young officer in a group, & the curtain drops" (fol. 14v; see *CM* 3:399). Later, however, the novelist apparently decided that such an ending was both abrupt and rather flat. As a new ending, he developed a theatrical metaphor and used it to generalize not only about Woolcomb's visits but also Philip's: "As in a theatre booth at a fair there are two or three performances in a day, so in Beaunash Street a little genteel comedy is played twice:—at four o'clock with Mr. Firmin, at five o'clock with Mr. Woolcomb; and for both young gentlemen same smiles, same eyes, same voice, same welcome. Ah, bravo! ah, encore!" (*CM* 3:399).

The large deletion removed the equivalent of almost sixty printed lines, while the three major additions totalled twenty-four printed lines, leaving a net decrease of about four-fifths of a printed page. The original text of chapter 9, therefore, extended well onto a tenth page of proof (391–400). For reasons that will be more fully apparent when we examine the next chapter, Thackeray wished not only to improve the text of chapter 9 but also, apparently, to reduce its length to nine pages. His long deletion would have provided a text of such reduced length, but his three additions helped produce a text that required somewhat more than nine pages to print. Further alteration, however, was made: most notably, through nine changes that removed a total of ten printed lines.[19]

This wish to shorten the text helped prompt Thackeray to identify and improve certain aspects of his narrative. In explaining to readers his reluctance to bestow Philip on a girl who had another suitor and was making her choice between them solely on the basis of their financial "eligibility," the narrator originally asserted: "I am not such a savage towards my readers or hero, as to make them undergo the misery of such a marriage, as that would assuredly be wh. united two such people" (fol. 7). One infers that several reasons prompted Thackeray to delete the last phrase: the inappropriateness of linking Agnes with Philip as "two such people," the stylistic infelicity of the third "such," and the wish to reduce the text by a line. Accordingly, the printed sentence ended with "marriage" (*CM* 3:392).[20] The alteration of "as loudly as some men do who may have a leg to be taken off" (fol. 8) to "as loudly as some men who may have a leg taken off" (*CM* 3:393) tightened the syntax at the same time that it saved a line; the same can be said of the replacement of "This one has been trotted to the market ever so long now: so long that she knows the way herself" (fol. 13) with "This one has been trotted to the market so long now that she knows the way herself" (*CM* 3:397). The saving of space seems to have been Thackeray's primary motivation as he changed "Reformatories in Grosvenor Square (or where you will that is most genteel and pleasant)" (fol. 9) to "reformatories in Grosvenor Square" (*CM* 3:394); as he deleted the last four words from "game as that of Assye" (fol. 12; see *CM* 3:396, where the context clearly identifies Assaye); and as he omitted the last three words of: "with her laces and flat iron" (fol. 12; see *CM* 3:396).

Considerations of style and character delineation operated heavily, however, in the remaining examples. Thackeray's allusion to "Sultan Philip" did not fit well with all of Philip's immediately ensuing statement to the girl he was pursuing: "I like mine ease and mine inn, and I'm an old Bachelor, you know" (fol. 10), for one usually associates polygamy, not bachelorhood, with sultans; hence Thackeray deleted the last seven words and improved the utterance as well as saved a line (*CM* 3:395). Similarly, he removed a largely irrelevant final phrase of five words from Woolcomb's statement: "*I'm* not going to be had in that way by Mrs. Grimdeath and her daughter—No not as I knows if you please and much obliged to you" (fol. 14; see *CM* 3:399). Since a reference to the gorgeousness of Philip's clothing apparently seemed an inappropriate reflection upon his character, Thackeray decided to end a sentence with emphasis upon the "most undeniable odour of cigars about his person" (*CM* 3:394) and to delete the ensuing manuscript phrase: "& somewhat careless, though gorgeous, got-up-without-expense, and generally well-made garments" (fol. 9); the novelist thereby saved two lines as well. Finally, in the process of deleting language he also significantly modified a connected expression, for Nixon's silly rebus repeated by Woolcomb was no longer accorded even the modest success of an appearance in *Punch*. Thackeray changed "and had a thing once in Punch Nixon had—I know he had for I heard" (fol. 14) to "and sent a thing once to *Punch*, Nixon did. I heard" (*CM* 3:399); the novelist thereby gave the riddle its deserved rejection and saved another line. As a result of these deletions, Thackeray's revised text, together with his three additions, took up exactly nine pages.

When the manuscript of chapter 10 went to the printer, it consisted of six leaves (fols. 1*a*–6*a*) containing a text that ended with Philip's news of having met Hunt at Mrs. Brandon's, with the doctor's fearful rage, and with Hunt's swaggering entrance into Dr. Firmin's house, where he first addresses Philip and then his father: "What *you* dine here? We rarely do Papa the honor of dining with him, says the parson with his knowing leer. I suppose, Doctor, it is to be Fatted Calf day now the Prodigal has come home. Theres worse things than a good fillet of veal—Eh?" It is difficult to say whether or not Thackeray originally intended to end his chapter and installment at that point. We can observe, however, that he later went on to write two additional leaves, fols. A and B,[21] which recounted a tense scene between Philip and Hunt, followed by one in which Philip hears Caroline Brandon promise Dr. Firmin, to the latter's great relief, never to do something—what it is remaining unspecified but somehow involving all three of them and Hunt. Unquestionably the material supplied by fols. A and B logically follows from what we learn on fol. 6*a* and provides a more dramatic ending. Whether planned all along, as very possibly it was, or written to fill out the number, it constituted an ending that Thackeray did not wish to delete when he was faced with the desirability of filling only the usual twenty-four pages. Furthermore, since this final chapter, like chapter 8, was more tautly written[22] than the installment's middle unit and could not easily be reduced in length by a page, Thackeray had an additional reason for concentrating on chapter 9 in his search for appropriately expendable matter.

The text of number five survives on twenty-six leaves, fols. 1–11 forming chapter 11 and fols. 13–19 and 21–28 forming chapter 12. Composition may well have begun with the text on what is now fol. 8, for the previous installment ended with Caroline Brandon's cry of "Never, my dear; no, never, never!" (*CM* 3:408), while fol. 8 begins: "Caroline's tender 'never never' rang in Philip's memory as he sate at Ridley's party" (see *CM* 3:563). After continuing this narrative, Thackeray may then have written the portion that precedes it and ends several inches from the bottom of fol. 7; in this narrative segment, Thackeray begins the chapter not with an account of Philip at Ridley's party, which follows in chronological sequence from the end of the previous installment, but instead with a portion of retrospective narration dramatizing the scene between Caroline and Dr. Firmin that immediately preceded Caroline's words, "never, never," but that we had not been given in number four.

Another anomaly in the manuscript of chapter 11 suggests that the present chapter begins with a leaf that was either composed by itself or recopied. The first surviving leaf in the *Philip* manuscript to be written in Thackeray's slanted hand, it opens with the words, "Philip had long divined," and continues in slanted hand, with somewhat more than a dozen brief alterations, to "falsehoods before Thee!" (fol. 1; *CM* 3:556–57), which left just over an inch of space at the bottom of the leaf. Thackeray then drew a vertical line through the remaining space; by that time he was either ready to continue composition on a fresh leaf or, more probably, he had prepared a revised introduction for what he had already set down in upright hand on an ensuing leaf or leaves. In either event, he later made a brief addition in upright hand at the bottom of fol. 1 by modifying the opening words of fol. 2—"Thus, my dear Sir"—to read, "And so, my dear Sir." He also added in upright hand a chapter title, "A SOIRÉE," which he then changed to the present version, "In wh. Philip is very ill-tempered" (fol. 1).

A final anomaly in the manuscript identifies an interpolated passage, for in the margin of fol. 9 and on its verso, Thackeray wrote a portion of text that he designated: "A to be inserted (& T.O for the remainder)" (fol. 9). Originally, on fol. 9 Thackeray had Pendennis announce that he would not contaminate the narrative with an account of the bachelor smoking party at Ridley's (*CM* 3:564); the narrator then went on with a new paragraph in which Philip observes Hunt's arrival at Caroline Brandon's apartment downstairs: "Phils head and cigar are thrust out from a window above, and he lolls there musing about his own affairs, as his smoke ascends to the skies. Who is that holding by the railings below, and talking in at Mrs. Brandon's window?" Afterwards, however, Thackeray decided to prepare the reader better for Philip's angry, violent treatment of Hunt and therefore lengthened the narrative of Ridley's smoking party to the extent of showing an exchange between Jarman and Philip. Here, Jarman's envious abuse of Ridley's picture begets Philip's insult and the narrator's comment: "Have I not owned that Philip was often very rude? And to night he is in a specially bad humour" (fol. 9v; *CM* 3:565). Besides offering us this preparation, Thackeray was also dramatizing the chapter's revised title. Since there was not to be a long narrative of Ridley's party, the chapter was not to be called "A Soirée"; instead the emphasis was to fall on Philip's "ill-humour"—a phrase both dramatized by this addition and climactically stated with the words, "a specially bad humour." The novelist then completed his addition with a transitional sentence that led into the mention of Hunt: "As he continues to stare into the street; who is that who has just reeled up to the railings?" (fol. 9v).

The text of chapter 11 ends in upright hand about two-thirds of the way down fol. 11; chapter 12, designated by another hand, presumably the printer's, begins at the top of fol. 13 in slanted hand. This writing continues until almost the middle of fol. 16, where, beginning with the words: "Marriage ceremonies" (*CM* 3:571), Thackeray went on in upright hand.[23] Except for a brief phrase in slanted hand, "The first person on whom he had to practise hypocrisy" (fol. 17; *CM* 3:572), writing in the upright hand extends to a point an inch from the bottom of fol. 19, concluding with the final words of Dr. Firmin's confession: "I fled the Country, and I left her" (*CM* 3:575).[24] From this point, Thackeray originally continued on several leaves, mostly in slanted hand, with narrative commentary, beginning: "If a gentleman is sentenced to be hung, I wonder is it a matter of comfort to him or not to know beforehand the day of the execution?" The first two of these leaves were numbered fols. 21 and 22; their text comments on Dr. Firmin's ignorance of his day of execution and tells of the improved relations between Philip and his father that followed the doctor's confession (*CM* 3:576–79). After composing these two numbered leaves and possibly several unnumbered ones that told of Hunt's vengeful collusion with Talbot Twysden against Dr. Firmin and Philip, Thackeray inserted a passage in his upright hand on two new leaves that he numbered fols. 21 and 22. Instead of following the last words of the doctor's confession with commentary that directs our attention to Hunt's vengeful pursuits, he provided, first, a speech in which Hunt promised to seek that revenge; second, an actual departure of Hunt's from the house; and third, an ensuing conversation between Philip and his father in which the latter outlines Philip's immunity from Hunt's revenge, as contrasted with his own vulnerability. Thackeray thereby smoothed a previously abrupt shift in his narrative by ending the dramatic scene more satisfactorily and by preparing more adequately for what is to follow. Philip, we are led to believe, is not to be proven illegitimate; instead, Hunt's revenge will destroy the doctor's professional career and leave him in a precarious financial condition. Part of the preparation, of course, is ironic, for although the doctor indicates he will leave Philip some increase of wealth, if not "much increase" (fol. 21; *CM* 3:576), we are later to learn that Dr. Firmin not only will leave debts, but has swindled Philip out of his mother's legacy, and will continue to rob his son.

After completing this new passage extending from "A sham marriage, a sham marriage! cries the clergyman" (fol. 21; see *CM* 3:575) to "The little Sister resigned her claims past, present, future" (fol. 22; see *CM* 3:576), followed by the vertical line that frequently marks an insertion, Thackeray went on to renumber the original fols. 21 and 22 as 23 and 24. The text continues in slanted hand from fol. 24 to fols. 25 and 26. This portion of the narrative ends three inches from the top of fol. 26 with Caroline's firm characterization of the legal tampering to which she has been subjected and with her brisk dismissal of Mr. Walls, the agent of that tampering: "I dont know what you're come about. I dont want to know, and I'm most certain it is for no good" (fol. 26; see *CM* 3:580). Thackeray may have considered ending his installment at that point, or he may simply have stopped in order to forward this portion to the printer. In either event, he went on to compose a lengthy additional passage, which survives only in part; written still in slanted hand, beginning on fol. 27, it recounts the scene that immediately follows Caroline's dismissal of Walls, concluding in mid-sentence at the bottom of fol. 28 with Caroline's words: "But if we both knew that" (*CM* 3:582).[25] The equivalent of about one leaf is missing at this point, but clearly it contained either the present ending or something related to it, in which Caroline triumphantly denied her knowledge and thereby protected Philip's legitimacy from further attack.

Number five was the first installment to diverge in length from the pattern of twenty-four printed pages. Though composed of only two chapters, like all installments except the first and fourth, its text of approximately twenty-seven manuscript leaves produced twenty-eight printed pages. So far as one can determine, this increase seems to be the result of two factors: Thackeray's wish to develop his material more satisfactorily and circumstances that permitted or perhaps even encouraged the printing of an installment longer than usual. At any rate, print it he did, making changes in press[26] that included the following:

reputable (fol. 1)	respectable (*CM* 3:557)
alimony (fol. 4)	a maintenance (*CM* 3:560)
name! and she clasps her hands, and thanks [blank space] (fol. 6)	name!" (*CM* 3:562)
of the [blank space] (fol. 8)	of the *Connoisseur* (*CM* 3:563)
Ah *Schwankende Gestalten* (fol. 8)	Ah, ghosts of youth (*CM* 3:564)
Mrs. Brandon went and sate (fol. 13)	Nurse Brandon sate awhile (*CM* 3:568)
wh. no housemaid had as yet visited, and where hung (fol. 13)	where hung (*CM* 3:568)
black velvet collar & cuffs (he always wore those ornaments) and of the poor faint lady who had been his wife and Philip's mother (fol. 13)	black collar and cuffs, and contemplated this masterpiece until an invasion of housemaids drove her from the apartment, when she took refuge in that other little room to which Mrs. Firmin's portrait had been consigned. (*CM* 3:568)
day (fol. [14])	night (*CM* 3:569)
Miss Ringwood (fol. 15)	Ellen Ringwood (*CM* 3:570)
are man (fol. 15)	are man and wife (*CM* 3:570)
intelligible (fol. 18)	unintelligible (*CM* 3:573)
had (fol. 24)	held (*CM* 3:579)
pretty quickly (fol. 24)	quickly (*CM* 3:579)
made (fol. 25)	had (*CM* 3:579)

With the making of adjustments such as these, the number was complete.

Number six for June 1861, like numbers two, three, five, and all succeeding installments, is made up of two chapters. Fols. [1]–9, which make up chapter 13, are all in Thackeray's slanted hand and reveal only one compositional development. Marked simply "CHAP." by

Thackeray, who included its title "ULYSSES AND ARGUS" (fol. [1]), it contains a cancelled passage that begins the scene in the "Admiral Byng" rather quickly. After an initial paragraph that now opens the chapter and that develops the metaphor of the monkey, the cat, and the hot chestnuts, Thackeray went on:

> There were only two gents in the parlor of the Admiral Byng on that afternoon when Mr. Wills went to persuade Mrs. Brandon to claim her husband, and disinherit her husbands son—and one of these was a tall slim old man engaged in perusing the Morning Advertiser a work of some small difficulty to that elderly student, and another guest a very harbitrary party, for he took no liquor to speak of, drummed with his fingers called in an imperious tone to the newspaper reader and troubled him for that paper, cursed the clock for being too slow, and exhibited a dozen signs of peevishness and impatience.
>
> To this arbitrary and impatient man, old Mr. Wills presently entered— on wh. he without patience cried out—Well, Sir, Well. Sir, what news Sir? And (fol. [1])

Thackeray decided, however, to cancel this passage and to rewrite it, at the same time setting the scene in a more careful, detailed, and indeed more comic manner. As a result, he went on to compose the four paragraphs we now know, beginning: "If you have ever been at the Admiral Byng, you know, my dear Madam, that the parlor where the Club meets is just behind Mrs. Rudge's bar, so that by lifting up the sash of the window wh. communicates between the two apartments that good-natured woman may put her face into the Club-room, and actually be one of the Society" (fol. [1]; see *CM* 3:642). In the new passage, Wills (later, as earlier, "Bond") and Twysden do not talk in front of Ridley; instead of being in the parlor, as we see in the first new paragraph, Ridley is now stationed in Mrs. Rudge's (later, as earlier, "Mrs. Oves's") bar, close to the window through which he can hear the conversation taking place in the parlor. The new passage continues by placing the scene in time, somewhat in the manner of the opening sentence of the cancelled passage: "On the day when Mr. Wills went to persuade Mrs. Brandon in Thornhaugh Street to claim Dr. Firmin for her husband and to disinherit poor Philip—a little gentleman . . . appeared" (fol. [1]; see *CM* 3:642). Now Thackeray provides further examples of Twysden's arrogant and anxious behavior and also explains the source of his knowledge, after which the novelist proceeds to develop the actual scene between Twysden and Bond.

Chapter 14, originally "YOUNG ROBIN GRAY,"[27] had its title changed in manuscript and became "Contains two of Philip's mishaps" (fol. 1a). Thackeray wrote it on fourteen leaves (fols. 1a–12a, 12b, 13a), beginning in slanted hand, then changing to upright in the middle of fol. 10a and continuing in upright thereafter, except for fols. 12b and 13a. Upright script also appears in a few minor corrections scattered throughout the installment on leaves otherwise composed in slanted hand. The only other notable aspect of the chapter's manuscript, aside from the absence of significant identifiable difficulties of creation,[28] is the existence of two leaves bearing the numeral 12: fol. 12a being an insertion written in upright hand on the upper portion of the leaf, followed by a vertical line, and fols. 12b and 13a—which contain Dr. Firmin's letter and close the chapter—being in slanted hand. From this evidence, one infers that the concluding letter, which so marvelously combines incriminating apology with incriminating hope and provides so effective an ending for the installment, was written before the rest of the chapter had been completed. On its appearance in print, number 6 covered one more page than usual—twenty-five—but it was the last installment to vary from the usual length.[29] Its passage through the press was not sufficiently notable for comment.

Like the last leaf composed for number six (fol. 12a), the first leaf and one-quarter of number seven for July 1861 are written in upright hand. The slanted hand then succeeds for a leaf (the lower three-quarters of fol. 2 and the top quarter of fol. 3), at which point upright hand continues on the chapter's remaining two and three-quarter leaves—most of fol. 4 being set down in pencil. All of the leaves contain the usual minor changes but no major alterations. In pencil Thackeray supplied the word "Chap" and the title, "Samaritans" (fol. 1), but as usual he omitted the chapter number, which was added by someone else—presumably the printer. Chapter 16, which seems to have been designated as a separate unit by Thackeray only after he had composed its first portion, comprises fourteen leaves with unusually repetitive numbering that requires several sets of italic letters to distinguish them: fols. [1a]–[3a], 1b–8b, and 1c–3c. All are written in upright hand. The first three leaves, which he never numbered, narrate Caroline Brandon's kindness to Philip, his taking up residence in the Temple, his nominal pursuit of the law, and his acquaintance with Cassidy, who writes as a

correspondent for the *Pall Mall Gazette* (*CM* 4:8–12).[30] Fols. 1*b*–3*b*
then treat of that journal, its owner, Philip's securing employment
with it, his journey to Boulogne to visit the Pendennises, and his account of his new employer (*CM* 4:12–15); in fols. 4*b*–8*b*, Thackeray
centers on Boulogne and the meeting of Philip with the Baynes family.
This portion, which ends several inches from the bottom of fol. 8*b*, is
then followed by the resolution of the Baynes's anxieties—as explained
by Mrs. Baynes's letter on fols. 1*c*–3*c* (*CM* 4:22–24).

In press Thackeray made over thirty verbal changes, of which several stand out. To the last page of chapter 15 he added a passage of
seven sentences that followed the generalization, "Never was a penniless gentleman more cheerful" (fol. 5), and provided the reader with
concrete instances of Philip's cheerfulness, including a high-spirited
and characteristically bad joke for the children: "As for his dinner,
Phil's appetite was always fine, but on this day an ogre could scarcely
play a more terrible knife and fork. He asked for more and more, until
his entertainers wondered to behold him. 'Dine for to-day and tomorrow too; can't expect such fare as this every day, you know. This
claret, how good it is! May I pack some up in paper, and take it home
with me?' The children roared with laughter at this admirable idea of
carrying home wine in a sheet of paper. I don't know that it is always
at the best jokes that children laugh:—children and wise men too"
(*CM* 4:7).

The most interesting alterations, however, concerned a touchy subject for Thackeray: the Grub Street fraternity as he had characterized
it on fol. [3*a*] in the paragraph beginning "When Pendennis and his
friends wrote in this newspaper" (*CM* 4:11). Thackeray originally
wrote: "They worked for the very smallest fee: but paid themselves by
impertinence, and the satisfaction of insulting their betters." In press,
however, he changed "the very smallest fee" to "very moderate fees"
and altered "insulting" to "assailing" (*CM* 4:11). Similarly, he modified the following manuscript passage: "The writers were unsuccessful
barristers, ushers, and college men, and piqued[31] themselves on their
elegance. They lived in Temple attics or basements, but they took a
Pall Mall strut as they walked westward, and they liked to tell this
writer or that that he was not a gentleman" (fol. [3*a*]). In the published version, however, Thackeray changed "unsuccessful" to "obscure" and concentrated on their amusing intellectual arrogance rather
than their unpleasant social pretensions: "The writers were obscure

barristers, ushers, and college men, but they had omniscience at their pen's end, and were ready to lay down the law on any given subject—to teach any man his business, were it a bishop in his pulpit, a Minister in his place in the House, a captain on his quarter-deck, a tailor on his shopboard, or a jockey in his saddle" (*CM* 4:12). The new passage was, in fact, more in keeping with Thackeray's original opening generalization about them, which concerned the amusing "airs wh. they occasionally thought proper to assume" (fol. [3a]; see *CM* 4:11) as journalists rather than as social snobs, and also their ability to laugh at their own rhetorical absurdities, as Pendennis himself does in recalling those days. In short, Thackeray disciplined a somewhat aberrant satirical impulse in order to achieve greater artistic coherence. The change also increased the printed text by about a line, but the addition was numerically insignificant: the installment fitted easily into its twenty-four pages.[32]

Only one chapter of number eight for August 1861 survives in manuscript—chapter 17, the title of which was revised from "The shortest (perhaps) in the whole Story" to "BREVIS ESSE LABORO" (fol. 1).[33] It has no major manuscript revisions, but in press had a passage of a half-dozen sentences inserted towards the end of the long final paragraph in which the mature Pendennis begins by mocking the absurdities of youthful love-making and then suddenly veers to recall and celebrate the remembered happiness: "Was it not rapture . . .?" After providing an example of how a young man would receive the notes in which his loved one "used to prattle," Thackeray had originally gone on with a concluding analogy of a lover and a braying donkey, but in press he decided to precede it with emphasis on the universality of the romantic impulse as well as on the persistence of that impulse even in mature people, through memory. His sentences take the form of an address to young lovers, the complex effect being to make them aware while they are young not only of the evanescence of their passion but of its tempered permanence:

> Young people, at present engaged in the pretty sport, be assured your middle-aged parents have played the game, and remember the rules of it. Yes, under papa's bow-window of a waistcoat is a heart which took very violent exercise when that waist was slim. Now he sits tranquilly in his

tent, and watches the lads going in for their innings. Why, look at grandmamma in her spectacles reading that sermon. In *her* old heart there is
a corner as romantic still as when she used to read the *Wild Irish Girl* or
the *Scottish Chiefs* in the days of her misshood. And as for your grandfather, my dears, to see him now you would little suppose that that calm,
polished, dear old gentleman was once as wild—as wild as Orson. . ..
(*CM* 4:137)³⁴

The extension provided by these lines is minimal—from thirty-one to
forty-one final lines—but the aesthetic effect is considerable, both in
added complexity and in the greater emphasis given to the final reductive analogy, whose ironic effect is all the stronger for having directly
proceeded out of a passage of sympathetic involvement.³⁵

Except for a few passages in slanted script, the manuscript of number
9 for September 1861 is written entirely in upright hand.³⁶ The first
unit, marked "Chap *Qu'on est bien à vingt ans*" (fol. 1), consists of
eight leaves, on only one of which was a passage of any length cancelled. After a paragraph concerning the dearness of some dinners,
like those given by Lord Ringwood for a spiritual price exacted from
his guests (*CM* 4:259), Thackeray originally went on in a new paragraph: "We are writing of times so early that young gentlemen, who
are five and twenty years old in the present year of grace, had only just
begun to walk on this this world wh. is now at their feet. In those days
Paris was actually a cheap dwelling place. Philip Firmin brags to this
hour of having lived in very sufficient comfort during a whole month
for five pounds, and bought a waistcoat with part of the money" (fol.
2). Thackeray cancelled this passage, however, because he found that
he was here repeating part of an earlier paragraph on fol. 1: "The
times of wh. we write, the times of Louis Philippe the King, are so
altered from the present, that when Philip Firmin went to Paris it was
absolutely a cheap place to live in; and he has often bragged in subsequent days of having lived well during a month for five pounds and
bought a neat waistcoat with a part of the money" (see *CM* 4:258).

The only other idiosyncrasy in the manuscript of this chapter is fol.
6, which contains only about a half dozen lines on its upper portion.
Before numbering his leaves, Thackeray may have ended what is now
fol. 5 with the words, "I am not surprized at Philip for announcing

that this was the happiest time of his life," and then gone on with a new paragraph at the top of what is now fol. 7: "The Baroness herself was what some amateurs call a fine woman" (see *CM* 4:264). If so, he later added a final line and a half at the bottom of fol. 5. Beginning "In later days," the passage continues in mid-sentence to the top of a new leaf, now fol. 6, and concludes somewhat later with the words: "People are still alive who knew her under [a] different name." Because of the distinctive coloration of fols. 5 and 6, however—a prominent blue, as opposed to the buff or pale gray of all other leaves of this installment— it seems more probable that Thackeray composed the texts of the two leaves in direct sequence, then paused, and ultimately took the un- usual step of continuing composition on a fresh leaf, fol. 7, instead of on the blank portion of fol. 6. In any event, it is clear that after beginning the paragraph at the top of fol. 7, Thackeray took its first two words and added them in pencil[37] together with a short vertical line, at the end of the final paragraph at the top of fol. 6; as a result, the present paragraph about the struggling impoverished lady now does not begin with a comment on her appearance as "a fine woman" but with an observation on her financial troubles.

The installment's other chapter, marked "Chap II., Course of True Love," continues with one leaf numbered in accordance with the pre- vious sequence (fol. 9) and then with seven additional leaves numbered in a new sequence: fols. 1a–6a by Thackeray, and fol. 7a by another hand. Thackeray apparently intended to send the first nine leaves to the printer as a separate relay, for he marked the top of fol. 1a, "con- tinuation of ⟨go on⟩ with Second Chapter," and began a new para- graph: "From my previous remarks" (*CM* 4:269). If he did send them as a relay, however, he probably soon followed them with fols. 1a and 2a, for the printer appears to have marked fols. 9–2a as a unit.[38] There are a fair number of minor modifications on each leaf that show Thackeray constantly at work to improve his text, but none calls for special comment.

As usual, Thackeray made a variety of brief changes as the install- ment went through the press; one change, however, stands out be- cause of its length. Besides creating two new paragraphs on what are now *CM* 4:276 and 280, beginning, "So you" and "The truth is"—both of which increased the chapter's length by one printed line—Thack- eray also created a third paragraph that commenced with the words: "And so the conversation goes on" (*CM* 4:276). After this sentence, and before ensuing mention of "the first ardour of the friendship which arises between Mrs. Baynes and Mrs. Boldero" (*CM* 4:277), Thackeray inserted in press a generous sample of their ardently snobbish blather ("If Mrs. Major MacWhirter . . . delightful news"). The passage is an amusing illustration of how "the conversation goes on," and if no one would call it essential to the novel, yet it has a certain relevance as well as humor; more important, it added twenty-six printed lines to the text of the chapter and, together with the two new paragraphs, lengthened the chapter by one printed page, thereby providing the installment with a full complement of twenty-four.

The manuscript of number ten for October 1861 does not seem to have survived intact. The Huntington manuscript contains the second chapter, "Pulvis et Umbra Sumus" (fols. 11–17), but not the first, chapter 21, "Treats of Dancing, Dining, Dying," which exists in the form of the lower half of fol. [2], at Texas, fol. 3 separately at the Huntington, fols. 4–5, 7–10 at Yale, and fol. 6 in the Berg Collection. The various brief changes in the manuscript of these two chapters are not so striking as several additions made in press, but a few connected instances of the former may call for brief comment: Thackeray's manuscript revisions of chapter 21's final scene, in which Talbot Twysden, in ignorance of Lord Ringwood's death, egoistically holds forth about his noble relative.[39] Although Thackeray cancelled language mentioning the delayed arrival of the *Globe* newspaper, one cannot assume that he originally intended to have Twysden arrive at his club before the newspaper, which was to undercut his posturing by announcing Ringwood's death. Such an assumption would ignore the implications of what Pendennis has just said: "It was two days before Christmas, and I took my accustomed afternoon saunter to Bays's, where other of the habitués of the club were assembled. There was no little buzzing and excitement among the frequenters of the place" (fol. 9; see *CM* 4:399). From this information it is possible to infer that the news has already arrived but that Twysden has not. Therefore Thackeray's subsequent passage—"On this day, when he reached the club, the arrival of 'the Globe' had been a little later than usual"—seems to indicate a change from the original conception, rather than to reveal the original conception itself. Consequently, it is possible to interpret Thackeray's alteration of this sentence as a return to his earlier idea: "On this day, some ten minutes after his accustomed hour, he reached the club." The novelist then wrote, "Other gentlemen were engaged in perusing the ⟨sheet⟩ Evening Journal," and thereby went on to carry out what seems to have been his earlier intention.

In press, two substantial additions were made to the installment— one for each chapter. The first concerned Philip's dinner at the home of Mugford, the proprietor of the *Pall Mall Gazette*. Originally, Thackeray had merely mentioned Mugford's profuse hospitalities and his pleasure at Philip's letters for the *Gazette*. The novelist had then dramatized the embarrassing frequency of reference by the Mugfords to Philip's noble relative, Lord Ringwood, and the punishment Philip inflicted on Pen's shins under the dinner table. Wishing to lengthen the chapter, however, Thackeray decided to add a passage at this point in order to provide a better indication of the lengths to which Mugford went to honor Lord Ringwood's great-nephew, and thereby to provide an even more ironic contrast to the immediately ensuing scene in which a gout-troubled Lord Ringwood quarrels with Philip, promises to cut him off financially, and orders him out of his presence. The humorously narrated addition not only prepares us for the ironic contrast, more- over, but also prepares us for Mugford's own future estrangement from Philip. Partly like Talbot Twysden, who is mentioned in the addi- tion, Mugford is a crude sycophant whose entertainment has a worldly motive and whose interest in an individual varies in proportion to his estimate of what that individual can do for him. Like Twysden also, Mugford pays out more in efforts (in his case, also in expense) than he receives. But unlike Twysden, Mugford's and Mrs. Mugford's quali- ties are more comical and harmless than sinister. It is here in this addi- tion ("We drove to the suburban villa . . . on my part" [*CM* 4:391– 92]) that we first fully receive these impressions. As a result of the addition, Thackeray not only achieved an artistic purpose but also, with these thirty-three lines, moved the chapter onto a sixteenth page (*CM* 4:400), which now contains twenty-eight lines.

The second passage inserted in press came in the middle of the fol- lowing chapter. Thackeray had originally written of the success of Mrs. Baynes's efforts to take Charlotte out a great deal to evening parties and to attract suitors more eligible than Philip. The novelist, however, had rather rapidly gone on to quote disparaging remarks made about Philip at these parties; he had not shown us what kind of suitors Charlotte attracted, nor that the unflattering remarks were addressed to Mrs. Baynes rather than to Charlotte, nor how they acted upon that snobbish mother. To remedy this matter and to fill out his number, Thackeray then wrote an additional passage, inserting it between the phrases "Charlotte was very much admired" and "What engaged to that queer red-bearded fellow . . .?" (fol. 15; see *CM* 4:405–6). In this instance, Thackeray did not actually extend the text on to a new page, for it already contained five or six lines; it seems probable, however, that he felt the twenty-one additional lines were desirable to fill out that page more satisfactorily and at the same time to create a better bridge between two portions of his narrative.

As one surveys the form of numbers one through ten, he can see that the first installment unfolds around the structural center of Philip's illness at school—itself a precursor of suffering he will undergo, but also of the care and love he will receive from others. The dominant organizing metaphor, as the novel's subtitle first informs us, is that of the man who fell among thieves and who was variously robbed, passed by, and helped. As we are soon told, "When the traveller (of whom the Master spoke) fell among the thieves, his mishap was contrived to try many a heart beside his own—the Knave's who robbed him, the Levite's and Priest's who passed him by as he lay bleeding, the humble Samaritan's whose hand poured oil into his wound, and held out its pittance to relieve him" (*CM* 3:11). The initial Samaritans are Mrs. Brandon and Dr. Goodenough, the latter's blunt-spoken and generous behavior forcefully contrasting (as will Philip's) with Dr. Firmin's courtly hypocrisy, and the former—herself befriended in need by Goodenough —revealed at the end of the first installment as a victim cruelly exploited and abandoned by a man who, when he finally appears at his son's bedside, is discovered to be Dr. Firmin himself.

In number two we see another life of sustained hypocrisy—that of Talbot Twysden. "If this Levite met a wayfarer, going down from Jerusalem, who had fallen among thieves, do you think he would stop to rescue the fallen man? . . . He would pass on . . . " (*CM* 3:167). The figure immediately contrasting with him, though only partly, is the blunt-spoken old Lord Ringwood, whose penchant for tongue-lashing the Twysdens is emphasized by a Thackerayan addition in press;

but, unlike Goodenough, Ringwood has no generosity, just brutal, often malicious, arrogance. The fundamental contrast to Dr. Firmin and the Twysdens is Philip, who is characterized as a bohemian Idle Apprentice rebelling against his father's busy obsequiousness. The foolishness of his courting the worldly Agnes Twysden is that he has committed his emotions, but she has none to offer. By the end of the installment, Philip has not discovered this danger to his future happiness, but he has acted so as to prevent his father from victimizing yet another woman in marriage.

Number three begins with a contrast—like that in *The Newcomes*—between the life of Vanity Fair and the life of J. J. Ridley, who finds fulfillment in his dedication to art. In this context we can see a further reason for Thackeray's addition in press of the passage where Philip castigates life in the fashionable world ("I have dangled about at fine parties . . . " [*CM* 3:279]), for we are given to understand that his rebellion comes to be directed not merely against his father but against the whole life of social aspiration. The merry days of Philip's early manhood are epitomized by the song he sings at his call-supper, "Doctor Luther," but the context is severely limiting, as the various conflicts during the evening, the foreboding presence of Hunt, and Thackeray's various revisions to that chapter—together with the brief, telling remark of the bill-discounters in number two concerning the Doctor's long history of stamped paper—remind us. These matters all prepare us for Philip's prophecy at the end of number three, which again comes in an important passage added in press: "the whole edifice of our present life will crumble in and smash" (*CM* 3:293). Philip's fatalistic acceptance of the upheaval, moreover, readies us for his later repeated acceptance of victimization by his father.

Number four opens by showing us the worldly, hypocritical behavior of the Twysdens, especially Mrs. Twysden, who, in promoting a marriage between Agnes and Philip, does not see that she is attempting to place him in spiritual imprisonment much like his father's, which is evoked by the chapter initial; in fact, even as Mrs. Twysden attempts to help Agnes rob and wound Philip, she imagines herself virtuous, "remembers her neighbour's peccadilloes to the third and fourth generation; and, if she finds a certain man fallen in her path, gathers up her affrighted garments with a shriek, for fear the muddy, bleeding wretch should contaminate her, and passes on" (*CM* 3:388). The antithesis of the Twysdens' house in Beaunash Street is Mrs. Brandon's house in Thornhaugh Street, as we are reminded by Philip's saunter from one to the other during the middle of number four, which is suspended between these two opposite poles. After Philip leaves the Twysdens, he is succeeded there by his dusky opposite, Woolcomb, and when Philip arrives at Mrs. Brandon's he finds another dark antagonist—Tufton Hunt, the drunken and malicious clergyman, who is in effect an anti–Dr. Luther, as the tippling monk in the chapter initial helps imply. Mrs. Brandon's Samaritan-like tending of Philip during the illness that opened Thackeray's narrative is evoked by the novelist (*CM* 3:401–2) just prior to Philip's arrival to find Hunt in Thornhaugh Street, however, since her love for Philip will help protect him against Hunt, as her embrace of Philip and mysterious promise to his father at the end of the installment also suggest. Amid these developments and in contrast to the prodigality of Hunt and Dr. Firmin, we see the prodigality of Philip, who is sardonically called "the prodigal" by Hunt (*CM* 3:406) but whose excesses take the form only of vehement physical gestures, bluntly honest speech, jovial bohemianism, and an instinctive repudiation of the way of the world. Philip, in fact, is an inverse prodigal: blunderingly comical but—like Colonel Newcome—a good-hearted, essentially incorruptible innocent.

Dr. Firmin's exploitation of Mrs. Brandon is more fully revealed in number five, which opens as he partly confesses to her and communicates his sense, which complements Philip's, of imminent destruction. Amid a bohemian Thursday night gathering at Mrs. Brandon's, with "modest and kindly refreshment" (*CM* 3:563), and good fellowship only partly marred by Philip's annoyance at the petty jealousy of Jarman (which Thackeray preparingly emphasized with a passage interpolated into the manuscript) comes the malicious Hunt, whose drunken behavior towards Mrs. Brandon causes Philip to throw him into the gutter and in turn provoke the cry of "BASTARD" (*CM* 3:566). The Bohemian smoker in the initial of chapter 11 finds his contrast in the ironically innocent initial of chapter 12 showing a boy with a pipe blowing a soap bubble beside a composed little girl, for the boy and girl turn out to emblemize the hopefully projective Hunt and the undaunted Mrs. Brandon at the climax of the installment. Meanwhile, the sword of Damocles (*CM* 3:568) falls as Dr. Firmin confesses to Philip his deception of Mrs. Brandon. Against this background comes an extension of her promise at the end of the previous installment, for Thackeray concludes the present number by having Mrs. Brandon lovingly repudiate her own honesty in order to protect Philip. Here the Samaritan-like act of loving mercy is implicit, for in her deed we can see how she is shielding Philip both from an evil consequence of his father's act and from Dr. Firmin's unscrupulous accomplice, who tries to rob Philip not only of his monetary inheritance but also of his very legitimacy. In harmony with the Samaritan of the parable—not a priest or a Levite, but something of an outsider—and with the ironic inversion typical of Thackeray's fiction, the merciful act is quite unorthodox; indeed, it is intentionally deceitful.

By her act Mrs. Brandon tries "to save Philip from ruin" (*CM* 3:583), but financial ruin inevitably follows, as we already suspect and as we learn at the end of number six. During the interval, Philip discovers that his uncle, Talbot Twysden, has been involved in the attempt to rob and wound him, and that his cousin, Agnes, has repudiated him for the wealthy Woolcomb. For all the pain this repudiation causes Philip, it is termed only a mishap (*CM* 3:651) and is ultimately a blessing. By implicit analogy, therefore, his second mishap will also turn out well. For the moment, however, the latter event appears to be devastating, as Dr. Firmin is called upon to pay the devil's due (*CM* 3:651) and as his son is financially ruined as well as he. The hidden disruptiveness in Dr. Firmin's nature and past that was revealed to us at the end of number one, checked at the end of number two, and ominously evoked in the conclusions of numbers three and four, and throughout number five, finally erupts at the climax of the sixth installment.

The novel's chief organizing metaphor reappears prominently at the start of the following serial number in the chapter "SAMARITANS" (*CM* 4:1). Philip's relatives, the Twysdens, of course pass him by, and Lord Ringwood, anticipating requests for money, orders that his doors be shut to Philip. But the robbed man's money cannot be restored; the Samaritan-like act is to minister to his wounded spirit with loving mercy—an act epitomized by the spontaneous fellow-feeling of the Pendennis children, whose willingness to give their bread and jam and meagre store of coins truly vivifies the spirit not only of Philip but of the onlookers too. Mrs. Brandon's gift is analogous: a room for Philip furnished with loving care, and the gift of her meagre hoard of £23. Philip's response, as the installment's concluding chapter reveals, is to show his mettle (*CM* 4:8) by going to work for the *Gazette* and especially by refusing to hold General Baynes responsible for his carelessness as trustee of Philip's inheritance. In short, Philip seeks to make his own way through the world and not to rob the unwitting accomplice of his father. By the end of number seven he has met his appalling future mother-in-law, Mrs. Baynes, but also his future wife, Charlotte, who will more than compensate Philip for her father's inept trusteeship. Indeed, it is Philip's mercy that enables him to find her love.

By the beginning of number eight Charlotte and Philip have begun to fall in love, the remarkable unworldliness of Philip being emphasized by Thackeray's causing Pendennis to argue at length, though not without tones of irony, the antithetical case for prudent calculation. Philip is like the happy lame beggar in the initial of the concluding chapter. In spite of poverty, uncertainty, and the ghastly Mrs. Baynes, he has discovered the "sweet uses of adversity" and, as the installment's concluding words also announce, has felt the comfort of hands "eager to soothe and succour" (*CM* 4:152).

Number nine begins with Philip's happy existence in Paris—comfortably bohemian, free from the anxieties of fashionable life, sustained by "many a good Samaritan ready with his twopence, if need were" (*CM* 4:263), and endowed with the daily rapture of seeing Charlotte. The latter half of the installment, however, begins to develop ominous overtones. Philip at last begins to see Mrs. Baynes for the unbearable person she is and Pendennis helps us to understand that Mrs. Baynes is likely to repeat the behavior of Mrs. Twysden by discovering it her "duty" to find a wealthier suitor for Charlotte. The woman's hostility begins to be apparent at the end of the installment, though not to Philip, who continues to be prodigally open in expressing his feelings, especially his laughter at the ridiculous. With complex irony we are told that "the poor fellow had not with his poverty learned the least lesson of humility, or acquired the very earliest rudiments of the art of making friends" (*CM* 4:280). No doubt we can all learn more of true humility, but it is especially Philip's incorrigibly naïve purity of heart that receives emphasis here—a virtue that keeps him free of the sycophantic respectfulness that afflicts so many people in the novel, especially his newest antagonist, Mrs. Baynes.

With number ten we come to the half-way point of the novel. Mrs. Baynes's future conduct towards Philip is epitomized in her treatment of the Vicomte de Loisy, whose association with her daughter she first encourages and then, upon discovering his poverty, insultingly terminates. Contrasted with her behavior is the Samaritan conduct of Philip's friends on their visits to Paris (*CM* 4:388). When friends like

Pen try to help Philip with calculatedly worldly advice, however, the incalculable inevitably emerges to disrupt these plans. Hence Philip's meeting with Lord Ringwood turns into a decisive quarrel, which is followed by the latter's determination to change his will and by his sudden death in his postchaise while journeying to Whipham. Philip's response to his unlegacied state is, of course, a cheerful puff on his cigar: "Was not Philip the poor as lordly and independent as Philip the rich?" (*CM* 4:403). The installment ends with further unpleasant developments and with Philip's imperviousness to change. Though Mrs. Baynes takes Charlotte out to fashionable evening entertainments, responds to a socially prominent admirer of her daughter, becomes increasingly dissatisfied with Philip, and begins nagging her husband about the proposed marriage, Philip continues to be incorrigibly content. The number then ends with a memorable contrast between two physical and spiritual states: the dissatisfied General and Mrs. Baynes lying sleepless in their bed, and, across the Seine from them, after a contemplative bedtime pipe and a prayer for Charlotte, the peacefully sleeping Philip. The latter image also has a premonitory quality, for we are prompted to infer that Philip, secure in his childlike serenity, will remain unvanquished by the anxieties entertained in the opposite bedchamber.

10

The Adventures of Philip

Installments 11–20

The manuscript of number eleven for November 1861 exists on fifteen leaves, fols. 1–9 composing chapter 23, "IN WH. WE STILL HOVER ABOUT THE ELYSIAN FIELDS" (fol. 1), and fols. 10–11, 20–[23] composing chapter 24, entitled: "Chap II. NEC DULCES AMORES SPERNE, PUER, NEQUE TU CHOREAS" (fol. 10). The odd numbering system suggests that Thackeray may have sent the first eleven leaves separately to the printer. The novelist apparently numbered three of the last four leaves faintly in pencil—one has considerable difficulty in positively identifying the "20" because the printer has pencilled a heavy "20" where Thackeray's numeral seems to be. Whoever began the final series of numbers, however, evidently started with the numeral "20," because most of that leaf was taken up with the text of the installment's twentieth printed page (*CM* 4:532).

Aside from the usual brief alterations, a lengthier change was made in the manuscript of chapter 23 by the insertion of a passage in the conversation of men at the British chancellery in Paris. Originally, Hely had announced disgust at his companions for their having entertained some aging actresses the night before; he had then sentimentally sighed for "Charlotte" and again denounced their debauched revelry, apparently ending with the characterization of one of the actresses as "that old Cerisette who has got a face like a *pomme cuite* and who danced before Lord Malmesbury at the Peace of Amiens. She did I tell you" (fol. 5; see *CM* 4:520). Thackeray then had Lowndes identify "Charlotte" as Charlotte Baynes. The conversation subsequently continued with a sally directed against O'Rourke and one against Lowndes. Ultimately, however, Thackeray decided to make the scene more comic by adding additional byplay and by repeating Hely's theatrical and sentimental cry of Charlotte's name. Hence Thackeray added "and before Lebrun the ⟨third cons⟩ second consul" after Hely's "She did I tell you"; the novelist then went on here and at the bottom of fol. 5 ("Insert above") with the following addition:

Mr. Chesham (looks up from his writing) Lebrun was third consul. Its of no consequence but

Lowndes. Thank you I owe you one: your a most valuable man Chesham, and a credit to your father and mother.

Mr *Chesham.* Well he *was* third Consul.[1]

Lowndes. I am obliged to you. I say I am obliged to you, Chesham and if you would like any refreshment order it meis sumptibus old boy,' at my expense.

Chesham These fellows will never be serious. he resumes his writing.

Hely *iterum, but very low.* O Charlotte Char!

The addition is not major but it does involve Chesham at the beginning of the scene, not just at its end, and it adds a playful tone that helps make Hely's sentimental sighs appear even more comical than before.

Thackeray added a whole paragraph in the manuscript of chapter 24, again on the bottom portion of a leaf (fol. 11). Originally he had written a paragraph about Mrs. Baynes's counsel to Charlotte to forget Philip now that she was going out into the world. He had then gone on with a paragraph about the Ambassador's ball ("Now the Queens birthday arrived" [see *CM* 4:531]). At this point, however, he evidently remembered that he had never treated the ball of Mrs. Hely's that he had already announced—indeed, prepared for—at the end of the previous chapter and at the beginning of the present one. Therefore at the bottom of fol. 11 he now went on to write about Mrs. Hely's ball in what he called "Paragraph A," marking it for insertion further up on the leaf, just ahead of his account of the Ambassador's ball. Since Thackeray's account of the ambassadorial function is to concentrate not on Hely and Charlotte but on Philip's collisions with Twysden, in this interpolated paragraph the novelist shows us "Prince Slyboots's" attentions to Charlotte at another social function: his mother's entertainment.

After carrying his narrative of Philip's adventures at the Ambassador's ball to a point several inches from the bottom of fol. 22, Thackeray may have paused, sent material to the printer, and considered ending his chapter there, with the ominous foreshadowing of "His Excellency caused Mr. Firmin's name to be erased from his party lists: and I am sure no sensible man will defend his [i.e., Philip's] conduct for a moment" (see *CM* 4:535).[2] If so, Thackeray found he needed one more page of material. Whatever the origin of the final three paragraphs, however, which Thackeray wrote on fol. [24], there can be no doubt of their success, for they focus on three significant matters: the strengthening of Mrs. Baynes's ambitions for her daughter because of Charlotte's success at the ball; the failure of Twysden to respond to Philip's kicking him; and the ironically contrasting reaction in the Baynes household, where the portentousness of Philip's disgrace— hinted at in the Ambassador's response—is made dramatically evident in the only way that matters to him: the Baynes's subsequent unwillingness to tolerate his courtship of Charlotte.

One substantial addition was made in press, also towards the end of chapter 24.[3] Originally Thackeray had ended the paragraph in which he narrated Philip's kicking of Twysden with the sentence: "And as for Philip's coat it was torn worse than ever." The novelist then had gone on with a new paragraph that turned to Philip's victim: "Mr. Twysdens hands coat-tails &c were very much singed and scalded" (fol. 22; see *CM* 4:535). In press, however, he began the new paragraph with the focus on Philip's attire and with an instruction to Frederick Walker that is reminiscent of those to Doyle in the text of *The Newcomes*, though here the emphasis falls on what *not* to illustrate.

> I don't know how many of the brass buttons had revolted and parted company from the poor old cloth, which cracked, and split, and tore under the agitation of that beating angry bosom. I hope our artist will not depict Mr. Firmin in this ragged state, a great rent all across his back, and his prostrate enemy lying howling in the water, amidst the sputtering, crashing oil-lamps at his feet. When Cinderella quitted her first ball, just after the clock struck twelve, we all know how shabby she looked. Philip was a still more disreputable object when he slunk away. I don't know by what side door Mr. Lowndes eliminated him. He also benevolently took charge of Philip's kinsman and antagonist, Mr. Ringwood Twysden. (*CM* 4:535)

The chief purpose of the added passage, as its tone suggests, seems to be to terminate the narrative of violence with comedy—and thereby both to reduce its melodramatic quality and, by contrast, to make the installment's ending come with increased effect. The event itself is not meant to be melodramatic; instead we are to see that its significance lies in the exaggerated effect contrived for it by the melodramatic Mrs. Baynes.

Greater complexity can be discerned in the surviving manuscript of number twelve for December 1861 than in most earlier portions of the

Huntington manuscript. Chapter 25, "INFANDI DOLORES" (fol. 1) is written on ten leaves (fols. 1–10) in Thackeray's upright hand. Only the bottom portion of fol. 4 is absent; the missing portion of about twelve lines presumably furnishes part but not necessarily all of the twenty-four printed lines that have no source in the manuscript (from "Yes, so reckless" to "the muddy Champs Elysées" [*CM* 4:646–47]). One insertion in the manuscript is notable, for after Madame Smolensk's visit to console Philip, Thackeray had concluded this portion of his narrative with a brief account of her return home and of the liveliness of her behavior, for all of her cares, explaining: "it is a wounded arm that bandages your's when bleeding." At the bottom of the same leaf, the novelist had shifted to a new subject: "(break a line) And now as the events of this history must be narrated in the order of time in wh. they occured, Mr. Firmin's biographer must take leave to insert in this place a letter wh. Philip received from an old acquaintance who has been absent for a brief space from this history, but who" (fol. 6). Thackeray continued on a new leaf with the final words of the sentence—"remembered his son though separated from him by wide oceans"—and then began to set down the letter itself, possibly continuing on an additional leaf to what is now the end of the chapter. He decided, however, that he had omitted necessary material. Hence he deleted the new beginning at the bottom of fol. 6 and, on an additional leaf and a half, wrote an insertion that came to be printed as three paragraphs (*CM* 4:650–51). Beginning with the comfort Madame Smolensk brought Charlotte from Philip, Thackeray went on to prepare for Charlotte's rebellion against her mother in the following chapter and for Mrs. Baynes's surprise at the insubordination; this he did by quoting the mother's lengthy letter to Mrs. MacWhirter, which expresses a belief in Charlotte's ability "to honour her father and mother," and by commenting on the steadfastness of Charlotte's love for Philip, "however time or distance might separate them" (fol. 8). Then, by writing a revised introduction to Dr. Firmin's letter, Thackeray completed his transition to that letter, which had previously been begun and perhaps finished; finally, the last two leaves were numbered, becoming fols. 9 and 10.

The manuscript of chapter 26 consists of nine and one-half leaves (fols. [1a]–6a, 1b–4b), the upper half of fol. [1a] being missing, together with the manuscript equivalent of forty-one printed lines of text ("Who was" to "call me cynic" [*CM* 4:655–56]). The first five and one-half leaves are in Thackeray's upright hand, the next three in Anne's,[4] and the final one in the hand of a secretary[5]; the last four appear to have derived from an earlier version.[6] After composing four leaves that carried the narrative to the midst of the quarrel between General Baynes and Colonel Bunch, Thackeray immediately went on in mid-sentence at the top of a fifth leaf with Bunch's words:

> it is a cowardly action!
> 'Colonel Bunch,' do you dare to use such a word to me? calls out the General, starting up to his feet
> 'Dare be hanged! I say its a shabby action roars the other rising too.
> 'Hush. Unless you wish to disturb the ladies. Of course you know what your expression means Colonel Bunch? and he drops his voice and sinks back to his chair
> I know what my words mean, and I stick to 'em Baynes—wh. is more than you can say, of yours, growls the Colonel.
> Very good Sir.

Later Thackeray inserted two more brief speeches after the Colonel's growl: Baynes's remark, "I am dashed if you shant answer to me for this language says the General in the softest whisper," which Thackeray then cancelled and replaced with, "The affair seems quite simple as it is without further bad language on your part Bunch says the General." Ultimately, however—apparently after having filled up the leaf —Thackeray decided to revise the passage, especially the last line that he had squeezed in. Lacking the room to do so, he deleted the whole passage preceding the words "Very good Sir," and copied it with modifications on the top part of a new leaf, which became fol. 5, the older one becoming fol. 6. Here the last portion of the exchange removes the excessively calm objection of the General to Bunch's taunt. Realizing that Baynes would have been enraged by Bunch's use of the words "cowardly" and "shabby," Thackeray made a modified return to the language of his cancelled insertion on the other leaf and added a response from Colonel Bunch:

> I am deed if any man alive shall use this language to me says the General in the softest whisper, without accounting to me for it.
> Did you ever find me backward Baynes at that kind of thing? growls the Colonel with a face like a lobster and eyes starting from his head[.]
> (fol. 5; see *CM* 4:661)

The result is an exchange that is effective for the characters and at the same time amusing to the reader, especially in the General's combination of swearing with extreme softness of voice, together with Bunch's heightened rage; the comedy, as is so often the case in Thackeray, effectively relieves the melodrama. The sequence of composition in the chapter's last four leaves is unclear; we can simply say that fols. 1*b*–3*b* seem to have been copied after fol. 4*b* was set down, for the text on fol. 3*b* ends only part way down the leaf, followed by the vertical line that usually connects a text to a preexistent one that follows it in narrative sequence.

The passage of this installment through the press also brought several notable changes. Two of these concern preparation for Charlotte's stay with her aunt in Tours. At first such a stay was mentioned only in brief general terms in chapter 25, just after the narrator had quoted Mrs. Baynes's letter to her sister and as a way of authenticating his knowledge of its contents: "Charlotte saw the letter some time after, when on a visit to her aunt at Tours, and when a quarrel occurred between the two sisters Mrs. Major and Mrs. General" (fol. 8). There was no mention of such a visit in the letter itself; instead, there was a closing allusion indicating that Mrs. Baynes had great hopes Mr. Hely would propose for Charlotte: "and I hope I hope—I am not at liberty Sister to say Why—a better fate for my dearest girl. The General sends regards to Mac: and I am &c." (fol. 8). It appears, therefore, that Thackeray may originally have intended to develop at this stage Hely's interest in Charlotte and to have her go to Tours sometime in the future. Later, in chapter 26, however, the novelist had Mrs. Baynes send "for ⟨her Sister and⟩ MacWhirter" (fol. 6*a*).[7] By the end of chapter 26 Thackeray had had Hely pay Charlotte only a single, unsuccessful visit and he had brought the MacWhirters to Paris to accompany their niece to Tours. Hence modifications had to be made in chapter 25. As a result, Thackeray made three further changes. First he inserted into Mrs. Baynes's letter a request that Charlotte be allowed to pay the visit: "I think if *she were to go to you and MacWhirter at Tours for a month or two*, she would be all the better for *change of air*, too, dear Mac. Come and fetch her, and we will pay the *dawk*" (*CM* 4:651). Second, he cancelled her allusion to her hopes regarding Hely. Finally, he deleted the now somewhat redundant mention of Charlotte's having seen the letter "when on a visit to her aunt at Tours, and" (fol. 8), substituting the words, "upon one of those not unfrequent occasions" (*CM* 4:651), ahead of the extant language: "when a quarrel occurred between the two sisters Mrs. Major and Mrs. General" (fol. 8; see *CM* 4:651–52). The chief alterations were thereby completed.[8]

Installment thirteen for January 1862 was written on sixteen consecutively numbered leaves, the first of which is now missing. The surviving manuscript of the first chapter—27, "I CHARGE YOU, DROP YOUR DAGGERS!" (fols. 2–8)—reveals several idiosyncrasies that are as tantalizing as they are illuminating.[9] On the bottom right corner of one leaf, just after the account of Charlotte's hysterical collapse into her uncle's arms and her mother's callous response, which begets Baynes's protest: "By George, Eliza, you are too bad! says the General quite white," Thackeray squeezed in a brief section of dialogue: "Eliza you are a Brute! cries Mrs. Macwhirter. *So she is!* shrieks Mrs. Bunch from the landing place over head. Eliza Baynes knew she had gone too far. Poor Charley was scarce conscious by this time & wildly screaming 'Never. Never'" (fol. 5). The novelist cancelled this passage, however, and recopied it at the top of a fresh leaf, adding only to the description of Mrs. Bunch's vantage point the phrase, "where other lady-boarders were assembled looking down on this awful family battle" (fol. 6; *CM* 5:8). The fact that the passage was squeezed in at the bottom of fol. 5 and then cancelled suggests that the present fol. 6 may be a recopied leaf or an inserted one, as does the fact that its text does not extend completely to the bottom. Fol. 7, moreover—the text of which begins with the words "Were your humble servant" (*CM* 5:10) and ends several inches from the bottom of the leaf with the words "where the rain is pouring; ⟨where we will not follow him⟩"[10] (see *CM* 5:11) and with an ensuing vertical line—also seems to be either a recopied leaf or an insertion into the manuscript.

If, as seems likely, fols. 6 and 7 have both been inserted, and fol. 6 later recopied, it will be apparent that Thackeray decided to complete his extended assemblage of persons in Madame Smolensk's passageway by bringing in Philip from outside the house. In any event, the narrator offered a comic summary of the group: "Here *is* a picture I protest. We have 1. The boarders on the first landing, whither too. the Baynes children have crept in their night gowns. Secondly we have Auguste. Francoise, the Cook & the assistant coming up from the basement; and 3. we have Colonel Bunch. Doctor Martin Major Mc. Whirter with Charlotte in his arms. Madame. General B. Mrs. Mac. Mrs. General B all in the passage, when our friend the bombshell bursts in amongst them." Besides introducing comedy to reduce the scene's melodrama, Thackeray also wished to provide Baynes with a sight that would strongly help to motivate his forthcoming change of mind—not simply the image of Charlotte weakly leaning on MacWhirter, but fainting on Philip: "and at the next moment she has fainted quite dead —but this time she is on Philip's shoulder." "And Charles Baynes felt he had acted like a traitor, and hung down his head" (fol. 6; *CM* 5:9). Thackeray also wished to emphasize, in advance of the conflict's resolution, that it would not issue in bloodshed, and he did this with narrative commentary at the bottom of fol. 6 and at the top of fol. 7, the latter passage indicating that not even Mrs. Baynes could bring about such a dire outcome. A final authorial purpose seems to have been the wish to tie up loose ends, for while the narrator had implied a dispersal of the assembled group, he had not clearly gotten everyone out of the passageway; furthermore, Philip had also to be gotten out of the house itself. These matters were all taken care of in the last fifteen lines of fol. 7 (*CM* 5:10–11).

In the case of chapter 28, "In wh. Mrs. Mc.Whirter has a new bonnet" (fol. 9), no particularly striking manuscript alterations are evident. In both chapters, however, it is again apparent that Thackeray made changes in ink at different times and also, on at least one occasion, made a number of alterations in pencil as well.

In press the installment's first chapter was extended in several instances. Of the two major additions, one shows MacWhirter's anger towards Baynes at somewhat greater, and in this case more convincing, length as well as scope, for it now includes allusions to Baynes's wife and past injuries. Instead of simply growling his news to Colonel Bunch—"I tell you, Tom Bunch I want to send a message to him—Invite me to his house, and insult me and Emily when we come! By . . ." (fol. 5)—the Major now continues: "'By George, it makes my blood boil! Insult us after travelling twenty-four hours in a confounded diligence, and say we're not invited! He and his little catamaran.' 'Hush!' interposed Bunch. 'I say catamaran, sir! don't tell *me*! They came and stayed with us four months at Dumdum—the children ill with the pip, or some confounded thing—went to Europe, and left me to pay the doctor's bill; and now, by——'" (*CM* 5:7–8). Thackeray thereby added eight printed lines of impassioned outcry. The other major augmentation added eleven more. In this instance, Thackeray decided to elaborate at comic length the military metaphor he had been intermittently using to characterize the quarreling of the fiery veterans; in the process he also indicated the importance of Charlotte's reappearance in the passageway, pointed mention of which had been made on the probably inserted fol. 6:

> The colonel, the major, the doctor, ranged themselves on one side the table, defended, as it were, by a line of armed tumblers, flanked by a strong brandy-bottle and a stout earth-work from an embrasure in which scalding water could be discharged. Behind these fortifications the veterans awaited their enemy, who, after marching up and down the room for a while, takes position finally in their front and prepares to attack. The general remounts his *cheval de bataille*, but cannot bring the animal to charge as fiercely as before. Charlotte's white apparition has come amongst them, and flung her fair arms between the men of war. In vain Baynes tries to get up a bluster, and to enforce his passion with by Georges, by Joves, and words naughtier still. (*CM* 5:11)

The passage, as we can see, has an artistic as well as quantitative purpose, however, for Thackeray wanted both to lighten the contentious scene and to prepare for the general's immediately ensuing capitulation to his only temporarily estranged friends.

Several minor changes also lengthened the text. A paragraph that needed to be created on *CM* 5:10 (beginning, "What a pity") added one line; a new sentence later in that paragraph added another ("The sad little vision has disappeared"). Somewhat further on, two new sentences extended Dr. Martin's brief utterance by two lines ("She has had . . . fellow" [*CM* 5:11]).[11] Altogether, then, twenty-four lines were added to a chapter whose last page contains twenty-eight.[12] A number of brief changes were also made in press to the text of chapter 28, but none requires singling out.

The manuscript of number fourteen for February 1862 consists of seventeen leaves—nine for chapter 29, "IN THE DEPARTMENTS OF SEINE, LOIRE, AND STYX (INFÉRIEUR)" (fols. [1]–9), and eight for chapter 30, "RETURNS TO OLD FRIENDS" (fols. 10–12, 1a–[5a]). Both chapter titles are absent from the manuscript, as are numbers for the first leaf and the last, fol. [4a] having been misnumbered "3."

The manuscript of chapter 29 does not conclusively reveal any area of significant development in its original composition,[13] but Thackeray seems to have had some difficulty in describing the scene in which Charlotte and Philip receive the dying Baynes's consent. Since a small portion of manuscript is missing from the bottom of fol. 8, statements about this scene's composition in manuscript must remain limited; it is clear, however, that the sentences immediately preceding and following this gap contain a somewhat higher than usual incidence of cancelled and revised language. Thackeray began by emphasizing the preeminence of love in Philip's thoughts and then went on to show how as Philip and Charlotte "were advancing" towards the bed of the dying general, "I have no doubt the love of those two young people had time to make its signal" (fol. 8). Unfortunately, however, the sentence ended by shifting attention from the general back to love and the lovers instead of vice versa; hence Thackeray deleted the last phrase, thereby revising the sentence so as to have it conclude with mention of "the bed where the poor father lay hopeless and in pain." Here followed the portion of fol. 8 that is now missing; it apparently ended with the narrator turning away from depicting the general's last hours, with the words, "I do not," for fol. 9 begins: "care to pursue this last ⟨season⟩. scene. Let us close the door as the children kneel by the ⟨old man's⟩ sufferer's bed side; and to the old man's ⟨prayer⟩ petition for ⟨pity and⟩ forgiveness, and to the young girls sobbing vows of love and fondness say a reverend amen." He then went on: "It is hard for those who expect love and reverence to have to own to wrong and to ask pardon: Old knees are stiff to bend. Brother reader, young or old, when our last hour comes, may we have grace ⟨enough⟩ given us to do as much" (fol. 9). He then cancelled this last passage, however, feeling that the commentary after "amen" had best be deferred until after an account of the general's last letter and Charlotte's response to it. Then he again set down these sentences, slightly revised, which now close the chapter.

The third leaf of chapter 30, ending with the words "*dixi*; and I wont cancel the words" (fol. 12; see *CM* 5:145) followed by a blank space and a vertical line at the bottom of the leaf, might represent an insertion into the manuscript (together with a few words at the bottom of fol. 11, beginning, "You know such" [*CM* 5:144]); more probably, however, the portion was sent to the printer before the rest of the chapter was completed, for the latter segment has a new numbering system. The chapter, marked off as such, originally opened with the words "When the service has been read, and the last volley has been fired over the buried soldier, the troops march to quarters with a quick step & to a lively tune" (fol. 10). Afterwards, however, Thackeray decided to enter ahead of this language a sentence that was once a continuation of chapter 29 but that is now cancelled at the end of the text on fol. 9: "Philip and the three old soldiers formed the little mourning company wh. followed the General to his place of rest at Montmartre." These words, with some modification, then were inserted at the top of fol. 10, where they now form the opening sentence of chapter 30.

Thereafter, so far as one can tell, composition seems to have proceeded along the line of the narrative's present development. Only one matter calls for notice: a brief cancellation at the bottom of fol. 3a. A single vertical stroke is drawn through the leaf's last three lines, which read as follows[14]: "We had an entertainment then, I own, We asked our finest company and Mr. & Mrs. Mugford to meet them. Of course I was about to invite Philip to this banquet wh. was given as it were for his benefit, but Mrs. Laura interposed. He might be a little loud you know; or restive; or contradict some one; or offend Mr. Mugford'—this artful woman remarked, and it was determined that he should"; composition may have continued on another leaf that was discarded, along with any additional numbering, for fol. [4a] begins with a new paragraph that explains how Laura's presence is enough to guarantee Philip's meekness. In short, Thackeray decided that Philip would indeed be present at Pendennis's dinner and that his meekness would be overcome when Laura withdrew from the men's company after dinner. The coming about of an explosion between Philip and Bickerton (or an equivalent figure) was inevitable; Thackeray merely seems to have speeded it up and to have removed a somewhat implausible wish to have Philip excluded—even for his own temporary good—from a dinner held on his behalf. Hence the cancellation of the above lines. What is somewhat odd, however, is the fact that only the third and fourth sentences quoted above failed to appear in print. It is readily understandable that the compositor should have set up the first sentence, but not the second, for the vertical cancelling line clearly cuts through "asked," its second word. One suspects, nevertheless, that their retention derives from the compositor rather than the author, and that it failed to attract Thackeray's notice because only the third and fourth sentences conflicted with his ultimate inclusion of Philip among the diners.

In press there were two main changes, one for each chapter. In the first instance, Thackeray again went back to the scene where Philip and Charlotte approach the dying general hand in hand, with "mutual love and faith." After these words, Thackeray's revised manuscript text had continued: "It is the first business of life, youthful love. It is stronger than all other hopes or passions. It wakes in the morning with the first act of consciousness. It is present all day, and through every action of life almost. It is the last waking thought ere the eyes close in slumber. It could accompany the young people walking in that sad chamber to the bed where the poor father lay hopeless and in pain" (fol. 8). A new paragraph then apparently followed on the portion of fol. 8 that is now missing. It is impossible to say what it contained, but the printed text reads as follows, ending with three words that connect with the words from the top of fol. 9, which are here given in brackets:

> The poor man laid the hands of the young people together, and his own upon them. The suffering to which he had put his daughter seemed to be the crime which specially affected him. He thanked Heaven he was able to see he was wrong. He whispered to his little maid a prayer for pardon in one or two words, which caused poor Charlotte to sink on her knees and cover his fevered hand with tears and kisses. Out of all her heart she forgave him. She had felt that the parent she loved and was accustomed to honour had been mercenary and cruel. It had wounded her pure heart to be obliged to think that her father could be other than generous, and just, and good. That he should humble himself before her, smote her with the keenest pang of tender commiseration. I do not [care to pursue this last scene.] (*CM* 5:140)

Although only limited inferences can be drawn from this portion of the text, one can observe that in press Thackeray cut the last passage on the surviving portion of fol. 8 ("It is the first . . . in pain"), and thereby saved seventy-six words. Whatever changes there may have been in the missing portion of text, it seems plausible to suspect that the above deletion may have been prompted by the wish to limit chapter 29 to twelve printed pages, which it now occupies with one line to spare.

If Thackeray made such a decision about the length of chapter 29, he made it largely on artistic grounds, for the manuscript version of chapter 30 produced almost exactly eleven printed pages; it now occupies twelve pages because of extensive augmentation. First, Thackeray added a few words at the end of the second cancelled sentence apparently retained by the compositor: "and we prayed that unlucky Philip to be on his best behaviour to all persons who were invited to the feast" (*CM* 5:149). Second, and more important, Thackeray added a long passage showing how Mrs. Mugford in effect returned Laura's visit to her and how her vote for Philip as sub-editor of her husband's journal was assured. (Incidentally, a contributing cause to the delay of the dinner and Laura's upset was assigned: the wreckage caused by the inept assistance of Mrs. Mugford's groom.) Thackeray had originally explained that Lady Hixie promised to be gracious to Mugford "and his wife; and surveyed Mrs. Mugford with a great deal of interest and good natured curiosity." He had then gone on concerning Mrs. Mugford: "I am bound to say that the good woman presented a remarkable appearance" (fol. [4*a*]). Between these two sentences, and after cancelling the last portion of the former ("and surveyed . . . curiosity"), the novelist made his lengthy insertion, thereby accomplishing his artistic as well as serial purpose.

Number fifteen for March 1862 consists of the usual two chapters, both with their titles given in the manuscript. Chapter 31, which "NARRATES THAT FAMOUS JOKE ABOUT MISS GRIGSBY," consists of ten numbered leaves, one of which is missing (fol. [7]), and two lettered inserts (fols. A and B). The first six leaves, which reveal no particular difficulties of composition, carry the narrative to Charlotte's arrival in London and to the beginning of her opera visit with Mrs. Mugford (*CM* 5:265). The missing fol. [7] presumably included an account of the visit of Charlotte and Philip to Westminster Abbey, where "they passed, and thought no ill" (*CM* 5:266). At this point, on an earlier fol. [8], Thackeray may have written a passage of commentary and preparation for the letter from Philip's father and perhaps a beginning of the letter itself, continuing with the words, "And so you are returned," that appear at the top of the next leaf, the present fol. 9. The letter, which lacks a salutation, now opens with these words (see *CM* 5:267) and continues without a break onto the present fol. 10, which was originally designated "9," perhaps by mistake. Thackeray may then have revised and recopied the narrative from the earlier fol. [8] onto the leaf now bearing that number, whose text ends several inches from the bottom with the dateline, "New York. April 1. 18—" (the date disappeared in press), together with a short vertical line drawn through the upper portion of the blank space. Alternatively, Thackeray may deliberately have skipped ahead to write the letter on the as yet unnumbered fols. 9 and 10 (together, perhaps, with an ensuing passage on fol. 10 concluding the chapter) and then gone back to write fol. 8, which then took on the appearance of an insertion.

Chapter 32, "WAYS AND MEANS," is written on seven leaves: fols. 11–15 (the middle portion of fol. 15 being missing) and [16]–[17]. Here there is further idiosyncrasy. After carrying the narrative at least as far as fol. 15, which begins, "Well, the speeches were spoken. The bride was kissed and departed with her bride groom. They had not even a valet & ladys maid to bear them company" (see *CM* 5:277), Thackeray apparently decided to revise and recopy the immediately preceding portion of narrative. Hence, on a fresh leaf (the present fol. 14) he set down a text beginning, "A melancholy little chapel" (*CM* 5:276). This text may have ended with the words "every day cogitation," for a long vertical line then follows. If so, Thackeray subsequently wrote another paragraph beginning "After the ceremony," together with a transcribed version of the first three sentences at the top of fol. 15. In any event, he also wrote for the printer "This to stand," so that the printer would ignore the long vertical line running through the text on the lower half of fol. 14. Thackeray completed this reworking by deleting the three sentences at the top of fol. 15.[15] He also composed the sentence that was to come before "A melancholy little chapel," penning its beginning at the bottom of fol. 13 ("Every respectable man . . . were running") and squeezing the remainder into the top of fol. 14.

A final idiosyncrasy appears towards the end of the chapter—again in proximity to a letter. Here the letter is Charlotte's and Philip's, which takes up fols. [16]–[17].[16] The text of the missing portion of fol. 15, presumably beginning with the words "voice. I walked" (*CM* 5:277) and ending with "how dreary that" (*CM* 5:278), was succeeded by the final portion of the short paragraph immediately preceding the letter. After the dateline, "Hotel du Rhin. Amiens. Saturday," Thackeray wrote down two lines that begin the letter, followed by a vertical line extending several inches to the bottom of the leaf. Here, then, Thackeray either inserted fol. 15 into the text as a desirable augmenta-

tion or, more probably, he composed the letter first, all the while intending to come back and write the intervening leaf. In either event,
after setting down the last two lines on fol. 15, he cancelled them with
three vertical strokes, but then wrote the word "Stet." Following this
direction, the printer set up type—with one main modification—from
these two lines rather than from the uncancelled lines at the top of the
following leaf.

In press, several notable changes were made to fill out the installment, all of them in chapter 31. The first added passage, inscribed
"Insert A," extended Dr. Firmin's letter to Philip. On fol. 9, Thackeray had Dr. Firmin ask Philip whether he could not write journalistic
letters for the "Colonel," "my friend the Editor of the New York
Emerald? He knows a part of your history." The "Colonel," of course,
was Colonel J. B. Fogle, proprietor and editor of the *New York Emerald*, as the Doctor had mentioned in number twelve. On fol. A, however, Thackeray decided to introduce a new paper and a new editor.
Hence Dr. Firmin's friend became the editor of the

> new Journal, called here the Gazette of the Upper Ten Thousand. It is
> *the* fashionable journal published here; and your qualifications are pre-
> cisely those wh. would make your services valuable as a contributor.
> Doctor Geraldine the Editor is not I believe a relative of the Leinster
> family, but a self-made man, who arrived in this country some years
> since, poor and an exile from his native country. He advocates repeal
> politics in Ireland: but with these of course you need have nothing to do.
> And he is much too liberal to expect these from his contributors. I have
> been of service professionally to Mrs. Geraldine and himself, My friend
> of the Emerald introduced me to the Doctor. Terrible enemies in print,
> in private they are perfectly good friends, and the little passages of arms
> between the two journalists serve rather to amuse than to irritate. 'The
> Grocers boy' from Ormond Quay (Geraldine once, it appears, engaged in
> that useful but humble calling) and the 'Miscreant from Cork' the Editor
> of the Emerald comes from that city assail each other in public but drink
> whiskey and water *galore* in private. If you write for Geraldine, of course
> you will say nothing disrespectful about *Grocers' boys. His dollars are
> good silver*, of that you may be sure. Dr. G knows[.] (see *CM* 5:268)

This passage not only lengthened the text by eighteen printed lines but
also added important premonitory detail for the reader—though,
ironically, not for Philip, who is overjoyed at the possibility of additional income. Because of this passage we see a suspicious similarity
between this editor, who is pointedly called "Doctor,"[17] and Dr.
Firmin, who is also poor and in "exile" from his native country. We

also see the continuing unscrupulousness of Dr. Firmin, who coolly endorses the unprincipled journalism exemplified by Geraldine and encouraged by him. For these reasons, we are encouraged to suspect that Philip will meet with equally unprincipled behavior from Dr. Geraldine and that he will receive no more payment than he did and does from his father. As a result we are given grounds for viewing Philip's ensuing actions, including the confidence of his rush into marriage, from a new, ironic, perspective.

Evidently at the same time, Thackeray made a second insertion: fol. B, which is marked "Insert at 268." Into a later portion of the same letter, he had Dr. Firmin advocate that Philip cultivate the new Lord Ringwood, of whom we have as yet heard almost nothing:

> You will of course pay your respects to your relative the new Lord of Ringwood. For a young man whose family is so powerful as yours there can surely be no derogation in entertaining some feudal respect and who knows whether and how soon Sir John Ringwood may be able to help his cousin? By the way Sir John is a Whig, and your paper is a conservative. But you are above all *homme du monde*. In such a subordinate place as you occupy with the Pall Mall Gazette, a man's private politics do not surely count at all. If Sir John Ringwood your kinsman sees any way of helping you so much the better and of course your politics will be those of your family. I have no knowledge of him. He was a very quiet man at College, where I regret to say your father's friends were not of the quiet sort at all. I trust I have repented I have sown my wild oats. And, ah, how pleased I shall be to hear that my Philip has bent *his* proud head a little, and is ready to submit more than he used of old to the customs of the world. Call upon Sir John then. As a Whig gentleman of large estate I need not tell you that he will expect *respect* from you. He is your kinsman: the representative of your grandfathers gallant and noble race. He bears the name your mother bore. To *her* my Philip was always gentle; and for her sake you will comply with the wishes of[.] (see *CM* 5:269)

Here Thackeray added twenty printed lines and also sounded a hitherto mostly silent key in preparation for later use: Philip's relationship with the new Lord Ringwood. Thackeray saw the connection between the hypocrisy of unprincipled journalism and the hypocrisy practiced on the wealthy and titled, who, though in a different way from editors, also encourage such behavior on the part of those whom lack of wealth and position places to some degree in their power. The continuity of Dr. Firmin's behavior is thereby emphasized in a new way, as is the continuity of Philip's difficulties, now that they are placed in yet a broader context of pressures.

With these two additions, Thackeray lengthened his text by thirty-eight lines, but he was not yet through. The printer's marks suggest that Thackeray sent fols. A and B to him together with fols. 12–14 of chapter 32, for the printer marked the former two leaves 1 and 2, and the latter three leaves 3–6 prior to subdividing them.[18] Therefore, probably to a later set of proofs, Thackeray added a third passage to chapter 31—once again to Dr. Firmin's letter, this time between the two other insertions. On fol. 9, Thackeray had made Dr. Firmin briefly indicate appropriate subject matter for the proposed letters to the New York newspaper: "personal news regarding the notabilities of London—anecdotes of men and women of fashion. . . . Who are the reigning beauties of London. . . . Has any one lately won or lost on the turf or at play? What are the Clubs talking about? Are there any duels? What is the last scandal? Does the good old Duke keep his health. Is that affair over between the Duchess of This and Captain That?" Needing to lengthen his text, however, Thackeray was prompted to see further possibilities. Hence, between the phrase, "personal news regarding the notabilities of London," and "anecdotes of men and women of fashion," he inserted the following:

> and these, I assured him, you were the very man to be able to furnish. You, who know everybody; who have lived with the great world—the world of lawyers, the world of artists, the world of the university—have already had an experience which few gentlemen of the press can boast of, and may turn that experience to profit. Suppose you were to trust a little to your imagination in composing these letters? there can be no harm in being *poetical*. Suppose an *intelligent correspondent* writes that he has met the D–ke of W–ll–ngt–n, had a private interview with the Pr–m–r, and so forth, who is to say him nay? And this is the kind of talk our *gobe-mouches* of New York delight in. My worthy friend, Doctor Geraldine, for example—between ourselves his name is Finnigan, but his private history is *strictly entre nous*—when he first came to New York astonished the people by the copiousness of his anecdotes regarding the *English aristocracy*, of whom he knows as much as he does of the Court of Pekin. He was smart, ready, sarcastic, amusing; he found readers: from one success he advanced to another, and the *Gazette of the Upper Ten Thousand* is likely to make *this worthy man's fortune*. You really may be serviceable to him, and may justly earn the *liberal remuneration* which he offers for a weekly letter. (*CM* 5:268–69)

The novelist thereby made clear that Philip was not expected merely to report news but—in the well-known tradition of American journalism, and to an extent English—to fabricate news. The hypocrisy of the whole enterprise is made even more apparent here by the decided un-masking of "Doctor Geraldine," who is revealed, ironically enough, by a similar mountebank unwittingly displaying his own true self in the process of uncovering another. Thackeray's narrative is thereby en-riched by further comedy as well as by further ironic point. Moreover, with these additions, together with a brief paragraph near the chap-ter's end pointing out the movement of time ("And so months . . . to sentiment?" [*CM* 5:270]), his chapter was lengthened by a total of sixty-one printed lines—well over a page of magazine text—and the final page now contained seventeen lines. The development of chapter 31 in press contrasts very much, therefore, with the development of chapter 32, for no significant additions and no major changes were made in press to the latter.[19]

The manuscript of number sixteen for April 1862, like those of num-bers nine and thirteen, consists of sixteen leaves. The leaves of chapter 33, "DESCRIBES A SITUATION INTERESTING BUT NOT UNEXPECTED" (fols. 1–5), reveal no complexities of composition, while those of the following chapter (fols. 1a–9a, [1b]–[2b]), "IN WHICH I OWN THAT PHILIP TELLS AN UNTRUTH," which also has its title in manuscript, contain several minor idiosyncrasies. Once again it appears that Thackeray may have composed a letter before writing or at least com-pleting its preparatory passage. At the top of fol. 2a, he began the body of Dr. Firmin's letter to Philip announcing the confiscation of his son's first and only wages from the New York newspaper: "And so I may congratulate myself on atchieving *ancestral* honors" (see *CM* 5:394). Later he either wrote fol. 1a or revised an earlier leaf on a fresh folio, ending only slightly more than half-way down the leaf with the letter's dateline and a new form of the opening previously written on fol. 2a: "And so, my dear Philip, I may congratulate myself on having."

Two other matters may be briefly noted. Fol. 9a was originally 8a, but it contained only the last twelve words of the incomplete sentence on the bottom of fol. 7a: "and his family, than I would ask her to join the Mormons." For some reason Thackeray set down a revised version of these words at the top of a fresh leaf: "than I would induce her to turn Mormon and accept all the consequences to wh. ladies must submit when they make profession of that creed" (see *CM* 5:402). He numbered the new leaf fol. 8 and then went on with composition, eventually continuing in mid-sentence onto the other leaf, crossing out its twelve superseded words and renumbering it fol. 9. The chapter's last leaf and a half were unnumbered and may have gone separately to the printer, who divided them into generally shorter stints and gave them a separate numbering system, a–e. [20]

As the installment passed through the press, Thackeray saw that it took up only twenty-three pages, chapter 33 having about ten lines on its final page and the last chapter having about forty-five. The novelist's response was to add a passage to each of the chapters. It is interesting to note that his addition to chapter 33 is closely related to Walker's full-page wood-engraving, "MUGFORD'S FAVORITE," which opens the number and which was suggested by Thackeray in a sketch accompanied by the following words: "Old gentleman in thick shoes scratching a pig's back over a pig-stye railing in his garden. Philip disgusted. Background, trees, cottages, villas, Hampstead Heath." [21] In the manuscript, Thackeray had already mentioned Mugford's scratching "one of his pigs on the back" while walking with Philip "round his paddock and gardens" (fol. 3; *CM* 5:389); now, however, we receive a more detailed verbal picture of Mugford among his outdoor possessions and an account of how his sense of ownership prompts his voluble boasting:

> Streets and terraces now cover over the house and grounds which worthy Mugford inhabited, and which people say he used to call his Russian Irby. He had amassed in a small space a heap of country pleasures. He had a little garden; a little paddock; a little greenhouse; a little cucumber-frame; a little stable for his little trap; a little Guernsey cow; a little dairy; a little pigsty; and with this little treasure the good man was not a little content. He loved and praised everything that was his. No man admired his own port more than Mugford, or paid more compliments to his own butter and home-baked bread. He enjoyed his own happiness. He appreciated his own worth. He loved to talk of the days when he was a poor boy on London streets, and now—"now try that glass of port, my boy, and say whether the Lord Mayor has got any better," he would say, winking at his glass and his company. To be virtuous, to be lucky, and constantly to think and own that you are so—is not this true happiness? To sing hymns in praise of himself is a charming amusement—at least to the performer; and anybody who dined at Mugford's table was pretty sure to hear some of this music after dinner. I am sorry to say Philip did not care for this trumpet-blowing. (*CM* 5:388)

The effect upon us, of course, is a strengthening of our awareness not only of the incompatibility between the two men but also of the obnoxiousness that makes inevitable his repudiation by Philip at the end of the number—an ending already written. In terms of the immediate scene into which the passage was interpolated, we can also see that Philip's boredom with Mugford is now given an immediate source. Originally Thackeray had written: "Philip went to this village retreat. He was frightfully bored at Haverstock Hill" (fol. 2). Now, however, we are made more clearly aware that the boredom arises not from the rural retreat but from the way Haverstock Hill acts upon Mugford and from Philip's reiterated experience of Mugford's trumpeting. By adding these lines, Thackeray did not extend the text onto a new page, but he did fill up more of the previously rather empty final page of chapter 33 and strengthen his artistic design.

In chapter 34 the novelist decided to create, in effect, the installment's twenty-fourth page by giving a fuller picture of the climactic evening on which Philip's annoyance at the presence of Mrs. Woolsey causes him to insult and enrage his employer. Originally we were told that Philip was ill-humored towards Mrs. Woolsey because he had believed falsehoods told about her by Trail and by others "whose testimony was equally untruthful. Remembering these wicked legends, then, Philip sate before this poor unconscious Mrs. Woolsey, silent, with glaring eyes, insolent, and odious" (fol. [1b]). Almost immediately thereafter, however, Thackeray had hastened on with an account of their departure and Philip's brief return to tell Mugford that the woman was no fit company for Charlotte. Presumably in looking for a portion of the narrative that needed amplification, he recognized that he had not made adequate preparation for Philip's particular exasperation on this evening. Therefore he inserted the following passage after the word "untruthful":

On an ordinary occasion Philip would never have cared or squabbled about a question of precedence, and would have taken any place assigned to him at any table. But when Mrs. Woolsey in crumpled satins and blowsy lace made her appearance, and was eagerly and respectfully saluted by the host and hostess, Philip remembered those early stories about the poor lady: his eyes flashed wrath, and his breast beat with an indignation which almost choked him. Ask that woman to meet my wife? he thought to himself, and looked so ferocious and desperate that the timid little wife gazed with alarm at her Philip, and crept up to him and whispered, "What is it, dear?"

Meanwhile, Mrs. Mugford and Mrs. Woolsey were in full colloquy about the weather, the nursery, and so forth—and Woolsey and Mugford giving each other the hearty grasp of friendship. Philip, then, scowling at the newly arrived guests, turning his great hulking back upon the company and talking to his wife, presented a not agreeable figure to his entertainer.

"Hang the fellow's pride!" thought Mugford. "He chooses to turn his back upon my company, because Woolsey was a tradesman. An honest tailor is better than a bankrupt, swindling doctor, I should think. *Woolsey* need not be ashamed to show his face, I suppose. Why did you make me ask that fellar again, Mrs. M.? Don't you see, our society ain't good enough for him?"

Philip's conduct, then, so irritated Mugford, that when dinner was announced, he stepped forward and offered his arm to Mrs. Woolsey; having intended in the first instance to confer that honour upon Charlotte. "I'll show him," thought Mugford, "that an honest tradesman's lady who pays his way, and is not afraid of anybody, is better than my sub-editor's wife, the daughter of a bankrupt swell." Though the dinner was illuminated by Mugford's grandest plate, and accompanied by his very best wine, it was a gloomy and weary repast to several people present, and Philip and Charlotte, and I daresay Mugford, thought it never would be done. Mrs. Woolsey, to be sure, placidly ate her dinner, and drank her wine; whilst, remembering these wicked legends against her, Philip sate before the poor unconscious lady, silent, with glaring eyes, insolent, and odious. (*CM* 5:406–7)

As a result, we are made actually to observe Philip's resentment at what he feels is an insult to his wife instead of merely to hear him announce it outside later without apparently having felt it in the drawing room; hence his later objection has no hint of contrivance or puzzling abruptness. So too, the vehemence of Mugford's later response to Philip's remark (addressed to him outside) is prepared for more adequately by showing not just a prior general alienation and an anger at the insult but also specific and increasing annoyance beforehand at Philip's behavior towards Mrs. Woolsey (and himself as host) in the drawing room. Thackeray thereby provided a doubly useful bridge across a gap in his narrative and completed the filling out of his installment.

The manuscript of number seventeen for May 1862 offers certain problems to an analyst of its composition, beginning with chapter 35, "RES ANGUSTA DOMI." Fols. 1–8, all in Thackeray's upright hand, reveal no special complexities of growth, nor does the genealogy appended as a note to fol. 5 (see *CM* 5:519), which is in the hand of Thackeray's secretary, Samuel Langley, and of the novelist himself.[22] Fol. 8, however, is only a half leaf, ending with Franklin's words: "But you dont have it often I suppose because you're so very poor &c." (see *CM* 5:523). Because the lower half of fol. 8 is missing, one cannot be sure whether the chapter originally ended here or whether it continued—and, if so, in what manner.[23] We can only see that four folios—all half-leaves—in the hand of Langley (fols. 1a–4a) complete the present text. Chapter 36 exists in three hands, with its own numbering system and a title that does not appear in the printed version: "In wh. Philip wears a wig" (fol. 1b). The first three leaves are in Thackeray's upright hand (fols. 1b–3b, to the words "and the agents" [*CM* 5:529])[24]; the next three are in Anne's hand (fols. 1c–3c)[25]; the ensuing two and one-third in Thackeray's upright hand again (fols. 4c–6c, ending with "smartest hotels just then opened" [*CM* 5:534]); and four in Langley's hand (fols. 7c–10c, as far as "brought me money herself" [*CM* 5:534]). At this point, in mid-sentence, marked by the catchword "but," the manuscript breaks off.

In press Thackeray made one major identifiable change to chapter 35. Although we can surmise that the short paragraph beginning "I am glad Philip's infant could not" (*CM* 5:523–24) may have been written on the missing portion of fol. 8, we can definitely see that the chapter's last two paragraphs were added in press, for the first of the four leaves on which they exist—in Langley's hand—was marked by Thackeray with the numeral "524," the number of the *Cornhill* page on which they were to be inserted. Thackeray's original text probably ended at about the second line of *CM* 5:524 with the comic observation: "As it was, the compliments charmed the mother, for whom indeed they were intended, and did not inflame the unconscious baby's vanity." Presumably the novelist wished to provide as a matter of course a fuller final page by adding material somewhere in the chapter. It must have been apparent, however, that the ending's mild humor did not save it from being flat; accordingly, Thackeray decided to make his addition at the end, with the result that he provided a much more satisfactory conclusion. Because he saw that the turn away from Franklin to the subject of the Firmin baby had been both abrupt and misguided, he came back to Franklin and introduced a subject that had aroused the reader's sympathetic wonder—not only the reaction of Franklin's mother and sister but also Philip's response to the boy's unwittingly cruel as well as comical remarks: "What would the polite mamma and sister have said if they had heard that unlucky Franklin's prattle? The boy's simplicity amused his tall cousin. 'Yes,' says Philip, 'we are very poor, but we are very happy and don't mind—that's the truth'" (fol. 1*a*).

A final paragraph that actually ended the scene by bringing Franklin's talk and the visit to a conclusion then followed:

Mademoiselle, that's the German governess said she wondered how you could live at all, and I don't think you could if you ate as much as she did. You should see her eat—she is such a *oner* at eating. Fred my brother— that's the one who is at college one day tried to see how much Mademoiselle Wallfisch could eat, and she had twice of soup, and then she said ⟨si vous plait⟩ sivoplay,[26] and then twice of fish and she said sivoplay for more, and then she had roast mutton—no I think roast beef it was, and she eats the peas with her knife and then she had raspberry jam pudding and ever so much beer and then"—but what came then we never shall know because while young Franklin was choking with laughter (accompanied with a large piece of orange) at the ridiculous recollection of Miss Wallfisch's appetite, his mamma and sister came down stairs from Charlotte's nursery, and brought the dear boy's conversation to an end. The ladies chose to go home delighted with Philip; baby, Charlotte—Everything was *so* proper . . . ; Everything was so nice; Mrs. Firmin was so ladylike. The fine ladies watched her, and her behaviour with that curiosity which the Brobdingnag ladies displayed when they held up little Gulliver on their palms, and saw him bow, smile, dance, draw his sword, and so forth—just like a man.[27] (fols. 1*a*–4*a*)

Besides ending the scene, instead of breaking it off, Thackeray's addition provided an effective generalizing keynote for the whole visit of Lady Ringwood and her children. They are indeed Brobdingnagian in their perceptiveness, Franklin only more overtly than his mother and sister, as his comments about Miss Wallfisch further emphasize; fineness of behavior exists mostly on the side of the Firmins, whose response to gross condescension—however well meant—is good-natured courtesy.

The incomplete manuscript of chapter 36 reveals only one significant change in press. In manuscript Thackeray's title, "In wh. Philip wears a wig," emphasized his good fortune in securing remunerative legal work—which led to a move into new and better quarters. The revised title, however, underlines the more fundamental truth that emerges in the last portion of the chapter with the revelation that Dr. Firmin continues to draw on his son and with Philip's discovery that his father has forged Philip's signature on a large bill. Consequently we can understand why this is a chapter "IN WHICH THE DRAWING-ROOMS ARE NOT FURNISHED AFTER ALL."

Number eighteen for June 1862 works out some of the immediate implications of Dr. Firmin's letter and the forgery it revealed. The first of its two chapters consists of eight leaves, all in Thackeray's upright hand. Originally he began it on what is now fol. 3 with the title "Holophernes." This portion of narrative extended from the phrase "Having frequently succeeded in extorting money from Dr. Firmin" (see *CM* 5:643) to at least as far as the first sentence of the following leaf, then numbered fol. 2, which began, "She would invent" (*CM* 5:644). In short, this portion detailed Hunt's pursuit of Dr. Firmin to America, together with Hunt's return to England and his first appearance at Mrs. Brandon's house. Thackeray decided, however, to begin the chapter in another way and to give it a new title—"NEC PLENA CRUORIS HIRUDO"—reserving the old title for modified appearance as the title of the installment's large illustration: "JUDITH AND HOLOFERNES." Therefore, on two fresh leaves (fols. [1] and 2) the same size as fols. 3 and 4 (which are smaller than the others used for this installment), he began the chapter by continuing the scene that closed the previous installment, so as to show us Pen's and Philip's responses to Dr. Firmin's letter—especially Philip's fatalistic decision to honor the forged bill drawn in his name. With this new opening and the significant orientation it provided, Thackeray increased the ominousness of Hunt's arrival with the bill and the drama of that narrative, for the reader now knows Hunt will find a willing victim in Philip. The reader now also understands the dilemma in which Philip finds himself and the implications of the unsatisfactory alternatives among which he has had to choose. The deprivation Philip is accepting will fall not only on him but on his children and his wife, who is innocently discussing new chintzes for a future that is not only threatened but apparently doomed. If Philip agrees to pay the forged bill, he will simply invite further forgeries, but if he refuses, he will send his father to jail and publicly advertise his own and his children's shame. Ending with the sentence, "The bearer of *the bow-string* we knew was on his way, and would deliver his grim message ere long" (fol. 2; see *CM* 5:643), Thackeray completed his preparation for the narrative on fols. ⟨1⟩ and ⟨2⟩ and his transition to it. He then renumbered fols. ⟨1⟩ and ⟨2⟩ as 3 and 4, and continued the chapter to its ending: "And so with resolute hearts we would prepare to receive the Bearer of the Bow String" (fol. 8; see *CM* 5:651).

Only a portion of the manuscript of chapter 38 exists: fols. 1*a*–11*a*. Fols. 1*a*–7*a* are in Anne's hand, though they contain a number of alterations and additions in Thackeray's upright hand, including the title: "Chap 2 THE BEARER OF THE BOW STRING." The top of fol. 8*a* is also in Anne's hand, but Thackeray's upright script then begins with "Her cheeks are like apples" (*CM* 5:655) and continues for three and three-quarters leaves, breaking off after "the terrified man" (*CM* 5:660).[28] No major alterations are visible.

During the passage of chapter 37 through the press, six new paragraphs were formed by dividing old ones; a number of significant verbal changes were also made, all of them in the chapter's last two paragraphs. In manuscript Pendennis had narrated Charlotte's attitude towards the forgery as follows: "And as for the little case of forgery, I dont believe the young person could ever be got to see the heinous nature of Doctor Firmin's offence. How dreadfully pressed he must have been when he did it poor man! Now theres little Philip's cake in the cupboard wh. Brandon brought him. Now suppose Papa was very hungry and went and took some without asking Philly? He wouldn't be so very wrong I think, do you?" (fol. 8). In press, however, Thackeray added several more sentences to this speech, with a resultant increase in subtlety. After Charlotte's opening statement ("And . . . offence"), he inserted the words: "This desperate little logician seemed rather to pity the father than the son in the business" (*CM* 5:650–51)—thereby deepening the effect with a wonderful complex of ironies. Charlotte is certainly not a "logician," and her argument is thoroughly one-sided and perverse, as the overt judgment indicates. At the same time that we perceive her argument to be desperately illogical, however, we hear the worldly tone of Pen's judgment upon her and recognize *its* limitations as well. Because of Charlotte, we can understand the pitiableness of Dr. Firmin's position as well as Philip's and can perceive more readily that her naïve outlook is not only inferior to Pen's but also, in its own way, morally superior.

Thackeray also made Charlotte's position more complex than originally, for after her cry of pity for the poor man, the novelist made her acknowledge her sense of the wrongness of Dr. Firmin's act: "To be sure, he ought not to have done it at all." However, Thackeray made the acknowledgement immediately lead to a further statement of her special awareness: "but think of his necessity!" Such a view, moreover, was articulated to her antagonist in the debate: "That is what I said to Brandon" (*CM* 5:651). At this point, she uses the naïvely inadequate analogy between Dr. Firmin's dishonesty and the taking of a son's piece of cake, but because of Thackeray's additions the analogy has less undermining effect than before. The analogy now serves less as her argument than as an amusing, unwitting qualification of it. A final change came in the last paragraph, where Thackeray recalled that Philip no longer worked for the *Pall Mall Gazette* and altered "We would have an advance from Pall Mall" (fol. 8) to "A friend might help with a little advance" (*CM* 5:651). Thackeray thereby also signalled a change in Pen's own attitude from his earlier position of "however generously Philips friends might be disposed towards him, they could not in this matter give him a helping hand" (fol. [1]; see *CM* 5:642). Thackeray's changes added a few lines to chapter 37, but they did not extend its text onto a new page; they only brought the text somewhat closer to the middle of the final page. No sizable changes appear in chapter 38 either, but the absence of its final leaves severely limits the observations one can make.[29]

Number nineteen for July 1862 was set down on nineteen leaves of manuscript: six for chapter 39, "In wh. several people have their trials" (fols. 1, 1a, 2–5), and thirteen for chapter 40, "In wh. the luck goes very much against us" (fols. [1a], 1b–10b, 1c–2c), of which fol. [4b] and the upper portion of fol. [2b] are now missing. All are in Thackeray's upright script, which shares space on one leaf with Langley's (fol. 1a).

In the case of chapter 39 the manuscript reveals considerable difficulty of composition, especially at its beginning. The earliest of these leaves appears to have been the leaf now numbered fol. 1a. Written both in Thackeray's upright hand and in Langley's characteristic slant,

it began with the police report itself: "Marylebone. Wednesday. An
individual professing to be a clergyman . . .." The opening of the sentence then became, "Thomas Edward Hunt an individual professing to
be a clergyman . . .," before Hunt received his correct middle name.
Thackeray later wrote a new opening at the very top of the leaf: "If
you read your morning paper two days after the occurrence of the circumstances described in the last chapter, you came on the following
police report wh. my clerk has been at the pains to hunt up and copy."
After this sentence came an account of Hunt's appearance before
Beaksby, containing a variety of additions and deletions too numerous
and generally insignificant to detail. Eventually Thackeray decided to
compose a new introduction, which he wrote on a fresh leaf:

> If Philip and his friend had happened to pass through High Street
> Marylebone on their way to Thornhaugh Street to reconnoitre the Little
> Sister's house, they would have seen the Reverend Mr. Hunt, in a very
> dirty battered crestfallen and unsatisfactory state marching to Maryle-
> bone from the Station where the reverend gentleman had passed the
> night. and under the custody of the police. A convoy of street boys fol-
> lowed the prisoner and his guard, making sarcastic remarks on both.
> Hunt's appearance was not improved since we had the pleasure of meet-
> ing him on the previous evening. With a grizzled beard and hair, a dingy
> face, a dingy shirt and a countenance mottled with dirt and drink, we may
> fancy the reverend man passing in tattered raiment through the Street to
> make his appearance before the magistrate.
> You have no doubt forgotten the narrative wh. appeared in the morn-
> ing papers two days after the Thornhaugh Street incident, but my clerk
> has been at the pains to hunt up and copy the police report in wh. events
> connected with our history are briefly recorded. Marylebone Wednesday.
> Thomas Tufton Hunt[.] (see *CM* 6:121)

As we can see, by writing this new opening for his chapter, Thackeray preceded his brief narrative summary with a paragraph that provided dramatic action and graphic detail. Now we actually see Hunt's
"very dirty battered crestfallen" condition as he is taken to the magistrate, and we get a detailed picture of the disreputable appearance he
presents to that official—an appearance that will make clearer to us
why his wild testimony is so quickly dismissed. The new leaf, a considerable improvement over the earlier opening, was numbered fol. 1,
and the previous fol. 1 became 1a—presumably because a fol. 2 already existed, and very possibly fols. 3–5 as well. Fol. 2 may have
been replaced by another leaf with that number, for the present fol. 2

contains writing only on its upper half, underneath which is a long vertical line; however, the gap possibly represents only a break in composition.[30]

After a false start that was immediately cancelled ("Do you believe in Fate") fol. 3 went on to recapitulate Philip's relatively good fortune during his married life, beginning, "In so far" (*CM* 6:123). Five lines from the bottom of the leaf, however, came a turn: "And now, I grieve to say, money became scarce for the payment of these accounts: and though Philip fancied he hid his anxieties from his wife, be sure she loved him too much to be deceived by one of the clumsiest hypocrites in the world. Only, being a much cleverer hypocrite than her husband, she pretended to be deceived. And thence arose a little sentimental quarrel between these two young people wh. I am pleased to think led to no long estrangement, but only to a confirmation of the great love between them. Whatever ill-fortune befel him, that love, he owns with a thankful heart, has never failed him: Nor can he be called poor on whom Heaven has bestowed such" (see *CM* 6:124). At this point Thackeray may well have continued composition on a new leaf now replaced by the present fol. 4; if not, he immediately cancelled the last half of this passage (from "And thence arose") and continued his sentence on the top of the present fol. 4 with an account of how successfully Charlotte pretended: "and acted her part so well that poor Philip was mortified with her gaiety and chose to fancy his wife was indifferent to their misfortunes." Instead, then, of narrating the outcome, Thackeray went on to recount their misunderstanding, the emphasis now falling on the comic nature of the contretemps. Moreover, instead of offering at this point the generalized commentary he had begun to write at the bottom of fol. 3 ("Nor can he be called poor on whom Heaven has bestowed such"), Thackeray saved it for effective placement at the very end of the chapter, in modified form: "If he had his troubles our friend had his immense consolations. Fortunate he, however poor, who has friends to help, and love to console him in his trials" (fol. 5; see *CM* 6:126).

In composing chapter 40, Thackeray apparently dispatched its unnumbered first leaf, fol. [1*a*], to the printer before sending the rest of the chapter. The novelist then continued composition, using a numbering system that again began with "1"; this relay—which may have extended only from fol. 1*b* to fol. 3*b*[31]—was sent to the printer after Thackeray had received proof for the earlier part of the installment, for he wrote at the top of fol. 1*b* "⟨Go on at⟩ 8 continued." (From *CM* 6:128 it can be seen that the text of fol. 1*b* commences toward the middle of the installment's eighth page.)

The absence of the upper portion of fol. [2*b*] (presumably from "'Your father'" to "and friendly" [*CM* 6:129–30]) and all of fol. [4*b*] (presumably from "for what" to "the last forty" [*CM* 6:132–33]) limits the observations one can make, but one idiosyncrasy does appear: the absence of writing on the lower half of fol. 6*b*, which begins, "teeth and gave a very fierce glare" (*CM* 6:135), and ends with the words "expensive for him" (*CM* 6:136), followed by a vertical line drawn through much of the remaining space. Perhaps the text of an earlier fol. 6*b* was recopied and modified, or perhaps Thackeray merely broke off composition. The present fol. 6*b* may have marked the end of a relay, for fols. 7*b*–10*b* seem to constitute another.[32] The latter segment is devoted entirely to the Richmond dinner at which Philip quarrels with his cousin and namesake. Two more leaves remained to be written, however; set down on the installment's only other two leaves with a Palace Green imprint, they detailed the results of the quarrel and told how the completion of the Ringwoods' alienation from Philip was accompanied by Tregarvan's termination of Philip's employment and by Mrs. Baynes's dismissal of Philip's and Charlotte's claims upon her with a ten-pound note. Thackeray concluded the two leaves with another version of the ending of chapter 39: "in the midst of his griefs, Philip Firmin was immensely consoled by the tender fidelity of the friends whom God had sent him. . . . Kind readers all, may your sorrows, may mine, leave us with hearts not embittered, and humbly acquiescent ⟨to⟩ in to the Great Will!" (fol. 2*c*; see *CM* 6:144).

At the proof stages, Thackeray made no notable changes in chapter 39, but he made a number in chapter 40. Several were brief alterations made in the interest of exactness—such as "third rank" (*CM* 6:128) for "second rank" (fol. [1*a*]), and "See, good sir, the men" (*CM* 6:128–29) for "See the men" (fol. 1*b*). Others were lengthier modifications made for several purposes. The first of these alterations was designed to prepare for Laura's disapproval and Philip's suspicions, as well as our own, of his namesake and cousin. Originally, in recounting the meeting of the two cousins, Thackeray had written as follows: "Philip Firmin, who had not set eyes upon his kinsman since they were at school together some score of years before, was quite surprised to find a man much smaller than himself in the upper boy whom ⟨he remembered So well) had once admired for his tall stature. One day when the friendship of his new found cousin was at its height, Philip and Charlotte dined with Sir John . . ., when his son entered and asked for dinner" (fol. 1b). Now, however, Thackeray deleted the passage about Ringwood's size and about friendship between the cousins ("some score . . . its height"), making in its place a telling insertion. On seeing Ringwood, Philip now "remembered some stories which were current about Ringwood, and by no means to that eminent dandy's credit— stories of intrigue, of play, of various libertine exploits on Mr. Ringwood's part" (CM 6:129). Thackeray thereby deleted an inappropriate reference to "friendship," especially because the two Philips had not met for years, and he also made adequate novelistic preparation for what ensues.

The other significant changes came towards the end of the chapter, but only some of them appear to have been prompted chiefly by the wish to lengthen the installment onto a twenty-fourth page. Similarly, the desire for clarity caused the change in the passage in which Caroline Brandon gives Philip her purse. It would have been quite out of character for Philip to have accepted money from her even at this point, yet that is what Thackeray's narrative appeared inadvertently to imply: "And Philip kissed her, and thanked God for sending him such a dear friend. Indeed he had but five pounds left in the world when this benefactress came to him" (fol. 2c). Thackeray's revised version made matters unmistakable, however, for the passage now reads: "And Philip kissed her, and thanked God for sending him such a dear friend and gave her back her purse, though indeed he had but five pounds left in his own when this benefactress came to him" (CM 6:143). A few lines further the novelist slightly amplified and clarified a terse reference to Charlotte's portion, which had not been paid "since the second quarter three years ago" (fol. 2c); this he changed to "since the second quarter after their marriage, which had happened now more than three years ago" (CM 6:143).

The wish to lengthen his narrative helped Thackeray to see that the report of Tregarvan's dissatisfaction might be made a fuller and hence more convincing expression for the effusive Welshman. In manuscript, Tregarvan's letter announced that though he "would not recapitulate" all his dissatisfaction with Philip's conduct of the Review, "He was much disappointed in its progress, and dissatisfied with its general management. He thought an opportunity was lost wh. never could be recovered for exposing the designs of a Powre wh. menaced the liberty and tranquillity of Europe" (fol. 2c); he then concluded with the terms of dismissal. In press, however, Thackeray preceded mention of those terms with an additional statement that more fully set forth Tregarvan's obsessive, unfulfilled hopes for the *Review* and his dissatisfaction with Philip: "Had it been directed with proper energy that Review might have been an aegis to that threatened liberty, a lamp to lighten the darkness of that menaced freedom. It might have pointed the way to the cultivation *bonarum literarum*; it might have fostered rising talent, it might have chastised the arrogance of so-called critics; it might have served the cause of truth. Tregarvan's hopes were disappointed: he would not say by whose remissness or fault" (*CM* 6:142–43). A further amplification took place when Thackeray had Pendennis comment on Laura's observation that "Lady Ringwood knows how dreadful the conduct of that Mr. Ringwood is, and . . and I have no patience with her" (fol. 1c); Pendennis did so by alluding to his previous wonder at Laura's knowledge of Ringwood's dissolute behavior (*CM* 6:130): "How, I repeat, do women know about men? How do they telegraph to each other their notices of alarm and mistrust? and fly as birds rise up with a rush and a skurry when danger appears to be near?" (*CM* 6:142).

All these additions, however, would have produced no more at best than a twenty-fourth page containing about one line of print; Thackeray's main augmentation supplied quite a bit more than all of them combined. He used the occasion to bring us up to date on a character who had dropped out of the narrative for some time but had just re-emerged to deliver a culminating blow at Philip. Originally Thackeray had written merely that "Mrs. General Baynes was living at Jersey at this time. She sent Philip a ten pound note open by Captain Swang of the Indian army, who happened to be coming to England. And that, Philip says, of all the hard knocks of Fate, has been the very hardest wh. he has had to endure" (fol. 2c). In order to emphasize her hypocrisy and the effect of her blow on those who know her well, among whom we are to be included by virtue of our newly refreshed memory, Thackeray added the following pointed exposition after the word "Jersey":

> in a choice society of half-pay ladies, clergymen, captains, and the like, among whom I have no doubt she moved as a great lady. She wore a large medallion of the deceased General on her neck. She wept dry tears over

that interesting cameo at frequent tea-parties. She never could forgive Philip for taking away her child from her, and if any one would take away others of her girls, she would be equally unforgiving. Endowed with that wonderful logic with which women are blessed, I believe she never admitted, or has been able to admit to her own mind, that she did Philip or her daughter a wrong. In the tea-parties of her acquaintance she groaned over the extravagance of her son-in-law and his brutal treatment of her blessed child. Many good people agreed with her and shook their respectable noddles when the name of that prodigal Philip was mentioned over her muffins and Bohea. He was prayed for; his dear widowed mother-in-law was pitied, and blessed with all the comfort reverend gentlemen could supply on the spot. "Upon my honour, Firmin, Emily and I were made to believe that you were a monster, sir—with cloven feet and a forked tail, by George!—and now I have heard your story, by Jove, I think it is you, and not Eliza Baynes, who were wronged. She has a deuce of a tongue, Eliza has: and a temper—poor Charles knew what *that* was!" In fine, when Philip, reduced to his last guinea, asked Charlotte's mother to pay her debt to her sick daughter, Mrs. General B. sent . . .. (*CM* 6:143–44)

As a consequence, we can understand more readily why this was the very hardest knock that Philip had to bear, and why Thackeray had chosen this event to be the climactic repudiation in the chapter.[33]

On 3 July 1862 Thackeray wrote in his diary, "6.15 p.m. Finis Philippi" (*Letters*, 4:403).[34] The manuscript of number twenty for August contains the usual two chapters. That for chapter 41 consists of fols. 1–3, while that for chapter 42 of fols. 4–15 and, after a gap of about a leaf and one-half, the final but unnumbered leaf, which I shall designate fol. [18]. The three leaves of the former chapter, "In wh. we reach the last stage but one of this journey" (fol. 1), reveal no special growth of composition, but evidence of somewhat complex genesis is to be found in the surviving leaves of the final chapter. For one thing, Thackeray made several decisions about its title. On fol. 4 he at first called it "The abode of Bliss and Halls of Prismatic Splendour," in keeping with the elaborate pantomime metaphor that he used, especially in its opening paragraph, where that phrase also appears (see *CM* 6:222). He later crossed out the phrase, however, and replaced it with the title, "In wh. the Fairy descends from her Chariot"—another pantomime reference closely related to his first paragraph and to the chapter's and

novel's climactic event, when Woolcomb descends from his chariot and unwittingly brings Philip good fortune.

The most interesting evidence of growth, however, is supplied by writing on the versos of fols. 10 and 11, from which we can see very clearly that Thackeray's relatively "clean" texts on fols. 7 and 10 in themselves tell us nothing about the existence or nonexistence of earlier versions of these leaves; such information can come only from the survival of actual antecedents, which here are to be found on the versos of fols. 10 and 11, thereby reminding us that the existence of such versions of all Thackeray manuscript leaves must be allowed as a theoretical possibility.[35] The text on fol. 10*v*, a version of the appearance of Philip, Pendennis, and J.J. at Ringwood's castle lodge, is brief: "⟨open⟩ and might people walk in the Park? Yes. any body might walk in the Park: and if the family was not to the house, ⟨any⟩ gentlemen might see it.' We walked up the great avenue undisturbed, and arrived at the Portico of the mansion, in wh. some of Philip's ⟨[word illegible]⟩ ancestors had been born." Thackeray saw further narrative possibilities, however, that made this version seem too simple and hasty; accordingly, he rewrote it on a fresh leaf. For one thing, with the innocent, permissive voice—originally that of "⟨A laborer with his jacket on his arm . . .⟩" (fol. 6) rather than a little red-cheeked girl—Thackeray contrasted a fierce voice of denial that symbolically enacted the family hostility, as the lodgekeeper's and later the porter's willingness to let money govern their decisions enacted the family's venality. For another, Thackeray had Pendennis, with ironically archaic language, mock both the aged lodgekeeper and Philip's attitude towards his mother's ancestors and this ancient family home.[36]

Even more, however, Thackeray went on to chasten Pen and then to show so marvellously the strange and moving power of the place upon Philip's imagination—both as a boy, when he fixed its image and description in his memory, and now when he first walks through the familiar though strange landscape and peoples it with the creatures of a comic yet magical force of his own:

Was ⟨†any body staying at†⟩ the house to be seen?
   Yes says a little red-cheeked girl with a curtsey. No! calls out a harsh voice from within: and an old woman comes out from the lodge and looks at us fiercely. 'Nobody is to go to the house. The family is a coming.' That was provoking. ⟨We⟩ †Philip† would have liked to behold the great house

where his mother, and her ancestors were born †'Marry, good dame,'†
⟨'This cavalier'⟩ Philip's companion said to the old beldam, †This goodly
gentleman† hath a right of entrance to yonder castle wh., I trow, ye wot
not of. Heard ye never tell of one Philip Ringwood slain at Busaco's
glorious fi * *

Hold your tongue. and don't chaff her's ⟨Pen⟩ growled Firmin.[37]

Nay an⟨d⟩ she knows not Philip Ringwoods grandson,' the other wag
continued in a softened tone 'This will convince her of our right to enter.
⟨Know you⟩ †Can'st recognize† this image, ⟨grand⟩ of your queen?

'Well I suppose 'ee can go up' said the old woman at the sight of this
talisman. There's on⟨y⟩ly two of them and ⟨the *Laryer*⟩ staying there,
and they're out a⟨can⟩ drivin'." Philip was bent on seeing the halls of his
ancestors. ⟨They⟩ †Gray and huge, with towers and vanes and porticoes,
they† lay before ⟨him⟩ †us† a mile off separated from us by a streak of
glistening river. A great chestnut avenue led up to the river and in the
dappled grass ⟨thed⟩ the deer were browsing. You know the house, of
Course. There is a picture of it in Watts bearing date 1783. A gentleman
in a cocked hat and pigtail is rowing a lady in a boat on the shining river.
Another nobleman in a cocked hat is angling in the glistening river ⟨over⟩
†from† the bridge, over which ⟨the⟩ a postchaise is passing. 'Yes the
place is like enough' said Philip, 'but I miss the post chaise going over
the bridge, and the lady in the punt with the tall parasol. Dont you remember the print in our housekeepers room in Old Parr Street? My poor
mother used to tell me about ⟨this⟩ †the† house, and I imagined it
grander than the palace of Aladdin

⟨Win⟩ It *is* a very handsome house, †Philip went on,† 'It extends two
hundred and sixty feet by seventy five, and consists of a rustic ⟨b⟩Base-
ment and principal Story with an attic in the centre, the whole executed
in Stone. The grand ⟨portico⟩ †Front† towards the Park is adorned with
a noble portico of the Corinthian order. and may with propriety be considered one of the finest elevations in the' * * I tell you I am quoting out
of Watts's Seats of the Nobility and Gentry,' ⟨p⟩published by John &
Josiah Boydell and lying in our drawing room. Ah dear me! I painted the
boat and the lady and gentleman in the drawing room copy, and my father
boxed my ears. and my mother cried out, Poor dear Soul! And this is the
river, is it? And over this the post chaise went with the ⟨dock⟩ †club†-
tailed horses: and here was the pig-tailed gentleman fishing: It gives one
a queer sensation, says Philip standing on the bridge, and stretching out
his big arms. ⟨P[illegible] Perhaps the⟩ 'Yes there are the two people in
the punt by the rushes. I can see them, but you can't, and I hope, Sir,
you will have good sport.' And here he took off his hat to an imaginary
gentleman ⟨angling⟩ supposed to be angling from the balustrade for
ghostly gudgeon. ⟨The painter listened half puzzled.⟩ We reach the house
presently: We ring at a door in the basement under the portico. (fols.
6–7; see *CM* 6:226–27)

The antecedent of fol. 10 also reveals a number of interesting changes, though they are somewhat less radical in nature. The two versions follow:

†a most† affectionate †of† parents. He has a large ⟨second⟩ family by his second marriage, and his estates go to his eldest Son. We must not quarrel with Lord Ringwood for wishing to provide for his young ones. I dont say that he quite acts up to the ⟨Republican⟩ †extreme Liberal† principles wh. he †once† was rather fond of boasting. But if you were offered a Peerage, what would you do? If you wanted money for your young ones, and could get it would you not take it? ⟨Mind. I⟩ †Come. Come† dont let us have too much of this Spartan virtue If ⟨y⟩You were tried, be sure you would be not much worse or better. ⟨Has the landlord no better Sherry? Ha. What is that in the window of the Ram?⟩ †You are going to dine? We pressed him to join our party but he declined he was going up to the house—where of course he should dine with them— But here he broke off, with a 'Ha! What is that paper they are putting up in the window of the Ram?—†

We looked across the way, and we saw ⟨a gentleman⟩ †one or two people† standing before the Inn Window of the Ram: and admiring a placar[d]³⁸ or proclamation there posted. '⟨An⟩ ⟨†As I live an†⟩ †As I live, cried Bradgate, an† Opposition! †Whose is it? Bedloe's of course.† How did ⟨they⟩ †he† ⟨now⟩ know that there was to be a Vacancy? In this case We must hang out our banners on the outer wall. And seizing the wafer box, the nimble lawyer speedily pasted

the most affectionate of parents' †Mr. Bradgate remarked†. He has a large family by his second marriage, and his ⟨†landed†⟩ estates go to his eldest Son. We must not quarrel with Lord Ringwood for wishing to provide for his young ones. I don't say that he quite acts up to the extreme Liberal principles of wh. he was once rather fond of boasting. But if ⟨you⟩ †we† were offered a peerage what would you do; what would I do? If you wanted money for your young ones and could get it, would you not take it? Come, Come. Dont let us have too much of this Spartan Virtue! If we were tried my good friends, we should not be much worse or better than our neighbours. Is my fly coming, waiter? We asked ⟨to⟩ Mr. Bradgate ⟨would he not share⟩ †to defer his departure & to share our† dinner. ⟨b⟩But he ⟨said thank you I⟩ †declined, and said he† must go up to the †great† House, where I ⟨suppose I shall stay to dinner. We have plenty of business to arrange. Ha What is that paper they have just put up in the window of the Ram⟩? †he and his client had plenty of business to arrange, and where no doubt he would stay for ⟨dinner⟩ the night. He bade the inn servants put his portmanteau into ⟨the⟩ his³⁹ carriage when it came. The old Lord had some famous Port wine, he said 'I hope ⟨the hous⟩ †my friends have the key of the cellar.'†

⟨Though t⟩ The waiter was just putting our ⟨dinner⟩ †meal† on the up his manifesto in the bow window of the Coffee room in wh. we were sitting.

This was very exciting. ⟨We⟩ †The Ringwood flag flying, we† ran across the way to the Ram and there read a placard ⟨announ⟩ denouncing in terms of unmeasured wrath the impudent attempt to ⟨def⟩ dictate to the free and independent electors, and saying that a friend of freedom, a friend to the borough, was determined to ⟨contest⟩ †rescue† it out of the hands of an insolent oligarch. The Freemen were invite[d][40] to ⟨be⟩ show themselves worthy of the name and submit to no CASTLE DICTATION— The placard was Signed a BRITON WHO WILL NOT BE A SLAVE. And when Mr. Bradgate read it, he pronounced at once that it came from Bedloe's office—⟨the local⟩ †an† attorney of the town. (fol. 11v)

table, ⟨we went out⟩ ⟨as we looked from⟩ †as we stood in† the bow window of the Ringwood Arms Coffee room ⟨towards the Opposit⟨⟨ion⟩⟩e Inn where we saw a great placard⟩ †engaged in this colloquy. Hence we could see the street, and the Opposition inn of the Ram, where presently a great placard† was posted. At least a dozen street boys shopmen and rustics were quickly gathered round this manifesto, and we ourselves went out to examine it. The Ram placard denounced in terms of unmeasured wrath the impudent attempt from the Castle to dictate to the free and independent electors of the borough. Freemen were invited ⟨to b⟩ not to promise their votes, to show themselves worthy of their name; to submit to no castle dictation. A county gentleman of property of influence of liberal principles No WEST INDIAN no CASTLE FLUNKEY but a TRUE ENGLISH GENTLEMAN would come forward to rescue them from the tyranny under wh. they laboured. On this point the electors might rely on the ⟨vor⟩ word of A BRITON. This was brought down by the clerk from Bedloe's. He and a newspaper man came down in the train with me: a Mr. * * (fol. 10; see CM 6:229–30)

Here, as we can see, Thackeray made a number of changes between the two texts. We remember that in the earlier surviving version of fol. 7 (fol. 10v), the novelist had cancelled mention that "the Laryer" was staying at the castle, but we do not fully know what was in Thackeray's mind when he made that change. We can only see that in the earlier surviving version of fol. 10 (fol. 11v) Bradgate was sipping the abominable sherry—perhaps just prior to dinner at the Ringwood Arms. If such was the case, Thackeray quickly cancelled this reference because he saw that he could use the subject of dinner as an ironic way of dramatizing further the arrogant parsimony of Woolcomb, who is to be the unwitting Good Fairy, and presumably of making possible a comic dramatization of the struggle in Bradgate between rage at Woolcomb and professional loyalty to his employer. In the revised version, the novelist injected Bradgate's allusion to the former Earl's port, thereby increasing Bradgate's expectations (as well as ultimate disappointment) and preparing for the eventual reintroduction of his annoyance at the landlord's fiery sherry, for which Bradgate finally has to settle when he is sent away from the castle without a bed or dinner. Thackeray removed from the earlier version the somewhat anomalous surprise of Bradgate's at the existence of a political opposition—a surprise that is immediately followed by the lawyer's identification of that opposition. In the latter text there is curiosity on the part of all concerning the contents of the opposition proclamation. Now, Bradgate's identification of its authorship derives at least in part from his awareness of the means by which it has been introduced into the town. Thackeray also rewrote the proclamation itself, shortening it slightly and improving its stylistic effectiveness. Finally, one can say that while both versions reveal a constant process of compositional revision, the greater part takes place not within each text but from one text to the other.[41] The most memorable narrative result of this complex creation—the evocative visit of Philip to the family home he has known only from an illustrated book, which impinges on the present in imaginative memory, generating the true grounds of future possession—serves as an epitome of Thackerayan continuity, both within the novel and without, since it gives us a model for taking our own possession of the imaginative worlds created by his fiction.

In surveying the form of the last half of *Philip*, we note immediately the appearance of the Samaritan theme at the beginning of number eleven, where it is inverted to characterize Mrs. Baynes. If Philip is intolerant of her relentless prattle, she finds her obligation to him even more unpleasant: "I wonder was that traveller who fell among the thieves grateful afterwards to the Samaritan who rescued him?" (*CM* 4:514). Her preparations for breaking her promise to Philip are again indicated, but so is the ultimate futility of her efforts to prevent the marriage (*CM* 4:515). Against this background Thackeray presents us with images of two contrasting couples: the pair now courting and destined to be happily married, and the Woolcombs, the sight of whom makes Philip even happier to have escaped Agnes and found Charlotte. Unhappiness is also to come, however, as the rest of the number begins to show. The narrator repeats his mention from two installments earlier (*CM* 4:264) of Philip's pain years later on recalling the unhappiness suffered under Mrs. Baynes, and he soon shows us one basis for Mrs. Baynes's interference: the well-to-do Hely's infatuation for Charlotte. Hely is the second string Mrs. Baynes tries to place on Charlotte's bow (*CM* 4:528). If this is the chief positive development in Mrs. Baynes's eyes, the major negative one is Philip's misbehavior at the Ambassador's entertainment, where after comically bursting out of his gloves and—as a result of Twysden's deliberate bump—out of his coat and vest as well, Philip learns of Twysden's malice and kicks him into the fountain—to the dismay of the respectful. The installment ends, therefore, as General and Mrs. Baynes confront their Samaritan: "But no Charlotte was in the room" (*CM* 4:536).

Numbers twelve and thirteen present the crisis, which is largely resolved when Charlotte departs from her mother's supervision at the end of the latter installment. In the former, after General and Mrs. Baynes break off the engagement, the merciful behavior is Madame Smolensk's in coming to Philip and giving him comfort: "The Samaritan who rescues you, most likely, has been robbed and has bled in his day, and it is a wounded arm that bandages yours when bleeding" (*CM* 4:650). She also, of course, gives comfort to Charlotte, whose loyalty to Philip not only causes her to suffer but also helps prompt Mrs. Baynes unwittingly to begin the process of freeing Charlotte by asking Mrs. MacWhirter to take the girl for a while. At the same time a new dimension is added to Philip's troubles, when his generosity towards his exiled father causes Dr. Firmin to begin a further series of thefts from him (*CM* 4:654). During the second half of the installment, Philip's troubles in Paris begin to take a comic turn as General Baynes, in attempting to defend himself to Colonel Bunch, only provokes the latter's denunciation.

With the arrival of Major MacWhirter at the end of number twelve, Baynes believes he has found an ally and second, but the opening of number thirteen undercuts this expectation as MacWhirter supports

Bunch against the general, causing the latter to quarrel with him too. One by one all the combatants come upon the stage with passions raging and the comedy riotously mounting until Charlotte's collapse in Philip's arms breaks the tension, disperses the group, and brings an end to the threatened violence. Although both the general and his wife have been defeated, only the general has apologized. Hence, when the second contrast is established between the soundly sleeping Philip and the wakeful pair across the Seine, we see a further division: while Mrs. Baynes is sleepless with "Baulked revenge and a hungry disappointment," her husband "is awake to the shabbiness of his own conduct" (*CM* 5:13) as well as that of his wife. The rest of the installment then traces the intimidating effects upon Mrs. Baynes of Charlotte's defiance and the general's guilt and anger at his wife. It is the general who now decisively arranges for Charlotte to visit the MacWhirters at Tours. The Samaritan theme closes the installment on this occasion, as Madame Smolensk brings Philip information about the planned departure, news of the MacWhirters' readiness to receive Philip's visits, and a banknote enabling him to take advantage of the opportunity. An end is thereby promised to his separation from Charlotte, which had begun at the end of number eleven.

When Charlotte moves away from her parents at the start of number fourteen, she makes a major break with her restrictive past. Whereas Philip had accompanied them all during the ride from Boulogne to Paris in number eight, here, not long after she recalls that former journey, she is suddenly reunited with Philip at a stop along the way as he reveals himself in Orleans to be journeying by a rival coach towards Tours (*CM* 5:132). The reestablishment of their association is then confirmed by the dying general, whose decline has been hastened by separation from Charlotte, but who manages to join their hands before he dies (*CM* 5:140). After Charlotte returns to her aunt, the remainder of the installment treats Philip's return to London, where he seeks an additional source of income that will make his marriage possible. Whereas the Twysdens live in fear of Philip's coming to borrow money, Mrs. Brandon continues to be "ready to relieve many a fallen wayfarer on her road" (*CM* 5:145), and when the sub-editorship of the *Pall Mall Gazette* becomes vacant, she and Laura go to work upon Mrs. Mugford to secure the position for Philip, as a passage added in press shows. Their warm-hearted artifices succeed for a time, for Philip gains the appointment, but a hint of the future is provided at the

close of the installment by Pendennis's dinner, where the editor, Bickerton, behaves insufferably and where Philip bluntly tells him of his
obnoxiousness.

The beginning of number fifteen announces Philip's actual installa-
tion as sub-editor of the *Gazette*, where he cheerfully accepts both his
light work and his light pay. As he tells Pendennis, "I am not at all a
clever fellow, you see; and I haven't the ambition and obstinate will to
succeed. . . . I am going seriously to learn the profession of poverty,
and make myself master of it" (*CM* 5:260). The intention is a sensible
one, though for a time the full degree of necessity for learning this profession is not apparent. Soon after his resolve, Charlotte is brought to
London by Major MacWhirter and installed in a spare bedroom of
Laura's. Then comes a climactic piece of news: a letter from Dr. Firmin proposing that Philip serve as London correspondent for a New
York newspaper. Innocently believing in this prospect of further income that will enable them to marry, Philip and Charlotte prepare for
that "event, with which the third volume of the old novels used to
close" (*CM* 5:274). But the wedding does not close the installment any
more than it does the novel. Instead, the last word is given to Charlotte and Philip, who write the Pendennises a long honeymoon letter
dramatizing their happy joining of spirits. This is the tone that sounds
at the three-quarter mark of Thackeray's novel.

The honey and moonshine imaged at the beginning of number sixteen by the chapter initial and text continue for a time, but the joyful-
ness evoked in the first half of the installment is conveyed to us with
tones of foreboding. Although Philip continues to work for the *Pall
Mall Gazette*, his social relations with Mugford come to be a problem.
As a Thackerayan addition in press emphasizes, Mugford's vocal appreciation of his own worth becomes increasingly difficult to endure. A
child is born and still Philip hopes to continue saving part of his salary;
Mrs. Baynes, however, stops payment of Charlotte's modest income.
"Poor as he was, this was his happiest time" (*CM* 5:391), we are told,
but as that language implies, a downturn is soon to begin—which it
does in the installment's other chapter, where the news is increasingly
bad. First, Dr. Firmin steals Philip's initial paycheck from New York.
Then, as Philip becomes more restive at working for Mugford, the editor of the New York journal absconds and Philip's income from that
source is permanently cut off. There are also hopeful notes, like the
prospect of employment with a new journal, the *European Review*,

and the continued presence of Samaritans, for as Philip recalls, "I wanted succour, and I found it. I fell on evil times, and good friends pitied and helped me. . . . Your good Samaritan takes out only two-pence maybe for the wayfarer whom he has rescued, but the little timely supply saves a life" (CM 5:403). The installment's final note, however, is one of comedy and disaster, as Philip quarrels with Mugford, during a scene augmented in press, and at the same time implicitly has his employment at the *Gazette* terminated.

The opening of number seventeen confirms this implication and reminds us: "So two of Philip's cables cracked and gave way after a very brief strain, and the poor fellow held by nothing now but that wonderful *European Review* established by the mysterious Tregarvan" (CM 5:515). Laura makes sure of Tregarvan's continuing support, however, and even succeeds in getting Philip several legal briefs to supplement his income. With the help and succor of Tregarvan (CM 5:526), Philip himself stumbles into good relations with his relative, Sir John, thereby contrasting again with the lick-spittle Twysdens, who not only try to cultivate Sir John but also to poison his attitude towards Philip. With the help of legal briefs Philip actually builds up a few savings, and Mrs. Brandon, who is ever ambitious for him, encourages him to take a house. Further developments bring serious threats, however, as his father repeatedly steals from him, the installment ending as Dr. Firmin forges Philip's name to a bill that passes into the hands of Philip's old enemy, Tufton Hunt. At the same time, however, the Doctor sends Mrs. Brandon what will prove to be an anodyne against Hunt's malice: a bottle of chloroform.

At the start of number eighteen, in a passage inserted into the manuscript, Philip accepts ruin as his fate and prepares again to be sacrificed by his father (CM 5:643). The violence of what is to be done to him is conveyed by the metaphor of Hunt as the bearer of the bow-string, but fortunately there is a counteragent of violence, who is capable of being Judith to Hunt's Holofernes (CM 5:645). Laura, Philip, and Charlotte all agree in Christian acquiescence, Mrs. Brandon alone rebelling against the looming fate, especially as it threatens not only Philip but his children. Mrs. Brandon does not, of course, premeditate violence, just rebellion, and it is Goodenough who offers her a peaceful mode of action by giving her money to tempt Hunt and by giving her tactical advice: "tell him plenty of lies, my dear" (CM 5:653). Only after Hunt refuses to sell the forged bill, after he leeringly approaches her, and as she shrinks back half hysterically, does she defend herself by striking him and then follow up her advantage by chloroforming him and destroying the forged bill. Goodenough enthusiastically praises "her glorious crime, and most righteous robbery" (*CM* 5:661), but the more persuasive authentication comes in another manner. It is appropriate for Laura, Philip, and Charlotte to acquiesce, but it is also appropriate for the militant Mrs. Brandon (and Goodenough) to defend against aggression: just as Mrs. Brandon had charitably lied to protect Philip from Hunt at the end of number 5, so here she charitably protects him by stealing and destroying a forged document, the previous act helping to authenticate this one. Even greater support for her conduct is provided by the final chapter's initial, for there we are asked to see her as a female Christian knight (though without the formal banner of the Cross) chivalrously on guard, ready to defend the vulnerable Philip and his family from the violent Turk who bears the bowstring (*CM* 5:652).

In number nineteen, even Laura and Charlotte, though with qualifying pity for Dr. Firmin, "loved and admired" Mrs. Brandon for her "lawless act in her boy's defence" (*CM* 6:123). The affair is settled as Hunt's disreputable appearance and behavior discredit his story to the magistrate, while Philip's denial of having given a bill of exchange effectively warns Dr. Firmin to cease his forgeries. Philip has a good deal of "succour and relief" (*CM* 6:123), but hereafter grim difficulties are to come. Now that Philip and his family have moved away from Mrs. Brandon's, Charlotte's poor handling of expenses becomes apparent. As his means shrink, moreover, Philip has the misfortune to renew acquaintance with Sir John's son, Philip Ringwood. When another bachelor dinner is held at which Philip sings "Doctor Luther," as he had in number three, he finds himself not only in the midst of good fellowship but in the presence of Philip Ringwood, whose snobbish and dishonorable behavior he bluntly denounces—as he had done with Bickerton's in number fourteen and Trail's in number seventeen. Philip goes further on this occasion, however, threatening to send a decanter at Ringwood's head and inviting him to come forward and be knocked down. The result is that Sir John breaks off relations with Philip, and his employer Tregarvan does the same; Philip's third and last cable has now given way and he is left without any income. The serial number ends with a final blow, as Mrs. Baynes ignores his request that she pay what she owes from Charlotte's portion; instead, she sends him by a messenger "a ten-pound note, open" (*CM* 6:144).

In the final installment, number twenty, Thackeray draws rather elaborately upon his central metaphor. Responding to Mrs. Baynes's contemptuous gesture, Philip wonders "whether the thieves who attacked the man in the parable were robbers of his own family, who knew that he carried money with him. . . . But again and again he has thanked God, with grateful heart, for the Samaritans whom he has met on life's road, and if he has not forgiven, it must be owned he has never done any wrong to those who robbed him" (*CM* 6:217). Though a third child has been born and Charlotte lies in a fever, Philip knows better than to "look or ask for . . . succours from his relatives" (*CM* 6:218)—the Twysdens, Sir John, or Woolcomb. "When he fell wounded and bleeding, patron Tregarvan dropped him off his horse, and cousin Ringwood did not look behind to see how he fared" (*CM* 6:219). But Mrs. Flanagan, Dr. Goodenough, J.J., Mrs. Brandon, Laura, and Pendennis are "ready with their sympathy and succour" (*CM* 6:218); so too, thanks to Mrs. Brandon, are the forgiving Mrs. Mugford and her dutiful husband, who gives Philip employment at the *Gazette* once more as the penultimate chapter closes. Finally, we enter "THE REALMS OF BLISS" (*CM* 6:222), for although in the previous number Philip had impatiently accused Charlotte of acting "as if life was a pantomime" (*CM* 6:125), it is the Good Fairy of the Christmas pantomime who presides at the novel's close (*CM* 6:222). Final succor for Philip and his family is provided by Woolcomb, who turns out to be the unwitting Good Fairy riding in the chariot—the late Lord Ringwood's postchaise, with the still valid will lying behind the side panel.

With the final words of this, his last completed novel, Thackeray evokes the inevitability of ending: "Good night. Good night, friends, old and young! The night will fall: the stories must end: and the best friends must part" (*CM* 6:240). These words do not occur by themselves, however, but in the context the author has just provided for them, in which he indicates the inevitability of ever-new beginnings and continuations. Seen in this context, the endings of his individual novels are not endings but temporal resting points in continuing processes. Like the individual serial installments, his novels themselves embody palingenesis, a continuous recurrence of birth, and like their present-day successors, modern serial poems, these individual embodiments give a temporal existence to the continuous life that inhabits them and us.

Afterword

The public dimension of Victorian serialization has been forcefully emphasized in a recent study which reminds us that "Critics from 1836 on have slighted the part played in the runaway reception of the novel by its unusual format; yet subsequent to Dickens's success with *Pickwick*, parts publication became for thirty years a chief means of dramatizing and enormously expanding the Victorian book-reading and book-buying public. Dickens and his publishers discovered the potential of serial publication virtually by accident. In so doing, they changed the world of Victorian publishing, and the Victorian novel, permanently. And, at the same time, their discovery yielded profits hitherto thought impossible for any publisher or author, transforming them all from minor figures in Victorian letters to titans."[1]

Thackeray reached his largest audiences with his serial contributions to the *Cornhill*, but, as Henry James witnesses for us, Thackeray's serial installments were titanic not only from their command of the collective sensibility but also from their own genial weight and force. Ultimately, they were large arrivals because they were recurring enrichments of life.

Scholars still need to learn more about the conditions under which Thackeray composed his serial numbers, especially the influences that led to the development of his original conceptions, the growth of his plans for illustrating the installments, his sketches or finished drawings, his communications with his illustrators and the craftsmen who executed the illustrations, details concerning the time required for their execution in wood and metal, and the circumstances of the passage of text and illustrations through the press—including the final adjustment of both to occupy a number's allotted space. Even with our present knowledge, however, we can gain fundamental insights into the conditions of his art and can therefore come to understand that art more profoundly. No one would deny that instances of inconsistency and even carelessness can easily be found in his work, but the claim that such instances require us to view him as a basically careless artist represents both a failure to argue logically and a failure to consider sufficient evidence. The more one studies his manuscripts and their passage through the press, the more one is struck by the constancy, scope, and variety of his efforts to discover and reveal the rich potential of his narratives, and by his success not only in purifying and developing this potential but also in giving it a unity both minute and far-reaching. Moreover, if the challenges and opportunities of serial publication—ranging from the exacting nature of the form itself to the generous latitude given him by his publishers for meeting those constraints—repeatedly stimulated Thackeray to modify his expression within that form, the interaction of these motives with Thackeray's commitment to the integrity of his art repeatedly gave his installments new richness and strength. Finally, then, what we can perceive is not simply the landscape of his fiction but the living processes that animate it. Timed, shaped, and ended by the strokes of the great clock, they are also stimulated by our awareness of those strokes to renew themselves and to renew those of us who respond.

Abbreviations and Symbols

Abbreviations

Adversity	Gordon N. Ray. *William Makepeace Thackeray: The Uses of Adversity*. New York: McGraw-Hill, 1955.
Arents	Arents Collection, New York Public Library
Berg	Henry W. and Albert A. Berg Collection, New York Public Library
British Lib.	British Library, London
Buffalo	Lockwood Memorial Library, State University of New York at Buffalo
Charterhouse	Charterhouse School, Godalming
CM	*Cornhill Magazine*
Fitzwilliam	Fitzwilliam Museum, Cambridge University
Harvard	Harvard University Library, Cambridge
Huntington	Henry E. Huntington Library, San Marino
Illinois	University of Illinois Library, Urbana-Champaign
Kansas	Kenneth Spenser Research Library, University of Kansas
Leeds	Brotherton Collection, University of Leeds
Letters	Gordon N. Ray, ed. *The Letters and Private Papers of William Makepeace Thackeray*. 4 vols. London: Oxford University Press, 1945–46.
Loyola Marymount	Loyola Marymount University, Los Angeles
Morgan	Pierpont Morgan Library, New York
NLS	National Library of Scotland, Edinburgh
NYU	Fales Library, New York University
Parrish	Morris L. Parrish Collection, Princeton University Library
Punch	Punch Publications, Ltd., London
Ray	Gordon N. Ray
Rochester	University of Rochester Library
Rosenbach	Rosenbach Museum, Philadelphia
South Carolina	South Caroliniana Library, University of South Carolina, Columbia

Taylor   Robert H. Taylor Collection, Princeton, N.J.
Texas   Humanities Research Center, University of Texas at
                          Austin
Washington   Washington University, Saint Louis
Wisdom   Gordon N. Ray. *William Makepeace Thackeray: The
                          Age of Wisdom.* New York: McGraw-Hill, 1958.
Yale   Yale University Library, New Haven

Symbols

† . . . . . . †   material inserted into a manuscript
⟨ . . . . . . ⟩   cancelled material
[. . . . . .]   inferential or otherwise supplied material

Notes

1: Introduction

1. Lionel Stevenson, "William Makepeace Thackeray," *Victorian Fiction. A Guide to Research* (Cambridge, Mass.: Harvard Univ. Press, 1964), p. 158. His single example is a misplaced paragraph in *Vanity Fair* about which Thackeray was in fact aware; there is no evidence to show that Thackeray failed to make the correction in proof.

2. John Hammond Schlacht, "A Critical Edition of William Makepeace Thackeray's *Denis Duval*" (Ph.D. diss., Univ. of Illinois, 1947). John A. Sutherland has also treated it in *Thackeray at Work* (London: Athlone Press, 1974), pp. 110–37. The first major study of the serialization of a Victorian writer's fiction, John Butt and Kathleen Tillotson, *Dickens at Work* (1957; rpt. London: Methuen, 1963), remains preeminent, though a fuller background for understanding the development of the Victorian serial novel has recently been provided by Robert L. Patten in "*Pickwick Papers* and the Development of Serial Fiction," *Rice University Studies* 61 (1975): 51–74.

3. The most recent study of this controversy is K. J. Fielding's "Thackeray and the 'Dignity of Literature,'" *Times Literary Supplement*, 19 and 26 September 1958, pp. 536, 552.

4. A few contrary statements made shortly after his death seem not to have had an appreciable effect on critical opinion. Although claiming that Thackeray gave the impression of "undervaluing his art," Dickens termed it a "pretense," not a reality. Dickens also mentioned a portion of the *Denis Duval* manuscript, saying: "The condition of the little pages of manuscript where Death stopped his hand, shows that he had carried them about, and often taken them out of his pocket here and there, for patient revision and interlineation" (*CM* 9 [1864]: 131). A few months later, Frederick Greenwood commented on the "too-hasty notion which we believe to have been pretty generally accepted: namely, that Mr. Thackeray took little pains in the construction of his works. The truth is, that he very industriously *did* take pains. We find . . . his designs for 'Denis Duval' . . . in the form of many most careful notes, and memoranda of inquiry into minute matters of detail to make the story *true*" (*CM* 9 [1864]: 656). It was unusually insightful for an anonymous writer at the turn of the century to point out the elaborateness of Thackeray's pedigrees and the artful care with which he made them consistent with one another across the entire body of his fiction. This writer went on to say: "In view of these considerations it is difficult to understand how certain of his contemporaries could have formed the idea that Thackeray took little pains in the

construction of his novels. The charge was of course utterly disproved by the publication of part of the contents of his note-books, and by the notes to his unfinished 'Denis Duval'—but the indirect evidence of the pedigrees alone should have been sufficient to make such criticism impossible" ("One Aspect of Thackeray," *Temple Bar* 124 [1901]: 76).

5. *Thackeray: The Humourist and the Man of Letters* (New York: Appleton, 1864), p. 188.

6. *Thackeray* (New York: Harper, [1879]), pp. 15, 119, 38, 119–21, 134, 56–57.

7. Herman Merivale and Frank T. Marzials, *Life of W. M. Thackeray* (London: Scott, 1891), pp. 28–29. One notices, however, the persistence of Trollope's misconceptions in a piece like Arthur Calder-Marshall's "Thackeray: A Spoilt Artist": "Rather lazy, rather self-indulgent, he usually set himself to write only when he knew that the printers were clamouring for copy" (*The Listener* 49 [1953]: 211).

8. *The Oxford Thackeray*, 17 vols. (London: Oxford Univ. Press, [1908]), 12:xxx. More recently, Donald Hawes has taken a similar position regarding *Pendennis*, pointing out that "Thackeray's revision mostly took the form of cutting," claiming that "This shortening was an improvement in every respect," and asserting that the deleted matter, which he identifies as "padding, crudities, and inconsistencies," had "arisen from his hasty, piecemeal method of composition for the monthly parts" ("Note on the Text," *Pendennis* [Harmondsworth, U.K.: Penguin, 1972], p. 23). I find the nature and significance of the deletions to be less simple a matter than does Hawes, and note that once again we are faced with a unique situation. These revisions form a poor basis for making generalizations about Thackeray's serial composition, for the 1856 edition of *Pendennis* is the only instance of a Thackerayan serial in which the revisions for a later edition take the form of frequent and extensive cuts.

9. I have given detailed consideration to these matters in "The Serial Structure of Thackeray's *Pendennis*," *Revue de l'Université d'Ottawa* 45 (1975): 162–80, especially 177–78.

10. *Pendennis*, 2 vols. (London: Bradbury and Evans, 1849–50), 2:v.

11. Two full-page illustrations might take four days to etch, a Thackerayan wood-block roughly a day to engrave. For further details see John Harvey, *Victorian Novelists and Their Illustrators* (New York: New York Univ. Press, 1971), pp. 182–98.

12. The two surviving leaves of number fourteen—fols. 1 and 4—identify either a new relay of manuscript or an addition made when the installment was shown to be too short. In either case, the addition was made when Thackeray had page proof, for fol. 1 (Huntington) was also numbered 432 by Thackeray, representing the page on which the insertion was to begin. Here Thackeray was adding what is now the final passage of chapter 48, beginning as Briggs looks up from the work table, continuing through Becky's brilliant stroke of getting from Steyne twice the amount she owes Briggs, and ending as Becky deposits the large banknote in the desk given her by Amelia (fol. 4 [Taylor]).

If this is the kind of carelessness and padding allegedly caused by the serial mode of writing, a reader can hardly get too much of it.

A leaf, now at the Rosenbach Museum, from the final double installment of *Vanity Fair* may have initiated a relay in that serial part, for it was numbered fol. 1 by Thackeray, though it begins the installment's second chapter, as was noted by someone—perhaps the printer—who marked at its top in pencil that it was chapter 2. The following leaf continues the numbering system: fol. 2, which survives in the Huntington Library. Almost the only extant bit of the *Pendennis* manuscript, a portion of number thirteen (Harvard), also reveals a repeated numbering system in the middle of an installment; here the installment's third chapter begins with 1, as does the first chapter. Thackeray's letters reveal that he did send portions of *The Newcomes* in relays.

13. Because of the difficulty of positioning wood-blocks at their proper place between certain lines of type, the galleys could be set with page divisions—as we can see in a fragment (p. 35) of the *Vanity Fair* manuscript—or the manuscript could be set directly into page proof.

14. An unpublished letter (privately owned in Great Britain) of 16 February 1857 to Bradbury and Evans, for example, contains Thackeray's annoyed complaints that the printer had not followed his written directions concerning the *Miscellanies*. For the failure of Thackeray's repeated instructions concerning the title page of *Rebecca and Rowena*, see my "Thackeray's 'Rebecca and Rowena': A Further Document," *Notes and Queries*, n.s. 24 (1977): 20–22.

15. Regarding *Pendennis*, Thackeray wrote that his work on number sixteen for May 1850 was "pretty well advanced" and that he expected to finish what appears to have been his basic manuscript on Sunday evening, 26 May. "Then comes printing & proof correcting & so forth, and by Thursday I hope to see you." After writing the basic manuscript for the final double installment, he said: "There are always 4 or 5 hours work when it is over: and 4 or 5 more would do it all the good in the world, and a second or third reading" (*Letters*, 2: 668, 709). The latter quotation is especially ambiguous. Does the first phrase refer to work special to the final installment, such as the writing of an introduction; does "4 or 5 more" mean further revision; and does "a second or third reading" refer to a single set of revises, later revises, or what?

16. The nearly complete manuscript of *Esmond*, it might be stated in passing, helps identify a number of alterations made in manuscript and in press, but fails to reveal any major changes in the novel's design.

17. Further details are given in my study, "The Challenges of Serialization: Parts 4, 5, and 6 of *The Newcomes*," *Nineteenth-Century Fiction* 29 (1974–75): 3–21.

2: *Vanity Fair*, Installments 1 and 2

1. See *Adversity*, pp. 384, 495; *Vanity Fair*, ed. Geoffrey and Kathleen Tillotson (Boston: Houghton Mifflin, 1963), pp. xvii–xix (hereafter cited as

Tillotson edn.); and John Sutherland, "A Date for the Early Composition of *Vanity Fair*," *English Studies* 53 (1972): 47–52. Sutherland's article lends support to Ray's belief that Thackeray began the novel shortly after his return to England in February 1845.

2. *Thackeray. A Personality* (1932; rpt. New York: Russell & Russell, 1966), p. 157.

3. Vizetelly, *Glances Back Through Seventy Years*, 2 vols. (London: Kegan Paul, Trench, Trübner, 1893), 1:284 (hereafter cited as *Glances*).

4. Kate Perry writes of meeting Thackeray at Brighton during the latter part of 1846 and being told by him that "he is now writing a novel, but cannot hit upon a name for it." She continues: Thackeray "told me some time afterwards that after ransacking his brain for a name for his novel, it came upon him unawares, in the middle of the night, as if a voice had whispered, 'Vanity Fair.' (He said,) 'I jumped out of bed and ran three times round my room, uttering as I went, "Vanity Fair, Vanity Fair, Vanity Fair"'" (*Reminiscences of a London Drawing Room* [n.p.: privately printed, n.d.], pp. 2–3). In the context of her remarks, "some time afterwards" may imply while they were both still at Brighton, where she indicates Thackeray would bring "his morning work to read to me in the evening" (p. 2).

5. The lower halves of fols. 31 and 32 are missing from the Morgan manuscript. The two upper halves were pasted on a single page by the person who made up the album in which the manuscript now exists; nevertheless, I treat these halves as separate leaves with missing bottom portions. The missing half of fol. 31 perhaps contains the source of a portion of text that appears in surviving proof and in printed versions. Joan Stevens, in 1964, identified the missing half of fol. 32 as being "in the possession of the Thackeray family" ("A Note on Photography: The MS of 'Vanity Fair,'" *Journal of the Australasian Universities Language and Literature Association*, no. 21 [1964]: 85); this half contains "Thirteen lines in sloping hand" (Tillotson edn., p. 671) that perhaps reappear in surviving proof and printed versions. I have not been able to locate the fragment.

In citing the manuscript of this novel, as in the case of all subsequent novels, I transcribe all errors and omissions of words and punctuation without comment. I do not, except in special instances, include cancelled variants within quotations or identify changes, but instead give Thackeray's final corrected manuscript versions. Printing costs have made it impossible to use superscripts. Hence, for example, what Thackeray set down as "M!" appears here as "Mr." and my verso designations appear in italics (e.g. fol. 8*v*). Similarly, instead of using a superscript to distinguish two manuscript leaves bearing the same numeral, here also I use italics (e.g., fol. 8 and fol. 8*a*). Unitalicized letters appearing with folio numerals (e.g., fol. 8a) represent actual manuscript designations that have been directly transcribed. Words with double underlining in the manuscript have been set directly into capitals and small capitals.

6. It will be clear, therefore, that I view statements like the following to be

unproved: "At this time [February 1845] he wrote half a dozen chapters or more in his earlier slanting hand." "Henry Colburn [was] evidently the last in this series [of publishers whom Thackeray tried]" (in fact, Colburn may have been the first). "By January of 1846 the manuscript . . . [was] entitled 'The Novel without a Hero: Pen and Pencil Sketches of English Society'" (*Adversity*, p. 384). For further discussion of the title, see my article, "Thackeray and His Publishers: Two Uncollected Letters Concerning *Vanity Fair* and *Esmond*," *Papers on Language & Literature* 12 (1976): 167–76.

7. *Vanity Fair* (London: Bradbury and Evans, 1848), p. 621. All subsequent citations to this novel, as to all subsequent novels issued in separate monthly parts, refer to the first book issue because of its greater accessibility than a set of the parts issue. Although the printing history of a given Thackeray serial is liable to be very complicated (as Peter L. Shillingsburg has shown in his excellent study, "The First Edition of Thackeray's *Pendennis*," *Publications of the Bibliographical Society of America* 66 [1972]: 35–49), collation of book issues with parts issues has revealed no variants in quoted passages except in the case of *Vanity Fair*, where they are duly noted.

8. Several times in this portion of the manuscript Thackeray wrote "Selby," but he corrected the name in manuscript.

9. It occurs on fol. 20*v*, which, like most of the initial leaves, is numbered in pencil—apparently not by Thackeray; the designation in this case is "19A." A proofreader has penned brackets around the passage and added the word "out," meaning "mistakenly left out." Thackeray's usual instruction to the compositor in such cases—"T.O." (turn over)—is missing from the bottom of fol. 20; hence the compositor evidently at first failed to set up the passage written on fol. 20*v*, but then had the omission called to his attention by a proofreader.

10. The proposal that these two omissions resulted from double eye-skip by the compositor seems to me farfetched. I therefore very much suspect that at least some of these ten fragments come from revised galley proof.

11. George's identity as a military officer is not emphasized until the second installment, but Jos has already said that George will marry Amelia "As soon as he gets his company" (fol. 22; p. 27).

12. As these statements suggest, the Tillotsons' assertion that there is "no hint of [Dobbin] in the early draft of Chapter 6" (Tillotson edn., p. xix) seems too emphatic.

13. I am indebted here to Peter Shillingsburg, who has pointed out to me, for example, that the type font consistently used for "y" and "?" in the ten proof fragments has been consistently replaced in the published forms and that the cost of composition at the Bradbury and Evans shop for thirty-two pages was only £4—not enough to warrant keeping type out of circulation for eight months.

14. The best-known deletion was the removal of a sentence hinting at Becky's literal illegitimacy: "Ill natured persons however say that Rebecca was born before the lawful celebration of her excellent parents' union" (fol. 8).

This sentence was replaced by one that identified the illegitimacy as meta-phorical and, indeed, self-created: "And curious it is, that as she advanced in life this young lady's ancestors increased in rank and splendour" (p. 10).

15. In discussing Thackeray's illustrations, I make the following distinctions: "etching" refers to the full-page illustrations for the separate monthly numbers, two for each serial installment; "internal wood-engraving" denotes an illustration inserted into the text of a chapter—as opposed to a "chapter initial," which is a wood-engraving that inaugurates a text, or an "endpiece," which is a wood-engraving that occupies the blank space on a chapter's final page. In the case of *The Cornhill Magazine*, the illustrations are of only two kinds: full-page illustrations and chapter initials; both are wood-engravings.

16. One should also observe that Thackeray prepared an additional wood-engraving; taking up about nineteen lines, it depicted George watching Amelia at the piano. The novelist evidently intended to insert it into the text of page 28, but found he could not do so because the twenty-seven-line wood-engraving near the bottom of page 29 could not then have been included on that page. As a result, the illustration of George and Amelia appeared, rather inappropriately, as an endpiece.

17. A considerable number of changes were made by the compositors, who corrected formal errors, made errors of their own, added necessary and unnecessary punctuation, introduced standardized spelling, expanded abbreviations, established regularity, and imposed their versions of appropriate word forms. In attempting to demonstrate this process, one can probably attribute to them, for example, the following variants from the brief portion of text appearing on the opening page:

its' (fol. 1)	its (p. 1)
gates	gate [an error]
Pinkertons	Pinkerton's
Academy	academy
ladie's	ladies,
coach	coach,
servant	servant,
Pinkertons	Pinkerton's
house,—nay	house. Nay,
recognized	recognised
drawing room	drawing-room
It	"It
coach sister!	coach, sister,"
Jemima, Sambo	Jemima. "Sambo,
servant	servant,

Coachman	coachman
waistcoat.	waistcoat."
Have	"Have
departure	departure,
Jemima?	Jemima?"
Hammersmith	Hammersmith,
M^{rs}.	Mrs.
The	"The
morning	morning,
sister,	sister,"
we	"we
bow pot.	bow-pot."

One should also note the following errors in the printed installment: "Diction-ary" (p. 3) for "Dixonary" (fol. 2); "humble" (p. 9) for "loveable" (fol. 7); "neckcloth" (p. 16) for "neckcloths" (fol. 13); "toxopholite" (p. 17) for "toxo-philite" (fol. 14); "but" (p. 20) for a somewhat oddly formed "and" (fol. 17); "said Joe" (p. 20) for "said Jos" (fol. 17); "first" (p. 23) for "just" (fol. 19); "Joe" (p. 25) for "Jos" (fol. 20v); and perhaps also "outrage" (p. 8) for "out-rages" (fol. 6); and "If he" (p. 24) for "If I" (fol. 19). Geoffrey and Kathleen Tillotson have identified three of these, printing "outrages," "just," and "If I" (Tillotson edn., pp. 19, 33–34). One should note that generally printers seem not to have returned copy with proofs. See chapter 4, note 5.

18. The upright hand appears in the "Explanation of the Allegory" at the bottom of his sketch for the frontispiece. Now in the Berg Collection, it has been reproduced in Lola L. Szladits and Harvey Simmonds, *Pen and Brush: The Author as Artist* (New York: New York Public Library, 1969), p. 16. The engraver did not include the language in his woodblock, however; it was set up in type and printed below the engraving.

19. T. J. Brown, "English Literary Autographs: II. *William Makepeace Thackeray*, 1811–63," *The Book Collector* 1 (1952): 97, also cites some of this evidence.

20. The importance of this event is emphasized by a plate that also depicts it: "*Mr. Joseph in a state of excitement*." Although the illustration appeared in the second installment, the drawing for it and perhaps the plate itself seem to have been executed during or after composition of the first version of chap-ter 6, but before the second version was completed, for the etching clearly shows the Hebrew gentleman, mention of whom was deleted from the text of the second installment.

21. This perspective also appears in the drawing Thackeray made to illus-trate the moment of meeting between Amelia and the awkward young officer. Ultimately, however, the printer could not "place" the illustration satisfac-

torily in the text; as a marking in the manuscript (fol. 10) indicates, it was originally meant to follow the words, "one of the clumsiest bows that was ever performed by a mortal," but evidently because there was insufficient room at the bottom of p. 40, he was forced to insert it near the top of p. 41, after the words, "When she held out her hand for him to shake . . . and as he let his cocked-hat fall," although the illustration shows Dobbin's hat in his hand and Amelia's hand at her side. The first internal wood-engraving of chapter 6 has also been moved, again presumably for lack of room. The manuscript shows its place of insertion next to the words, "THE NIGHT ATTACK" (fol. 12; p. 43), but it actually appeared just after Vizard hears the click of a pistol (p. 44). In a final instance, lack of space seems to have forced a wood-engraving to be moved forwards. Thus Jos gazing tenderly at Becky does not follow "said Joseph, with a most killing tenderness" (fol. 16; p. 49), but rather follows "Miss Rebecca Sharp and her stout companion lost themselves" (p. 48). Joan Stevens's generally appropriate injunction that future editions of the novel emulate the first edition's positioning of illustrations, therefore, must be qualified by the phrase: "to the degree that the first edition appropriately follows the manuscript directives or clear indications of the text itself." See Stevens, "Thackeray's 'Vanity Fair,'" *Review of English Literature* 6 (1965): 19–38.

22. I have treated some aspects of this subject in two companion studies: "The Fields of Mars in *Vanity Fair*," *Tennessee Studies in Literature* 10 (1965): 123–32, and "The Function of Mock-Heroic Satire in *Vanity Fair*," *Anglia* 84 (1966): 178–95.

23. See, for example, *The Examiner*, 26 December 1846, p. 831.

24. The lengthy nature of the stints suggests that the two chapters were set up without heavy pressure of time.

25. Several apparently compositorial errors in the second installment require correction, notably the following: "Princess Peribanou" (fol. 5) for "Prince Peribanou" (p. 36); "last wishes" (fol. 5) for "best wishes" (p. 37); and "*Mon Seigneur*" ("*Mon ⟨Prince⟩* †Seigneur†" [fol. 13]) for "Monseigneur" (p. 45). Additionally, "talked of" should replace "talked off" (p. 46), which repeats a manuscript error (fol. 14). The Tillotsons identify "Princess," but they restore an error by substituting "byeword and reproach" (Tillotson edn., p. 50) ("byeword & reproach" [fol. 8]) for "byword of reproach" (p. 38). "Byword" here means "by name," a "nickname" of reproach: thus "the name of Figs which had been a byword of reproach became as respectable and popular a nickname as any other in use in the school" (p. 38).

26. For an outline of this structure and a brief discussion of it, see my article, "The Discipline and Significance of Form in *Vanity Fair*," *PMLA* 82 (1967): 530–41.

27. In this instance I use the term "section" in referring to those portions of each chapter that are marked off by the break of a line in the text. Though chapter 1 has only two sections, it offers parallels to the three sections of chapter 5, just as the three chapters of number two pair off with the four chapters of number one.

3: *Vanity Fair*, Installments 3 and 4

1. Fol. ⟨39⟩ was once ⟨40⟩ and fol. ⟨40⟩ was once ⟨37⟩, but these cancelled designations may represent only misnumbering, for the latter continues in mid-word from the bottom of the former.

2. The subject of Sir Pitt's relationship with Miss Horrocks is treated by Myron Taube, "Thackeray at Work: The Significance of Two Deletions from *Vanity Fair*," *Nineteenth-Century Fiction* 18 (1963–64): 273–79, the argument of which is partly modified by Peter L. Shillingsburg, "Miss Horrocks Again," *NCF* 28 (1973–74): 92–95.

3. *Thackeray at Work*, pp. 24–25.

4. In the printed version, the last six words are also given to Miss Crawley instead of to Becky, perhaps as a result of a compositor's error.

5. These leaves provide the chapter's ending except for the final three sentences, which were written on a leaf formerly in the Lambert Collection (no. 902, "Catalogue of the Sale of Major William H. Lambert's Collection of Thackerayana at the Metropolitan Art Association, February 25–27, 1914"). The leaf apparently remains in private hands.

6. This information was inserted as a brief aside, but the compositor evidently misplaced it, for it should follow the words, "she sang," not precede them (p. 95).

7. This is the only watermarked date I have been able to find in the entire manuscript.

8. I have treated this subject at greater length in "The Serial Structure of Thackeray's *Pendennis*." See chapter 1, note 9.

4: *The Newcomes*, Installments 4, 5, 6, and 10

1. A total of twenty-four leaves, several of them quite fragmentary and one of them ultimately rejected, are known to exist at Harvard University, the Huntington Library, the Berg Collection, and the Robert H. Taylor Collection. Portions of them have been treated by Sutherland, *Thackeray at Work*, pp. 45–55, and Peter L. Shillingsburg, "Thackeray's *Pendennis*: A Rejected Page of Manuscript," *Huntington Library Quarterly* 38 (1975): 189–95. Two pages of corrected proof also are to be found in the Berg Collection.

2. The Charterhouse manuscript, which contains most of what survives, consists of numbers four through six, ten, fourteen through fifteen, seventeen through twenty, and a portion of the final double number, twenty-three/twenty-four—a total of 457 leaves. The only surviving fragment of an early monthly part seems to be in the Robert H. Taylor Collection: two leaves numbered A1 and A2 that apparently were added in press to the second installment. Providing two paragraphs (beginning, "With that fidelity which was an instinct of his nature"), these leaves by themselves did not change the page count but added a memorable passage that placed the Colonel's longing for his

absent child in the context of the "strange pathos [that] seems to me to accompany all our Indian story" (*The Newcomes. Memoirs of a Most Respectable Family*, 2 vols. [London: Bradbury and Evans, 1854–55], 1:52).

3. This conjecture seems further supported by a passage from a letter written in October 1854 to Mrs. Procter: "If I were to lose a number of the Newcomes I don't know what I should do. I never could write it over again: the idea of the calamity frightens me; and when we were abroad I never used to let the MS out of my sight" (*Letters*, 3:394).

4. Gordon Ray describes Leigh as "a genial man of scholarly tastes known as 'The Professor' among his colleagues, . . . Thackeray's closest friend after Leech and Doyle among the *Punch* writers" (*Letters*, 2:105n).

5. Leigh may not have checked the revises against copy, however. As Philip Gaskell points out: "It does not appear . . . that copy was normally returned to the author with the proof until the later nineteenth century, and even when it was the author did not necessarily compare the two" (*A New Introduction to Bibliography* [Oxford: Clarendon Press, 1972], pp. 352–53). As we have seen, roughly half the novel's manuscript is missing.

An example of what Thackeray also expected Leigh to do appears in an unpublished letter of 23 January 1854, now in the *Punch* office, which reveals further evidence of Thackeray's wish to safeguard his manuscript:

> Rome. January 23.
>
> My dear B. & E.
>
> I send No VII. by a private hand and pray it may go safe as I have no copy thereof. That will be the April number.
>
> Please tell Leigh I have omitted
>
> The housekeepers name at Colonel Newcomes Fitzroy Square
>
> The ——— Dragoons charging the ——— guns at Assaye—a life of Wellington will tell him what dragoons & what niggurs were charged.
>
> I'm getting better of my illnesses & the weather is just heavenly. If I can do good work next month here we shall go to Naples. I shake every body by the hand & am
>
> Yours always   WMT.
>
> Proofs on thin paper might be sent care of MacBean & Co.

Leigh supplied the necessary details, for we now read of "the 19th Dragoons charging the Mahratta Artillery" (1:204), and find the housekeeper identified as "Mrs. Irons" (1:215)—evidently because Leigh supplied the name himself, having failed to discover that Thackeray had identified her in chapter 16 as "Mrs. Kean," the wife of Colonel Newcome's man (1:160).

6. In a letter of 24 June 1854, Thackeray is quite specific about Leigh's authority to make cuts in the page proofs or their revises: "There will be a little too much letter press in No XI. for August. Will you kindly snip off the extra sentence or two in case I should not be here?" (*Letters*, 3:378). John Forster performed a similar, though perhaps more substantial, function for

Dickens, as John Butt and Kathleen Tillotson have indicated in *Dickens at Work*, pp. 23–24.

7. See G. D. Hargreaves, "'Correcting in the Slip': The Development of Galley Proofs," *The Library* 26 (1971): 295–311, Gaskell, *A New Introduction to Bibliography*, pp. 194–95, 351–53, and John Bush Jones, "British Printers on Galley Proofs: A Chronological Reconsideration," *The Library* 31 (1976): 105–17. See also Butt and Tillotson, *Dickens at Work*, for evidence that in the case of *David Copperfield* (1849–50) Bradbury and Evans probably sent Dickens galley proof only for the opening installment. To Butt and Tillotson, however, a lack of time was the essential reason for the printers' decision to take only page proof: "for time was short; and . . . the bulk of correction was necessarily done in page" (p. 21). As we have already seen in the case of *Vanity Fair* and as a letter quoted immediately below will reveal, however, Thackeray was familiar with galley proof of his serial fiction.

8. Although Thackeray indicated in the manuscripts of *Vanity Fair* and *Pendennis*—novels he himself illustrated—where wood-engravings were to be placed, he made no such notations in the manuscript of *The Newcomes*. In an unpublished letter (privately owned in Great Britain) written from Berne c. 10 August 1853, when Thackeray proposed to Bradbury and Evans that Doyle illustrate *The Newcomes*, the novelist suggested that Doyle do a colored etching for each installment and the chapter initials, but no other wood-engravings; Thackeray promised to furnish Doyle with portraits of the characters and with hints for the etchings and chapter initials. As Anthony Burton has pointed out in "Thackeray's Collaborations with Cruikshank, Doyle, and Walker," *Costerus*, n.s. 2 (1974): 156–61, Thackeray gave Doyle at least some sketches and instructions; in the case of the first installment, he supplied a sketch of the Colonel leaving the Cave of Harmony and also apparently provided the idea for the emblematic initial of chapter 2, which "was intended to represent Hogarth's industrious apprentice" (*Letters*, 3:321). After Doyle had illustrated Belsize in the printed number, Thackeray commented: "Belsize does not look buck enough, and his beard is too long: but that's a trifle." For Doyle's response, compare "*An incident in the life of Jack Belsize*" (number nine, opposite 1:280) with "*'To Rome'*" (number ten, opposite 1:301) and especially with "*The old love again*" (number seventeen, opposite 2:159). In the same letter Thackeray wrote, "If you do Lord Kew make him smart handsome & like a young swell—a square faced brisk blue-eyed bushy whiskered fellow is the gentleman I have in my mind" (*Letters*, 3:373).

Aside from this evidence, the clearest sign of Thackeray's communication with Doyle exists in the novel itself. The final plate of number two for November 1853, "*Mr. Barnes Newcome at his Club*," for example, reveals Barnes's mistress and one of his illegitimate children—characters whose identity Thackeray had obviously communicated to Doyle but who were not to be introduced verbally until number 10, which would not be written until February 1854 (*Letters*, 3:673). Thackeray also provided Doyle with challenges or hints in the text—such as that in number five ("I have turned away one artist . . . , and I doubt whether even the designer engaged in his place can make such a portrait of Miss Ethel Newcome as shall satisfy her friends and her own sense of justice" [1:150]) or that in number eight, which introduces a description of Clive at a family party ("For being absent with his family in Italy now, and not likely to see this biography for many many months, I may say that he is a much handsomer fellow than our designer has represented; and if that way-ward artist should take this very scene for the purpose of illustration, he is requested to bear in mind that the hero of this story will wish to have justice done to his person. . . . And now let the artist, if he has succeeded in drawing Clive to his liking, cut a fresh pencil, and give us a likeness of Ethel" [1:231–32]). Doyle, in fact, responded with illustrations for these two passages. When the novel was prepared for republication without illustrations, these passages were deleted.

As Thackeray's characterization suggests, Doyle could be annoyingly "way-ward" in preparing his illustrations for press, the normal deadline apparently being the 15th of the month. George and Edward Dalziel, for example, report the following incident concerning *The Newcomes*: "Doyle . . . was singularly deficient as to the value of time . . . ; but little reliance could be placed upon him even when working for periodical publications. On one occasion when illustrating a story by Thackeray, the number had to be issued short of certain pictures that had been arranged for. Thackeray was a good deal annoyed and asked Doyle if he could give any reason why he had not done the drawings. He replied in his cool, deliberate manner: 'Eh—er—the fact is, I had not got any pencils'" (*The Brothers Dalziel* [London: Methuen, 1901], p. 58). June 1854 was apparently a crucial stage in Doyle's relations with his author and pub-lisher, for Bradbury and Evans were on the point of dismissing him and Thack-eray was prepared to take over the illustrating (*Letters*, 3:375). An unpub-lished letter, now in the *Punch* office, shows the novelist interceding on Doyle's behalf, however. Evidently written on 19 June 1854 from London after the publication of number nine, it reads:

Monday 19

Dear B & E.

Doyle was with me yesterday and showed that with respect to the plates for this month the fault was not his. He had written for them & they were not sent until 3 days before the 15th His blocks were all but ready—finally, I have agreed subject to your approval to continue him

He has signed a paper owning that he has been constantly late, that he has had many warnings from you, & 3 distinct ones from me: and ac-knowledging that on his very first delay hereafter he puts himself out of our undertaking.

Be the next time then the final leave-taking. Had the dismissal taken place now he would have had some ground for complaint against B & E, for keeping him to the letter of his agreement and not providing him with means for its fulfilment.

B & E were too busy with the Crystal Palace to attend to his affairs, and to certain others—I go to Boulogne at the end of this week with my family and should like a talk before our departure.

Yours ever

WMT.

In spite of these warnings, however, Doyle continued to be rather wayward (*Letters*, 3:384).

9. Thackeray wrote fols. 25b–25d and presumably an earlier version of fol. 25a in pencil in his upright hand on an unsteady surface—perhaps in bed. Subsequently he seems to have replaced fol. [25a] with a larger leaf written in his slanted hand without any distortion of script; this is the present fol. 25a, which has some blank space at its foot but connects with fol. 25b in mid-sentence.

10. The passage has been cited by John Sutherland in "The Inhibiting Secretary in Thackeray's Fiction," *Modern Language Quarterly* 32 (1971): 186. Sutherland, assuming that all passages in Anne's writing were dictated to her rather than copied, argues that the presence of Anne distracted Thackeray from the artistic needs of his narrative, so that Thackeray later had to cancel portions of the manuscript text like this one about Ethel. The few passages quoted in the article, however, must also be placed within the context of similar passages that are retained and of deletions necessitated by the requirements of the serial form.

11. Since chapter 16 begins without the customary chapter initial, lacks other wood-engravings, and covers the final page to the very last line of available space, it is here that the question of Leigh's control over the text comes to its sharpest focus so far. Although Thackeray returned corrected proof and could at this stage make close estimates of how much the text was short or long, in the case of a chapter like 16, which uses up every bit of space, Leigh may well have made the last cut: a phrase concerning the growth of Pen's friendship with the Colonel. Unless one can demonstrate that Leigh made the deletion, however, one must assume that it is authorial.

12. 1:166 is set up as a page of forty-six lines, though it actually prints only forty-four because two lines of poetry require additional spacing.

13. It is twenty-three lines high and somewhat more than half a line wide.

14. No chapter in the novel contains more than three internal wood-engravings and only two other chapters—4 and 5, both from number two—contain that many. Two other chapters each have two internal wood-engravings and an endpiece; only four other chapters contain as many as two wood-engravings and they lack endpieces.

15. Leigh also supplied two lines (1:166) from Cowper's "Boadicea: An Ode" that Thackeray had indicated in manuscript only as follows: "When the [blank space] ⟨Roman⟩ †British† Queen," (fol. 7).

16. Thackeray's letter of 25 February 1854 to Leigh from Naples mentions receiving the proofs, which went by way of Rome and took unusually long to reach him, on February 21st—"Four days ago" (*Letters*, 3:349). If he corrected them immediately and sent them to London on the day following his

receipt of them, they could have arrived in London on Monday, 27 February; in fact, his letter sent to Leigh from Naples on 8 March—also a Wednesday—took exactly that length of time—five days—as the postmark indicates (*Letters*, 3:354). (The appearance of the March number may also have been delayed, but I have not found evidence to support this hypothesis.) Thackeray would have sent the proofs directly to Bradbury and Evans, of course, not to Leigh, to whom he sent his somewhat lengthy letter on the 25th. Thackeray's deletions might be more understandable if one knew that he thought Leigh would discover the purpose of the three leaves and realize that number 6 had sufficient copy; however, given his characteristic wish to improve the text, they would be comprehensible even without this uncertain assumption. The three leaves were apparently discarded by Leigh, for the Charterhouse manuscript is consecutively numbered, with no later insertions or additions, and the printed text contains none either, aside from the passage taken from within the manuscript of number five. With the problem of number 6 satisfactorily settled, numbers 7 and 8 could be printed without special difficulties.

17. These errors include the following: "Also of course drew" (1:163) for "Also of course Clive drew" (fol. 3); "fine turns" (1:163) for "fine tones" (fol. 4); "old heart bobbing" (1:178) for "old head bobbing" (fol. 19); "Todmoreton" (1: 181, 183) for "Todmorden" (fols. 26, 28); and "here virtue" (1:186) for "here Virtue" (fol. 30).

18. In a letter of 8 March 1854 from Naples to Percival Leigh, Thackeray asks that he alter the name "Montaign" to "d'Ivry" (see *Letters*, 3:355, which adds a final "e" to "Montaign" that does not appear in the original letter in the Morgan Library); the name first appears in number seven for April. Thackeray apparently assumed that he himself and Leigh would detect subsequent uncorrected references in proof and he did not bother to change all of them in the manuscript of number ten. Some were in fact altered in proof, but other references to "Prince," "Princesse," and "Princess" persisted into the published text (1: 301, 302, 304, 308, and 310).

19. Anne's rather idiosyncratic handwriting presents certain difficulties. Her initial "c's" and "s's" of words within a sentence, for example, tend to be larger in size than the rest of the word; I transcribe them and other doubtful examples in lower case, reserving upper case for letters clearly formed as capitals, even though she may habitually use them even in the middle of a sentence—like the initial "E" of "Eyes."

20. In "The Inhibiting Secretary in Thackeray's Fiction" (p. 185) John Sutherland cites this passage, which was not dictated but was set down by Thackeray himself. The strength of Thackeray's wish to find an appropriate expression of the idea in the earlier cancelled passage about the squeamish *reader's* inhibiting effect on an artist attempting to paint "modern pictures of life" (fol. 19) becomes manifest not only on this leaf but also in number eleven. There, after alluding to Kew's Don Giovannian victories, the printed text reads: "If we have told or hinted at more of his story than will please the ear of modern conventionalism, I beseech the reader to believe that the writer's purpose at least is not dishonest, nor unkindly" (1:333).

21. Above the words "she has taken the idea that she resembles Mary Queen of Scots" Thackeray inserted "more than ever to" (fol. 25). Since there has been no prior mention of this idea in the *numerically* preceding leaves of manuscript, however, Thackeray was recalling material *written* earlier: "Do you know the Princess calls herself the Queen of Scots and she calls me Julian Avenel! says Jones" (fol. 28; see 1:310). It is instructive to see how the brief allusion to Scott is succeeded by the more telling citation of Bothwell, Rizzio, and Darnley (fol. 25; 1:307).

22. An addition in Thackeray's hand, later cancelled in manuscript, constitutes his first attempt to remove this ambiguity. Immediately after the taunt to Barnes, Thackeray wrote: "and added in a louder voice, I beg your pardon. I am very clumsy" (fol. 11).

23. On 28 June 1855, setting down the last leaf of the novel, Thackeray wrote: "Two years ago, walking with my children in some pleasant fields, near to Berne in Switzerland, I strayed from them into a little wood; and, coming out of it presently, told them how the story had been revealed to me somehow, which for three and twenty months the reader has been pleased to follow" (2:373). He perhaps refers to 10 August 1853, before any of the novel had appeared and while he was in the midst of composing number three during a week's visit to Berne with his daughters, for his diary records a "very nice walk with the children" on that day (*Letters*, 3:669). Since the diary does not even allude to a sudden revelation concerning his novel, exactly what he meant remains unclear. Sophia Alethea's pointing to Orme may have been inserted into the manuscript or proofs of number one, or the Colonel's emblematic appearance at Greyfriars in number three may have been added to the manuscript, but it seems clear that by August 1853 Thackeray intended to have Colonel Newcome end his days as a poor pensioner at Greyfriars.

24. In "The Pygmalion Myth in *The Newcomes*," *Nineteenth-Century Fiction* 29 (1974–75): 22–39, R. D. McMaster perceptively discusses the ways in which so many characters in this novel seek, like the Colonel, to impose their own imaginative patterns upon others or, like Ethel for a time, to fashion their own behavior according to a fiction of their own creating.

5: *The Newcomes*, Installments 14–15, 17–20, 22, 23–24

1. Fol. 4, which is missing from the Charterhouse manuscript, may have contained the conclusion of the scene in which Hannah explains to Clive the reason for Miss Honeyman's anger and the latter's assertion that her house is not intended for assignations (2: 36–37).

2. About a dozen brief corrections appear in the manuscript in a distorted hand that I take to be produced by Thackeray writing on an unsteady surface. In composing fol. 5, for example, Thackeray was apparently unable to recall the name of a Brighton lodging-house keeper, who had been identified in number three; he left a blank space and later, in the unsteady hand, inserted the proper name—Bugsby—though the whole passage was later deleted in press.

The other insertions generally involved slight corrections or refinements. Thus the earlier phrase, "prevented her from going out ⟨or so⟩ †receiving at him or† this season," was corrected to read: "prevented her from going out or receiving at home this season" (fol. 7; 2:39). In addition, an occasional sequence like "conversed . . . conversation" was changed to "conversed . . . dialogue" (fol. 9; 2:41), and "remarked . . . remarked" became "remarked . . . observed" (fol. 10; 2:41).

3. We know, however, that Doyle made a drawing for another internal wood-engraving that was not included in number fourteen: Clive walking in Brighton with two of his younger cousins (see Note 4). It seems probable that the illustration was rejected for want of space. One may also suspect that the wood-engraving of Clive sitting amid a group of Life Guards officers and painting one of them, which now appears in number fifteen (2:65), may originally have been intended for the previous installment to illustrate the phrase "Clive drew portraits of half the officers of the Life Guards Green; and was appointed painter in ordinary to that distinguished corps" (2:52).

4. Only four other chapters of the novel's eighty lack a chapter initial: chapters 5 and 6 (number two), chapter 16 (number five), and chapter 28 (number nine). No space was left in two cases, the equivalent of only six and four lines being available for the others. Here in number fifteen, space for the equivalent of only two lines was left. The Centenary Biographical Edition of *The Newcomes* prints six of Doyle's wood-engravings that were not included in the 1854–55 edition. Five of these could not have been printed in the remaining space: an initial for chapter 5 (number two), and four internal wood-engravings—two for chapter 28, one for chapter 29 (both number nine), and one for chapter 4 in the second volume (number fourteen). The sixth is printed as an endpiece for the final chapter of this edition.

Peter Shillingsburg points out to me that Bradbury and Evans records at the *Punch* office list charges for the following unused engravings (to which I have added, in parentheses, the presumed installment number): initial D, initial C, and "A Bouquet," 3 December 1853 (number three); "Two Gentm," 3 June 1854 (number nine); "Four Gentlemen" and "Ethel in Galley," 30 June 1854 (number ten); "Clive and Children" and another, unnamed, 4 Nov. 1854 (number fourteen); initial O, 31 March 1855 (number nineteen); initial IN, 2 June 1855 (number twenty-one).

5. By the time Thackeray composed number seventeen—a month before number fifteen was in press—he remembered what he had written here about the Colonel's payments for the subscription but in seeing number seventeen through the press he may have forgotten that he had cancelled this passage, for Madame de Florac reports that she has been reading "marvels of [Clive's] works in an English Journal, which one sends me" (2:146).

6. Four leaves of number sixteen, which is entirely missing from the Charterhouse manuscript, survive in the Berg Collection: fols. 13–16, containing the end of chapter 10 and the beginning of 11. Fol. 14v contains a matter of special interest—a brief notation that shows Thackeray's efforts to keep a clear time scheme in mind.

The Colonel goes away	August	41.
Rome		
Clive goes to ⟨Baden⟩.	October	41.
returns to England	June	42.
Lord Highgate & Lord Dorking die	———	42
meets Ethel at Paris	May	43.
Sir Bryan dies	June	—
Pendennis marries	September	43.
meets the company	May	44.

By the end of number sixteen, all the events have taken place except "meets the company," which does not culminate in a specific occasion when Pendennis meets members of what I take to be the B.B.C.; by the end of the installment, however, Pen has learned about the company and its shareholders. Two additional leaves of number sixteen were sold at Sotheby's on 27 June 1977: fols. 18 and 23, containing portions of chapters 11 and 12.

7. Nine other installments also lack internal wood-engravings: numbers nine, eleven, twelve, and, increasingly as the novel draws towards its close, seventeen, nineteen, twenty, twenty-one, twenty-two, and twenty-three/ twenty-four.

8. Some writing by Thackeray himself in his slanted hand on the verso of fol. 1a may help date this addition to the manuscript: "My dear Sir. Will you give me the pleasure of your company at dinner on the 1 April." It may be a joke directed at himself, or an actual invitation to someone else that he never sent, or even a testing of his pen, but it suggests as an approximate period of composition the middle of March.

9. Number seventeen has one such page (2:132), though it is not needed.

10. In a letter of 4 May 1855 to Mrs. Bray, Thackeray informed her that these two passages were written in her house during his visit to Coventry to deliver a lecture on April 24th. He speaks of them as a single "interpolation" (*Letters*, 3:449), making no mention of the final added passage. One should also notice that Doyle's final plate, "'*Sir Barnes Newcome on the Affections*,'" in this case anticipates the future, for the passage it illustrates was to appear only in chapter 28 of installment 21.

11. The following leaves of number twenty-one exist: fols. 20–21 (British Library), fols. 27 and 48 (Texas), fols. 34–38 (Berg), and fol. 49 (Huntington); all are in Thackeray's hand. In the case of number twenty-two, aside from identifying seven missing leaves, fols. [1], [2], [18], [20], [21], [59], and [60], one should also point out misnumbering by Thackeray's secretary in the manuscript of chapter 33. The secretary attempted to correct it by adding numerals in blue ink but did not entirely succeed in doing so, as one can see from an account of the relevant leaves: fol. ⟨29⟩ 22; fol. ⟨28⟩ 23; fol. ⟨27⟩ 24; fol. ⟨26⟩ 25; fol. ⟨25⟩ 26; fol. 24; fol. 23; fol. 22; fol. 21; fol. ⟨20⟩ 30; fol. ⟨21⟩ 31. For fols. 24–21, one should probably assign the designations [27], [28], [29], and [29a].

Because chapter 34 begins towards the bottom of fol. ⟨21⟩ 31, the lower portion has been separated from the upper part, probably by the printer; I treat the two portions as a single leaf in my description of the manuscript.

12. The two leaves in the Berg Collection, fols. 8 and 9 from chapter 39, are in Thackeray's hand as well. Here again we have evidence that Thackeray sent the manuscript to the printer in relays, for in an unpublished letter of 16 June 1855 (privately owned in Great Britain) to Bradbury and Evans, Thackeray indicated that he had taken proofs of a portion of the installment with him to Paris, from where he promised to send the remainder of the manuscript.

13. The quotation from Orme, however, is not transcribed with absolute accuracy—a fact that can be attributed to Thackeray's exercise of the novelist's privilege of condensing a source, or to the Colonel's failing memory, or to both. The Colonel's version, which emphasizes the defensive aspects of the British action, is consistent with Thackeray's softening of the Colonel's more militant outlines in this portion of the novel, but one should also note that the Colonel's version is not really clear. Orme reads as follows: "The two battalions advanced against each other cannonading, until the French coming to a hollow-way, halted on the opposite side, imagining that the English would not venture to pass it under the disadvantage of being exposed to their fire; but Major Lawrence ordered the Sepoys and artillery to halt and defend the convoy against the Morattoes, still hovering about, and pushed on briskly with the main body of Europeans across the hollow way" (Robert Orme, *A History of the Military Transactions of the British Nation in Indostan, From the Year MDCCXLV*, 3d ed., rev., 2 vols. [London: Nourse, 1780], 1:279).

14. This hypothesis receives some support from Anne Thackeray Ritchie's recollection: "I remember writing the last chapters of 'The Newcomes' to my father's dictation." The "last chapters" could therefore mean the last two, the following qualification being understood: "I wrote on as he dictated more and more slowly until he stopped short altogether, in the account of Colonel Newcome's last illness, when he said that he must now take the pen into his own hand, and he sent me away" (*The Works of William Makepeace Thackeray*, 26 vols. [1910–11; rpt. New York: AMS Press, 1968], 12: li).

15. The omission cannot be accounted for by any wish to reduce the length of the text, for the final double installment did not have any fixed number of pages: *Vanity Fair* had forty-eight, *Pendennis* fifty-two, and *The Newcomes* fifty-five. In fact, the final page of the latter is blank, as is most of the penultimate page.

16. Gordon Ray first published this outline (*Wisdom*, p. 469), which is now in the Robert H. Taylor Collection. Ray, however, tabulated the rupture as a part of number sixteen, which seems a possible but improbable interpretation, since Thackeray did not add the words in the blank space after "for Clive."

17. Juliet McMaster astutely discusses the significance of fable-land and the unity of *The Newcomes* from another perspective in *Thackeray: The Major Novels* (Toronto: Univ. of Toronto Press, 1971), pp. 153–76.

6: *The Virginians*, Installments 1–10

1. The letter, which is in the Library of the University of Illinois at Urbana-Champaign, appears in its entirety in my article, "Thackeray and His Publishers: Two Uncollected Letters Concerning *Vanity Fair* and *Esmond*," *Papers on Language and Literature* 12 (1976): 167–76.

2. *Letters of Dr. John Brown*, ed. J. Brown and D. W. Forrest (London: Black, 1907), p. 325.

3. Gerald C. Sorensen, "A Critical Edition of W. M. Thackeray's *The Virginians*," (Ph.D. diss., Univ. of Minnesota 1966), tabulates most of these variants but, partly because he worked only with a photocopy, fails to indicate seventeen of them, records three incompletely, and lists two that in fact do not exist. Accordingly, I draw on my own collation throughout.

4. Thackeray's instructions to the printer have survived in this case: "Please send a corrected proof with the blocks, or the space for them, let in —." On the same leaf he also included the titles for the two steel etchings: "The family pew" and "A welcome to old England" (leaf following fol. 37). Like *The Newcomes*, the manuscript of *The Virginians* does not include indications of where wood-engraved illustrations were to be inserted within the text—with a single exception. At the end of the third paragraph of the first chapter, Thackeray originally sketched two crossed swords, as if for a wood-engraving, and added a set of dates: "1736" and "1776" (fol. 2). None of these details appeared in the printed version, however, possibly because Thackeray intended them to go together but found the printed format left him insufficient space at the bottom of page 2 for an illustration and therefore gave up the whole idea. Thackeray's sketch was based upon his sight of two crossed swords upon the library wall of the American historian, W. H. Prescott. For details see *Wisdom*, p. 213.

5. Thackeray either could not entirely erase this original idea from his mind, or he could not always remember when Washington was promoted, for at times in the second installment Washington is called "Major" (1: 57, 59, and 60), as if he had not yet set off as a Lieutenant Colonel on the venture that was to end at Fort Necessity—though that battle is mentioned on 1:49, where Washington is first called "Colonel," and in the entire subsequent narrative it is clear that he has returned from that expedition.

6. It is interesting to note that fol. C's text was somewhat modified in a further stage of page proof, when Thackeray deleted two separate phrases in removing mention that Castlewood overlooked the Potomac.

7. An uncancelled but apparently rejected version of these sentences appears on the verso of fol. 63*a*: "His servants led his horses away to their well-known quarters, and his valises were carried to the apartment usually set aside for him. Another bed or two had been placed in this room, for the company expected was numerous, and the" (fol. 63*av*). If, as is usual with cancelled or rejected readings on the verso of Thackeray's manuscript leaves, this passage was written before the one on the recto of fol. 63*a*, which ends

the chapter and number (1:63–64), then the printed version of this passage represents a modified return to an original thought.

8. Thackeray may also have wished to avoid offending an American audience, though Franklin's *Autobiography* (1791) mentions his sexual licence.

9. Thackeray also followed this numbering procedure in making an insertion into the page proofs of number seven. I refer to "revised page proof" because the texts of fols. [A], [B], and [C] have evidently been inserted into the previous page proof setting, thus yielding this revise, containing proof pages 33–63.

10. One might also point out that Thackeray nowhere gives us a better insight into the unconscious depths of George's oedipal rage and hatred than through George's choice of this song, for Malbrouk never returns to his lady but dies as a result of warfare. The destiny that Washington escapes, moreover, ironically becomes one that for a considerable time threatens George himself.

11. Letter of 3 December to Henry Reeve, in the Fales Library, New York University.

12. In the brief Yale notebook devoted to jottings for *The Virginians*, a copy of a letter dated 11 December 1857 to S. Low and Sons, who were acting in London for Harper Brothers, contains the following postscript: "I am just advised of your payment for No I & II & hope to send you No III next week" (fol. 14). In the letter he actually sent, which is now in the Berg Collection, Thackeray wrote and then crossed out the entire postscript—presumably because he was sending the installment directly to Harper for the American serial appearance.

13. In the same letter, which is in the Morgan Library, Thackeray also wrote: "We dont sell 20000 of the Virginians as we hoped, but more than 16000 and should have done better but for the confounded times. I have thought proper to knock 50 £ a month off my pay from Bradbury & Evans till we get up to a higher number— . . . I never hear the book mentioned except in stray kind notices from country friends, from you, from Prescott at Boston who is delighted." As Peter L. Shillingsburg has pointed out, Bradbury and Evans had printed 20,000 copies of the first installment but only 16,000 of the second —the same number they were to print of the January installment (see "Thackeray and the Firm of Bradbury and Evans," *Victorian Studies Association of Ontario Newsletter*, no. 11 [March 1973]: 13).

14. The correct form of her name is used here. Later in the printed text it appears as "Curtis" (1:101), but not in the manuscript (number four, fol. 7), nor, Sorensen points out (p. 95n), in the revised edition of 1863; the reading of "Curtis," therefore does not seem to be the misinformation that Jay B. Hubbell thought it was ("Thackeray and Virginia," *Virginia Quarterly Review* 3 [1927]: 85), but an undetected compositor's error, as Sorensen indicates.

15. Knowing that the battle was fought on "the 9th July" (1:96), Thackeray apparently believed that Braddock died on July 12th, "three days after the battle" (1:97), though Bancroft and other sources had made the actual date clear.

16. These reproaches seem unduly severe, however, since, aside from his diversions and sicknesses, when not actually writing he was of course recurrently thinking about his novel, reading for it, taking notes, and sketching for it. After the copy of the letter of 11 December, the Yale notebook contains a number of brief extracts from the *Public Advertiser* of 1756 concerning coaches, dancing schools, horse races, Marybone Gardens, Virginia volunteers, theatres, and other matters, together with sketches of public figures and of contemporary dress. Even though considerable reading might yield him only a single sentence, he continued to strive for historical verisimilitude. Understandably, he said: "These Virginians take me as much time as if I was writing a History" (*Letters*, 4:70). The day after finishing number four, he exhibited his concern about details ranging from the color of Washington's livery to George Warrington's experiences "after he was knocked down at Braddock's defeat" (*Letters*, 4:66). The answer to the first, which came back from America too late, was "scarlet and white. . . . I see you say 'blue and white'" (*Letters*, 4:73). This detail may have eluded Thackeray's vigilance as a reviser, for he had deleted from the proofs of number three a similar mention, changing the manuscript reading, "in blue and white liveries" (fol. 84), to "in livery" (1:66).

Thackeray had already sketched the outlines of the answer to the second question by means of the steel etching that closed number three, for "THE WILDERNESS" showed George saved by a military sword thrust that dispatched the Indian attempting to scalp him (opposite 1:96). Therefore the comment of Frederick S. Cozzens that "You can by no means fulfil the dreams of Madam Esmond by making G. W. a prisoner in the hands of the Indians" (*Letters*, 4:73; see 1:100), told Thackeray little he did not already know, no matter how desperate a hope he had given to Madam Esmond, for Harry's guide had already said, "The French might possibly respect them, but the Indians would not" (1:98). Thackeray later carried out his original intention of having George "taken by Indians into a French fort" (*Letters*, 4:66), but may have increased Florac's supervisory role in this action as a result of Cozzens's letter.

17. Fol. 8 was originally designated 7, but this seems to have been a numbering error.

18. An entry in the Yale notebook from the *Public Advertiser* of 1756 contains the information Thackeray used in chapter 15: "August 2. The 4 year old Plate at Huntingdon was won by the D of Ancaster ch. c. by Cartouche out of Miss Langley. The Six Year old & aged Plate was won by Jason beating Brilliant Pytho & Ginger. The odds were 5 to 4 on Brilliant against the field. 3 to 1 agst Jason. 7 to 2 agst Pytho & 20 to 1 agst Ginger" (fol. 15). Subsequently Thackeray conflated this information by making Cartouche and Miss Langley the sire and dam of Jason (1:113–14) and, unwittingly, by having Jason run in both "the 4 year old Plate" (fol. 19) and "The Six Year old plate" (fol. 23; see 1:118); in proof, however, he changed the first numeral to read "Six" (1:113).

19. Fol. A has been made up of two half leaves pasted together and num-

bered A.1 and ⟨A.2⟩. For the sake of convenience I term the whole leaf fol. A. Similarly, I refer to the two and one-half leaves of the second interpolation as fols. C1, C2, and C3, though their manuscript designations are fols. "C," "C, continued," (a half leaf), and "C continued."

20. The verso of fol. B contains a brief cancelled passage that may represent the beginning of a projected but abandoned addition: "Between you both you make my life miserable, that's what you do exclaims Lady Fanny. I wish it was ended. I wish I were married to some quiet man, and could live away in the Country. I shall grow as old as Maria."

21. The Morgan manuscript also contains page proof (printed on both sides) for the end of chapter 15 (pp. 115–18) and the whole of chapter 16 (pp. 119–26), page 115 beginning with the last three lines of what is now 1:115. The difference of a page is to be accounted for by the addition of the three paragraphs at the end of chapter 13, but the discrepancy of three lines is less clear. Since there were no deletions in press totalling three lines from the text of chapter 15 up to this point, one can only postulate a change in the format of the chapter's opening page—presumably when the woodblock was inserted. A space equivalent to thirty lines was left for the internal wood-engraving of Sampson (p. 116), but the actual block came to take up only twenty-nine lines (1:117); in the latter instance the existing lines of type were locked in place and the page was printed with only seventeen lines of text instead of eighteen.

22. A final word—"Harry!"—was added later.

23. Writing to an American friend on 25 February, Thackeray both complained about the difficulty of writing an historical novel and mentioned a possible remedy: "I often hope that I may come over and finish it on the ground itself, and certainly mean to do so if health & circumstance will let me" (*Letters*, 4:70).

24. Here, as in every other instance where italic letters follow folio numbers, I have added them for the sake of clarity. Fol. 23 is in the Robert H. Taylor Collection.

25. The words remain in the text—"Twere a consummation devoutly to be wished!" (1:155)—but Garrick's tragic tone and gestures would have been inappropriate at this obsequious moment, when Sampson is flattering Lord Castlewood with the hope that the supposedly wealthy Harry will marry the impoverished, elderly Maria. Garrick had first played Hamlet in the early 1740s.

26. George Berkeley married Lady Suffolk, George II's former mistress, in 1735; this would hardly have been "the common talk of the town" twenty years later.

27. Thackeray later made use of this allusion, however: "Have you not read of the fine lady in Walpole, who said, 'If I drink more, I shall be "muckibus!"?' As surely as Mr. Gough is alive now, our ancestresses were accustomed to partake pretty freely of strong waters" (1:303).

28. Letter of 17 February in the Robert H. Taylor Collection.

29. Fol. 1*a* survives in the Humanities Research Center of the University of Texas at Austin, and the detached top of fol. 2*a* in the Berg Collection.

30. The latter phrase was apparently rejected because it was historically inaccurate. Edward Wolfe did serve in the Netherlands under Marlborough, but as a second lieutenant of marines. James Wolfe (b. 1726/27), in turn, was commissioned as a second lieutenant in his father's regiment of marines, then designated the 44th foot. He obtained a majority in the 20th foot in January 1748/49, but the regiment became Kingsley's only after the appointment of William Kingsley to its colonelcy in May 1756 (*Dictionary of National Biography*).

31. I have corrected an error in *Letters* by reference to the original in the Berg Collection. As happened on a number of other occasions, Thackeray later revoked the decision to begin a new chapter at this point. In the printed version, the sentence begins a paragraph in the middle of chapter 26—not on 1:208 (the sixteenth page of the installment), but on 1:205, as follows: "These feats of activity over, the four gentlemen now strolled out of the tavern garden."

32. This suggests that John Blackwood's letter of 23 May to G. H. Lewes, if it refers to the May rather than to the forthcoming June installment, must have been based upon a partial misunderstanding of what Thackeray said in indicating "he was desperately pushed with the last No., having written the last 16 pages in one day, the last he had to spare" (Mrs. Gerald Porter, *John Blackwood*, vol. 3 of Margaret Oliphant and Mrs. Porter, *William Blackwood and His Sons*, 3 vols. [Edinburgh and London: Blackwood, 1897–98], p. 42; also quoted *Letters*, 4: 79–80n). Such a prodigious feat of composition was doubtless possible—though it seems a unique achievement for the novelist—but it seems to have been quite unnecessary for either number. Manuscript evidence given below also requires that Blackwood's statement be to a moderate degree discounted.

33. The voyage took a little less than two weeks and the June 1858 issue of *Harper's New Monthly Magazine*, containing number seven, appeared shortly before Friday, 14 May, on which date a version pirated from it appeared in New York in the semi-weekly *Tribune* (see James Grant Wilson, *Thackeray in the United States 1852–3, 1855–6*, 2 vols. [London: Smith, Elder, 1904], 2:399, and J. Henry Harper, *The House of Harper. A Century of Publishing in Franklin Square* [New York: Harper, 1912], pp. 115–16).

34. These leaves were apparently copied by Anne from a corrected earlier version, for the original text—from "Had he not seen the best company" to "how cd. he resist" (fols. [13]–[15]; see 1:223–24)—survives on an unnumbered leaf in the Berg Collection written and corrected by Thackeray. There is one instance of substantive change—apparently made in error: Thackeray wrote, "all his days," but Anne wrote, "his days," and the printed text, which was of course set up from her copy, followed her reading (1:224). Thackeray intended to add further language to his leaf, for he marked it: "T.O.," but nothing is written on the verso; a final sentence appears in Anne's and the printed version.

35. In spite of Blackwood's letter, therefore, it seems impossible for Thackeray on a single day to have composed half his May number, had that final half

set up in page proof, corrected it, dictated five additional leaves, corrected them (as he did), had them set into proof, and then sent the proof sheets or had them sent (even without final rereading) to Liverpool.

36. Thackeray created a hiatus in the numbering system at this point, perhaps by replacing two leaves with one; there is now no fol. 11.

37. At the top of fol. 17 Thackeray wrote the following comment to himself, later cancelled: "[Mind in regard of Harry's cakes and ale | only mean good honest."

38. The manuscript for the last fourteen pages of the monthly number is missing; these leaves, together with the fifty-six lines added in press, make up almost half of the monthly installment and could conceivably be the portion mentioned by Blackwood. Qualifications similar to those cited in the discussion of number seven for May, however, must also be made here.

39. Already in manuscript Thackeray had written and then cancelled a sentence mentioning, with comic euphemism, how "very few persons" at the entertainment emulated the satirical behavior of "The stout old Queensberry" (fol. 7). He had continued to characterize her as "the stout Queensberry," however, for that phrase, which recurred further down on fol. 7, was only cancelled in press—presumably with the insertion of this second passage, where the narrative perspective slightly but significantly changed, her excesses now being made quite clear.

40. MS letter of 21 September 1859, to Mrs. Baxter (South Caroliniana Library, University of South Carolina).

41. For a fuller discussion of this document, which is at the State University of New York at Buffalo, see my article, "A Partial Plan for Thackeray's *The Virginians*," *Journal of English and Germanic Philology* 75 (1976): 168–87.

42. It should be noted that Maria has had an intrigue not only with an august personage but also with a dancing master, as both the Chaplain and the Baroness know. Maria's later infatuation for an actor seems latent in this attachment, though we cannot say with certainty when Thackeray identified the latency. In carrying out such a development, he gave her attachment to illusion a revealing emblem, for she does not break away from her family's values so much as embrace them in a new, if partly modified, form.

7: *The Virginians*, Installments 13, 17–18, 20–24

1. Henry T. Tuckerman, *The Life of John Pendleton Kennedy* (New York: Putnam, 1871), p. 296.

2. Quoted by Jay B. Hubbell, *"The Virginians* of William Makepeace Thackeray," *South and Southwest: Literary Essays and Reminiscences* (Durham, N.C.: Duke University Press, 1965), p. 164. Hubbell remarks on the same page that "Kennedy could hardly have committed" the error about the sugar maples. In fact, the topographical details are essentially limited to the following:

Our way . . . lay through a level tract of forest . . . upon the right bank
of the Monongahela. By daylight we came to a clearer country. . . . It
was the fatal field where Braddock had fallen. . . . We presently crossed
the river . . ., taking our course along the base of the western slopes of
the Alleghanies; and through a grand forest region of oaks and maple,
and enormous poplars that grow a hundred feet high without a branch.
. . . At this time of year, the hunters who live in the mountains get their
sugar from the maples. . . . So we passed over the two ranges of the
Laurel Hills and the Alleghanies. The last day's march . . . took us down
that wild, magnificent pass of Will's Creek, a valley lying between cliffs
near a thousand feet high—bald, white, and broken into towers like huge
fortifications, with eagles wheeling round the summits of the rocks, and
watching their nests among the crags. (2:32)

3. The historical detail concerned scalp money. In the brief Yale notebook,
Thackeray had evidently copied from the *Public Advertiser* of 1756 the following information: "Rewards for Indians Scalps 130 dollars or pieces of 8" (fol.
[15]). Subsequent research led to a note Thackeray made for himself on the
verso of fol. 12 of the present installment: "The Pa. Govt. offered for Indian
male scalps 1⟨3⟩50 $ women 50." He then incorporated the latter information
into George's narrative, reintroducing the figure of $130 for male scalps (2:22).
Just above the notation, there is a preliminary sketch for the wood-engraved
initial of chapter 1.

4. Because of the absence of a fol. [8], it is impossible to say whether the
Lamberts were a part of George's original audience. One can see, however,
that their responses, which appear on the newly added bottom of fol. 10, on
16a, and on 18, became more important as the writing of the chapter progressed. The family's presence, as we shall see, was established on fols. G–H.

5. The different systems of numbering help to indicate various stages
of composition and also suggest that Thackeray sent his manuscript to the
printer in relays. Besides evidence already cited, one might also note the
presence of pencilled insertions by Thackeray on fols. 24–27, which were also
numbered in pencil, presumably at the same time, and perhaps when he had
only 23 pages of proof. Fol. 16a was also numbered in pencil, but by a different
hand, apparently the printer's; a similar hand wrote on the verso, "Page 24,"
the printed page on which its text begins. On 18*v*, Thackeray wrote to the
printer: "Send back proofs as soon as poss."

One hitherto unnoticed makeshift is the misplacing of the steel etching,
"A YOUNG REPROBATE," which does not represent Sir Miles telling his wife
about Harry in number thirteen (2:9), but Virginians gossiping about George
and La Biche in the following installment (2:51). Thackeray first intended to
include the latter passage in George's original narrative, then found he could
no longer squeeze it into the thirteenth installment (see below), but for lack of
time had to use the already etched plate and partly disguised its inappropriateness by placing it opposite to Sir Miles's gossip.

6. Fol. A survives in the Fales Collection, New York University, and fol.

[22] in the Boyes Album at the Morgan Library. The lower half of fol. 20, missing from the Morgan manuscript, is also in the Boyes Album. The final leaves of chapter 19 are missing (2:152–60).

7. Fol. 2 also has the cancelled marking: "Chap. Horrida Bella." On its verso fol. 3 has the words: "Nevertheless, Sir, he said." Two separate cancelled readings appear on fol. 14v: first, "[word or words illegible] he was right in sending back those trinkets, hurt as I was at his doing so. Go down to him, will you be"; and second, "Some few [?] days ago as I walked in a certain garden on the outskirts of London, where a vast multitude of." The former had presumably been written on this leaf before its appearance in the manuscript of number thirteen at the top of fol. 4 (2:5), while the latter may have been an early beginning of the passage that presently opens chapter 18 (fol. 14; 2:142).

8. Alternatively, the numeral "14" could have been used because Thackeray knew that the text of chapter 18 would begin on the installment's fourteenth page—which it presently does. If such we   , Thackeray would not only have received page proof but also have written the two additional passages that, as we shall see, extended chapter 16's printed length by one page.

9. As this and a number of other examples in *The Virginians* show, one cannot agree with John Sutherland's implied judgment that before Thackeray began writing serials with shorter installments for the *Cornhill*, he "rarely made changes in proof and then hardly ever additions" ("The Composition of Thackeray's *Philip*," *Yale University Library Gazette* 48 [1974]: 196). As we have seen, his statement is also incorrect for *The Newcomes*, which it specifically mentions.

10. The place where 2:145 begins—"and pleasure-parties"—is marked in ink on fol. B, apparently by the printer, with a bracket ahead of "and," together with the number "145"; corresponding markings for the beginning of 2:151 appear on fol. [21], except that the bracket is pencilled.

11. The manuscript of chapter 21 is marked in several places with page divisions, apparently by a printer's proofreader, thus suggesting that the manuscript was set directly into page proof, but these markings do not correspond with present divisions. The beginnings of line forty-three on what are now 2: 167 and 170 are designated in ink as the beginnings of "Page 169" (fol. 8) and "Page 172" (fol. 11), probably because the earlier proof had a fuller text, from the missing fols. [1]–[4], than was later printed. The unusual, if fragmented, survival of earlier and later page proof at the Morgan Library shows that all changes discussed in the body of my text were made to the earlier page proof. The Morgan proofs are made up of the following four portions: (1) pp. 189–92 and [193], apparently set directly from the manuscript, all of them containing added pencilled changes, and p. [193] containing a final thirteen lines of text; (2) pp. 161–76, representing a complete sheet, with machine-cut edges, unlike the three other portions, which have torn and hand-cut edges; (3) pp. 177–88; and (4) pp. 191–92. Portions (2) and (3) embody changes made during the earlier stage of proof, while (4), which may form a common set with (2) and (3), embodies the corrections pencilled on the corresponding segment of (1).

12. This paragraph, which serves as a transition between the texts of fol. 14 and fol. A, was apparently composed before fol. A on the bottom of a proof sheet, now missing. Thackeray then marked fol. A for insertion "at 175."

13. In addition to making these changes, Thackeray had to straighten out one major confusion in the earlier proofs. His last apparent manuscript relay, we remember, was fols. 1a–3a. The printer evidently divided fols. 1a and 3a in half, but not fol. 2a, which had a short text; only then did he add pencilled numberings of his own to the resultant five pieces of paper. He failed to see, however, that his numbers were mistaken, for he had designated the two halves of fol. 3a as "1" and "2," the two halves of fol. 1a as "3" and "4," and fol. 2a as "5." By following these mistaken numbers, therefore, the compositor set up a wrong sequence of text on pp. 191–[193] of the early proof, which Thackeray had to unscramble. It is worth noting that four dozen brief changes to the text of the later proof were made before the installment's publication; they include a do͟z͟e͟n substantive changes as well as alterations in punctuation and word form.

14. The letter, which was addressed to Lady Hardinge and which was, I assume, written on Sunday, 13 March 1859, but partly misdated, reads as follows:

36 Onslow Sqr. S.W.
Sunday. March 12.

Dear Lady Harding

Thanks for the Wolfe orders. They are, I think, very characteristic of the man who drew his sword and swaggered so oddly in Pitt's dining room. I like the Quixotism in his character, wh. helped him perhaps to be a hero; and fancy a sort of gasconading and military strut not in the least unbecoming a good and brave man. But I daren't draw the character quite as I fancy it: for I may be utterly in the wrong, and have no right to take liberties with such great names. I am sure Pitt Sr. was a prodigious quack and think he did an immense mischief but who am I to dare to say as much, or to fling mud at the tall Statue wh. History has chosen to elevate to him? Some day or other I may perhaps try & treat this subject quite seriously, or find it too high for me, and leave it alone.

Very faithfully yours
W M Thackeray.

During the time when Thackeray lived at Onslow Square, 12 March never fell on a Sunday. The letter, which is now in the University of Rochester Library, offers further evidence that Thackeray himself obviously possessed the quality he admired in Macaulay: the repeated willingness to read widely in historical material, even if the final product was only a passing phrase.

15. Fol. 10½, numbered in pencil by another hand, was set down after fol. 10 and before fol. 11 but by mistake never originally given a number. The absence of a fol. 12 may be accounted for either by this misnumbering or by the disappearance of an actual fol. 12 containing the text of a final six lines ending with the word, "shoulder" (2:234). The latter eventuality would make the

six lines a part of Thackeray's manuscript insertion, while the former would identify them as an insertion made in press.

16. The lower corner of the leaf is torn away at this spot—hence the hypothetical last letter of "newspaper[s]" and the first letter of "[m]anner," below.

17. The former hypothesis seems the more likely, since there has been a partial attempt at redesignation: fols. 31–33 were numbered in ink in the upper left-hand corners and then were given the additional numbers in pencil of 32–34 in the upper right corners, perhaps by Thackeray; the ensuing leaf, which I have called fol. [34], received a similar designation of 35, and the last two were numbered in the upper right corners in pencil as fols. 37 and 38 by the same hand. Later the pencilled numerals 32 and 35 were largely erased.

18. An earlier version of the last part of fol. 4c and the presumed first part of an earlier fol. [5c] exists in the Humanities Research Center of The University of Texas at Austin, together with a note from Robert Evans to an unidentified correspondent in which he mentions enclosing a manuscript paragraph of *The Virginians*. The leaf is in Anne's hand with a few corrections by Thackeray and his marginal notation concerning the last eight manuscript lines, which narrate the Baroness Bernstein's final outburst. The first four words of the first of these lines, "frightful hysterical shrieks & laughter," have been crossed out and replaced by the word, "strange," in Thackeray's hand, though the correction was apparently revoked elsewhere. This portion of the passage continued to the words at the bottom of the leaf: "& the pitiful," but the last five or six lines were then cancelled. Thackeray's notation reads: "See 14 where this is more clearly written." The reference to a fol. 14 (itself the number written on this leaf) is puzzling; one can only posit that it refers to a missing fol. [5c], which would be the fourteenth leaf of chapter 25 if two leaves and not just one are missing from the first sequence: a fol. [6a] as well as a fol. [5a].

19. In the printed version the words "with their battle-axes" begin the "quotation," which very freely conflates Smith's account rather than quotes from it. A modern photographic reprint of the 1910 Edinburgh edition reads as follows:

The challenge presently was accepted by *Bonny Mulgro*.

The next day both the Champions entring the field as before, each discharging their Pistoll (having no Lances, but such martiall weapons as the defendant appointed), no hurt was done; their Battle-axes was the next, whose piercing bils made sometime the one, sometime the other to have scarce sense to keepe their saddles: specially the *Christian* received such a blow that he lost his Battle-axe, and failed not much to have fallen after it; whereat the supposing conquering *Turk*, had a great shout from the Rampiers. The *Turk* prosecuted his advantage to the uttermost of his power; yet the other, what by the readinesse of his horse, and his judgement and dexterity in such a businesse, beyond all mens expectation, by Gods assistance, not only avoided the *Turkes* violence, but having drawne his Faulchion, pierced the *Turke* so under the Culets thorow backe and body, that although he alighted from his horse, he stood not long ere hee lost his head, as the rest had done. (*The True Travels, Adventvres, and Observations of Captaine Iohn Smith* . . . [London: Slater, 1630; rpt. Edinburgh, 1910; rpt. 2 vols., New York: Franklin, n.d.], 2:839–40.)

Thackeray's final sentence comes from Smith's next chapter: "*Sigismundus* comming to view his Armie, . . . hee was made acquainted with the service *Smith* had done at *Olumpagh, Stowle-Wesenburg* and *Regall*: for which with great honour hee gave him three *Turkes* heads in a Shield for his Armes, by Patent, under his hand and Seale, with an Oath ever to weare them in his Colours, his Picture [i.e., *Sigismund's portrait*] in Gould, and three hundred Ducats, yearely for a Pension" (2:841).

20. On fol. 8 the words that now initiate the thirty-first line on 2:263 are designated as the beginning line of that page, suggesting the insertion into chapter 32 of eight lines in addition to the passage concerning Smith (which represents a net gain of about twenty-three lines); however, I cannot identify any such insertion. Similarly, the marking on fol. 11 of what is now the third line on 2:266 as the beginning of 2:265 reveals the extension of chapter 32 by one page; the additional discrepancy of two lines may perhaps be accounted for by a change from the format of the proof, for the full text of chapter 33 up to this point is contained in the manuscript. A marking much later in the manuscript (fol. 3*b*) correctly indicates the beginning of 2:284.

21. The last leaf of the previous chapter is also numbered 12; here as elsewhere the italic letter is mine. The number [⟨18⟩] is inferential, since the top of this leaf, later presumably renumbered fol. [22], is missing, corresponding to ten lines of printed text.

22. The forty-fourth line on 2:301 is marked (fol. 13) as the first line of 2:302, but the first lines of 2: 303 and 305 are correctly indicated (fols. 15— with a bracket but no numerals—and 18).

23. Beginning with fol. 6, someone—apparently the printer—has renumbered the installment's leaves fols. "9"–"25," for a reason that remains unclear. Thackeray numbered fols. 1, 4–17, originally giving fol. 17 the numerals 15 and 16. The top of the following leaf is missing, together with the manuscript source for two and one-half lines of printed text. I have designated the surviving fragment fol. [17*a*] because of the original numbering error on fol. 17 and because the ensuing leaf is numbered 18 (by Anne). Fols. 19–21, also numbered by Anne, were redesignated fols. "23"–"25" by the same hand as above.

24. An ink spot covers all but the first two letters.

25. Fol. 12 is in the Berg Collection. Fol. 6 is in the Morris L. Parrish Collection, Princeton University Library, and fol. 15 is owned by Gordon N. Ray; both have kindly provided me with a copy. The Parrish leaf shows that Thackeray once intended to begin a new chapter with the words, "His previous rank" (2:362).

26. The top of fol. 9 is marked in pencil by another hand: "Ch. 44. p 363"; the text begins in the middle of the twenty-seventh line of that page. The top

of fol. 10 is similarly marked: "Ch 44 364"; the text begins near the start of the forty-third line of 2:363.

27. The final number also contained thirty-two pages, but the equivalent of eight were taken up by the title, dedication, contents, and list of plates, the text occupying only twenty-four pages.

8: *Lovel the Widower*

1. The background of Thackeray's association with the *Cornhill* is provided by Spencer L. Eddy, Jr., *The Founding of The Cornhill Magazine* (Muncie, Indiana: Ball State Univ., 1970).

2. Sixteen pages were the equivalent of one printed sheet, the whole magazine issue taking up eight sheets. The surmise is confirmed by a memorandum of agreement between Thackeray and Smith, Elder, dated 20 August 1859 (NLS), which provided that the novelist was to contribute six installments of sixteen pages each, submitting them at monthly intervals beginning on 1 December 1859. An unpublished letter of 5 December 1859 to George Smith, which includes evidence concerning Thackeray's final relay for number one, shows that Smith later suggested twenty-four pages, at least for the first installment, but Thackeray objected: "I am strongly against giving more than 16 pages of my story. Unless we give 24 in every succeeding number: the public will cry out against you & me. The additional copy wh. I send will fill the vacant space of the sheet" (NLS).

3. In "I AM REFERRED TO CECILIA" and "BESSIE'S SPECTACLES," however, Thackeray drew a figure who resembled Pendennis in appearance and who seemed to be in his thirties or very early forties. An unpublished, only partly dated letter to Smith, apparently of 21 November 1859, indicates that Smith may have urged Thackeray to narrate in his own voice: "I should rather like to make Mr. Pendennis the author of my story; and let him walk through it. He can talk more freely than Mr. Thackeray. But if you prefer Mr. T. of course he is Yours very truly W" (NLS).

4. "In fact I learned quadrilles on purpose to dance with Her that Long vacation, when I went to read with my young friend Lord Viscount Poldoody at Dub—psha! Be still, thou foolish heart!" (fol. 15; see *CM*, 1:54). Probably at the same time the following insertion was made on fol. 13, where an earlier reference to an emerald green tabinet waistcoat was now extended: "and wh. I wore at the L——d L——t—n—nts Ball, Ph——n—x Park D—blin once when I danced with *Her* there!"

5. On the verso of fol. 3a is the following cancelled note in Thackeray's hand:

A.

Print immediately, & send with corrected proofs of Mr. Thackeray's article.

B. Footnotes for Mr. Higgins's article.

C.

This was apparently cancelled because Thackeray decided to complete his text on another leaf, fol. [4a], which would then have been the outside leaf. Thackeray continued to refer to this insertion as "A" on the Huntington galleys of this chapter. By "Mr. Higgins's article," Thackeray presumably meant "Invasion Panics," which was not published until February; nothing by Higgins appeared in the January issue. See Walter Houghton, ed., *The Wellesley Index to Victorian Periodicals 1824–1900*, vol. 1 (Toronto: Univ. of Toronto Press, 1966), p. 325. "Mr. Thackeray's article" presumably refers to his January Roundabout Paper, "On a Lazy Idle Boy."

6. With a rather broad-leaded pencil, someone has made a caret on fol. 18 at the place where the text of fols. 1a–[4a] was inserted and has underlined certain words that were changed by Thackeray in proof. I assume these marks were made by someone after the text was set up in corrected proof—probably by an annotator long after the text had appeared in published form. I take it the same person wrote "omitted" in pencil over Thackeray's cancelled passage on fol. 16, and I have ignored similar markings scattered through the manuscript.

7. Batchelor alludes to Rossini's opera, *La Gazza Ladra* ("The Thieving Magpie"), which had London premieres in March 1821 (Italian), February 1830 (English), and October 1838 (a new English version). The plot concerns a servant girl who is wrongly accused of stealing from her mistress a silver spoon that is later found in a magpie's nest. Like Elizabeth, she becomes engaged to a man above her in station—in her case, the son of her mistress, who, like Lovel's mother-in-law, opposes the match.

8. Five pages of a later set of publisher's page proof (pp. 44–48), including the chapter initial, survive at the Humanities Research Center (Texas). They are congruent with the published *Cornhill* text.

9. Anne Thackeray Ritchie, who reproduces Thackeray's original sketch for the chapter initial, reveals, as one would have expected, that Thackeray did the drawing before completing the serial installment, for George Smith had "asked him to send his drawings in by a certain date, before the arrival of the MS., so as to give the engravers more time to complete their part of the work" (*The Works of William Makepeace Thackeray*, 18:xlvi).

10. This sentence appears in earlier form upside down on fol. 7v: "I fear Mamma Prior had not been unaware of the love passages between her daughter and the fugitive Bombay Captain." Thackeray copied a portion of fol. 8 (*CM* 1:240) onto a separate leaf (NYU), which he entitled "The Syrens and their Mothers," and signed—evidently for a friend.

11. Ensuing dialogue indicates that Batchelor is already in evening dress. The deletion made a later reference to his bus ride more oblique but still understandable: "I had thought, until Bedford spoke, that the ride on the top of the Putney omnibus had left me without any need of brushing" (*CM* 1:247).

12. The seventeen leaves of chapter 3, fols. 1–17, survive in the Morgan Library, while three sets of publisher's galleys are to be found at Yale: two duplicate sets of early galley proof with no provision for the chapter initial, and a later set—marked "Duplicate of this revise sent to M Thackeray 13/2/60"—with the initial in place (though mistakenly including the title, "WHERE THE SUGAR GOES TO") and with various minor changes in the text. A few further alterations appear in the published version that correct minor errors.

13. Yale owns two and one-half sets of publisher's page proof. The first (YA) is an early set (pp. 394–407) containing the text of fols. 1–[13] but lacking a chapter initial. An intermediate set (YB) contains in its beginning portion an identical text (except for two reset lines). It too lacks a chapter initial, and it reveals an editorial decision to print the installment as the opening piece of the monthly issue. Hence it contains an additional heading ("THE CORNHILL MAGAZINE. APRIL, 1860"), a resulting displacement of eleven printed lines, and new page numbers for the previous text (pp. 385–99), which had ended with the word "sh-sh-shugarbaker!" near the top of the page. An ensuing half set (YC) begins with the new ending on a fully printed page 399 and extends to page 403. Five portions of such proof exist at Texas: one complete version and two fragments of the early set, plus two copies of the later half set.

Thackeray's surviving correspondence concerning number four for April 1860, much of it unpublished, is rather extensive, though at times frustratingly undated. By 21 February he had made arrangements with Edwin Landseer about the wood-engraved initial, and on 8 March requested "My Lovel proofs as soon as possible. A couple of pages remain to be written" (NLS). Copy for the April *Cornhill* was apparently a bit short, for on 14 March Thackeray volunteered to write two extra pages, at first saying, "I can add 2 pages to Lovel more easily than to the Jane Eyre" [i.e., his introduction to "The Last Sketch" by Charlotte Brontë], but then proposing a page for each (NLS). Apparently not long after, however, he faced constraints of space: "I shall go to 18 pages I should think—It would be a pity to cut it out, as the end seems to me odd & pleasant" (NLS). Finally, as we shall see, he had to prune, but only a bit.

14. The original figure survives early in chapter 5 (fol. 1 and *CM*, 1:584) but four hundred appears again later (fol. 10 and *CM*, 1:591).

15. The Morgan manuscript contains a pencil sketch by Thackeray of the lion and snake with the following words underneath it, written in his upright hand: "This lion was sketched from the bronze and is a little better than that on the paper." Below this is a note by Anne: "I remember my Father drawing this sketch one morning at Mentmore from a bronze Lion in the grounds there." (Mentmore Park is the seat of the Earl of Rosebery.) Thackeray's sketch does not conform with the published initial, for among other differences it lacks Batchelor's head and has the "I" over the lion's tail. The manuscript also includes pencil sketches for the full-page wood-engravings of number one (untitled); number four, "Miss Priors Reflections" ("BESSIE'S REFLECTIONS," in the printed version); and number five (untitled), as well as a proof for that of number six with the title, "Lovel's Mothers," added in pen by Thackeray.

16. His original continuation began on what is now fol. 5*v*: "we used to sit, the same but how different! The bench was a bank then of roses and jasmines in the midst of wh. my young Affection sprang up and bloomed fragrantly." Thackeray cancelled this language, however, turned the leaf over, and wrote the present version.

17. A set of publisher's proof congruent with the *Cornhill* text exists at Texas (pp. 652–68).

18. A deleted insertion immediately below the word may have helped the compositor's eye pass over the underlining.

9: *The Adventures of Philip*, Installments 1–10

1. MS letter (Harvard). In an undated letter of 1860–61, Thackeray suggested that Smith bring out *Lovel* as a separate book: "It amused me when I read it: and others—a few others have spoken well of it" (NLS).

2. Samuel Langley, MS diary for 1860, fols. 109, 111 (Berg). Several other relevant documents have also survived. In a letter of 27 November to Smith, Thackeray wrote: "No 1. of Philip comes herewith. May he prosper! I have marked the size of the letters, 3 chapters, and the chapters had best be set up allowing for them. I'll send the initials, & the illustration to Swain immediately. Some episodical twaddle I shall excise in proof" (NLS). The specimen title page was laid out as follows:

How do you like

The adventures of

PHILIP

on his way through the world
Showing who robbed him, who helped him, and who passed him by.

The book will be called Philip, and it is as good a name as any other.

(NLS)

Thackeray's original agreement involving *Philip*, dated 9 April 1859 (NLS), mentions two novels depicting contemporary life, each of sixteen numbers thirty-two pages in length, the first novel to be submitted beginning 1 December 1859. The agreement permitted Smith, Elder to publish the works in a monthly periodical. When a subsequent agreement of 20 August 1859 (NLS) was signed, provision was made for the appearance of *Lovel* and *The Four Georges* in a monthly periodical, for the appearance of the two novels in separate monthly form, and for their possible extension to twenty numbers each if Thackeray so wished. A third agreement of 8 December 1860 (NLS) returned *Philip* to the *Cornhill*, stipulating that each of the sixteen monthly submissions was to furnish matter for twenty-four printed pages, and include a full-page illustration and two chapter initials. A later addition to the agreement provided for *Philip*'s extension to twenty numbers.

3. These leaves are the following: fol. 1 (Loyola Marymount Univ.), fol. 7 (Fitzwilliam Museum), fol. 8 (British Lib.), fol. 9 (Washington Univ.), fols. A and B (Yale), fol. 20 (Texas), fol. 21 (Univ. of Kansas), fol. 26 (Huntington), and fol. 27 (Leeds). Fol. 9 has the cancelled designations "8" and "10," the meaning of which cannot be determined until more of the manuscript is recovered; fols. 7 and 26 both contain a pencilled "4."

4. F. L., "A Human Skull," *CM* 2 (July–December 1860): 718.

5. A note of Thackeray's to Swain, the engraver, which does not appear in *Letters*, contains instructions for details of the full-page illustration that accompanied the first installment, "What Nathan said unto David":

Boy in bed looking wild with fever
Woman fainted with fair hair.
Little Doctor like Collingwood in the volume I send.
Tall Doctor same as on block (neat feet & hands
                                            a middle-aged Swell
He has just come in from the outer room wh. is
seen in perspective.

(*A Shabby Genteel Story and The Adventures of Philip*,
The Harry Furniss Centenary Edition [London: Macmillan, 1911], p. xi)

Furniss also prints a number of Thackeray's sketches, including his original sketch and instructions for the second installment's full-page illustration, which Swain or an assistant also redrew (p. xii).

6. The proofreader, for example, questioned "more better-tempered" on proof page 5, as a result of which Thackeray deleted "more." The former also called attention to a blank space that the compositor had left on proof page 8 for a missing word; accordingly, Thackeray supplied the word "he." Thackeray cancelled the third query, on proof page 14, for the proofreader apparently failed to understand the meaning of the colloquial word "punter."

7. Alternatively the Baxter volume may have failed to print accurately the second, third, and fourth last sentences of Thackeray's letter by omitting to place them in quotation marks; the letter's current location is unknown.

8. Here Thackeray must temporarily have forgotten that by cancelling the passage at the bottom of fol. 12, he had swept away his earlier "Phil's cousin —Philip Ringwood" (originally "Phil's mothers cousin—Bayle Goring"), for he made Philip address "Philip Ringwood" (originally "Bayle Goring," of "Goringburg" [fol. ⟨18a⟩]), before deleting Ringwood's name and having Philip address Hunt instead.

One should note parenthetically that Thackeray's compositional difficulties with chapter 7 apparently derived especially from the fact that he was partly incorporating material that had been composed several months previously. In an unpublished letter to Smith of 4 February 1861, he wrote: "I am in a hash with my last chapter in wh. I have been trying to work in a portion written 4 months ago—and have bothered my brains over it until I am ½ crazy. But I shall be done to day. D.V." (NLS).

9. A manuscript correction; on this leaf Thackeray first called Ascot "Egham," the name under which he was introduced in the first number: "young Lord Egham (the Marquis of Ascot's son . . .)" (*CM* 3:4). In the present number the names were reversed (*CM* 3:282).

10. Fol. ⟨17⟩ originally ended: "Philip looked very dismal in the midst of the festivity—and when I asked him what was ailing him? He said in an undertone that he had had another terrible row with his father in the morning." After setting it down, however, Thackeray recalled that he had written something similar about Philip's demeanor just prior to the Doctor's entrance and had made Philip explain to Pendennis the reason for it (fol. 14; *CM* 3:283). Hence Thackeray inserted "still" after "Philip," deleted everything after the word "festivity," and added instead: "He was thinking of his differences with his absent parent."

11. Fols. 25 and 26 were originally designated 26 and 27, but the reason is not clear; it may have been a misnumbering.

12. Various portions of page proof exist in the two collections, comprising earlier and later sets, which I designate A and B. Arents A, consisting of proof pages 1–11 and 17–22, is author's proof and contains corrections by Thackeray; Texas A, consisting of proof pages 1–22, is publisher's proof, containing an occasional proofreader's query. The later sets are all publisher's proof: Arents B, consisting of proof pages 1–24, and four sets of Texas B, the first containing proof pages 1–24, the second 1–15, the third 1–16, and the fourth 9–16.

13. In a letter of 21 January 1861 to Frederick Walker, who executed the finished drawing for "THE OLD FOGIES" (opposite *CM* 3:270), Thackeray also mentioned this detail:

> Can you copy the faces on this block as accurately as may be on to another block improve the drawing of the figures furniture &[c] and make me a presentable design for woodengraving?
>
> Faithfully yours
> W. M. Thackeray.

> The less work the better. The 2 tumblers touching each other. The old man red-nosed & a wig. The young man light hair large whiskers moustache.

The letter, mostly in the hand of Samuel Langley, and with the postscript set down by Thackeray, is now in the Morgan Library. *Letters* prints it from a somewhat inaccurate transcript. It is interesting to note that the letter antedates the publication of number 3 by over a month; publication date for the March *Cornhill* was announced as 26 February.

14. An unpublished undated letter to Smith written in early February informed the publisher: "I filled out one page of my wanting matter with a song and had luckily a page written on Wednesday; wh. can carry on—but I think still I had rather leave the song out, and fill up when I am better tomorrow with a page of better surplusage" (NLS). Thackeray's diary for 1861 shows

that he was ill on Thursday and Friday, 7 and 8 February, and again the following week, 13, 14, and 15 February (*Letters*, 4:395).

15. In an unpublished letter of 6 March 1861 in the hand of Langley, Thackeray tells Smith: "I spent five precious days last week in a vain endeavour to do a large woodblock for 'Philip.' I am ill with one of my attacks, cant think of any work for three days, have only 8 or 9 pages of 'Philip' done, room must be left for me, and the moment I have strength enough I will set to work" (NLS). Thackeray had recovered by Friday morning, 8 March (*Letters*, 4:396), and four days later wrote Smith: "I am very sorry I have been so late but from circumstances you know, Philip & all his friends history &c went clean out of my mind and it is only just now that I have been able to get hold of them & bring them back." As an afterthought he proposed going away for a time in order to get ahead, indicating also further recurring difficulties: "I had best go away somewhere and not return without at least 2 numbers of Philip in my portfolio. It takes me a week always to get the steam up, and in doing those Roundabouts I let it go down. Then comes an attack mayhap. or some other cause of delay" (NLS).

16. Thackeray made three rather unusual markings in the margin of three leaves: they seem to have been made at moments when composition temporarily halted, as notes to himself for future development. On fol. 10, opposite the phrase, "suppose Mamma leaves the room at this juncture" (see *CM* 3:395), he wrote "(mem)"; on fol. 11, he wrote, "Phil begins on poetry &c. Black Prince on racing &c"; and on fol. 13, opposite the words "mistake country" (*CM* 3:397), which are followed by a large blank space, he wrote: "Arcadia." In the printed text, the word "Arcadia" appears after the above words, followed by mention of Tityrus and Amaryllis.

17. I have added italic letters to distinguish these leaves from those with the same numbers in chapter 8.

18. The last three words connect with an earlier phrase and modify it: "'As I came by Apsley House,' says he," becomes "As I passed by Apsley House."

19. In a further instance, Thackeray apparently added a few words in press, but he had left a large gap in his manuscript and the printer may well have followed his example in setting up type. Thackeray had written: "She will leave JACOB or even [blank space]: but . . ." (fol. 10). In the published version, this became: "She will leave REUBEN, the eldest born, with her daughters: but . . ." (*CM* 3:395).

20. In making this change, the printer neglected to remove the original comma preceding the last phrase; hence the printed reading of "marriage,.."

21. Fols. 2a–6a, A, and B were cut into pieces for the compositors, the pieces corresponding to marked compositorial stints. The other leaves were divided in two, but fol. A originally had at least one more piece, which is now missing and which presumably contained the text of the short paragraph beginning: "The doctor's patients" (*CM* 3:407).

22. Thackeray, of course, did not neglect to refine details of the final chapter, but none of these brief modifications calls for special notice.

23. The omission of a fol. 12 indicates either a cancelled leaf or a numbering error. Fol. 13 is the only blue leaf in the chapter, except for fol. 18. Fol. [14] is a composite leaf, a piece of paper with a black margin having been pasted over a slip of plain paper. The upper portion of the black-margined piece is missing, together with the text for the paragraph beginning: "A name?" (*CM* 3:569). Fol. 15 has the additional number "3."

24. Two undated letters to Smith seem to refer to this installment, as well as a dated letter, also unpublished. The first, which may have been written after fols. 1–11 were completed, tells Smith that Thackeray has "done ½ my next number. It is bitter & more stirring than the last   I must see an attorney before I send in the number though—so as to keep the law right" (NLS). The second, in the hand of Langley and dated 11 April 1861, informs Smith: "I am prostrated with one of my attacks and five pages of "Philip' remain to be done. It was the lawyers delayed me this time. Let me know the latest day I can have" (NLS). His estimate of five pages might indicate that nineteen of an expected twenty-four were done at this point, while his mention of "the lawyers" refers to the maneuvering in chapter 12. The third letter explains that "Fladgate the lawyer" has certified "that the law was all right." Thackeray then pointedly remarks: "This is the kind of Trouble wh. conscientious writers take" (NLS).

25. Fol. 28 was originally numbered "2."

26. Several other changes seem to be compositors' errors that escaped detection: "houseless" (*CM* 3:559) for "harmless" (fol. 3), "trust you" (*CM* 3:562) for "trust *you*" (fol. 7), "kept" (*CM* 3:563) for "kep" (fol. 7), "you know" (*CM* 3:566) for "*you* know" (fol. 10), "Firmin's" (*CM* 3:568) for "Firmin" (fol. 13), and "frequently" (*CM* 3:577) for "presently" (fol. 23).

27. In the chapter's text Thackeray alludes several times to the Scottish ballad, especially: "And before Philip came, poor Agnes could plead 'My father pressed me sair'—as in the case of the notorious Mrs. Robin Gray" (fol. 5; see *CM* 3:656). Since Woolcomb rather than Philip was the analogue to Robin Gray, however, Thackeray had to change his inappropriate chapter title.

28. Thackeray completed the last sentence of fol. 6a on what is now the verso of fol. 7a and later recopied it at the top of what is now the recto of fol. 7a—an action responding to what was apparently only an oversight partly brought about by a pause in composing his chapter. On the verso of fol. 1a, he composed a letter to Lady Shelley, declining an invitation because of illness.

29. In an undated letter of May 1861, Thackeray advised Smith: "I expect we shall go into 25 pages—23 are at the printers and the 2 last I have had copied, and will leave At the Printing office to send with the proofs to Low" (NLS); S. Low and Sons were English agents of Harper, which was publishing *Philip* serially in America.

30. The third last line on fol. [3a], with the last four words of the preceding line, appears also at the top of fol. 4b, where it has been cancelled: "their post and the public made sport of the victims contortions. The writers were unsuccessful barristers ushers and college men and piqued" (see *CM* 4:12). This

suggests that some or all of fols. [1a]–[3a] may represent leaves copied from an earlier version or versions, and that fol. 4b may be a part of that earlier group, the composition of which ended for a time with this sentence. If so, the version of this sentence on fol. [3a] would have been copied from fol. 4b. Thackeray apparently sent fols. [1a]–[3a] to the printer as a separate unit. In the printer's shop the first two leaves were numbered 1 and 2 in red pencil. All three leaves were then renumbered with an ordinary pencil and cut in half, the six fragments being designated 1, 2, 2½, 3, 3½, and 4. Fols. 1b–6b apparently followed as the next relay, being subsequently cut into sixteen fragments numbered in red: 1–3, 3a, 4–6, 6a, 7–8, 8a, 9–10, 10a, 11–12. When Thackeray sent fols. 7b–8b, the printer crossed out the numerals and created seven fragments numbered 1, 1½, 2, 2½, 3, 3½, and 4. The final relay was apparently made up of fols. 1c and 2c (both half leaves), plus fol. 3c; these were divided into fragments designated 1, 1½, 2, 2½, 2¾, 3, 3½, 4, and 4½.

31. This, as we recall, is the sentence Thackeray wrote at the top of what is now fol. 4b and then cancelled, apparently after copying it on fol. [3a].

32. The printer added several brackets and page numbers to the manuscript. On fol. 2, just ahead of "countenances" he added a bracket and the numeral "3"; the marking coincides with the present beginning of page 3, line 14, not line 1, as one might expect; most of these thirteen lines were presumably taken up by the magazine heading, since *Philip* opened the July *Cornhill*. On fol. [1a], after the "self-" of "self-sacrifice," he added a terminal bracket; the spot presently marks the last short line of text alongside chapter 16's wood-engraved initial. On the same leaf he set down a bracket and "13" at the beginning of the present second line on *CM* 4:13; this discrepancy may have been caused by an extra line on a page of proof. He also added a bracket and "17" at the beginning of what is now page 17, line 1, and a bracket and "20" at the beginning of what is now page 20, line 3. The subsequent forming of two new paragraphs apparently produced the change of two lines; the paragraphs now beginning "Indeed" (*CM* 4:17) and "What" (*CM* 4:19) were originally joined to the paragraphs preceding them. A bracket and "21," which, unlike the chapter's previous markings, are in pencil and were apparently added some time later, coincide with the present beginning of page 21, line 1.

33. On 9 July, Thackeray had already informed Smith: "Philip is unfortunately going into poverty & struggle but this cant be helped; And as he will entre nous, take pretty much the career of WMT in the first years of his ruin and absurdly imprudent marriage at least the portrait will be faithful" (NLS; also quoted in *Wisdom*, p. 388).

34. The sheet of page proof on which Thackeray penned this insertion, which he designated "A," survives in the Morgan Library. Since this change came towards the end of the chapter, it did not contribute to the discrepancy between the beginning of *CM* 4:4, and the printer's bracket with the numeral "4" that mark the beginning of the twelfth line on *CM* 4:120—the installment's fourth page; the discrepancy may have been caused by a change in the format of the initial page, for *Philip* opens the *CM*'s monthly issue.

35. John Sutherland offers a contrasting view, terming this addition "a little moral digression" included "so as not to leave an unsightly blank on the last page of one of the magazine's installments" ("The Composition of Thackeray's *Philip*," *Yale University Library Gazette* 48 [1974]: 196).

36. On Wednesday, 31 July, Thackeray wrote Smith from Folkestone that he had done "13 pages of Philip. I hope the other 11 will be done on Saturday" (NLS).

37. Minor pencilled alterations apparently made by Thackeray also occur on fols. 2–5, 7–9, 3*a*, and 4*a*.

38. On the verso of fol. 5*a*, Thackeray wrote the following note, apparently to George Smith: "My dear S　I have sent a Roundabout, and Chap 1. Containing near upon 15 pages of Philip to 65 CornHill. and shall finish the number tomorrow D. V." The text of fols. 1–9 takes up nearly thirteen printed pages, while the text of fols. 1*a*–2*a* extends the printed length to nearly sixteen printed pages, ending in mid-sentence: "she had learned to" (*CM* 4:272). A description of all the printer's markings on these eight leaves would be excessively intricate, but the chief characteristic seems to lie in the difference with which he numbered the fragments he produced by dividing Thackeray's leaves. In the case of fols. 9–2*a*, he retained Thackeray's "9" and supplemented it in ink with 10–14; in the case of fols. 3*a*–6*a* (the lower half of fol. 7*a* is blank), he followed the extant numbering system by pencilling corresponding half-numbers on the lower portions. This difference may suggest, therefore, that fols. 3*a*–7*a* went to the printer as a separate relay. Several markings in the manuscript of chapter 19 should also be mentioned: a pencilled bracket and "5" that correspond with the beginning of *CM* 4:261, the installment's fifth page, and a pencilled bracket and "265" that indicate the beginning of *CM* 4:265. As before, these two different markings suggest the existence of at least two sets of proof. Fol. 5*av* also contains a set of figures, as does fol. 6*av*:

$$
\begin{array}{r}
4200 \\
4 \\
\hline
\end{array}
$$

$$24\,|\,\overline{16800.}$$
$$168.\qquad \text{(fol. } 5av\text{)}$$

$$
\begin{array}{r}
120 \\
35 \\
\hline
600 \\
360 \\
\hline
4200 \\
4 \\
\hline
\end{array}
$$

$$24\,\langle 00\rangle\,|\,\overline{168\,\langle 00\rangle}$$
$$
\begin{array}{r}
7 \\
\hline
168 \qquad\qquad \text{(fol. } 6av\text{)}
\end{array}
$$

On the inside flap of an envelope postmarked 5 August 1861 at Folkestone and 6 August at London, addressed to someone "at Smith Elder & Co's Printing Office Little Green Arbour Court," Thackeray wrote: "You got the remainder of Philip, didn't you? I find this opened envelope, and am in a fright lest something should have gone wrong" (NYU). The addressee's name has since been erased.

39. John Sutherland has treated the Yale leaves somewhat differently in "The Composition of Thackeray's *Philip*," 195–99.

10: *The Adventures of Philip*, Installments 11–20

1. Thackeray later changed this reference because it contained two historical inaccuracies instead of an intended single one. Lebrun was created Third Consul only after the Treaty of Amiens. Hence, in the printed version Hely says that Cérisette danced "before Napoleon," and Chesham replies, "There was no Napoleon then" (*CM* 4:520), for the First Consul signed official documents "Napoleon," instead of "Bonaparte" only after being elected Consul for life—which followed the Treaty of Amiens by several months.

2. A further scrap of evidence that may lend some support to this hypothesis follows from Thackeray's revision of names in the manuscript of this installment. In referring to the British Ambassador and his wife in the manuscript of chapters 23 and 24, Thackeray had written "Bagwig" (fols. 6, 11, 21) instead of "Estridge"—the version used in chapter 19 and in the printed text of chapters 23 and 24. Since the error in the text of these leaves was corrected only in press and since the sole appearance of "Estridge" in the manuscript occurs on fol. [23], the rest of the installment—at least as far as fol. 21 and perhaps further—may well have gone into proof and been corrected by the time the final leaf was written.

3. Two printer's markings should be mentioned: an inked bracket and "518," corresponding to the beginning of the tenth rather than the first line of *CM* 4:518, and an inked bracket and "521" corresponding to the beginning of the twelfth rather than the first line of *CM* 4:521. The ten-line change was presumably caused by the extra space required for the initial page, since *Philip* opened the November *Cornhill*.

4. Fols. 1*b*–3*b* were originally designated fols. 7a, 7b, and 7c; 7b then apparently became 8, and finally Thackeray himself appears to have redesignated them and to have numbered fol. 4*b*. An earlier version of a portion of fol. 2*b* in Thackeray's hand exists at New York University.

5. Both Thackeray's numbers and the additional ones supplied by the printer are rather complex and suggest that the manuscript of the installment may have been sent to the printer in at least three relays. The printer cut the leaves of chapter 25 into two or three portions each, thus producing twenty-two segments with the following numbers: 1–6, 6½, 7–21. The leaves of chapter 26 were divided into twenty-three segments: fols. [1*a*] and 2*a* became [1]–4, and the rest became a–i, k–t.

6. Fol. 1*b* has no blots or corrections and only one brief insertion, the adverb "still," which easily could have been omitted. Fol. 2*b* has a similar insertion, a corrected misspelling ("fourty"), a verbal change in Thackeray's own hand, and a joint correction: Anne's change of something very like "Moira" to that word and Thackeray's change of the immediately preceding adjective

from "inenuous" to "ingenuous." Fol. 3b contains two apparently omitted, then inserted, words, an erroneously repeated and then deleted phrase, and a correction of something like "long" to that word. The secretary's only correction resulted from what looks like an improperly formed "a" in "ora"; he deleted the word and rewrote it.

7. Just prior to this, an indication that "her Sister MacWhirter and the Major were expected" (fol. 6a) remained uncorrected until the text was in press.

8. Perhaps the most striking error attributable to the printer is his failure to incorporate Thackeray's revision of "disappear" to "retire" (fol. 2b; see CM 4:663). It suggests again that Thackeray did not normally read proof against copy.

9. One of them does not seem to derive from Thackeray. On fol. 4, around the words, "cries Emily flinging open the door of the dining room where the two gentlemen were knocking their own heads together—MacWhirter!," someone else has placed brackets and written the word "out." The marking represents the identification by a publisher's proofreader of language that a compositor mistakenly failed to set up into type, evidently because his eye skipped down from "MacWhirter!"—the word that immediately precedes the omitted unit—to the "MacWhirter!" that is written directly beneath the earlier word and that concludes the overlooked unit. The bracketed words appear in the published version (CM 5:6).

10. These last six words were presumably cancelled because, although they formed a true assertion, the already completed (but unnumbered) fol. 8 began with language that focussed on Philip and momentarily made it seem that he *would* be narratively followed: "While Philip, without Madame Smolensk's premises, is saying . . ." (fol. 8; CM 5:11).

11. Other changes brought such developments as the inclusion of a new phrase, "the gentle rain" (CM 5:11), which looked ahead to the chapter's final paragraph (CM 5:12), but this did not affect the line count; Thackeray also made a revision that reduced the number of words by twelve, though it did not alter the number of lines.

12. Two proofreader's marks added to fols. 11 and 15 call for notice. On these leaves, brackets and the numbers "15" and "21," respectively, were added in front of the words that now begin the first lines of CM 5: 16 and 22, thereby suggesting that Thackeray's textual additions extended by one page the installment's original length in page proof. Since Thackeray's additions were four less than twenty-eight lines, however, a further account is required to explain the discrepancy. The likeliest possibility is a change in format of the first page, which ultimately required extra space not only for the title of the novel, but also for the title and date of the magazine issue, since it was to open the January Cornhill. A bracket without a number marks the beginning of what is now the eighteenth line of CM 5:9.

13. Fol. 7 was originally numbered 6, but this may simply have been an error, for its text could not have followed directly from what is now fol. 5.

The present fols. 5 and 6 may be recopied leaves, but if so that process would apparently have been completed before all but the first ten words of fol. 7 had been set down. The cancelled phrase with which the latter leaf begins—"Since the departure of the dear Miss, Madame Smolensk said"—is succeeded by not dissimilar language: "He was so gravely ill, Madame said, that his daughter had been sent for" (see *CM* 5:137). The original idea seems to have reappeared below: "he has never been well, since Charlotte went away" (fol. 7; see *CM* 5:138).

14. The first word of these three lines supplies the ending of the previous sentence: "hypocrisy" (*CM* 5:149).

15. He also drew a horizontal line through the first five words of the following sentence ("Their route was to be"). As a result, a new opening was later required for the sentence. Thackeray presumably supplied it on a set of proof and someone else—perhaps the printer—set it down in pencil on the manuscript: "The route of the happy pair was to be." The same hand also set down in pencil two words—"had we"—at the bottom of fol. 4 and completed Thackeray's partial cancellation of "and rogueries" by deleting "and"; the following reading thereby emerged: "What artifices and hypocrisies ⟨and⟩ ⟨rogueries⟩ had we not to practice previously, so as to keep our secret from our children who assuredly would have discovered it!" (fols. 4–5; see *CM* 5:263).

16. In Thackeray's only partly published diary for 1862 (British Library), he has made the following calculation and note to himself concerning a detail in this letter—Mrs. Baynes's first and only payment of Charlotte's quarterly income:

24 Sheets = 3 vols of a novel.
Philip 279. Remember the 5 Sous (fol. 45*r*)

He also made a notation concerning the *Gazette*:

Pall Mall Gazette.

printer
Mugford. Proprietor. Bince ⟨Publisher⟩. Burjoice Publisher
Bickerton   Principal Contributors.
Mr. & Lady Mary Tregarvan.
Jack & Charles Lambert. (fol. 124*v*)

Only the Lamberts are not included in the published novel.

17. When the name first appeared on fol. A, Thackeray initially wrote "Colonel" but then replaced it with "Doctor."

18. The markings on fol. 11 bear a close resemblance to the partly inconsistent markings that appear on fols. 8–10. Fol. 15 has its own system (1, [2], 3), while fols. [16]–[17] have theirs (1–4).

19. One should mention several sets of ink numbering by Thackeray on the verso of two leaves:

```
    104                                          —
      5 : 4                                   2=3
                                           _____
    52                                   18 . = . 27
     6                                        —
   ____                                    16=24
   312.            (fol. 10v)
                                                (fol. 15v)
```

The meaning of the first set does not seem clear, but the second set appears to indicate his calculating the number of large sized leaves (often *Cornhill* stationery, measuring approximately 9 × 7 inches) he will need to fill an installment. Two of his leaves will yield three printed pages; sixteen will give the desired twenty-four; eighteen will produce twenty-seven.

20. One should also indicate three notations on the verso of fol. 1. The first is a draft letter to George Augustus Sala from 36 Onslow Square, dated "Saturday":

Dear Mr. Sala
    I will with great pleasure be your backer

Always yours
W M Thackeray

The second, also in ink, is a short list of "Queries. Pendenniss footmans name. Mugfords Xtian name." The third is a faintly pencilled set of calculations:

```
    896
    180
    ___
    716                  380
                         340
                         ___
                         700
```

The meaning of the draft letter is clarified by fol. 1b, which is written on the verso of an announcement, dated 7 March 1862, sent by the secretary of the Reform Club to Thackeray, telling him that Sala, seconded by Thackeray, will be balloted for on 13 March (see *Letters*, 4:256).

21. John George Marks, *Life and Letters of Frederick Walker, A.R.A.* (London and New York: Macmillan, 1896), p. 24.

22. This genealogy was apparently copied by Langley from an earlier version set down by Thackeray in his diary for 1862 (British Library); the novelist then made further changes in Langley's copy and some additions. Yet another genealogy, in Thackeray's hand, together with a fragment containing a few sketchy notations concerning time, is at Yale. At the top of fol. 5 Thackeray wrote "See Note." After the phrase "legends about his ancestry" someone pencilled an asterisk; after the words, "prodigious number of quarterings," someone also pencilled the numeral "5a." In proof Thackeray apparently placed the asterisk indicating this footnote at the end of a genealogically ex-

planatory sentence. The presence of the genealogy on a separate half leaf may originally have caused Thackeray to write what appears to have been a 7 at the top of what is now fol. 6; a change of 7 to 6 has no other apparent significance.

23. Thackeray was again delayed by illness. On 11 April 1862 he wrote to Smith: "It was a second attack wh. smashed me and made me incapable of work. But I have rallied from it and getting on pretty well. I shall not stop D. V. when the number is done but carry Philip on and to an end" (NLS). His diary for 1862 indicates that he completed the installment on 18 April (*Letters*, 4:400).

24. Thackeray originally began fol. 3*b* with the words: "No one was more elated at this circumstance than Charlotte's and Philip's constant friend." Soon, however, Thackeray decided to compose a transition. Hence, he apparently added the word "Philip" at the bottom of fol. 2*b* and wrote a passage designated "A" at the bottom of fol. 3*b*, extending from "had all our good wishes" to "body suffer? But" (*CM* 5:528). He then cancelled the first nine words at the top of fol. 3*b* and penned in their place "Insert A," together with a pointing hand. Insert A is presently joined to the top of fol. 3*b*.

25. Nine words completing the last sentence on fol. 3*c* were set down by Anne at the top of fol. 4*c*, but Thackeray copied them with slight augmentation at the bottom of fol. 3*c*: "once in her life before had she known so exquisite a pain" (*CM* 5:530).

26. This word is in Thackeray's hand; Langley used it as a model shortly thereafter in the same sentence. Langley writes a rather poor hand, which is not always possible to reproduce; the following "and," for example, omits a portion of the "n" and a portion of the "d."

27. In the published version, "peas" became "pease" and "so forth" became "take off his hat," indicating a further proof stage.

28. Fol. 11*a* survives in three separate fragments: the upper portion is to be found at Texas, the middle portion in the Berg Collection, and the bottom portion at New York University. The verso of the Texas fragment contains the following sets of calculations:

$$\langle 3 \,\big|\, \underline{144} \qquad\qquad 3 \,\big|\, \underline{72}$$
$$48.) \qquad\qquad\quad 24$$

29. We do know, however, that Thackeray had to supply additional copy, for he wrote Smith sometime during May: "I thought all was done when I went down to the printing office yesterday. My stars what a state I was in, when I found there were 3 pages wanting!" (*Letters*, 4:267).

A surviving sheet of page proof for *CM* 5:657 at Texas reveals that Thackeray saw at least two sets of such proof for this page. It contains five changes made by him in pen, all of them to readings set up from the manuscript: "he must." for "he must!"; "the pail!" for "the pail."; "reason to like 'em." for "reason." (all 3 on fol. 9*a*); "cotched you!" for "cotched you."; and "tell me?"

for "tell me." (both on fol. 10*a*). This sheet of page proof also gives several readings that were replaced in the published version:

fols. 9*a*–10*a*	p. 657	*CM* 5:657
that I daresay	that I dare say	which I daresay
and that that	and that, that	and that—that
both! Here	both! Here	both!—here
you, what I've got?	you, what I've got?'	you what I've got?"
glass. for	glass; for	glass—for
No you	No, you	"No: you
Caroline, I've	Caroline. I've	Caroline—I've
a bill.	A bill.	A bill?

One might also note the existence of over 125 variants in punctuation and word form between the manuscript and the sheet of page proof, most or all of which may be compositorial.

A sheet of page proof containing p. 658 and the headline, page numeral, and first seven lines of p. 659 exists in the Morgan Library. It contains nine notations in Thackeray's hand, eight of them representing changes: "Three hundred and eighty six, four, three" for a blank space; "where that" for "where they"; "from!" for "from"; "give me that!" for "give me that."; "three hundred pound" for "two hundred and fifty pound" (all 5 on p. 658); "tell. You" for "tell. *Vetabo qui vulgârit arcana.* Won't have him *sub iisdem trabibus*, by George. You"; "I say!" for "I say." and "money?" for "money." (all 3 on fol. 10*a*; p. 659). In the ninth Thackeray had originally begun a new paragraph, "Then poor Caroline went" (fol. 10*a*), but apparently the compositor set up "When" instead of "Then." On the page proof Thackeray first changed it back again but ultimately crossed out his change and added "Stet." Here too, alterations were made on subsequent proof, including, interestingly, a further modification of the sum offered Hunt by Mrs. Brandon:

fol. 10a	pp. 658–59	*CM* 5:658–59
[blank space] thas all.	⟨[blank space]⟩ Three hundred and eighty six, four, three that's all,	Three hundred and eighty-six four three— that's all;
I'll I'll	I'll, I'll	I'll—I'll
you you	you, you	you—you
Discountess—And	discountess? And	discountess?" And
two hundred and fifty pound	⟨two hundred and fifty pound⟩ three hundred pound	two hundred pound

What have	"What, have	"What? have
Alcaics	Alcaics	alcaics
brain. 'If	brain, "If	brain: "If
bond! And	bond! And	bond!" And
scoundrel—Thats it.	scoundrel. That's it.	scoundrel! That's it!
tell no no *I* wont	tell; no, no, I won't	tell. No, no, I won't
tell.	tell.	tell!

Thackeray appears to have sent fols. 8*a*–10*a* to the printer as the end of a relay, for the latter subdivided them (unlike fols. 1*a*–7*a*) as follows: 8, 8¼, 8½ (fol. 8*a*); 9, 9½, 9¾ (fol. 9*a*); and 10, 10½, 10¾, 11, 11¼ (fol. 10*a*). Two other pieces of evidence also indicate that the relay ended with fol. 10*a*: first, the printer's division of fol. 11*a* according to a different system—11, 11¼, 11½, 11¾; second, the nature of the Morgan sheet of page proof, which includes the upper portion of p. 659 and ends about four spaces from the end of a line with the words, "Look here"—the same words that conclude fol. 10*a*. In the published version, this line has been rejustified so as to use up the four spaces.

In the manuscript a printer's proofreader has penned in brackets that mark the beginnings of lines two and five of *CM* 5:648 and line one of *CM* 5:657.

30. Because Thackeray used so many different kinds of paper, one must be very cautious in using the paper as evidence. It is worth mentioning, however, that fols. 1*a* and 2 are written on the same kind of paper—Palace Green stationery—while fols. 1 and 5 contain a blue *Cornhill* signet; fol. 3 is the only leaf of blue paper, and fol. 4 is approximately the same size as the Palace Green stationery, but without the imprint.

31. I base this speculation on the printer's designations, for after dividing the first two leaves into halves and numbering in ink the lower portions 1½ and 2½, he divided fol. 3*b* into thirds and numbered the bottom portion 4, as he probably would not have done had fol. 4*b* also been present, since he tended to adopt Thackeray's numbering for the uppermost portions of the divided leaves. Fol. [4*b*] is missing, but the bottom portion of fol. 5*b* contains the normal printer's marking for this installment: 5½.

32. The latter four leaves were marked 1–4 in pencil by the printer, who then divided fol. 10*b* into thirds, numbering the two bottom portions 11 and 12.

33. After completing his work on this installment, Thackeray prepared to pay a day's visit to a friend but still asked that a copy of what was apparently a final set of page proof for chapter 40 be sent him there:

16/6/62

If the proof of the last chapter is ready by post-time send it to me at J. Coningham's Esq.
> Heathfield Lodge
> Bracknell

I shant send it back except in case of great need.

WMT
(MS letter, NYU)

34. Before this time Thackeray, with the assistance of his secretary, had begun to prepare *Philip* for book publication. Already on Thursday, 24 (?) November 1859, Thackeray had commented on Langley's abilities as a proofreader: "Langley has valuable qualities he fastens on a comma or a doubtful word & doesnt leave it. He told me how he had been surreptitiously looking out the French words used by yours truly" (NLS). A letter of late May or early June 1862, just before the completion of number 19, shows the beginning of their work on the republication of *Philip*: "I have read through the first 4 numbers with Mr. Langley this morning & you can print as soon as you please" (NLS). From his new home on 1 July Thackeray wrote Smith about the book's title, proposed that it include running headlines, and memorably epitomized for us his relations with his publisher:

Palace Green. July 1
1862.

My dear S.

I think 'Philip' *tout court* is better than the Adventures of &c, and that a running title on every other page as in Esmond will give a little freshness to the reprint.   I shall have done D. V. to day or tomorrow.

Sitting in this beautiful room, surrounded by ease and comfort and finishing the story, I stop writing for a minute or two, with rather a full heart.

Will you let Laurence make another drawing of you? I should like to hang it here.

Always yours
W M Thackeray.
(NLS; see *Letters*, 4: 269–70)

35. There is no reason, of course, to assume that the texts on fols. 10*v* and 11*v* represent the only antecedents of fols. 7 and 10.

36. This house is an imaginative composite but is chiefly taken from a description and illustration of Wansted House ("Wanstead" in the illustration), which was first published by William Watts in 1783. The description, which accompanies plate 56 in *The Seats of the Nobility and Gentry. In a Collection of the most interesting & Picturesque Views, Engraved by W. Watts* (Chelsea: Watts, 1779–[86]), reads in part as follows:

WANSTED HOUSE is situated upon the Western Part of *Epping Forest*, about six Miles North East of London. It was begun by Sir *Josias Child*, who purchased the Manor of *Wansted*, and finished by the late Earl Tylney, from Designs of *Colin Campbell*, (Author of the Vitruvius Britannicus) It extends 260 Feet by 75, and consists of a rustic Basement, and principal Story, with an Attic in the Center; the whole executed in Stone.—The grand Front towards the Forest is adorned with a noble Portico of the *Corinthian* Order, and may with Propriety be considered one of the finest Elevations in the Kingdom.

·   ·   ·   ·   ·   ·   ·   ·

> The Park, though handsome and well planted, is not proportionably magnificent with the House; but as the Earl of Tylney is hereditary Ranger of Epping Forest, the whole of that extensive Tract may be considered as his Park. The grand Approach is through a long and beautiful Vista, which extends to the high Road at *Layton Stone*, and is terminated by a large Piece of Water, at a little distance from the Front of the Building.

The illustration shows a house set in a park containing a lake, horses, two women, a man, and a dog; there is no bridge, balustrade, fisherman, or boat, and there are no deer, though other plates contain various combinations of these details.

37. After cancelling "Pen," Thackeray neglected to correct "her's"; the compositor seems to have made the correction but ignored the cancellation, thereby producing the reading: "her, Pen" (*CM* 6:226).

38. The "d" is conjectural because the leaf's mounting covers its extreme left edge.

39. This word was inserted into the insertion.

40. The "d" is conjectural because the leaf's mounting covers its extreme left edge.

41. Evidence of an earlier, now discarded, version of fol. 8 appears on fol. 9, for on the latter leaf, Phipps and the newspaper man from the *Daily Intelligencer* are given speaking roles without having been introduced. Thackeray later gave the speeches to Bradgate. Fol. 9, which is noticeably smaller than all the other leaves of the installment, also has a cancelled passage at its foot that suggests Thackeray may have planned the climactic discovery of the will in a slightly different way, perhaps through the rental of the coach by Philip, Pendennis, and J.J., one of whom would have found it in the vehicle's sword-case. Bradgate originally explains to them not that the present Lord Ringwood is one of the most affectionate of parents but that he is "one of the most economical magnates adorning the baronetage or peerage. He has sold off all the superfluities at the Castle. Half the pictures have gone to Christies—all the good ones—and all the good wine. He and Mr. Ringwood are not on good terms, or he wants ready money for the second family—He has let the gardens. He has let the Park. He has sold the horses and carriages. Why the very [word or several letters illegible] chaise in wh. old Ringwood died was bought by Mugwell of the Ram and you can hire it and a pair of posters at eighteen pence a mile to take you back to Periwinkle Bay—"

Afterword

1. Robert L. Patten, "*Pickwick Papers* and the Development of Serial Fiction," *Rice University Studies* 61 (1975): 51.

Manuscript Sources

Vanity Fair

Numbers 1–4: 113 leaves (Morgan)
Number 11: 1 leaf (Huntington)
Number 14: 1 leaf (Huntington), 1 leaf (Taylor)
Numbers 19–20: 1 leaf (Rosenbach), 1 leaf (Huntington)

The Newcomes

Number 2: 2 leaves (Taylor)
Numbers 4–6, 10, 14–15: 226 leaves (Charterhouse)
Number 16: 4 leaves (Berg)
Numbers 17–20: 184 leaves (Charterhouse)
Number 21: 2 leaves (British Lib.), 2 leaves (Texas), 5 leaves (Berg), 1 leaf (Huntington)
Number 22: 54 leaves (Berg)
Number 23-24: 47 leaves (Charterhouse), 2 leaves (Berg)

The Virginians

Number 1: 39 leaves (Morgan)
Number 2: 29 leaves (Morgan), 1 leaf (Arents)
Number 3: 31 leaves (Morgan)
Number 4: 34 leaves (Morgan), page proof (Morgan)
Number 5: 34 leaves (Morgan), 1 leaf (Taylor)
Number 6: 31 leaves (Morgan), 1 leaf (Texas), 1 leaf (divided between Morgan and Berg)
Number 7: 25 leaves (Morgan), 1 replaced leaf (Berg)
Numbers 8–10, 13, 15: 86 leaves (Morgan)
Number 17: 19 leaves (Morgan), 1 leaf (NYU)
Number 18: 19 leaves (Morgan), page proof (Morgan)
Number 20: 30 leaves (Morgan)
Number 21: 47 leaves (Morgan), 1 replaced leaf (Texas)
Number 22: 30 leaves (Morgan)
Number 23: 18 leaves (Morgan), 2 leaves (Huntington)
Number 24: 12 leaves (Morgan), 1 leaf (Parrish), 1 leaf (Berg), 1 leaf (Ray)

Lovel the Widower

Number 1: 25 leaves (Morgan), galley proof (Yale), galley proof (Huntington), page proof (Texas)

Number 2: 17 leaves (Morgan)

Number 3: 17 leaves (Morgan), galley proof (Yale)

Number 4: 6 leaves (Morgan), 12 leaves (Huntington), 1 leaf (NYU), 1 leaf (Berg), page proof (Yale), page proof (Texas)

Number 5: 16 leaves (Morgan), page proof (Yale), page proof (Texas)

Number 6: 16 leaves (Morgan), page proof (Texas)

The Adventures of Philip

Number 1: 1 leaf (Huntington), 1 leaf (Fitzwilliam), 1 leaf (Kansas), 1 leaf (British Lib.), 1 leaf (Leeds), 1 leaf (Texas), 1 leaf (Loyola Marymount), 2 leaves (Yale), 1 leaf (Washington Univ.)

Number 2: page proof (Arents)

Number 3: 27 leaves (Huntington), page proof (Texas)

Numbers 4–7: 90 leaves (Huntington)

Number 8: 6 leaves (Huntington), page proof (Morgan)

Number 9: 16 leaves (Huntington) ·

Number 10: 8 leaves (Huntington), 1 leaf (Texas), 6 leaves (Yale), 1 leaf (Berg)

Number 11: 15 leaves (Huntington)

Number 12: 20 leaves (Huntington), 1 replaced leaf (NYU)

Numbers 13–17: 92 leaves (Huntington)

Number 18: 18 leaves (Huntington), 1 leaf (divided among NYU, Berg, & Texas), page proof (Texas), page proof (Morgan)

Numbers 19–20: 35 leaves (Huntington)

Letters

7 December 1852, to George Smith (Illinois)

23 January 1854, to Bradbury and Evans (Punch)

8 March 1854, to Percival Leigh (Morgan)

19 June 1854, to Bradbury and Evans (Punch)

16 February 1857, to George Smith (NLS)

3 December 1857, to Henry Reeve (NYU)

11 December 1857, to S. Low and Sons (Berg)

21 December 1857, to John Blackwood (Morgan)

17 February 1858, to William Macready (Taylor)

9 April 1858, to Mrs. Carmichael-Smyth (Berg)

13 March 1859, to Lady Hardinge (Rochester)

21 September 1859, to Mrs. Baxter (South Carolina)

15 October 1859, to Charles Lever (Harvard)
21? November 1859, to George Smith (NLS)
24? November 1859, to George Smith (NLS)
5 December 1859, to George Smith (NLS)
8 March 1860, to George Smith (NLS)
14 March 1860, to George Smith (NLS)
March 1860, to George Smith (NLS)
27 November 1860, to George Smith (NLS)
3 December 1860, to George Smith (NLS)
19 December 1860, to George Smith (NLS)
1860–61, to George Smith (NLS)
21 January 1861, to Frederick Walker (Morgan)
4 February 1861, to George Smith (NLS)
February 1861, to George Smith (NLS)
6 March 1861, to George Smith (NLS)
12 March 1861, to George Smith (NLS)
11 April 1861, to George Smith (NLS)
April ? 1861, to George Smith (NLS)
April ? 1861, to George Smith (NLS)
9 July 1861, to George Smith (NLS)
31 July 1861, to George Smith (NLS)
5 August 1861, to unidentified recipient (NYU)
11 April 1862, to George Smith (NLS)
late May–early June 1862, to George Smith (NLS)
16 June 1862, to unidentified recipient (NYU)
1860–63, to unidentified recipient (NLS)

Other Documents

Chronology for a portion of *The Newcomes* (Berg)
Outline for Numbers 16–24 of *The Newcomes* (Taylor)
Notebook for *The Virginians* (Yale)
Outline for a portion of *The Virginians* (Buffalo)
MS diary for 1862 (British Lib.)
Samuel Langley, MS diary for 1860 (Berg)

Index